D1032980

Indexed in

EGLI 1991

Modernism to Realism on the Soviet Stage

Modernism to Realism on the Soviet Stage

TAIROV – VAKHTANGOV – OKHLOPKOV

NICK WORRALL

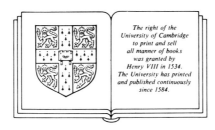

The right of the
University of Cambridge
to print and sell
all manner of books
was granted by
Henry VIII in 1534.
The University has printed
and published continuously
since 1584.

CAMBRIDGE UNIVERSITY PRESS

CAMBRIDGE

NEW YORK   NEW ROCHELLE   MELBOURNE   SYDNEY

Published by the Press Syndicate of the University of Cambridge
The Pitt Building, Trumpington Street, Cambridge CB2 1RP
32 East 57th Street, New York, NY 10022, USA
10 Stamford Road, Oakleigh, Melbourne 3166, Australia

First published 1989

Printed in Great Britain at
the University Press, Cambridge.

British Library cataloguing in publication data
Worrall, Nick
Modernism to realism on the Soviet stage:
Tairov – Vakhtangov – Okhlopkov. – (Directors in perspective).
1. Russia. Theatre. Directing. Biographies.
Collections
1. Title
792'.0233'0922

Library of Congress cataloguing in publication data
Worrall, Nick.
Modernism to realism on the Soviet stage: Tairov – Vakhtangov –
Okhlopkov/Nick Worrall.
p.   cm. – (Directors in perspective)
Bibliography: p.
Includes index.
ISBN 0-521-24763-2
1. Theater – Soviet Union – History – 20th century. 2. Tairov,
Aleksandr IAkovlevich, 1885–1950 – Criticism and interpretation.
3. Vakhtangov, Evgeniĭ Bagrationovich, 1883–1922 – Criticism and
interpretation. 4. Okhlopkov, Nikolaĭ Pavlovich – Criticism and
interpretation. 1. Title. 11. Series.
PN2724.W67 1989
792'.0947 – dc 19   88–15975

ISBN 0 521 24763 2

For
Ellen

Contents

Illustrations

Acknowledgements

This study could not have been undertaken without a British Council Scholarship, which facilitated a ten-month period at the Leningrad Institute of Theatre, Music and Cinematography. Considerable thanks are owed to members of the theatre research department at the Institute but, in particular, to the late Sergei Vasilevich Vladimirov and Yuri Alexandrovich Golovashenko for academic support and advice. Thanks for friendship, sustenance and encouragement are owed to Irina Malyutina, the late Alexander Gladkov and Professor A.G. Obraztsova of the VNII in Moscow, especially, but also to many other Soviet, British and American colleagues and friends. Thanks, finally, to Middlesex Polytechnic for periods of sabbatical leave and a respite from other duties to permit full-time work on this project; and to my wife.

A note on transliteration

As this study is intended for the general reader, I have not been pedantically purist as far as the transliteration of Russian names is concerned and have preferred to stick to established variants, where these exist, or to transliterate in a way more readily acceptable to English-language readers (e.g. Alexander is preferred to Aleksandr; Alexei to Aleksei).

Table of historical and theatrical events

Historical events	Theatrical events
1859 Birth of Nemirovich-Danchenko.	
1860 Birth of Chekhov.	
1861 Emancipation of the serfs.	
1863 Birth of Stanislavsky.	
1868 Birth of Gorky.	
1870 Birth of Lenin.	
1872 First Russian translation of Marx's *Das Kapital*.	
1874 Birth of Meyerhold.	
1879 Birth of Stalin.	
1881 Alexander II assassinated.	
1882	Repeal of Imperial Theatre monopoly.
1883 First organised group of Marxist Social Democrats. Birth of Vakhtangov.	
1885 Birth of Tairov.	
1886 Death of Ostrovsky.	
1887 Attempt to assassinate Alexander III by Lenin's brother, Alexander Ulyanov.	
1888	The Society of Art and Literature opens in Moscow.
1890	Meiningen Company visits Russia.
1894 Nicholas II becomes tsar.	
1896	First production of Chekhov's *The Seagull*.
1897	Moscow Art Theatre founded.
1898 First Congress of Russian Social Democratic Workers' Party.	Opening of Moscow Art Theatre.
1900 Birth of Okhlopkov.	
1902	Premiere of Gorky's *The Lower Depths*. Meyerhold leaves Moscow Art Theatre.
1903 Second Congress of Russian Social Democratic Workers' Party. Formation of 'Bolshevik' faction.	
1904 Death of Chekhov.	Premiere of *The Cherry Orchard*
1905 General strike and 'Bloody Sunday' in St Petersburg. Moscow uprising.	Stanislavsky opens Povarskaya Studio for Meyerhold's experimental work
1906 First Duma constituted	Meyerhold joins Komissarzhevskaya's Theatre.
1908	Meyerhold appointed head of Imperial Theatres in St Petersburg.
1909	Vakhtangov enters Adashev acting school.
1911 Prime minister Stolypin assassinated.	Premiere of Craig/Stanislavsky *Hamlet*. Vakhtangov joins Moscow Art Theatre.

Historical events	Theatrical events
1912	Formation of Art Theatre First Studio.
1913	First production at First Studio – *The Wreck of 'The Hope'* (dir. Boleslavsky). Official opening of First Studio with Vakhtangov's production of *The Festival of Peace*. Foundation of Free Theatre. Premiere of Tairov's production of *The Veil of Pierrette*. First meeting of Vakhtangov's Mansurov Studio Group.
1914 Germany and Austria–Hungary declare war on Russia.	Premiere of Vakhtangov's production of *The Lanin Estate*. Premiere of Sushkevich's production of *The Cricket on the Hearth*. Opening of Kamerny Theatre with Tairov's production of *Shakuntala*.
1915	Premiere of Vakhtangov's production of *The Deluge*.
1916 Assassination of Rasputin.	Premiere of *Thamyris Kitharodos* at the Kamerny Theatre. Formation of Art Theatre Second Studio. Death of Sulerzhitsky.
1917 February (old style) and October (old style) revolutions. Abdication of Nicholas II. Armistice with Germany.	Premiere of Meyerhold's production of Lermontov's *Masquerade*. Premiere of Stanislavsky's production of *Twelfth Night* at First Studio. Theatres placed under aegis of Narkompros (People's Commissariat of Education and Enlightenment) headed by Lunacharsky. Okhlopkov joins the local theatre in Irkutsk. Premiere of *Salomé* at the Kamerny.
1918 Introduction of new (Gregorian) calendar. Treaty of Brest/Litovsk. Foreign Intervention. Red Army organised by Trotsky. Royal family executed. Assassination attempt on Lenin.	Opening of the Jewish Habimah Studio. Premiere of Vakhtangov's production of *Rosmersholm* at First Studio. Premiere of first version of *The Miracle of St Anthony* at Vakhtangov's Mansurov Studio. Opening of the People's Theatre. Premiere, in Petrograd, of 'the first Soviet play' – Mayakovsky's *Mystery-Bouffe* (dir. Meyerhold).
1919 First congress of the Communist International in Moscow. White offensive launched.	Meyerhold captured by Whites and imprisoned in Novorossisk. Theatres nationalised.

Historical events	Theatrical events
	Bolshoi Theatre in Leningrad founded (later renamed Gorky Theatre in 1932).
	Premiere of Mardzhanov's production of Lope de Vega's *Fuente Ovejuna* in Kiev.
1920 End of Western Powers blockade.	Premiere of Stanislavsky's production of Byron's *Cain* at Moscow Art Theatre.
	Premiere of Vakhtangov's production of Chekhov's *The Wedding* at Mansurov Studio.
	Mansurov Studio incorporated within Moscow Art Theatre as its Third Studio.
	Premiere of *Princess Brambilla* at the Kamerny.
	Meyerhold appointed head of the theatre section of Narkompros. Launches 'October in the Theatre' movement.
	Meyerhold stages Verhaeren's *The Dawns* at the RSFSR Theatre No. 1.
	Evreinov stages mass spectacle *The Storming of the Winter Palace*.
	Mardzhanov stages mass spectacle *Towards the World Commune*.
1921 Kronstadt uprising. Tenth Party Congress. New Economic Policy put into effect.	Premiere of Stanislavsky's production of *The Government Inspector* with Michael Chekhov at the First Studio.
	Art theatre Fourth Studio founded.
	Premiere of *Romeo and Juliet* at the Kamerny.
	Tairov's *Notes of a Director* published.
	Okhlopkov stages mass spectacle, *The Struggle of Labour and Capital*, in Irkutsk.
	Premiere of second version of *The Miracle of St Anthony* at the Third Studio.
	Premiere of Vakhtangov's production of *Erik XIV* at the First Studio.
	Official opening of Third Studio.
1922 The RSFSR becomes the USSR. Stalin becomes general secretary of the central committee of the party. Death of Vakhtangov.	Premiere of Meyerhold's productions of *The Magnanimous Cuckold* and *Tarelkin's Death*.
	The Theatre of the Revolution founded in Moscow.
	Moscow Art Theatre embarks on European and American tour.

Historical events	Theatrical events
	Premieres of *Phaedre* and *Giroflé–Girofla* at the Kamerny.
	Okhlopkov enters Meyerhold Workshop in Moscow.
	Premiere of Vakhtangov's production of *The Dybbuk* at the Habimah Studio and of *Princess Turandot* at the Third Studio.
1923	Meyerhold Theatre founded.
	First European tour of Kamerny Theatre.
	Lunacharsky coins slogan 'Back to Ostrovsky'.
	Eisenstein stages eccentric production of Ostrovsky's *Enough Stupidity in Every Wise Man* at the Proletkult Theatre.
	Premiere of *The Man Who Was Thursday* at the Kamerny.
	Censorship body, Glavrepertkom, established.
1924 Death of Lenin.	Stanislavsky's *My Life in Art*
Britain establishes diplomatic relations with USSR	published in English translation.
	Art Theatre returns to Moscow.
	First Studio becomes MAT 2 (Second Moscow Art Theatre).
	Art Theatre Second Studio incorporated within main theatre.
	Moscow Theatre of Satire founded.
	Premiere of *St Joan* at the Kamerny.
	Premiere of *The Forest* at the Meyerhold theatre.
1925 Tsaritsyn renamed Stalingrad.	Second Kamerny European tour.
Association of Proletarian Writers (RAPP) formed.	Premiere of Erdman's *The Mandate* at the Meyerhold Theatre.
	Premiere of Seifullina's *Virineya* at the Vakhtangov Studio (dir. Popov).
	Premiere of Bill-Belotserkovsky's *Storm* at the Mossoviet Theatre (dir. Lyubimov-Lanskoi).
1926	Premiere of *The Government Inspector* at the Meyerhold Theatre.
	Soviet edition of *My Life in Art* published.
	Third Studio renamed Vakhtangov Theatre.
	Premiere of Stanislavsky/Sudakov productions of Ostrovsky's *Burning Heart* and Bulgakov's *Days of the Turbins* at the Art Theatre.

Historical events	Theatrical events
	Premiere of Trenyov's *Lyubov Yarovaya* at the Maly Theatre, Moscow.
	Premieres of *The Hairy Ape* and *Desire Under The Elms* at the Kamerny.
	Meyerhold Theatre becomes State Meyerhold Theatre.
1927 Britain breaks off diplomatic relations with USSR.	Fourth Studio renamed Realistic Theatre.
Trotsky and Zinoviev expelled from the party.	Premiere of Stanislavsky's production of Beaumarchais's *The Marriage of Figaro* and the Stanislavsky/Sudakov production of Ivanov's *Armoured Train 14–69* at the Art Theatre.
	Premiere of Hasenclever's *Antigone* at the Kamerny.
	Okhlopkov directs and stars in the film *Mitya*.
1928 First five-year plan implemented.	Stanislavsky's final appearance as an actor.
	Okhlopkov directs film *The Sold Appetite*.
	Premiere of Bulgakov's *The Crimson Island* at the Kamerny.
	Michael Chekhov emigrates.
	Meyerhold stars in Protozanov's film *The White Eagle* alongside Kachalov.
1929 Mass collectivisation decreed.	Premiere of *All God's Chillun* at the Kamerny.
Trotsky expelled from the USSR.	Premieres of *The Bedbug* and *Army Commander 2* at the Meyerhold theatre.
	Central Theatre of the Red Army founded.
1930 Death of Mayakovsky.	Premiere of Nemirovich-Danchenko's production of Tolstoy's novel *Resurrection* at the Art Theatre and Sudakov's production of *Othello* based on Stanislavsky's director's plan.
	Okhlopkov directs film *Way of the Enthusiasts*.
	Premiere of Brecht's *The Threepenny Opera* at the Kamerny.
	Third Kamerny European tour.
	Meyerhold's company perform in Paris.
	Premiere of *The Bathhouse* at the Meyerhold Theatre.
1931 Gorky returns semi-permanently to USSR.	Okhlopkov becomes artistic director of Realistic Theatre (renamed Krasnaya Presnaya Theatre).

Historical events	Theatrical events
	Premiere of Afinogenev's *Fear* at the Art Theatre (dir. Sudakov). Premieres of Vishnevsky's *The Last Decisive* and Olesha's *A List of Benefits* at the Meyerhold Theatre.
1932 End of first and beginning of second five-year plan. RAPP wound up.	Premiere of Bulgakov's dramatisation of *Dead Souls* (dir. Stanislavsky/Sakhnovsky) at the Art Theatre. Premiere of *Running Start* at the Krasnaya Presnaya Theatre. Premiere of Akimov's eccentric production of *Hamlet* at the Vakhtangov Theatre. Premiere of Zakhava's production of Gorky's *Yegor Bulychov* at the Vakhtangov theatre.
1933 Diplomatic relations established between the USSR and the USA. Gorky settles permanently in the Soviet Union. Death of Lunacharsky.	Premiere of Sophie Treadwell's *Machinal* at the Kamerny. Premiere of *Optimistic Tragedy* at the Kamerny. Premiere of Gorky's *Mother* at the Krasnaya Presnaya Theatre. Premiere of Gorky's *Into the World* at the Art Theatre (dir. Kedrov). Okhlopkov rehearses Brecht's *St Joan of the Stockyards*.
1934 USSR joins League of Nations. First Soviet Writers' Congress. Socialist realism promulgated. Leningrad party secretary, Kirov, assassinated.	Moscow Theatre Festival. Krasnaya Presnaya Theatre reverts to being called the Realistic Theatre. Premiere of *The Iron Flood* at the Realistic Theatre. Premiere of *Egyptian Nights* at the Kamerny. Premiere of *The Lady of the Camellias* at the Meyerhold Theatre. Premiere of *Yegor Bulychov* at the Art Theatre (dir. Nemirovich-Danchenko) Tairov attends International Congress of the Royal Italian Academy in Rome.
1935 Franco-Soviet and Czecho-Soviet Mutual Aid Pacts signed. Stakhanov movement launched. Opening of Moscow metro.	Opening of Stanislavsky Opera–Dramatic Studio. Premiere of Gorky's *Enemies* at the Art Theatre (dir. Nemirovich-Danchenko). Premiere of *Aristocrats* at the Realistic. Premiere of *King Lear* at the State Jewish Theatre (dir. Radlov) with Solomon Mikhoels. Premiere of Meyerhold's production of Tchaikovsky's *The Queen of Spades* in Leningrad.

Historical events	Theatrical events
1936 New Stalin Constitution adopted. Beginning of Moscow Trials. Death of Gorky.	MAT 2 closed down. Attack in *Pravda* on Shostakovich's opera *Lady Macbeth of Mtsensk*. Premiere of Bulgakov's *Molière* at the Art Theatre (dir. Gorchakov). Meyerhold speaks out against 'Meyerholditis'. First mention by Stanislavsky of the 'method of physical actions'. *An Actor Prepares* published in English translation in the United States. Premiere of *Othello* at the Realistic. Premiere of Borodin's *The Epic Heroes* at the Kamerny.
1937	First issue of theatre journal *Teatr*. Kamerny and Realistic Theatre merged. Meyerhold's production of *One Life* prohibited. Premiere of *Anna Karenina* at the Art Theatre (dir. Nemirovich-Danchenko). Premiere of *Colas Breugnon* at the Realistic.
1938 Third five-year plan inaugurated. Death of Stanislavsky.	Meyerhold Theatre closed down. Meyerhold takes up post at Stanislavsky Opera Theatre. Okhlopkov leaves Kamerny and joins Vakhtangov Theatre.
1939 Molotov replaces Litvinov as Commissar for Foreign Affairs. Nazi–Soviet Pact signed. Mutual assistance pacts signed with Estonia, Latvia, Lithuania. USSR invades Finland. USSR occupies Western Ukraine and Western Belo-Russia, formerly part of Poland.	First Soviet Directors' Conference. Meyerhold arrested. Premiere of *Tartuffe* at the Art Theatre (dir. Stanislavsky, Kedrov, Toporkov).
1940 Soviet–Finnish Peace Treaty signed. Estonia, Latvia and Lithuania vote in general elections for union with USSR. Death of Meyerhold.	Premiere of *Madame Bovary* during Kamerny Far East Tour. Premiere of Nemirovich-Danchenko's revival of *Three Sisters* at the Art Theatre.
1941 Germany invades USSR. Italy, Rumania, Finland and Hungary declare war on USSR.	Theatre companies evacuated from Moscow.

Historical events	Theatrical events
French Vichy government breaks off diplomatic relations with Moscow. Anglo-Soviet agreement signed in Moscow: Churchill declares that 'Russian people are now our allies'. German forces occupy Kiev. Siege of Leningrad by German and Finnish forces begins.	
1942 First Moscow Conference – Stalin, Churchill, Harriman. Battle of Stalingrad commences.	Okhlopkov stages premiere of *Cyrano de Bergerac* in Omsk. The Art Theatre stages premieres of Pogodin's *Kremlin Chimes* and Korneichuk's *The Front*.
1943 German forces at Stalingrad capitulate. Leningrad siege raised. Third International (Comintern) dissolved. Teheran Conference – Stalin, Churchill, Roosevelt.	Premiere of Leonov's *Invasion* at the Mossoviet. Okhlopkov appointed artistic director of The Theatre of Drama (formerly the Theatre of the Revolution). Kamerny Theatre Company returns to Moscow.
1944 Leningrad blockade lifted. Soviet troops enter East Prussia	Premiere of *The Seagull* at the Kamerny.
1945 Yalta Conference – Stalin, Churchill, Roosevelt. Berlin surrenders to First White Russian and First Ukrainian armies. Soviet troops enter Hungary, Poland, Czechoslovakia and Austria. Potsdam Conference. Soviet Union declares war on Japan.	Premiere of *An Inspector Calls* at the Kamerny. Tairov awarded the Order of Lenin.
1946 Fourth five-year plan.	Publication of party document 'On The Repertoire of the Dramatic Theatres and Measures for their Improvement'.
1947	Premiere of *The Young Guard* at the Theatre of Drama.
1948 Soviet blockade of Berlin begins. Stalin breaks with Tito.	Okhlopkov made a People's Artist.
1949 First Soviet atom bomb. Establishment of Comecon. Mao Tse-tung visits Moscow for Stalin's seventieth birthday celebrations.	Okhlopkov's theatre tours Poland and Czechoslovakia. Tairov transferred to Vakhtangov Theatre.
1950 Sino-Soviet Friendship Treaty. Death of Tairov.	
1953 Death of Stalin. Khrushchev becomes first secretary of the party. First Soviet hydrogen bomb.	Premiere of Ostrovsky's *The Storm* at the Theatre of Drama.

Table of historical and theatrical events

Historical events	Theatrical events
1954 Okhlopkov designated deputy minister of culture (post held for a year). Beginning of 'thaw' in East–West relations. Warsaw Pact signed.	Theatre of Drama renamed the Mayakovsky Theatre. Series of Mayakovsky revivals at the Moscow Theatre of Satire begins with the Yutkevich/Pluchek production of *The Bathhouse*. Premiere of *Hamlet* at the Mayakovsky Theatre.
1955 Meyerhold officially rehabilitated by a military court of the USSR.	Okhlopkov participates in International Shakespeare Conference held at Stratford. Tovstonogov revives *Optimistic Tragedy* at the Pushkin Theatre, Leningrad.
1956 Twentieth Party Congress. Khrushchev's secret speech denouncing the 'cult of personality'. Soviet intervention in Hungary.	Founding of Sovremennik Theatre under Oleg Efremov. Tovstonogov becomes artistic director of the Leningrad Gorky Theatre. Premiere of *Hotel Astoria* at the Mayakovsky Theatre.
1957 First artificial satellite launched by Soviet Union.	
1958	Moscow Art Theatre pays first ever visit to Britain.
1960 Yuri Gagarin first man in space. U2 spy plane shot down. Eisenhower–Khrushchev summit abandoned.	Yuri Zavadsky directs *The Cherry Orchard* in New York.
1961 Twenty-second Party Congress. Stalin's body removed from Lenin Mausoleum. Stalingrad renamed Volgograd.	Premiere of *Medea* at Tchaikovsky Concert Hall.
1962 Cuban missile crisis.	
1963	Reuben Simonov revives Vakhtangov's production of *Princess Turandot* at the Vakhtangov Theatre.
1964 Khrushchev forced to resign. Brezhnev becomes first secretary, Kosygin prime minister.	Okhlopkov takes part in Shakespeare Quarter-centenary celebrations held in London and Stratford. Yuri Lyubimov and a group of Shchukin Acting School students take over the Theatre of Drama and Comedy on Taganka Square. Moscow Art Theatre performs at World Theatre Season in London.
1965	Soviet premiere of *Look Back in Anger* at the Sovremennik.
1967 Fiftieth anniversary of the revolution. Death of Okhlopkov.	

General introduction

Between the opening of the Moscow Art Theatre in October 1898 and the Bolshevik revolution in October 1917[1] the theatrical situation in Russia underwent a number of important changes. However, these changes did not represent major breaks with the past but, rather, shifts in a theatrical tradition which was marked by a significant degree of continuity. In the major capitals, Moscow and St Petersburg, there continued to exist important so-called 'Imperial' Theatres, such as the Alexandrinsky in St Petersburg and the Maly in Moscow.[2] Their titles meant that, although they were self-governing and had an independent administrative system, they were ultimately dependent on royal patronage as they had been throughout the nineteenth century. Their repertoire tended to be conservative, in that they usually confined themselves to the production of great classic dramas of the nineteenth century by Russian authors – Pushkin, Gogol, Lermontov, Turgenev, Ostrovsky. Occasionally, they would experiment with new work by unknown, or untried playwrights such as Anton Chekhov, whose *Seagull* was given its first, disastrous production at the Alexandrinsky in 1896.[3] The reason for the failure owed much to the unusual nature of the dramatic material but was also attributable to the absence of a directorial tradition in the Russian theatre of the time. Added to this, the established theatre was a victim of hidebound conventions and its attitudes towards acting and staging tended to be untheoretical and generally lacking in rigour. However, the basis for the resurgence of theatre as a seriously conceived and executed art form, commensurate with the quality of the best dramatic material at its disposal, had already been established, both in their writings and in their theatrical practice, by such important innovators as Gogol, Turgenev, Shchepkin and Ostrovsky.[4] It was this tradition, which conceived theatre art as a high-minded, moral and educative cultural form, which was subsequently developed by Stanislavsky and has since become established as a *sine qua non* of theatre practice in the Soviet Union.

Co-existing with the Imperial Theatres were the ordinary commercial theatres run by independent entrepreneurs, who performed the standard classics of the Russian and Western European repertoire, but who tended to rely for commercial success on stock melodramas and farces which were mainly imported from abroad, as well as the vaudeville.[5] It was in provincial theatres such as these that Chekhov's Arkadina[6] would have performed. Rehearsals in these theatres were perfunctory affairs. The star reigned at the expense of the ensemble and, often, at the expense of the play.[7] Dialogue would be improvised rather than learned. Sets would be taken from stock, rarely refurbished or renewed, and plays were frequently staged less for their intrinsic artistic merit than to provide profitable benefit nights for the leading actor or actress – a fact which also contributed to the debacle of Chekhov's *Seagull*.[8] Theatres of this order existed in the larger regional centres such as Kiev or Kharkov but could also be found in distant outposts of the Russian empire such as Vologda, or Kerch, from whence the itinerant actors in Ostrovsky's play *The Forest* are journeying when they first meet.

I

Mention of Ostrovsky's play is a reminder of a kind of theatre which also served the smaller towns and the countryside. This was a more broadly based popular theatre centred on markets and fairs during public holidays and broadly categorised as the *narodnye gul'yanya*. This kind of popular entertainment included everything from travelling puppet theatres to pantomime and circus-style entertainment, as well as the native Russian *balagan*, with its stock characters whose origin went back to the eighteenth century when theatre in an organised form was first introduced to the country via travelling *commedia dell'arte* troupes, as well as through visiting French and German professional companies. This popular form exerted an increasing influence on mainstream theatre after the turn of the century, its types and its subject matter being taken up by dramatists, directors and musicians. Igor Stravinsky's ballet *Petrushka* (1911), for example, based its subject matter on a typical Russian Shrovetide fair, while Alexander Blok's highly influential 'symbolist' work *Balaganchik* (The Puppet Show)[9] drew its inspiration from the Russian clown show or *balagan*. *The Puppet Show* was first staged in 1906 as part of Meyerhold's struggle to promote an anti-naturalistic theatre and it was in this production that Alexander Tairov played the part of 'a masker in pale blue'.

The turn of the twentieth century, as well as heralding Russia's 'Silver Age' in the arts[10] also saw the establishment of a number of independent theatres inspired by the naturalist movement in Western Europe and influenced by the examples set by the companies of the Duke of Saxe-Meiningen and Otto Brahm in Germany and by André Antoine in France.[11] Their Russian equivalents, usually patronised and financed by wealthy industrialists with an interest in the arts, succeeded in establishing a number of serious theatre enterprises. Based mainly on a tradition of realism, they sought to refine it and extend its range to encompass varieties of new drama. Up until 1898 there existed few, if any, professional theatre companies in Russia capable of staging the serious new drama which was being produced within its own borders by Chekhov and Tolstoy and, beyond them, by Ibsen, Strindberg, Zola and Hauptmann. That deficiency was repaired with the establishment, by Stanislavsky and Nemirovich-Danchenko, of the Moscow Art Theatre, which set out to implement the ideas of Saxe-Meiningen, Shchepkin and Ostrovsky and to establish Gogol's ideal of a theatre which, as well as being a place of entertainment, was an institution of educational and moral concern.[12] The Art Theatre, from the outset, revolutionised concepts of staging and costume design, rehearsal procedures and production techniques. Probably their most important revolutionary innovation related to Stanislavsky's concept of acting and the role of the actor. The theories which he was to conceive and elaborate from 1907 onwards, and which came to constitute the basis of the so-called Stanislavsky 'system', were to have far-reaching effects on twentieth-century theatre. They also came to figure centrally in the ideological struggle between an actor-centred and a director-centred theatre; between a 'realistic' theatre and a 'theatre of convention'; between 'humanist' and 'formalist' conceptions of theatre art and even between apparent acceptance or apparent rejection of the political 'status-quo' – of 'reality' itself.

Stanislavsky and Nemirovich-Danchenko were not alone in regarding the acting profession as something other than a dilettante occupation for amateurs, or in seeing the theatre as something more important than a mere branch of the entertainment industry providing work for educated and semi-educated people of doubtful respectability. Their example and their watchword were taken up by proselytisers with just as much seriousness and dedication. Chief among these were actors and directors such as Vera Komissarzhevskaya and her brother Fyodor and the actor-managers Korsh and Nezlobin.[13] However, the most significant influence of the Moscow Art Theatre between 1898 and the first revolution of 1905 was in generating a theatrical opposition to the naturalism which it so assiduously espoused and which, in broad terms, became reflected in the dominant anti-naturalist art movements of the inter-revolutionary period which flourished in Russia, such as symbolism, futurism, cubo-futurism, suprematism and the like.[14] In theatrical terms, the way was led at home by the artists of the 'World of Art' movement,[15] the theorists and practitioners of the symbolist movement and the futurists. Among those whose theoretical work inspired from abroad were Richard Wagner, Edward Gordon Craig, Adolphe Appia and Georg Fuchs.[16]

Alexander Tairov's contribution to theatrical 'modernism' in Russia between 1913 and 1930 deserves to be seen alongside the work of such figures as Diaghilev and Meyerhold with whom he had much in common. Tairov was someone who wished to raise the art of theatre to the level of its sister arts such as ballet, painting and music. With Meyerhold he shared an antipathy towards post-Renaissance theatre which had culminated in the *cul-de-sac* of late nineteenth-century naturalism. They both sought to resurrect the archetypal theatre forms of pantomime and the harlequinade; the Roman *mimi*, and the improvisatory spirit of Italian *commedia dell'arte*. Tairov also sought to derive new theatre forms from ancient Greek and Eastern myth and trained his actors to handle their bodies on stage in such a way that distinctions between a *corps de ballet* and a *corps de drame* were broken down and where the art of the designer, the musician and the actor merged in a unified, aesthetic whole. His work at the Kamerny Theatre in Moscow, which he founded in company with his actress wife Alisa Koonen in 1914, became the forum for experiment in 'pure' theatre, but where the formalism never degenerated into *fin de siècle* decadence or sterile 'art for art's sake'. Tairov's essentially modernist theatre, influenced by symbolist poetry, cubo-futurist painting and the music of avant-garde composers became, in his hands, one of the world's great theatres with Tairov now acknowledged as one of the world's great directors.

Anti-naturalist theatre practice was supported by a whole range of theories, many of which drew their authority from Renaissance, pre-Renaissance, Greek and Roman theatre practice. It was Tairov, in his own theoretical work, *Notes of a Director* (1921) who quoted the symbolist theorist Fyodor Sologub[17] in describing the transformation of the theatre of Dionysus into a 'cosy tomb for rabbits'.[18] Another theorist, Vyacheslav Ivanov,[19] sought to resurrect the spirit of that very same theatre of Dionysus – a theatre of religious ecstasy which brought about a spiritual merging between audience and actors. Valeri Briusov,[20] an advocate of symbolist theatre, in an important essay, *Unnecessary Truth* (1902), advocated a means of theatrical production which eschewed true-to-life appearances. He argued for a theatre which could express abstract, poetic feeling in the spirit of the Belgian poetic dramatist, Maurice Maeterlinck, who was himself an important influence on the anti-naturalist theatre movement in Russia during this period.[21] Ivanov also inveighed against the 'deathly influence of the material in art' in the pages of the symbolist journal *The Balance* (Vesy)[22] which first appeared in 1904. The spirit of his declarations was supported by, among others, the novelist and essayist Andrei Bely[23] in an essay entitled *Theatre and Modern Drama* (1908) and by Fyodor Sologub in his essay *The Theatre of a Single Will* (1908). Sologub advocated the wholesale adoption of the devices of a conventionalised theatre and felt that the living reality of the actor was an unhelpful distraction from the essence of theatrical representation. These last two essays appeared as part of a collection published in St Petersburg,[24] which also contained significant contributions from Alexandre Benois,[25] Anatoli Lunacharsky[26] and Meyerhold.[27] Meyerhold's essay was of seminal importance in furthering the cause of a non-representational, anti-naturalist, aestheticised theatre. The former Art Theatre actor (he had left the company in 1902) levelled serious criticism at that theatre for its excessive reliance on the external trappings of naturalist performance which, in the case of its productions of Chekhov, had led to an inability to comprehend the 'symbolist' elements in the dramatist's work.[28] Another important theorist/practitioner in this context was Nikolai Evreinov,[29] who founded the Antique (Starinny) Theatre in St Petersburg in 1908, devoted to the resurrection and reconstruction of mediaeval theatrical forms and whose theory of 'monodrama' was first introduced in 1908. He also drew inspiration, as did many others, from the archetypal theatrical forms of pantomime and the harlequinade.

Even Stanislavsky became disillusioned with naturalism as a method and, in 1905, invited Meyerhold to return from the provinces where he had established his own company, to direct a theatre studio in Moscow devoted to experimentation in new, 'symbolist' methods of acting and stage presentation.[30] The experiment was not successful and Meyerhold transferred his experimental researches to St Petersburg, where Vera Komissarzhevskaya had established her own theatre, equally determined to devote her energies to the stage-realisation of the emergent forms of theatre art. Stanislavsky was left, virtually on his own, at the Moscow Art Theatre to forge the practical means whereby symbolist works could be staged. His efforts led to interesting, yet never wholly satisfactory, attempts to stage works by Maeterlinck, Leonid Andreyev and Knut Hamsun,[31] before he reverted to his earlier, realist style. Now, however, he sought to deepen, broaden and refine his method by investing that earlier naturalism with psychological and spiritual inwardness, a greater reliance on inner emotion and genuineness of feeling rather than emphasis on external manner and visual effectiveness. The first production to put the beginnings of his 'system' into effect was that of Turgenev's *A Month in the Country*, in 1909.[32] Stanislavsky was to continue his attempts to extend the experimental range of the Art Theatre's work, a significant example being his invitation to Edward Gordon Craig to stage *Hamlet* at the Art Theatre.[33] Another important step was his decision to open a theatre studio and to invite the young Evgeni Vakhtangov to conduct experiments in Stanislavsky's own 'system' – a remarkable act of faith in the talent and ability of someone whose eventual reputation would rival that of Stanislavsky himself.

Despite the comparative brevity of Vakhtangov's theatrical career – a total of about ten years spent as a professional artist – he has left a permanent mark on the history of world theatre establishing himself, with extraordinary rapidity, as a director of genius. If one seeks for analogies in the contemporary world which approximate to Vakhtangov's place in the theatre of his day, one thinks of the leaders of religious sects whose influence on their followers is as much personal as it is ideological, a compound of love, fear and intellectual respect. In many ways, Vakhtangov was an artistic fanatic whose standards were maximalist and absolutist. The theatre for Vakhtangov, as it was for Stanislavsky and had been for that fanatical genius of the nineteenth-century theatre, Nikolai Gogol, was a moral institution. It is not unusual to discover among Vakhtangov's writings connections between the actor's calling and a 'sense of mission', references to Stanislavsky as a 'god' and a theatrical art which needed to be 'served' as part of a 'service to the people'. Acting groups are referred to as 'sects' and the atmosphere of studio work is frequently compared with that of a monastery. The theatre is a place where 'the truth' can be sought and 'the soul purified' of the imperfections of living and where, eventually, the 'meaning of life' can be discovered. Vakhtangov was himself seen as a spiritual leader in the realm of art much as Lenin was regarded as a spiritual leader in the realm of politics.

Meanwhile, in St Petersburg, Meyerhold had succeeded in realising some of the dreams of an anti-naturalist theatre with important 'symbolist' productions at Komissarzhevskaya's theatre of work by Ibsen, Blok and Andreyev as well as work by other symbolist dramatists.[34] When, as a consequence of disagreements with Komissarzhevskaya, he was forced to leave her theatre in 1907, it was a complete surprise to everyone when the then head of the Imperial Theatres in St Petersburg, V.A. Telyakovsky, (apparently committed to the dominant mood of innovation and experimentation) appointed Meyerhold to head both of the Imperial Theatres and provided him with an almost unlimited budget. Meyerhold's subsequent pre-revolutionary work, mainly at the Alexandrinsky, can be said to have incorporated everything marvellous and sumptuous in the 'Silver Age' of Russian culture, bringing together the greatest designers, actors, singers and musicians of the age and staging some of the most magnificent productions in the history of this or any other theatrical epoch.[35] However, equally important (if not more important in the long term) was the experimental work which Meyerhold conducted under the pseudonym 'Dr Dapertutto', establishing acting studios and directing productions at various small-scale venues in and around the city. It was here that he experimented with styles which drew their inspiration from the ancient *mimi*, from *commedia dell'arte* and from the Russian *balagan*. It was here, also, that he laid the basis for the 'bio-mechanical' acting theories which he was to elaborate after the revolution.[36] It was as a result of witnessing some of Meyerhold's 'fringe' productions during this period that Vakhtangov, who had joined the Moscow Art Theatre in 1911, began to reassess his commitment to the total validity of those theories of Stanislavsky's which he was seeking to implement, both in his own Mansurov Studio and in the Art Theatre's First Studio. It was also as a result of seeing Meyerhold's production of Lermontov's *Masquerade*, staged on the eve of the revolution in 1917, that the young Sergei Eisenstein, decided to enter the theatre.[37]

In the immediate aftermath of the February revolution in 1917 very little changed in the theatrical situation. However, two weeks after the October (Bolshevik) revolution, the Council of People's Commissars issued a declaration which transferred responsibility for the theatre administration to the newly organised People's Commissariat for Education and Enlightenment, whose leader was Anatoli Lunacharsky. The government had been faced with a difficult situation. It could either have granted complete autonomy to all institutions involved in the arts, knowing that the majority were potentially hostile to the new government, or it could seek to implement a policy which would convert the consciousness of old-established institutions to a gradual acceptance of the new regime. The Bolsheviks knew full well that the arts, and especially the theatre, were an important means of extending their influence but that the system needed some form of central organisation to administer the entire artistic network via specially established regional organisations.

Responsibility for theatres throughout the RSFSR[38] was placed in the hands of a Theatrical Section within the Commissariat, with regional leaders in each part of the Federation. One of the first leaders in Petrograd[39] was Leon Trotsky's sister, while Meyerhold, who had welcomed the revolution by staging a production of what has become known as 'the first soviet play' (Mayakovsky's *Mystery-Bouffe* in November 1918),[40] was appointed head of the Moscow Theatrical Section. Traditionalists in the theatre, as well as those uncommitted to Bolshevism, were amazed and angered by the apparent change which then overcame Meyerhold. The erstwhile theatrical aesthete cast aside his top hat, cape, white gloves and patent-leather shoes[41] and donned the uniform of a Red Army man. In this new guise he proceeded to conduct a ruthless campaign against the established theatres, including the Moscow Art Theatre and the old Imperial Theatres. Between 1920 and 1921 (when he resigned his post as head of the Moscow Theatrical Section), Meyerhold ushered in what he called the 'October in the Theatre' movement[42] under whose banner he sought to organise the theatres along semi-military lines as part of an attempt to bring them all within a propagandist, revolutionary orbit, subject to governmental diktat. He even went so far as to seek to change their well-established names, substituting numbers in their stead, so that Meyerhold's own RSFSR Theatre No. 1, was to be followed by the renaming of other theatres as RSFSR Theatre No. 2, 3 and so on.[43] Needless to say, Meyerhold's onslaught was strenuously resisted by those organisations and institutions to whom Meyerhold appeared most hostile, including the Moscow Art Theatre and the Kamerny Theatre.

In addition to leading the attack against the old 'bourgeois' theatres, Meyerhold staged a 'revolutionary' production of Verhaeren's *The Dawns*, in 1920,[44] virtually rewriting the Belgian poet's play so as to adapt it to the circumstances of the Russian revolution and, in the process, bringing down on his head the sarcastic wrath of Tairov and others.[45] He also sought to stress the connection between theatrical and industrial production by incorporating 'constructivist' elements in the staging of both this and subsequent plays.[46] At the same time, he was attempting to establish a training ground for future actors and directors in a revolutionary Russia. He recruited students of the quality of Sergei Eisenstein[47] and Nikolai Okhlopkov to his directors' workshop. At his actors' workshop he experimented in 'bio-mechanical' acting techniques and mounted daring and startlingly innovative productions of traditional plays – such as his constructivist versions of Crommelynck's *The Magnanimous Cuckold* in 1922 and of Sukhovo-Kobylin's *Tarelkin's Death* in the same year.[48]

The way in which actors, directors and dramatists accepted or rejected the Bolshevik revolution varied widely. Apart from Meyerhold, only Mayakovsky[49] and Blok, among major artistic figures of the day, pledged total support to the Bolsheviks.[50] For the rest, they tended to co-exist as so-called 'fellow-travellers', were won over gradually (as were Vakhtangov, Tairov and Stanislavsky), or else they emigrated. After 1917, the Art Theatre went into a temporary decline with no new productions being staged. In response to encouragement from Lunacharsky, Stanislavsky insisted on artistic freedom, declaring that art which was worth anything at all could not be created by official decree. The Art Theatre's problems were exacerbated by the fact that, whilst on tour during the Civil War, half the company had been cut off from Moscow by a White Army advance. Some members of that group then emigrated rather than return to Moscow in which the Bolshevik government appeared secure by 1921. Stanislavsky staged little apart from a production of Byron's *Cain* (1920), in which he meditated on the trials and tribulations of civil war. Nemirovich-Danchenko turned his attention, for the time being, to the staging of operetta and musical comedy.[51] Fyodor Komissarzhevsky, Nikolai Evreinov, Leonid Andreyev and Fyodor Chaliapin emigrated. They were to be followed by many others during the course of the 1920s, one of the more significant being Michael Chekhov, nephew of the dramatist and an outstanding actor, who had headed the Second Moscow Art Theatre (MAT 2).[52] Former futurists, such as Mayakovsky, found little problem in integrating their artistic beliefs with their political convictions, and his establishment of the Left Front of the Arts (LEF)[53] reflected a broadly based fusion between the spirit of avant-garde artists and the revolutionary mood of the time. Even former symbolists, such as Vyacheslav Ivanov and Andrei Bely, took an active part in the work of the Theatrical Section and sought to place their theories at the service of the revolution. Before he emigrated, Evreinov tried his hand at staging a mass spectacle, *The Storming of the Winter Palace*, which was a far cry from his pre-revolutionary theory and practice.

Such mass performances, which often involved tens of thousands of participants, including detachments of the Red Army and Navy, were usually called 'actions' or 'mysteries'. They recalled the popular spectacles of the Middle Ages and were part of an attempt to return theatre to the public square. They were often staged according to mediaeval principles of 'simultaneous' staging, or on motorised 'pageant waggons' processing through a city. The action of these plays sometimes extended over centuries and frequently tended to modernise or parody biblical legend. Their main significance lay in the fact that they attracted and involved vast crowds who enacted, or saw enacted, in generalised, schematic terms, the main political themes of the day embodied in the allegorical figures of Labour, the Priesthood, Capital or Revolution. The names of the presentations were an indication of their content – 'The Pantomime of the Great Revolution', 'Hymn to the Liberation of Labour', 'The Flame of Revolution', 'The Action of Free Peoples', 'The International', 'Red Days', etc. Vakhtangov also felt drawn towards the idea of staging a mass spectacle based on the Bible, especially 'A Life of Moses'. Meyerhold adapted a production at his theatre in 1923 of *Earth Rampant*[54] as a mass spectacle which he staged on the Lenin Hills overlooking Moscow, involving military and naval detachments. Meyerhold's pupil Sergei Eisenstein, was also attracted to such mass entertainments which he eventually realised on film when he re-staged the taking of the Winter Palace as part of the film *October* (1927). Tairov's former colleague at the Free Theatre, Konstantin Mardzhanov,[55] planned a mass-spectacle version of Mayakovsky's *Mystery-Bouffe* (which parodies the 'Noah' legend) to be staged on a mountain top near Tbilisi in Georgia. The first production ever staged by the young Nikolai Okhlopkov was just such a mass spectacle – 'The Struggle of Labour and Capital' – which he mounted with a cast of thousands on the central square of his home town, Irkutsk, in 1921.

Okhlopkov's major contribution to Soviet theatre practice dates from the 1930s, rather than the 1920s, but the effect of the revolutionary period on the mental outlook of a young man who was seventeen years old in 1917 was permanent and ineradicable. Compared with his great counterparts – Stanislavsky, Vakhtangov, Meyerhold, Tairov – all of whom were born in the nineteenth century, Okhlopkov was quintessentially twentieth-century man, born into a world on the brink of epic events to which his consciousness was uniquely attuned. Okhlopkov was always interested in theatre on an epic scale. His dream was to resurrect a Soviet equivalent of the dramatic festivals of fifth-century Athens, to rival open-air performances like those of the mediaeval mystery plays, or the festivals staged by Leonardo da Vinci with their giant floats, some depicting models of the universe. He wanted a theatre of communal passions which could speak in a universal language to thousands simultaneously. Although Okhlopkov's experiments were restricted to the limits of the small Realistic Theatre during the 1930s, it was here that foreign visitors such as Bertolt Brecht recorded a sense of authentic theatricality and where the American director, Norris Houghton, experienced an excitement unlike any other he had felt in the theatre.

The background to all this exciting activity, between 1918 and 1921, was poverty, war, cold and starvation. The general effect of the civil war had been to bring the country close to economic ruin. At the Tenth Party Congress, held in

March 1921, Lenin put forward a proposal designed to alleviate the situation and provide the revolution with a breathing space. The measure in question was the New Economic Policy (commonly referred to as NEP) which marked a change from war communism to a new economic politics involving the reintroduction of limited forms of free enterprise. It was hoped that, by encouraging free trade in consumer goods between town and country, the nation would be enabled to survive until some future time when full socialist policies could be implemented. The re-establishment of the principle of private enterprise meant that, in practice, many regional theatres drifted away from control of the local branch of the Commissariat and back into the hands of private entrepreneurs. Types of play and methods of play production then arose which were seen directly to reflect the tastes and preoccupations of what were referred to as 'NEP people'. The aesthetic extravagances of Tairov's theatre in the early 1920s were said to be attributable to the NEP tastes of its audiences. As well as including plays in his repertoire which satirised NEP people, such as Nikolai Erdman's *The Mandate* (1925), Meyerhold was accused, in his productions of *Bubus the Teacher* (1925) and, to a certain extent, of *The Government Inspector* (1926), of reflecting or pandering to NEP tastes.[56]

If the Bolsheviks were experiencing difficulty in establishing a degree of political hegemony on the local and regional front (civil war continued to be fought in parts of the Far East until the late 1920s), the same was true, in the ideological sense, on the artistic front. Here, the source of the problem lay in Proletkult (the Proletarian Culture Organisation) which, together with the organisation which later became known as RAPP (The Association of Proletarian Writers), remained a thorn in the flesh of the party until the early 1930s.

The enormous broadening of a participatory theatre created by amateur performers, which marked the years of the civil war and afterwards, was one which was supported on firm ideological grounds by Proletkult. The organisation officially came into existence in 1917, before the October revolution, and its platform, very basically, rested on the belief that the culture of the past was so much useless lumber as well as being ideologically alien to the proletariat. Any future socialist culture and any future socialist art would take its form and substance from the working class acting independently, and in isolation, from the cultural and artistic forms of any other social group. This isolation was necessary to ensure the ideological purity of the new forms. The Proletkult theoreticians on the theatrical front included someone like Platon Kerzhentsev[57] (instrumental in Meyerhold's eventual downfall) who saw no place in the artistic future of the Soviet Union for members of the intelligentsia, or even for any artist whose origins stemmed from the peasantry, like the poet Sergei Esenin.[58] In supporting the amateur manifestations of theatrical activity, Proletkult was also striking a blow against any form of professionalism in the arts. However, being so absolute in theory, the Proletkult movement was often exposed to blatant contradiction in practice. For example, the forms which it took to most readily in the post-revolutionary period were those with which its anti-traditionalist ideology had most in common, namely futurism and constructivism. It was also forced, in its more official activities, to employ the services of artists such as Sergei Eisenstein, who staged outstandingly original productions at the First Proletkult Theatre in Moscow during the early 1920s, based on his theatrical concept of 'montage'. Eisenstein's personal credentials were far from being authentically proletarian, hailing as he did from a bourgeois background and possessing decidedly cosmopolitan tastes and interests.

In 1922, an article appeared in *Pravda* by one of the leaders of Proletkult, V.F. Pletnyov,[59] entitled 'On the Ideological Front', in which he referred to the need for the proletariat to reconstruct the basis of art from the very root, having broken with all previous cultures, especially bourgeois culture. Pletnyov's main point was that the intelligentsia should stand aside from the affairs of the cultural revolution. Lenin himself took Pletnyov to task over this article, which he described as 'a falsification of historical materialism'. He also considered nonsense Pletnyov's idea that 'the proletarian artist will simultaneously be both worker and artist'. It was Lenin, together with Lunacharsky, who led the attempt to retrieve the major achievements of the historical past as models for the further advance of a specifically socialist art. The basis for this was seen to be essentially grounded in realistic forms. Neither Lenin, Lunacharsky nor Trotsky felt that futurism, constructivism, cubism or any other fashionable 'ism' had anything significant to offer the revolution.[60] The immediate consequence of this was Lunacharsky's coining of the slogan 'Back to Ostrovsky', designed to make artists aware of the importance of a 'critical realist' inheritance which went back to the nineteenth century and great Russian artists of the past. The struggle between 'realism' and 'formalism' can be seen to intensify from here onwards. By 1934 and the First Writers' Conference[61] the struggle had become one between 'socialist realism' and a decadent 'modernism', although the essential terms of the conflict remained the same.[62] It is interesting to note that the immediate responses of Meyerhold and Tairov to Lunacharsky's call were for each to stage productions of plays by Ostrovsky – *The Forest* and *The Thunderstorm* – in styles which were uncompromisingly idiosyncratic and non-realistic.[63]

On the socialist realist front, the major breakthrough is officially seen to have occurred in 1924 with productions of Bill-Belotserkovsky's play *Storm* at the Moscow Trade Union Theatre, and of Lidya Seifullina's *Virineya* at the Vakhtangov Theatre.[64] These plays, and their methods of stage realisation, were firmly within a tradition of realism which, henceforth, would be officially encouraged. The content was also specifically that of Soviet reality, firmly rooted in the historical events of the recent past – in these instances, of civil war. Both the themes and manner of presentation of these plays were in marked contrast to the, seemingly, self-indulgent and irresponsible work being conducted, for example, by Kozintsev and Trauberg at the Factory of the Eccentric Actor[65] or the expressionistic experimentation of Sergei Radlov[66] (both in Petrograd) or the 'theatricalised dances' being performed at his Moscow workshop by the company led by Nikolai Foregger,[67] or the grotesque versions of Gogol being staged by Zavadsky and Igor Terentyev.[68] The changing climate towards formal experimentation in the theatre was to have far-reaching consequences for the better-known directors of the day, such as Tairov and Meyerhold, especially when the Moscow Art Theatre, having returned from a two-year world tour in 1924[69] took up the realist gauntlet. Under Stanislavsky's guidance, and with close support from Nemirovich-Danchenko, the theatre staged significant, socially-committed realist plays during the next six years, probably the most significant of them being the 1927 production of Vsevolod Ivanov's civil war play *Armoured Train 14–69*.[70] The Art Theatre also responded to Lunacharsky's call for a responsible attitude towards the staging of classic works of the past through the style and manner of their productions of Ostrovsky's *Burning Heart* (1926), Beaumarchais's *The Marriage of Figaro* (1927) and the stage adaptation of Tolstoy's *Resurrection* (1930). In so doing, the theatre was seen to be following an example already set by the former Imperial (now 'Academic')[71] Maly Theatre, where Konstantin Trenyov's civil war play *Lyubov Yarovaya* had been staged in 1926.[72]

The Fourteenth Party Congress took place at the end of 1925. Here a policy of rapid industrialisation, centred on the development of heavy industry and the collectivisation of agriculture, was first promulgated. In 1928, the NEP period was declared to be at an end and the first five-year plan for the development of the national economy was announced. RAPP had also come into existence in 1925 and was to conduct a running battle with members of the Left Front of the Arts, as well as with theatrical 'formalists' such as Meyerhold and Tairov. RAPP was not itself based on any particular aesthetic position and sheltered behind a series of slogans about the struggle for the ideological leadership of proletarian literature and art. Its methods were quite unprincipled and included political accusations against practitioners of the arts at every level. Like the Proletkultists, RAPP was especially suspicious of the intelligentsia. By 1930, its power and influence were such that, to many, the only way to beat them appeared to be to join them. Even Mayakovsky did so immediately prior to his death, whilst simultaneously conducting an ongoing dispute with one of RAPP's theorists, V. Ermilov, in his play *The Bathhouse*, which Meyerhold staged in 1930. This particular production was accused by the RAPPists of being 'anti-Soviet'. They applied the same label to Tairov's production of Bulgakov's *The Crimson Island* (1928). They even turned their fire on Stanislavsky and the Moscow Art Theatre. The Stanislavsky 'system' was declared to be 'idealistic' (i.e. too theoretical) as well as being 'metaphysical' and suffering from an excess of 'biologism'. Even *Armoured Train 14–69* was described as a 'reactionary' play, whilst the production of Bulgakov's *Days of the Turbins*[73] (which Stalin enjoyed so much he saw it on several occasions) RAPP categorised as 'a statement by a class enemy'. Vakhtangov was posthumously discovered to have 'mystical-idealist' roots to his philosophy, while Meyerhold was accused of 'mechanism', 'subjective idealism', 'fetishism' and of possessing 'reactionary restorative tendencies'.[74] RAPP survived until 1932 when, in April of that year, the party adopted a resolution 'On the Restructuring of Literary Artistic Organisations', declaring that 'all writers supporting the platform of Soviet power and striving to participate in socialist construction would be entertained within a single Union of Soviet

Writers'. This, by 1934, had brought all factions under a single authority. This was the year in which Okhlopkov's Krasnaya Presnaya Theatre was, significantly, re-named the 'Realistic' Theatre, and where he continued to interpret the meaning of realism in distinctly unconventional ways. In so doing, Okhlopkov succeeded in proving that the spirit of RAPP was alive and well and had his theatre taken away from him in 1937.

The 1930s saw an acceleration of the industrialisation programme and the pushing through of the collectivisation policy. This was reflected in many of the plays and productions of the period, including those of Krishon's *Bread* (1931) and *The Miraculous Alloy* (1934) at the Art Theatre; of Nikitin's *Line of Fire* (1931) at the Kamerny Theatre, as well as in Okhlopkov's version of Stavsky's *Running Start* (1932) at the Realistic Theatre. Although Tairov's and Okhlopkov's productions retained aspects of a genuinely experimental spirit, true experiment was becoming increasingly rare in the Soviet theatre during this period and tended to occur on the periphery or in the regions. Wherever it occurred it was liable to be branded as 'formalism', 'Meyerholditis'[75] or 'Turandotism' (after Vakhtangov's 1922 produc-tion of Gozzi's *Princess Turandot*). In the circumstances, with the avant-garde in retreat, productions such as Nikolai Akimov's eccentric version of *Hamlet* at the Vakhtangov Theatre in 1932[76] were exceptions which paid the price for their boldness by being severely (some would say, in this instance justly, criticised).

In the conservative atmosphere of the mid 1930s, the rediscovery of Shakespeare was proceeding apace. Shakespeare's popularity lay as much in his uncontroversial status as in the intrinsic merits of his work. Productions of *Othello* were staged by Stanislavsky at the Art Theatre and by Okhlopkov at the Realistic, as well as at the Maly. Among the most successful were considered those of *Much Ado About Nothing* at the Vakhtangov Theatre (1936) and of *The Taming of the Shrew* at the Central Red Army Theatre in 1937.[77] This was also a period when a 'safety first' policy led to the adaptation for the stage of, similarly non-controversial, classic works of world fiction, such as Balzac's *The Human Comedy*, staged at the Vakhtangov Theatre (1934), Dickens's *The Pickwick Club* (adapted from *The Pickwick Papers*) (1934) and a dramatised version of Tolstoy's *Anna Karenina* (1937), staged by the Moscow Art Theatre, and Flaubert's *Madame Bovary* at the Kamerny (1940). The period also saw a wide range of productions of plays by Maxim Gorky, who had returned to the Soviet Union in 1931 and who died in 1936.

The late 1930s also saw the canonisation of Stanislavsky's theories and the wholesale imitation of Art Theatre productions (about which Okhlopkov publicly protested). The initiative of theatre artists was being sapped and weakened. Rather than be accused of formalism, writers and directors turned out what was expected of them, or paid lip-service to the standards and values of the Art Theatre. This had the effect of, temporarily, devaluing the real significance and importance of Stanislavsky's theories, which had been published immediately prior to his death in 1938.[78] The culmination of this period of passivity in the arts was the emergence of the so-called 'no-conflict' theory, both in the drama and in the productions themselves.

The struggle against 'formalism' had intensified during the mid-1930s and reached a peak in 1936. A series of articles in *Pravda* concluded with one which attacked Nemirovich-Danchenko's production of Shostakovich's opera *Lady Macbeth of Mtsensk*, which had been running successfully at the Bolshoi Theatre for the previous two years.[79] The attack on formalist tendencies in the theatre also resulted in the closure of the Second Studio of the Art Theatre in 1936 and of Meyerhold's theatre in 1938. Building work on Meyerhold's new 'universal' theatre on Mayakovsky Square came to an abrupt halt and, when it was resumed, the plans were converted into those of the present Tchaikovsky concert hall.[80] Okhlopkov's Realistic Theatre was closed in 1937 and the company merged with Tairov's at the Kamerny. Following the first All-Union Directors' Conference held in Moscow in mid June 1939, Meyerhold was arrested on 20 June and died, probably in prison, the following February.[81] Other important theatrical figures met their fate during this terrible period of the 'purges', which came to a head in 1938–9, and in which the avant-garde Ukrainian director, Les Kurbas, and the playwright and Brecht translator, Sergei Tretyakov, lost their lives.[82] These tragic events were followed by the horrors of war when Hitler's armies invaded the Soviet Union in June 1941,[83] and, by 1945, had added a further twenty million dead to the number who had already perished in the purges. Theatrical life in Leningrad came to a halt during a prolonged siege of that city, while most of Moscow's theatres were evacuated beyond the danger zone.

The death of Stalin, in 1953, began the 'thaw' which was to lead to the revival of vitality in the Soviet theatre. It was heralded by productions of Mayakovsky's three plays at the Moscow Theatre of Satire, in 1954.[84] Greater boldness in the choice of repertoire was officially encouraged and the bounds of what could be contained within the parameters of socialist realism became more flexible. The year 1955 saw the official rehabilitation of Meyerhold by a military court of the USSR, which was followed by a reassessment of his place in Soviet theatre history, from which his name had virtually been eliminated since his demise. Almost as a response to the arbitrary closure of Tairov's theatre in 1949, and as a gesture of homage to him, Georgi Tovstonogov[85] staged a production of *Optimistic Tragedy* at the Leningrad Pushkin (former Alexandrinsky) Theatre in 1955, very much in the spirit of Tairov's original, 1933, production. Inspired and encouraged by the changing climate, new theatres such as the Sovremennik (Contemporary) sprang up, with official approval, in Moscow and elsewhere. Here, a group of young actors under equally youthful leadership staged new Soviet plays[86] which stressed a need to value human feeling and to cherish the significance of personality and individuality within a collective context. A former hostility to the Western repertoire, which had existed under the aegis of Stalin's cultural commissar, Andrei Zhdanov,[87] was replaced by a greater degree of openness to what was happening in the West. Here the way was led by Oleg Efremov[88] at the Sovremennik, who staged seminal productions of important British and American plays. The plays of Tennessee Williams, Arthur Miller and Edward Albee began to establish themselves as standard components of the Soviet repertoire. Brecht, whose work had first been staged by Tairov in 1930, but who had since been allowed to lapse into oblivion, was rediscovered and given vivid and imaginative productions by Yuri Lyubimov at the revitalised Theatre of Drama and Comedy on Taganka Square.[89] The pattern was set for the re-establishment of what was officially termed 'cultural normality' in the sphere of the arts and which, with various high points and troughs, has continued into the late 1980s.

The year 1967, which saw the death of Nikolai Okhlopkov, also saw the publication in *Pravda*, on 25 June, of a statement by the central committee of the Communist Party, which referred to the 'cult of personality' of Stalin as having been alien to Marxism/Leninism. It also referred to the 'illegal repression' which had taken place and to breaches of 'socialist legality', as well as to the 'flouting of the basic principle of collective leadership'. Okhlopkov had, himself, anticipated the spirit of these denunciations in the anti-totalitarian message inscribed in his productions of *Hamlet* (1954) and *Medea* (1961).

It is against this general background that the following account of the work of Tairov, Vakhtangov and Okhlopkov needs to be read.

I

Alexander Tairov, 1885–1950

If there is one name which has never achieved the international recognition it deserves in the pantheon of twentieth-century Russian theatre directors, it is that of Alexander Yakovlevich Tairov (real name Kornblit), founder and chief director of the Kamerny (Chamber) Theatre in Moscow from 1914 to 1949. During the 1920s and 1930s, as a result of three tours to Europe and one to South America, the work of Tairov's theatre became more widely available than that of either the Moscow Art Theatre or the Meyerhold Theatre. It was hugely praised by critics as diverse as Lunacharsky and Jean Cocteau and their opinions were echoed by artists as different as Fernand Léger and Eugene O'Neill. Of all the major Soviet directors, Tairov did most to popularise the repertoire of Western European and American dramatists, especially during the 1920s, staging the work of, among others, O'Neill, Shaw, Hasenclever and Racine. He is the author of one of the best and most readable theoretical works on the theatre ever written, *Zapiski rezhissyora* (Notes of a Director), 1921,[1] and his theatre was one of the most popular in the Soviet Union after the revolution of 1917. Despite this, he remains among the least familiar names of all the great Soviet directors as far as Western audiences and the English-speaking world are concerned.[2]

Dissatisfied with the means of both the naturalistic theatre and the theatre of convention, Tairov, together with his wife Alisa Koonen, created the Kamerny Theatre in 1914 as part of an independent attempt to forge a theatre of pure aesthetics, founded on the basis of the 'master actor' – someone armed with rhythmical and musical sensibility and capable of handling all the dramatic genres from tragedy to operetta and pantomime. The emphasis was to be on an aesthetic synthesis of form in which the ingredients were plasticity of physical movement, musical rhythm and the use of the stage area as a structural 'keyboard' designed for movement in space.

In the immediate post-revolutionary period, despite the theatre's avant-garde status and the fact that the Kamerny can be seen to have led the way in introducing stage constructivism, the radical element among the cultural activists tended to share a common antipathy towards Tairov and his work on both artistic and political grounds. Whilst essentially apolitical, Tairov had welcomed the revol-

1 Alexander Tairov in 1908

ution in which he saw a parallel between the world of political action and what he was trying to achieve in the theatre. 'How did we judge matters?', Tairov asked in 1936, and answered: 'The revolution was destroying the old forms of life and we were destroying the old forms of art. It followed that we were in step with the revolution. This was, of course, an illusion but, at the same time, we sincerely believed ourselves to be revolutionaries.'[3]

Nevertheless, the Kamerny repertoire remained singularly unaffected by the revolution and, as late as 1921, included Kalidasa's Hindu classic, *Shakuntala*, Oscar Wilde's *Salomé*, Scribe's *Adrienne Lecouvreur*, two plays by Claudel as well as work by E.T.A. Hoffmann and Arthur Schnitzler. Most of these productions excited controversy where they were not condemned outright by such as the Proletkultists, Meyerhold, and the advocates of the 'October in the Theatre' movement. Less controversial in terms of generally acknowledged artistic success were the theatre's productions of Racine's *Phaedre* and Charles Lecocq's *Giroflé–Girofla*, both staged in 1922. Otherwise, the story of Tairov's theatre in the 1920s consists of a struggle with its critics and a courageous attempt to pursue an independent artistic course. The political turning point for the theatre, as it was for many others, came at the end of the 1920s and the beginning of the 1930s when, in a radically changed artistic climate, experimentation and artistic high spirits were seen as inimical to the serious political tasks facing the country. This was especially the case after the first Writers' Conference of 1934, when the state began to intervene more directly in matters of artistic policy and practice as part of an attempt to curb the self-proclaimed hegemony of certain artistic factions and to promulgate an officially sanctioned 'socialist realism'.

In the grimly serious climate of these years, when the revolutionary gains of the previous ten years were seen to be under threat, an attempt was made to harness all the forces of art to assist in the rapid industrialisation process and the agrarian revolution based on the collectivisation of a formerly independent peasantry. Anyone who was not a 'realist' during this period was, by definition, an 'unrealist' or, in contemporary jargon, a 'formalist'. To be designated as such was not merely construed as potential hostility to officially promulgated artistic tenets, but was likely to be interpreted as hostility to the communist state itself.

Tairov, in common with Meyerhold and others, had to answer criticism levelled at the 'formalist' methods of his theatre and, in response, made strenuous efforts to come to terms with the new mood of the 1930s. In at least one instance (his production of Vsevolod Vishnevsky's *Optimistic Tragedy*, 1933) he succeeded triumphantly in not only fulfilling what was required of a Soviet artist, but in establishing a model for socialist realist theatre production. In addition, as part of his work as a Soviet director, Tairov abandoned the apparent eclecticism on which his choice of a predominantly Western-oriented repertoire had been based and, in response to the increasingly introspective times, began to stage a number of plays by new Soviet writers – Semyonov, Kulish, Vishnevsky and many others. Much of this work was, he himself recognised, of inferior artistic quality, whilst the drive against 'formalism' inhibited the possibilities of retrieving the work in theatrical terms through the brilliant inventiveness of his production methods. Many of these productions were subjected to serious criticism and, in the case of his version of Alexander Borodin's *The Epic Heroes* (Bogatyry), 1936, was condemned in a way no previous production of Tairov's had ever been. His theatre was merged with Okhlopkov's Realistic Theatre in August 1937, a step which, bearing in mind the incompatible temperaments of the two men and the radically disparate styles of their work, was tantamount to closing both theatres. The uneasy alliance broke up after a little over a year. Despite all these setbacks, Tairov continued to receive financial support from the Soviet government, his acting school attached to the Kamerny continued to be funded and he himself was made a People's Artist and awarded both the Order of Lenin and the Red Banner of Labour.

The 1940s saw a return to the classic Russian repertoire at the Kamerny Theatre with productions of Chekhov, Ostrovsky and Gorky. The German invasion of the Soviet Union also provided the need to stage a number of plays with either patriotic or war themes and, in common with other Moscow-based theatre groups, the Kamerny was evacuated to the east of the country. The last six years of Tairov's artistic life were spent in his own theatre staging, in the main, rather indifferent productions of unremarkable plays by mainly indigenous authors. He died in 1950 before the process of liberalisation which followed the death of Stalin had got under way, having suffered the final bureaucratic indignity of having his theatre taken away from him and handed to someone else.

The revival of interest in Tairov's work during the late 1960s and early 1970s was marked by the publication of Alisa Koonen's memoirs, the appearance of a full-length study of his work, and the publication of Tairov's own selected writings, including a reissue of *Notes of a Director*. It is noticeable that, in Soviet estimates of Tairov's contribution to the theatre of his time, stress is laid on those productions which have a pro-socialist or anti-capitalist emphasis and which, in either tragic or comic form, celebrate human potential. Nevertheless, it is probably fair to say that, in comparison with the attention accorded other major Soviet directors, Tairov has suffered, and still suffers, a degree of critical neglect. There are reasons for this. Firstly, there would seem to be little in the way of archive material comparable with that of either Stanislavsky or Meyerhold. There appear to be few detailed records of actual productions on a moment-by-moment basis. Tairov was not constantly surrounded by a group of assistants who recorded every word he said during rehearsals and no extensive photographic record of individual productions exists. Any reconstruction, therefore, is based mainly on contemporary reviews or statements which Tairov made to the press or theatre journals about aspects of his work.

Unlike Stanislavsky, Vakhtangov or Meyerhold, Tairov's theatre did not produce any outstanding individual actor or director who subsequently went on to make their own uniquely important contribution to the history of Soviet theatre. In the best sense his theatre was a collective, with few outstanding individuals. As a possible consequence of this fact, very few temperamental quarrels appear to have disrupted the continuity of the theatre's history or led to constant changes of personnel. Compared with his great counterparts, Tairov appears to have been singularly gentle, humane and undictatorial in his dealings with his colleagues and never inspired the fear and trembling of a Vakhtangov, the awe of a Stanislavsky, or the terrified respect of a Meyerhold. There is also little doubt that Tairov's personal success owed a great deal to his unbroken artistic partnership with Alisa Koonen, which lasted from his time at Mardzhanov's Free Theatre, through the founding of the Kamerny, until his death.

Tairov's contribution to Soviet theatre is unique in another important sense in that he enables us to understand better an entire historical period. Of all the major directors, he is the only one who worked, almost without interruption, through revolution, civil war, violent internal political upheaval, foreign invasion and the cold war which followed. His productions chart a course through one of the most turbulent periods in world history and provide a mirror which reflects these events. Whilst doing so, Tairov remained faithful to certain abiding principles. The first was the principle which he learned from the Greeks – the fact that the harmony of the universe is posited on the co-existence of tragedy and comedy. The second, related principle, consisted in the simultaneous unification and transcendence of these oppositions through the power of an earthly love which is both human and divine.

Alexander Tairov was born on the 24 June (old style) in the town of Romna in the Ukrainian province of Poltava. His father was a teacher. As a child he had been impressed by performances he saw given by the travelling theatre troupe led by the brothers Adelgaim,[4] who were both products of the German school of acting. His first stage appearance was at the age of sixteen when he acted in an amateur production of Ostrovsky's drama *More Sinned Against Than Sinning*, which is set in the world of provincial actors. However his first thoughts of a career were directed more towards the legal profession than the stage and, in 1904, he entered the Law Faculty of the University of Kiev. At the same time he maintained his connection with the theatre and joined an amateur touring group, led by L.N. Lepkovskaya, during the summer months. Among the roles he played during this period were Trofimov in Chekhov's *The Cherry Orchard* and Vaska Pepel in Gorky's *The Lower Depths*. In 1905, he joined a troupe in Kiev led by M.M. Borodai, a well-known entrepreneur who managed theatres in various provincial capitals. During his short spell with the company, Tairov acted Lysander in *A Midsummer Night's Dream* and the part of the mayor in Gerhard Hauptmann's *Hannele*. It was the year in which provincial centres such as Kiev suffered much the same kind of revolutionary disturbances as did Moscow and Petersburg. Tairov is reported to have taken part in organising a general strike in the theatres of Kiev and is also said to have been arrested on two occasions.

Whilst in Kiev, Tairov took advantage of a visit paid to the city by Vera Komissarzhevskaya and her Petersburg-based company to present himself to her for audition. The result was that she invited him to become a member of her troupe and, in 1906, having transferred his studies to Petersburg University, he joined Komissarzhevskaya's theatre on Ofitserskaya Street, where the newly appointed director was Vsevolod Meyerhold, fresh from his frustrated attempts to establish a symbolist experimental studio attached to the Moscow Art Theatre. Tairov appeared in the production of Alexander Blok's *The Puppet Show* in the small part of one of the Maskers in blue. He also appeared as a beggar in Maeterlinck's *Sister Beatrice* and as an extra in Andreyev's *The Life of Man* – all key productions in the history of Meyerhold's work during that period. It was around this time that Tairov was beginning to formulate his own theories of theatre and dramatic production which were to form the basis of his *Notes of a Director*. One of his starting points became a rejection of the kind of work which Meyerhold was engaged in, which seemed to Tairov to be based on insufficient regard for the actor as well as being at the mercy of the scenic artist, to whom the entire production appeared subordinate. The result was that Tairov left Komissarzhevskaya's theatre and joined the Mobile (Peredvizhnoi) Theatre headed by Pavel Gaideburov. This group had been formed in 1905 on the basis of Gaideburov's former company, the Accessible (Obshchedostupny) Theatre, which had a permanent base in the workers' quarter of St Petersburg. The company toured almost the entire country during its 23-year existence, conveying the classical repertoire to far-flung reaches of Russia. However, during this period of his life, Gaideburov had also become interested in the current symbolist phase of Russian dramatic activity and staged works by, among others, Björnson and Andreyev. Whilst with Gaideburov, Tairov acted roles in plays by Chekhov, A.K. Tolstoy, Sophocles, Ibsen, Shaw (Dick Dudgeon in *The Devil's Disciple*) and in Molière. However, more important than this acting experience, was the opportunity Gaideburov gave the young man to try his hand at direction.

The first play Tairov was given to direct was *Hamlet*, in which he was also to act Laertes. Gaideburov himself played Hamlet. A contemporary reviewer complimented the production on its lack of cliché, on the beautiful and stylish setting and on the director's attempt to break with tradition. The critic noted that the 'To be, or not to be . . .' soliloquy was delivered from the throne and was not accompanied by the usual extravagant gestures and eye-rolling. Tairov's Laertes was complimented on his movement and on the quality of his voice, 'full of noble pathos'.[5] The following season he staged Yuri Zhulavsky's play *Eros and Psyche* in which he had already acted (the role of Eros) and commissioned special music from M.M. Chernov. The importance of music in Tairov's developing theories of theatre production became even clearer during rehearsals of his next production, of Chekhov's *Uncle Vanya*, which he conducted to uninterrupted accompaniment of music by Chopin and Tchaikovsky. An observer noted that Tairov's ideas seemed to be based on Nietzsche's theories about the musical origins of drama.[6] It seemed as if the director wished to evoke a single unifying mood and to awaken spontaneous inner feeling in the actors as part of a total effect of inner, emotional ensemble. This practical work was followed by a letter-cum-article published in the magazine *Theatre Review* the day before the premiere of *Uncle Vanya* and entitled 'Music and Drama' in which Tairov explained why he conducted rehearsals to musical accompaniment as part of an attempt to generate and sustain 'inner emotional feeling':

> Body movements in drama occur as a final stage of creative work: they have the right
> to exist only when they serve as external expression of inner emotional feeling – only
> in this case do they receive justification and become artistically essential.[7]

In 1909, Tairov left Gaideburov's company and worked for a while in Latvia (at the Russian Drama Theatre in Riga) before moving to the Drama Theatre in Simbirsk, where he staged Chekhov's *Three Sisters*. Whilst in Riga he had staged Andreyev's *Anathema*, Ibsen's *The Vikings at Helgeland* and acted roles in plays by Byron (*Sardanapulus*), Ibsen (*The Lady From The Sea*) and Ostrovsky (*The Thunderstorm*). In 1910 he re-staged his earlier production of *Uncle Vanya*, in Riga, on the occasion of the fiftieth anniversary of Chekhov's birth and, in 1911, moved back to St Petersburg where he worked for a time at A.K. Reineke's theatre acting the role of Robert Chiltern in Oscar Wilde's *An Ideal Husband*,[8] Andrei in *Three Sisters*, as well as roles in plays by L. Tolstoy, Schiller, Schnitzler and Ostrovsky. His final role on any stage before he became a full-time director was as Mizgir in Ostrovsky's *The Snow Maiden*, directed by Evtikhi Karpov, who had been the director of the first, disastrous, performance of *The Seagull* in 1896. In 1913, the year in which he completed his law studies at Petersburg University and took up legal practice in Moscow, two crucial events took place which were to determine

Tairov's future career – one was an invitation from Konstantin Mardzhanov to direct at his newly-established Free Theatre. The second was his meeting with an actress of that theatre, Alisa Koonen, who was to become his partner for life.

Mardzhanov (real name Mardzhanishvili) was a Georgian by birth who commenced his theatrical career in 1894, became chief director at the Nezlobin Theatre in Moscow in 1910 (where he established a Georgian Drama Studio) and, a year later, joined the Moscow Art Theatre where he worked until 1913. Whilst at the Art Theatre, he directed Knut Hamsun's *In the Grip of Life* (1911) and Ibsen's *Peer Gynt* (1912), in which Alisa Koonen played the part of Anitra. He also collaborated with Nemirovich-Danchenko on the latter's production of *The Brothers Karamazov* (1910) and acted as assistant to Leopold Sulerzhitsky and Edward Gordon Craig on the famous, Craig-inspired production of *Hamlet* in 1911. He left to establish his own theatre, the Free Theatre (Svobodny Teatr) in 1913. This was conceived as a 'synthetic' theatre uniting all aspects of the art of the stage, employing actors capable of performing tragedy, farce, opera and pantomime with equal facility. Mardzhanov's aim was to do away with the specialising tendency which separated the functions of a singer from those of the actor and placed the dancer in a different category from the acrobat. Like Tairov, Mardzhanov dreamed of a 'universal' artist who would be a singer, dancer and actor in one, a type who had existed in classical antiquity and even during the Middle Ages, but whose art the post-Renaissance theatre had destroyed. Mardzhanov proceeded to try and reverse current trends in the theatre as he saw and understood them by breaking with clichéd patterns (particularly in the realm of operetta)[9] and by changing the singer into an actor. Similarly, 'the dancer was to possess the actor's power of expression, while certain acrobatic properties were to be shared by all in common'.[10]

The Free Theatre lasted for little more than a year but, during that time, it staged first performances of Mussorgsky's comic opera *Sorochinsky Fair* (based on Gogol), Bizet's *L'Arlésienne* and a pantomime by Schnitzler/Dohnanyi entitled *The Veil of Pierrette*, the last directed by Tairov. However, the most notable production was Mardzhanov's own staging of Offenbach's *Belle Hélène*, which broke totally with the canons and clichés of the past and for which V.A. Simov designed sumptuous settings. K. Somov's equally magnificent design for the permanent curtain of the Free Theatre stage gave a powerful indication of the theatre's artistic standards and its aesthetic priorities. Unfortunately, Mardzhanov's talents as a director were not matched by his entrepreneurial abilities and, following disagreements over the financial running of the theatre with the businessmen V.V. Sukhodolsky, the building was forced to close, having survived from October 1913 until May 1914.

Among the outstanding acting talents who joined Mardzhanov at the Free Theatre were N.F. Monakhov[11] and Tairov's future wife, Alisa Koonen. Koonen was born in 1889 and entered the Art Theatre School, where she proved to be one of Stanislavsky's favourite pupils. Her first professional stage appearance was as one of the guests in Stanislavsky's production of Griboyedov's *Woe from Wit*, in 1906, and she followed this with the role of Mytyl in Maeterlinck's *The Blue Bird* (1908), Masha in Leo Tolstoy's *A Living Corpse* (1911), and Anitra in *Peer Gynt*. Despite the success she scored in these roles, she felt the need to pursue her own creative path and, for the moment, this seemed to her to lie with Mardzhanov. Her leaving the Art Theatre was a bitter blow to Stanislavsky, who considered her a star pupil and was thinking of casting her as Anya in *The Cherry Orchard*. However, having made the traumatic break, Koonen was disillusioned and dismayed to find that, having chosen to ally herself creatively with Mardzhanov, the latter promptly handed her over to the completely unknown Tairov, who had been assigned responsibility for a production of an adaptation of a drama by Schnitzler, to music by Dohnanyi, entitled *The Veil of Pierrette*.

The interest in forms of drama which owed their origin to the Roman *mimi*, to *commedia dell'arte* and to the related art forms of music and dance, was something which Tairov shared with Mardzhanov and with many other Russian theatre practitioners before 1914. When he spoke of the importance of what he called 'pantomime', Mardzhanov was fond of quoting Arthur Symons who, in his essay 'Pantomime and the Poetic Drama' (1898) wrote: 'It is an error to believe that pantomime is merely a way of doing without words, that it is merely the equivalent of words. Pantomime is thinking overheard.'[12] Tairov would have felt sympathy with this statement and with those other remarks which Symons made to the effect that the pantomimic art was something which united comedy and tragedy in possessing 'that mystery which is one of the requirements of true art' as well as 'gracious, expressive silence, beauty of gesture, a perfectly discreet appeal to the emotions, a transposition of the world into an elegant, accepted convention'.

In his very first major, independent production of a play in which he himself did not simultaneously have an acting role, Tairov sought to get to the heart of what he termed serious 'mime drama' within the lighthearted framework of the 'pantomime'. In effect, he sought to convert Pierrot and Pierrette into Romeo and Juliet. In doing so, he adopted alternative means to those used by Meyerhold, who had staged his own version of the same play, called *Columbine's Scarf*, in 1910, eschewing the device of the 'grotesque' in favour of an attempt at tragic depth – a 'striving towards inner monumentality and the weighting of the work with deepened and refined emotion' as a contemporary critic expressed it.[13]

Schnitzler's original play, *Der Schleier der Beatrice* (Beatrice's Veil) served simply as the basis for the scenario of a mime-drama re-styled *The Veil of Pierrette*. The original play is a complicated five-act drama about the fate of the beautiful Beatrice who has passed from the arms of her lover into those of another and from him into the arms of the Count of Bologna, who decides to marry her. On her wedding day, prompted by passion, Beatrice goes to see her first lover, Filippo, who commits suicide. Beatrice returns to the wedding, leaving her bridal veil in the room where her meeting with Filippo has taken place. When this is discovered by her brother, he cannot bear what he interprets as disgrace to the family honour and so kills her. Tairov discarded most of the plot and reduced the quartet of lovers to three – the 'eternal triangle' – consisting of Beatrice (Pierrette), the count (Harlequin) and

Filippo (Pierrot). The 'realistic' characters of Schnitzler's play were replaced by the conventionalised, universal types of the Italian comedy of masks. The whole emphasis of the production was on movement justified by inner feeling, on a sense of tragedy which could be communicated most forcibly in statuesque poses and through gesture without speech. In rehearsal, Tairov constantly sought expressiveness of movement, but not aesthetic stylisation for its own sake. It had to accord with inner feeling and with the inner rhythm of the production as a whole, which the actors needed to grasp through the music. Tairov constantly urged his actors to listen to the music and respond emotionally to its mood – to move *in response* to the music rather than merely in time to it. Asked about the differences between pantomime and mime drama, Tairov explained:

> In the pantomime, the actor projects the image from the mask which determines the conventionality and stylisation of his movements. In a ballet-pantomime, illustrative gesture is employed which has its own particular alphabet. For mime-drama, neither the one nor the other will do. Now this certainly does not mean that we shall have recourse to everyday, life-like gesture of a kind used in drama productions. Here, in mime-drama, we shall seek for general collectivised gesture but in its concrete, maximised expressiveness. Gesture has to be volumetrical and possess three dimensions, like sculpture.[14]

For example, Tairov emphasised the need for the sense of horror which engulfs the action to be expressed in strong, broad, but at the same time, short gestures without anything fussy or extraneous. The more laconic the gesture, the greater the degree of expressiveness. It struck Tairov during rehearsal, for example, that there was something wrong with Koonen's gesture at the moment when she handed the poison to Pierrot. The kind of gesture she was using was only possible in drama, where there were words to accompany and support the movement. As there were no words in this case, what was felt could only be expressed through the movement of the arm itself. According to Tairov, an audience needed to be able to feel the cold of death in the way that the hand, especially the fingers, held the poison.[15]

Tairov had this to say about his production of *The Veil of Pierrette*:

> Yes, this was an entirely different sphere, on a different plane than our everyday life. Here eternal figures were locked in combat; the primordial images of the human creature, having done away with the world of everyday, were in the throes of the last engagement, the struggle between love and death.[16]

It was his first exploration of what was to become a permanent theme in his work – the conflict between eternal categories expressed in archetypal terms where living beings became representative carriers of eternal, abstract principles, whether they be Pierrot and Pierrette, Romeo and Juliet, Salomé and Jokanaan, Phaedre and Hippolytus or Antony and Cleopatra. The composer Scriabin said of the production that it could have induced him to write for the theatre – this, despite the fact that Tairov felt that he had accomplished only a fraction of what he was seeking and of which he felt that his actors were capable. Others were more critical and pointed to the fact that there was too much of the 'suffering woman' of naturalist drama in Koonen and too little of the archetypal, and that the conjunction of the lyrical in her and the tragi-grotesque in Shabrov's Harlequin had a discordant effect. Others felt it was a mistake to try and invest a play of this order with depth of tragic feeling and that the 'grotesque' approach adopted earlier by Meyerhold had been both more appropriate and more successful.[17]

During 1913, Tairov published some articles on pantomime and rehearsed *The Yellow Jacket*, a play by J.H. Benrimo and J. Hazelton based on a Chinese folk-tale. The production had its premiere at the Free Theatre on 21 December, with designs by A.A. Arapov, who had collaborated with Tairov on *The Veil of Pierrette*. No attempt was made to recreate, in scrupulous detail, the substance of Chinese theatre or Chinese reality. Instead, the production was intended as a parody of Chinese theatre and as a stylisation of its elements. Two stools with a board laid across them represented a flowing stream. An ordinary wooden ladder stood for the road to Heaven up which the hero's mother ascended to the Kingdom of the Righteous. Mountain tops were represented by an ordinary table with stools placed on top. The 'decapitated' hero carried his own severed head in the shape of a household cushion. Flowers strewn on the floor denoted the fact that the action was taking place in Paradise. By leaping in the air and beating himself about the legs the hero suggested that he was galloping along on a milk-white steed. The props man acted as a kind of silent executant, instigating the changes and transformations and facilitating the development of the action, scattering confetti to suggest a snowstorm,[18] holding out a stick to represent a door, creating the illusion of a boat journey and raising a lighted candle in a hoop on a stick to suggest moonlight.[19] By parodying 'the device' and emphasising its conventionality, Tairov's actors appeared to be ironic in their attitude towards events enacted on stage. It became customary to compare this production with Vakhtangov's 1922 version of Gozzi's *Princess Turandot*, which adopted a similarly ironic and 'alienated' attitude towards its subject matter.

The interest in forms of oriental theatre was fairly widespread in Russia and is traceable in the work of many outstanding theatre practitioners during this period.[20] It is, therefore, not surprising to find Tairov turning his attention from China to India and contemplating production of a work by the fourth-century poet, Kalidasa, for the opening of a new theatre in converted premises at no. 23 Tverskoi Boulevard, where the present-day Pushkin Theatre has its premises. The Pushkin is a small theatre with a balcony and a seating capacity of around 750, but in Tairov's day, the theatre's capacity was even less, hence the name adopted of 'Chamber' theatre, which stressed its intimacy and made it akin to serious, experimental studio theatres like those attached to the Art Theatre or to the Intima Teatern founded by August Strindberg in his native Stockholm. The opening repertoire was to consist of Synge's *The Playboy of the Western World* (called *The Irish Hero*) to be directed by a young protégé of Tairov's, Zonov, whom he had invited to join him from Komissarzhevskaya's theatre, Goldoni's *The Fan*, Mikhail Kuzmin's *Whit-Monday in Toledo*, Beaumarchais's *The Marriage of Figaro* and the opening production, Kalidasa's *Shakuntala* – the last four to be directed by Tairov.

Having arranged the details for the opening of their theatre, Tairov and

Koonen set off for Western Europe – she for a holiday in Brittany, he to visit his aunt, Zinaida Vengerova, who lived in London. This also meant that Tairov could research materal for his production at the British Museum as he had found little in the libraries in Moscow to help him penetrate the mysteries of ancient Hindu culture. He returned to Russia armed with a whole array of materials – sketches of ancient Indian ornaments, household utensils and the like which he hoped would help his designer, Pavel Kuznetsov, to convey the atmosphere of ancient India.

The plot of *Shakuntala* concerns the love of a royal person, King Dushyanta, for a commoner, Shakuntala, the daughter of a famous sage and foster-child of a hermit. The atmosphere is lyrically fantastic and takes place both in Heaven and on Earth. The central figure is a poor, simple girl who lives in complete harmony with the natural world. In order to create this sense of primordial innocence, Tairov decided that the actors would not wear conventional Indian costumes but would be half-naked and painted with body-paint. He wanted the actors' nakedness to assist them in arriving at the purity and primacy of each emotion. As he expressed it later:

> A tremendous amount of work was necessary to get the actor to accept his body and learn to carry it with that uninhibited chastity in the presence of which the eye of the spectator did not dwell on the nudity but accepted it as an original and pleasing theatrical costume . . .[21]

At a time when pessimism was very fashionable, especially in the Russian theatre, Tairov strove to assert the possibility of a different, very real and glorious world in which beauty and human wisdom reigned triumphant. The sense that human beings, animals and plants lived in some kind of ideal unity in a fabulous landscape was conveyed in the settings and through the beautiful language of Konstantin Balmont's translation.[22] Huge backdrops filled the stage – green, pink, sky-blue. Tiny fallow deer and mysterious flowers were integrated into these backdrops which seemed to be transparent with flowing light. The prologue took place in a setting which resembled a cathedral, in the depths of which sat immovable, silent gods in majesty while the inextinguishable sacrificial fire burned on the central altar. Four colossal rampant sky-blue horses framed the proscenium as if to demonstrate, through their gigantic proportions, the insignificance of the earthly, transcient plane of the drama.[23]

Because of delays caused by building work, rehearsals of this very demanding play had to be conducted piecemeal at various locations in the city, including Tairov's own flat. The plaster on the walls was still damp, the building was not properly heated and the acoustics were poor. Conditions were scarcely favourable for launching a venture of this order but, despite this, the opening night was a success and the production held its place in the Kamerny repertoire for a long time. This is more than can be said for the other productions which formed the basis of the first season's repertory, with the single exception of Goldoni's *The Fan*. The production of Synge's *Playboy* was savaged, and for much the same reasons as it had been criticised in Dublin, where its theme of parricide had been considered immoral. In Tairov's production of *The Fan*, the director's imaginative inventiveness was the equal of the magnificent setting by Natalya Goncharova and Mikhail

2 Setting for Kalidasa's *Shakuntala* (1914)

Larionov.[24] The design for the courtyard was especially successful with its two balconies at different heights providing separate levels for the action. The stage floor was covered with black canvas, which gleamed as though it had been lacquered and a striking effect was produced by the way in which the coloured heels of the actors stood out against this background and made a sharp noise as they walked or ran. Tall, elegant white buildings with arches and with bright red pantiled roofs dominated the setting against a background of a bright blue sky. The feeling of a sun-soaked square in 'a little village near Milan' was evoked with sparkling freshness. Tairov's approach to the production was on the basis of improvisation with many of the mime scenes and even some of the text being evolved in rehearsal.[25]

The principle adopted for the setting of *The Marriage of Figaro* was that of the fairground show-booth associated with strolling entertainments – the *balagan* of Russian markets and fairs, with its traditional proscenium and pavilions on each side. The magnificent setting for the final scene, at night in the park, was dominated by what looked like a tented pavilion of blue and purple, with rich rococo decoration, garnished with cupids and with the statues of Harlequin and Columbine posed against a deep-blue, starry sky. The theatre had been fortunate in securing the services of one of the 'younger generation' of the World of Art group, Sergei Sudeikin, who had worked with Meyerhold in St Petersburg. Tairov was also fortunate in acquiring the services of the talented actor Nikolai Tseretelli,[26] who came to the Kamerny from the Moscow Art Theatre and who was to become the leading male actor of the theatre and an equal partner for Koonen. In addition, the production also marked the beginning of a fruitful collaboration between Tairov and the composer Henri Forterre.[27] The production as a whole left Tairov feeling rather dissatisfied. It had been dominated by the decor to such an extent that he felt obliged to invent a correspondingly bold *mise-en-scène* and acting style to counter-balance it. This lent the production an air of stylisation and gave it an aesthetic varnish beneath which the rhythms and forms he was experimenting with were barely detectable.[28] One of the most important features of this production, as far as it affected Tairov's future work, was his decision to break up the floor of the stage into different sections at different levels. He was to elaborate his reasons for doing this when he came to write up his notes for his book *Notes of a Director*. Suffice to say that it was one of the first steps to be taken along the road to constructivism on the Russian stage.

The crowning point of the year 1916, which had seen a revival of *The Veil of Pierrette* at the Kamerny in October, was the premiere, in November, of Isidor Annensky's 'Bacchic drama' *Famira Kifared* (Thamyris Kitharodos),[29] for which Tairov solicited designs from Alexandra Exter, who was to prove another important collaborator in the immediate post-revolutionary period.[30] This was her first work for the theatre and she exploited the opportunity to explore her own interest in constructivist levels and sculptural form in costume design. This joint collaboration between Exter and Tairov was to produce the first authentically 'constructivist' approach to the staging of a play, in which there was complete unity between emotion, rhythm, metre and structure. Apart from being a testing ground for his own theories, Tairov's choice of Annensky's play would appear to have been influenced by several factors. There was a general interest among symbolist theorists, led by Vyacheslav Ivanov, in the possible revival of a 'theatre of ecstasy' with its roots in Ancient Greece and the drama in celebration of the god Dionysus. Annensky's play (based on the legend of Thamyris the musician's challenge to the Muses that he has no peers, and his punishment by blindness and loss of talent for this act of 'hubris') seemed to contain all the necessary elements. The play also contained choruses of satyrs and bacchantes, with the opportunities this provided for dance and music, as well as interesting variations of verse and prose.

Tairov attempted to solve the problems which the production presented by constructing his plan on the basis of rhythmic action. This involved a need to arrange the stage floor in such a way as to provide the maximum possibility for movement and for the display of such movement. Stage levels had to be constructed to correspond to the rhythm of the action so that the rhythmic intervals between stage levels needed to be assessed musically, in keeping with the rhythm of the actors' movements. Thus, a slow, dignified descent needed to be reflected in the evenly-spaced intervals between the levels of the setting, just as a dance in honour of Dionysus demanded an irregular scenic structure with levels of varying heights. In this instance, Tairov was faced with two rhythmic tasks at once – the one requiring an irregular scenic solution which corresponded to the Dionysian elements in the play, the other requiring a scenic structure of a counter-balancing order corresponding to the Apollonian.

3 Poster for *Thamyris Kitharodos* (1916)

Colour also played an important part in pointing these oppositions and was based on black and gold – the black representing the dark tragedy of Thamyris's blindness, the gold his sun-bright striving towards Apollo. Tairov told his actors that their speech needed to be simple but with total observation of the rhythms of the verse. The problem was made more complicated by the fact that the verse was frequently interspersed with passages of *zaum* (transrational language)[31] which were designed, if not to be totally unintelligible, to communicate feelings through the quality of verbal sound alone. During rehearsal, Tairov began to convert some of the verse passages into half-sung recitative which, when accompanied by the orchestra, produced beautiful results. Important contributions to the overall success of the production were made by the music of Henri Forterre and the system of stage lighting invented by A.A. Salzmann,[32] which Tairov had learned of while in Paris. Salzmann dispensed with footlights (nothing new in itself at this time), as well as floods, but managed to achieve an effect which was bright and clear like morning sunlight but which could be made to 'cloud over' to suggest an overcast day.[33]

In December 1916, the owners of the building in which the Kamerny Theatre was housed sold out to an entrepreneur whose future plans for the theatre did not include Tairov. On the eve of the first revolution in February 1917, the Kamerny left one home and settled in another on Bolshaya Nikitskaya Street. Their stay was only temporary. Following the nationalisation of the theatres after the October revolution, their former premises on Tverskoi Boulevard were restored to them. In the meantime, the new Kamerny Theatre opened on 9 October 1917 with a production of Wilde's *Salomé* – rather an incongruous choice when seen against the background of world-shaking events such as the revolution but an obvious choice for Tairov's aesthetically oriented theatre. Another factor determining the choice was that the play had become available for performance in Russia for the first time, having previously been banned by the Holy Synod (the old censorship laws had been lifted after the February revolution). The production also saw Tairov's second major collaboration with Alexandra Exter, with music provided, on this occasion, by I. Gyutel.

The play was interpreted as a clash between earthly feeling (Salomé) and the spiritual negation of the flesh which, literally, inflames Jokanaan. Tairov wanted to get away from the Aubrey Beardsley-influenced versions of the play which had previously been staged by Nikolai Evreinov and Max Reinhardt, which both presented Salomé as perverse and unnatural. Tairov felt that Salomé was a divided soul, full of inner contradictions, desperately searching for something pure and good. He also saw her as someone who had inherited an uncontrollable erotic element in her nature from Herodias which caused her to suppress whatever was whole and decent and redolent of girlish purity in herself. The birth of tender love in her was automatically accompanied by wild outbursts of frenzied passion which plunged her into an abyss of excitement, despair and horror. Her addresses to Jokanaan were a compound of all these feelings, angry reproaches, erotic ecstasy, tenderness and prayer. The 'Dance of the Seven Veils' was not played as an exercise in erotic arousal, but performed as if Salomé had a single *idée fixe* – to obtain Jokanaan's head as reward. The dance combined the inevitability of her cruel love for the prophet with her hatred of Herod who persecuted her with his incestuous lust. The production attempted to incarnate a tragic legend in which the poetry of passion resounded with great power. The threatening cries of Jokanaan which cut through the action, the quarrelling of the Jews and Nazarenes, Salomé's inflamed love for the prophet – all this was intertwined in the action and expressed with great strength, 'giving the production the ring of tragedy'.[34]

Different coloured drapes of differing shapes and sizes, each lit varyingly, appeared and disappeared in front of the cyclorama on a set which was given over to levels and areas of action. A vivid red and blue colour scheme was employed as part of an attempt to control and vary the emotional moods of each scene. As Tairov expressed it: 'In the production of *Salomé* I took the first steps on the path to a solution of the *problems of dynamic transformation of scenic atmosphere*' (his italics).[35] Costumes were decorated with paint. Their lines were emphasised either through colour or through rigid frameworks to retain the forms and rhythms of the designer's lines. The weave and fabric of the costume became part of the method of composition and provided the costumes with a definite and clearly expressed rhythm. Exter believed that every material had its own dynamic potential and that this could be varied by piecing a costume together from different sorts of material – velvet was associated with delay, silk with agility and speed. Differing textures could create impressions of heaviness, lightness, dullness, and so on – 'the delaying velvet, the speedy agile silk, the heavy-paced brocade'.[36]

A connection between Salomé and his next production, of R. Lothar's *King Harlequin*, was made by Tairov during the course of a lecture given in 1931, when he explained how his theatre approached the events of the Russian revolution from a subjective viewpoint, without any sense of class struggle but with a feeling for the pathos of revolutionary conflict.[37] The harlequinade was concerned with the unmasking and dethroning of kings, and in establishing in their stead the actor as revolutionary activist, unmasked despite his make-up, his open face constituting his revolutionary pathos. Salomé had performed an equivalent unmasking operation as far as religion was concerned – of its traditions and prejudices. The gods had been tumbled from their heavenly seats in the name of Life. Tairov considered his theatre's method at the time to be anarcho-revolutionary and that these two contrasting productions – the tragedy and the harlequinade – expressed the creative evolutionary method of the first phase of the Kamerny Theatre's development. The design for *King Harlequin*, by B. A. Ferdinandov,[38] consisted of a combination of portable geometric forms each of which functioned as an 'acting implement' with working parts. These 'implements' could be dispositioned in any space and could be transported for performance elsewhere – in clubs and factories, for example. Great attention was paid in the costuming to the 'eccentric' spirit of the harlequinade, combining elements of circus. Columbine in her elaborate costume and wig seemed to anticipate, in her outward appearance, the tragic figure of Adrienne Lecouvreur while Harlequin, Pantalone and Scapino, with their white faces and motifs emblazoned on their cheeks, exaggerated mouth make-up and thickly drawn brow lines, hailed clearly from the world of circus and clowning. The emphasis of the production was less on the anti-monarchical theme than on the 'capricious play of masks'.[39]

The premiere of Debussy's *The Toybox*, also with decor by Ferdinandov, took place a month later on 21 December 1917. Tairov himself composed the libretto and built the entire production on the basis of marionette movements, in such a manner as to blur the distinction between actors playing the part of dolls and the doll-like representation of human beings.[40] Mikhail Kuzmin, whose *Whit-Monday In Toledo* had been performed by the theatre, referred to

> the enchanting music of Debussy, and . . . the delightful performance of Miss Koonen and the touching production . . . The scene with the doll's dance, the handling of the flowers, the death and resurrection of the soldier, the prayer and rejoicing of Koonen in the second scene were, in my opinion, perfect. Her doll-like expressive face and gestures, half-childish, a surprised and spoilt coquettishness, a wooden 'flightiness' – all this was communicated by Miss Koonen with peculiar grace, both with deliberation and with freedom.[41]

The production of Claudel's *The Exchange*, which opened at the Kamerny on 20 February 1918, was notable for three reasons. The first was the collaboration between Tairov and Meyerhold on the staging; the second was the involvement of the designer Georgi Yakulov,[42] who was to collaborate fruitfully with Tairov on subsequent occasions. The third reason was the fact that this production was considered to be the first major failure among all of Tairov's immediate, post-revolutionary work. The cause of this lay, undoubtedly, in the fact that having invited Meyerhold to work at his theatre, Tairov discovered that their artistic personalities were incompatible. The production became a tug-of-war between divergent methods and conceptions. The grounds for the choice of play are unclear. Tairov possibly knew of earlier productions by Copeau and Pitoëff in 1914 and 1917. He may have been attracted by the play's faintly anti-capitalist theme, involving the American 'captain of industry', Thomas Pollock, with his 'Blessed be the Lord who hath given the dollar to Man', or Tairov may have discovered in the play something which he had also found in *Salomé* – a struggle between paganism and religion, between the human savage (Louis Laine) and the divine Marthe, whose path leads to God and the discovery of grace through evil. However, the inflated declamatory mode adopted by the actors had the effect of drowning any connection the production sought to establish with anything human, while Yakulov's elaborate geometrical setting also served to swamp any subtleties there might have been in the realisation. Following this failure, Tairov and Meyerhold parted company and remained on hostile terms for the rest of their lives.

On 3 April 1919, an example of Tairov's work on the operatic stage was seen when he mounted a production of Anton Rubinstein's version of Lermontov's *Demon* at the opera house of the Soviet Workers' Deputies, with designs by A.V. Lentulov. But, undoubtedly, the major event of the theatrical year was his staging of Scribe's *Adrienne Lecouvreur*. Tairov's collaborators on this occasion were the designer, Ferdinandov and A.N. Alexandrov, who provided the musical score.[43] The play, like the opera (by Francesco Cilea), is based on incidents in the lives of actual people prominent in the theatrical world of eighteenth-century Paris. It concerns the love affair between the leading actress at the Comédie Française during the early part of the reign of Louis XV (1710–74), Adrienne Lecouvreur, and Maurice, Count of Saxony, who later became Marshal of France. The intrigue-melodrama is extremely complicated and involves a double affair between the count, Adrienne and the Princesse de Bouillon. The political ambitions of the count are entangled with love affairs and involve him in having to hide his ex-mistress in one room while entertaining the unsuspecting Adrienne in another; secret doors, dropped bracelets, dramatic faintings on curtain lines, jealous treachery, revenge, a poisoned bouquet and Adrienne's eventual death in the arms of her lover. It is hackneyed, stereotypical stuff, a *pièce bien faite* out of which Tairov and Koonen between them created great theatre, even a great play. As Jean-Richard Bloch said on the occasion of the 75oth anniversary performance in Moscow:

> Tairov and Koonen have made of this play a creative miracle. They have revealed the
> fact that . . . a production is a work of art. We gave them a straightforward melodrama

and they have made of it a shattering tragedy. We offered them Scribe and they have given us Shakespeare.[44]

The production provided the theatre with the opportunity to steep itself in the age of the baroque. Tairov was fascinated by the decorative possibilities of the eighteenth century as well as the opportunities it afforded the actors to parody a world of superficial decorum which merely glossed an undercurrent of decadence and perfidy. The preciosity and refinement of the rococo style was stretched to its limits. The stage was divided into two sections. Three or four steps led from the proscenium to a platform bordered with high screens. The screens changed colour from act to act in accordance with the emotional mood (an extension of the principle employed with curtains in *Salomé*). In the first version of the production the tops of the screens were decorated with convoluted scrolls, cut-outs and the weird and sensuous luxury of the spirit of rococo. The colours of the screens changed from gold (the princess's salon) to brilliant blue (a night scene in a hunting lodge), were draped in mourning or lit by the light of candelabras. The stage furniture was of the most original and fantastic design, combining the spirit of baroque with art nouveau and a hint of the surreal, which contributed powerfully to a general sense of strange exoticism. At times the stage items resembled mushroom-like growths from another planet. The costumes were also given a heightened, grotesque character. The men's jackets were padded round the hip so that their hems appeared to flare out as if in a perpetual dance, even when the actors were standing still. Just as the furniture seemed to take on a life of its own, so the characters seemed like the spiralling twists and curlicues decorating the tops of ionic columns, mere extensions of their wigs and the elaborate decorations on their costumes. Even Adrienne's fan was fantastic in its contours as were the hairstyles of the princesses and countesses. The only human face amongst all this artificiality was that of Adrienne herself. An enthusiastic supporter of the Kamerny Theatre, Leonid Grossman, writing in 1930, said of Koonen's performance:

> In this magnificent interpretation of an actress in love, in this synthesis of love and creativity, of feminine passion and strict art, of tender entreaty and classical poetry – Koonen presents us with an image which is exceptional in its maturity. The profound heartbreak in suffering and pure pathos of this servant of Melpomene are here united in an artistic event of rare power and accomplishment.[45]

The production remained in the theatre's repertoire for twenty-nine years (it was revived in 1930) and was last played on the day the Kamerny closed for good in 1949.

The year 1920 saw the Kamerny Theatre promoted to the ranks of the Academic theatres alongside the Moscow Art Theatre and the Maly Theatre. The year also saw two Tairov productions each of which exemplified contrasting aspects of his theatrical philosophy and methods. E.T.A. Hoffmann's *Princess Brambilla* was a genuine attempt at a 'synthetic' theatre uniting all aspects of theatre – ballet and pantomime, comedy and tragedy, circus and operetta. Claudel's *The Tidings Brought to Mary*, on the other hand, was a solemn mystery play which made totally different demands on the 'master-actor' Tairov was seeking to develop.

At the centre of the overall conception of *Princess Brambilla* was the idea of carnival and the phantasmagorical life of the imagination. Yakulov constructed a set which combined the spirit of Venetian carnival with the 'carefree spirit' of those who have tasted of the spring which flows in milky currents from 'wondrous Lake Urdar'.[46] The setting was an intensely colourful vision in pink and gold which looped and folded, jutted and whirled in a kaleidoscope of levels, abutments, friezes, columns decorated with flaming white fire, and baroque curvature. The action of the play unfolded in carnival time and the production resembled a fizzing and sparkling firework. The carnival glittered and flickered before the audience's eyes in an endless exchange of masks which combined the fantastic and the real. Reality was represented in the spontaneous love of the actor Giglio Fava for the poor seamstress Giacinta – a love which, overcoming all obstacles and surviving all kinds of experiences and unusual events, established its own reality in opposition to the world of illusion, deception and dream. Tairov described the production as a *capriccio* in praise of E.T.A. Hoffmann. The idea was the pursuit of a dream which, in the end, turns out to be actual reality itself. Against a background of carnival, the drama of the two lovers was played out. In this pursuit of shadows, the central characters changed their appearance and their personalities so that they could rid themselves of fruitless fantasising and fall in love with reality once again. Dances, interludes, pantomime episodes, duels, tragi-comic burials, comic processions, all formed the basis of the action. The head-spinning changes of mask, together with the faerie-like complexity of the scenic design, the brightly coloured carnival costumes, all combined with the extraordinarily inventive *mise-en-scène*. Especially fine was a pantomime episode staged in a fairground theatre on the town square in which the admirers of Columbine 'killed' their successful rival, Harlequin, cut his body into pieces and hurled the bits about the stage. Columbine, weeping inconsolably, proceeded to gather them up in a huge basket. Suddenly a 'good fairy' appeared and gave her a magic wand, with a wave of which Columbine succeeded in reviving her loved one. Life defeated the phantoms and the love of Giglio and Giacinta became reality as, in the finale, caught up in a general rejoicing, the actors danced, tumbled, juggled flaming torches, crossed the stage on stilts, dressed as giants, camels and ostriches 'in a single wild rhythm.'[47]

An important corollary to the productions of the 1919/20 season was the gradual development at the Kamerny of an acting school which was eventually to be granted official status in 1923. The training programme consisted of classes in improvisation, make-up, dance, diction, movement, juggling, acrobatics, fencing, gymnastics as well as in theatre history. It was through the theatre school that Tairov sought to train the 'Über' actor, a polymath master performer, versed in all the theatrical disciplines and destined to create the synthetic theatre of the future.

Tairov's production of Claudel's *The Tidings Brought to Mary* opened on 16 November 1920, with music by Forterre and with designs by an important newcomer to the already famous Kamerny stable of designers, Alexander Vesnin.[48] The design scheme was one of cubist austerity and severity, both in terms of setting and costuming. The set itself was reminiscent of a cathedral, with a towering carved statue of the Virgin down-stage right, pillars which soared in geometrically straight lines, and with a cluster of five huge candles of differing sizes placed on an octagonal plinth dominating the stage. The severe, horizontal lines of steps leading to a number of platforms, the vertical lines of the setting, and the square forms of the stage architecture were then echoed in the lines and folds of the costumes which appeared to have been sculpted in the way that the material fell in folds to give a frieze-like appearance of mediaeval iconography. A brilliant architect, Vesnin was also a fine artist. His fresh and sappy colours spoke of the strength of life and the force of earthly passions. The gothic style of the Middle Ages was carried over into the depiction of the actors themselves who were turned into images in stained glass, stylised from head to foot.[49]

Speaking of this production later, in 1929, Tairov described the play as a 'mystery' incarnated in the titanic images of those who cultivate the soil and that this demanded a form which could convey man's unity with the poetry of the earth.[50] The two sisters, Mara and Violaine, were the twin poles of love, and the mystery grew out of the opposed origins of active and demanding love (Mara) and sacrificial, giving love (Violaine). 'We need the mystery now more than ever', Tairov had said in 1921, 'for it awakens great love and summons creative enthusiasm to overcome the insuperable.'[51] In this context it is interesting to note how the spirit of the mystery play also appealed to artists as dissimilar as Mayakovsky, whose *Mystery-Bouffe* was performed in 1918 and 1921; to Vakhtangov, who dreamed of staging the Bible, and to Stanislavsky, who staged Byron's *Cain* in 1920 using a setting by N. Andreyev[52] which was reminiscent of the interiors of gothic cathedrals, complete with stained glass. Some commentators said Tairov's production had little to offer the revolution as it was permeated with a spirit of pessimistic stoicism – a mood strengthened by the music of Forterre, composed in the style of Scriabin.

Shortly after this production had been premiered, Tairov joined in a polemic with Meyerhold over the latter's production of Verhaeren's *The Dawns*. Tairov's attack on Meyerhold was partly in defence of the Academic Theatres which Meyerhold, as head of the Theatrical Section of Narkompros,[53] had attacked in the name of the 'October in the Theatre' movement. Tairov described Meyerhold's actors as 'pitiful marionettes' and Meyerhold as an 'administrator–bureaucrat' who wanted to hang RSFSR signs on all theatres like numbers on prison cell doors. He described bio-mechanics as both decadent and pseudo-scientific. Tairov claimed that his production of *Tidings* was 'revolutionary' and, just as Meyerhold in *The Dawns* had taken a play with a semi-religious message and had altered it to accord with revolutionary reality so he, Tairov, had altered and rewritten *Tidings* (he had, in fact, jettisoned the whole of the fifth act). Another interesting fact is that Meyerhold had been associated with the revival of the mystery play long before the revolution. His first post-revolutionary production was of *Mystery-Bouffe*, which a committee of Narkompros had proposed should, in fact, have been staged by Tairov. The latter had refused on grounds (attributed to him scathingly by Mayakovsky) that a 'pure temple of the arts' had no place for a 'tendentious spectacle'.[54] All this was a useful polemical prelude to the publication, in 1921, of Tairov's own theatrical credo, *Zapiski rezhissyora* (Notes of a Director).

The book expressed Tairov's rejection of both the naturalistic theatre of the nineteenth century and what he termed the *uslovny* theatre (a stylised theatre of convention), which had constituted one of the main lines of revolt against naturalism. At the same time, the kind of theatre which Tairov was working towards may be said to have had more in common with Meyerhold and his *uslovny* school than with the realistic school of Stanislavsky. Tairov based his own credo on a revival of the spirit of the Roman *mimi* and of *commedia dell'arte*. He was very much aware of the classical origins of European theatre and never ceased to wonder how it was that the theatre of Dionysus had, by the end of the nineteenth century become, in Sologub's words, 'a cozy tomb for rabbits'.[55]

In the world of pantomime, however, genuine scenic action was born through the eternal figures of eternal passions embodied in Pierrot, Pierrette and Harlequin. Only pantomime would provide the key to the discovery of form saturated with creative emotion, where words die, and scenic synthesis is achieved through emotional gesture and emotional form.[56] To assist this process, the theatre needed to enlist the sister arts, that of music in particular, but also song and dance in an effort to fuse organically elements which were formerly separate, into a single unified work.

Having insisted on a synthetic unity of the arts, Tairov appreciated how dilettante and amateur was the art of the actor compared with that of the musician or the dancer. Rather than replace him with a Craigian Übermarionette, it was necessary to rediscover the actor's art. Actors needed to be taught how to care for the material of their art – their own natures and their own bodies. The *corps de ballet* ought to have its theatrical counterpart in a *corps de drame*. The actor needed to learn to be a master of his 'instrument' through a mastery of internal and external technique. Real scenic emotion was not part of an attempt to trigger off a corresponding appeal to the spectator's most easily accessible responses. '*The scenic figure is a synthesis of emotion and form brought to life by the creative fantasy of the actor*'[57] (Tairov's italics). The actor's body must be to him as the violin is to the performer, embodying in clear-cut forms the delicate vibrations of his own creativity. Together with mastery of the body went mastery of the voice and of diction. Tairov stressed that there was a particular timbre, key, tonality for every role and that it was the actor's task to find the necessary key and scale for each individual character.

Because the theatre is a collective art, the actor needed to subject himself to voluntary self-restraint and subordination to the director who creatively strives towards an overall harmonious result. The task of the director was to discover an appropriate form for the production as a whole, then to find literary material and transform it into an effective production structure for which there was need to enlist the help of the poet. The third task involved the use of music. Just as the theatre needed the poet, it also needed the composer. The final stage of the work involved the scenic atmosphere in which the actor had to function. This could only be worked out in a definite cubic capacity (for which the scale model was needed)

4 Scene from *Romeo and Juliet* (1921)

and the stage floor needed to be broken up into a series of horizontal or sloping surfaces of varying heights. This structure was based on rhythm. The playing area had to be a place where the actor could be incorporated and displayed, as well as somewhere he could play freely – a structural keyboard on which he could express his creative will.

Colour composition needed to be in accord with the design of the scenic construction and harmonise with the costuming. It was necessary to find for the modern actor the kind of costume which was an integral part of him – the equivalent to the archetypal costumes of Harlequin and Pierrot. Style and period entered the basic motif only as an accompaniment. The costume had to fit the actor, not vice-versa.

With regard to the audience in the changed circumstances of post-revolutionary Russia, Tairov set his face against the idea of a theatre of communal action based on a collectivist ideology. This, in his opinion, was tantamount to depriving the theatre of independent value, making it an adjunct of mass ideology, religious or social. What was needed was the reconstruction of the auditorium to enable the spectator to view creatively. *Notes of a Director* concluded with a series of crisp slogans:

Theatre is Theatre.

It is high time we learned this simple truth once and for all.

Its strength lies in the dynamism of scenic action.

He who acts – is the Actor.

His strength lies in his mastery.

The actor's mastery is the highest and most authentic *content* of theatre.

The permeation with emotion of that mastery is the key to its dynamism.

The scenic image is the form and essence of its expression.

The rhythm of the action is its organisational basis.

And so, Theatre is Theatre.

And the way to make this seeming truism become a joyful reality is single and unavoidable.

That way is through the *Theatricalisation of the Theatre*.[58]

Tairov's production of *Romeo and Juliet*, premiered on 17 May 1921, exemplified many of the principles outlined in *Notes of a Director*. According to Tairov, the 'tragic sketch' as he termed it, required a piece of stage architecture commensurate with its structure and, for this purpose, seven different acting stations were rhythmically calculated to represent the numerous obstacles in the path of the lovers. The central characters were not to be played as bodiless dreamers but as strong, healthy people whose hearts spoke to each other in unison. They were young, passionate lovers in whose striving towards each other lay concealed the tragic outcome of their tempestuous love.[59] Exploring the 'dynamic use of immobile form',[60] and following the example set by Appia and others, Exter exploited the architectural possibilities of the stage by using a combination of arches and steps in order to maximise scenic space. Developing and going beyond her work on *Famira Kifared*, Exter continued to replace the idea of decoration as a visual image of reality with the idea of rhythmically organised space[61] arriving at a concept of the spatial modulation of forms and achieving a perfect balance between mass and space through a complex of horizontal planes and verticals. The impulse behind the setting was abstract and constructivist although within the overall scheme, there were realist elements – canal bridges which seemed to turn Verona into a version of Venice, balconies and portals all cohering as part of a cubist design. The original setting was inlaid with mirrors (later replaced by tinfoil) which flashed and glittered in the light and accentuated the pace and exuberance of the action, which poured over the levels, or 'stations', of action only three of which were at floor level. At moments, as in the opening fight scene, the stage architecture was almost obliterated in the swirl of capes as the set became swamped by a constantly ebbing and flowing tide of figures dressed in sumptuously brilliant colours reminiscent of a Renaissance painting.

The coloured masses of materials, the gleam of their surfaces and the style of their cut – some smooth, others rough or transparent, some reflecting the light – the play of volumes in the cascading steps, some jutting out while others fell like the folds of a fan, the fractured structure of the bridges, one on top of another in the centre of the setting, the design of which was repeated in the broken structure of the balconies and levels – all had the effect of multiplying the movement of the figures. The complicated, multi-layered costumes, furiously whirling, rising and falling all over the framework of the stage structure was too much for some critics. The general feeling was that both Tairov and Shakespeare had become sacrificial victims of the stage designer. 'How could the story of Romeo and Juliet breath in this hodge-podge of furious movement? The answer is it suffocated.'[62]

The following season saw the first official success on the stage of the Kamerny Theatre with the production of Racine's *Phaedre*, which opened on 8 February 1922, in a version adapted and translated by Valeri Briusov and with designs by

5 Scene from *Phaedre* (1922)

Alexander Vesnin. Even before the premiere, Tairov was declaring that it would be
the first production of his in which the emotional side would be given pre-eminence
and in which many of the subsidiary elements, such as music and a complicated
setting, would be subordinate, thus 'permitting the actor to stand before the public
fully-armed with his mimetic means, his plasticity and his declamatory art, all
directed towards the revelation of a profound and deeply significant tragic idea.'[63]
The actors did not attempt to recreate the form and substance of classical theatre
with its panoply of masks, etc., but were transformed simply by a certain stylised
fashioning of costume and make-up and by being placed on low *kothurni*, which
gave a Japanese Noh rather than a classic Greek slant to the production.

Having discarded at least three design schemes, Tairov and Vesnin eventually
arrived at the idea of a listing ship, with a suggestion of sails and rigging in which a
gold colour predominated against a background suggestive of a light-blue sky and
the wide expanse of the sea. The stage floor was broken up into three planes
patterned on a sloping, diagonal structure. Phaedre's first entry was made along
this broken diagonal, very slowly, on low *kothurni*, trailing a heavy purple cape
which streamed out behind her. The theme of the play, according to Tairov, was
the fatefulness of passion – a passion which consumed the whole person. This was
evident in the way Koonen held her hands across her throat as if stifling a scream.
She moved slowly, as if having difficulty in orientating herself, then discovering a
ray of sunlight, fell helplessly into the arms of her maid Oenone.[64]

The scene of ardent confession between Phaedre and Theseus was also boldly
staged. Phaedre crawled from the wings on her knees, moving with the broad

movements of a wounded bird. Her blood-red cape, revealing bared shoulders, spread out behind her like a blood trace. During the confession, she straightened to her full height before falling like a broken reed.[65] Another remarkable moment was Theramenes' account of the death of Hippolytus. Having rushed on stage he spoke his monologue, leaning on his staff, motionless as if the sense of horror rooted him to the spot as he described the vision of the terrible punishment he had just witnessed. The costumes and head-dresses made a powerful impact in the production, cohering with the aesthetically stylised gestures. Phaedre's costume consisted of a classical tunic made of gold brocade covered by a cloak while over her entire appearance there lay the imprint of ecstasy and cruelty. From her first entrance the audience was struck by the masculine profile, the flame-coloured hair, and the distracted gestures. She moved rapidly about the stage, now bending towards the earth, now extending her arms heavenwards. She spoke her monologues in a song-like fashion which would rise to an agonised wail accompanied by shrieks of pain. She acted someone who had been reduced to ash by a burning emotion.[66]

Lunacharsky felt that there was true greatness about Koonen's performance, reminiscent of the French tragedienne Rachel. 'This is what a monumental production is all about,' he wrote in a review for *Izvestia*, leaving behind it a sense of 'beautiful cataclysm'.[67] Lunacharsky's reaction was shared by the sophisticated Paris audience before which the theatre performed on its first foreign tour in 1923. Jean Cocteau thought Tairov's *Phaedre* 'a masterpiece', while the ageing André Antoine thought it a dangerous example of what Bolshevism could do to the 'productions of our national heritage'.[68]

True to his principles, Tairov turned directly from Racinian tragedy to operetta and comedy. Described as 'the most ebullient' piece of buffoonery 'the Soviet theatre has ever known',[69] Tairov's production of Charles Lecocq's operetta, *Giroflé–Girofla*, opened on 3 October 1922, with settings by Yakulov. Nothing could have been more different from his designs for *Brambilla* than the scenic devices which Yakulov provided for this production, with its folding ladders, screens, revolving mirrors, trap doors and 'acting accessories' reminiscent of Meyerhold's production of *Tarelkin's Death*. The musical side of the production was in the hands of A.N. Alexandrov and A.K. Metner. The subject of this French operetta was a most unlikely one. Twin sisters are so alike that even their own parents cannot tell them apart, except by the colours of the ribbons in their hair – pink for Giroflé and blue for Girofla. Koonen played both parts. Both sisters are being courted – the one by the elegant Maraskin and the other by the ferocious moor, Murzuk. There occur a series of amusing adventures. Just before her wedding, Girofla is kidnapped by pirates (an elongated slot in the 'acting machine' opened and the 'pirates' swarmed on to the stage). Papa and mama, in despair, persuade Giroflé to act the part of her sister in order to pacify Murzuk. In the end all concludes happily. The bold admiral Matamoros rushes off in pursuit of the pirates and returns Girofla to her fiancé and the play ends with two happy marriages.

6 Setting for Lecocq's *Giroflé–Girofla* (1922)

At more or less the same time as Tairov was working on this production, Nemirovich-Danchenko was staging Lecocq's *The Daughter of Madame Angot* at his Musical Studio. Nemirovich described his production as a comic opera. Tairov retained the term 'operetta'. Both directors were up in arms against clichéd tradition, although Tairov defended his emphasis on 'convention', where Nemirovich sought to approximate the comic opera to real life, discovering subtle psychological approaches for the actors.[70] Tairov was not interested in the logic of character but in the logic of the genre. A critic close to the Kamerny explained why the theatre had chosen to stage something so diametrically opposed to *Phaedre*. He argued that:

> Operetta is the quintessence of authentic, genuine theatricality which is of value in itself; of that theatricality which, stemming from the *balagan*, is sustained by the poetic qualities of the actor . . . Operetta contains everything – music, the sharp sting of satire which permeates it and the everyday quality of its theatrical origins . . . The ideal operetta is soaked through with movement, dance, temperament, irony, quips, interests of the moment – it is all-action and not for a moment does it lose the energetic abandon of play.[71]

Tairov spent eight months working on this production, in which he leaned on the experience of *Princess Brambilla*. The style resembled a 'montage' of eccentric 'attractions', and provided Tairov with splendid opportunities for handling his favourite form of the harlequinade – the idea of the 'double', the mixture of the sinister and the joyful (as in *Brambilla*), transformation scenes, miraculous appearances and the like.

It was the most carefree and joyous production in the whole of Tairov's creative biography. The actors had 'quicksilver in their legs and champagne in their blood' wrote one critic.[72] Even the accessories and properties danced – a long-handled sunshade in the hands of one actor, fans in the hands of another, folding chairs, hats. Someone 'dances until he can't go on, until he can no longer stand on his feet. He sinks on to a chair and continues to dance sitting down. Devoid of strength he falls to the floor and, prone, continues to dance nonetheless. The top half of his body gives out, but one leg carries on dancing by itself. One foot begins to die down, but loses its shoe which continues to dance on its own. The owner of the shoe tries to nail it to the floor but fails to do so. The possession of the dance must exhaust itself to the end.'[73]

On 21 February 1923, Tairov and his company set off on the first of what were to be three European tours. It was an altogether eventful year. Not only was the Kamerny a resounding success but Tairov's *Notes of a Director* was published in Potsdam, in German translation, as *Das entfesselte Theater* (The Liberated Theatre). It is interesting to speculate as to the reasons why the Soviet authorities felt that the honour of a foreign tour should fall to the Kamerny rather than, say, to the Meyerhold Theatre or any of the other theatre groups which had been born almost simultaneously with the revolution and, in that sense, were unlike the more traditional Moscow Art Theatre who were currently touring America. There is little doubt that the authorities considered the Kamerny would provide less intimidating fare than the Meyerhold Theatre, that it was less obviously a revolutionary theatre in a directly political sense and that its aesthetic ideology tended to conform with Lenin's dictum that the best of the bourgeois heritage should be preserved. A performance of, for example, Eisenstein's version of Ostrovsky's *Enough Stupidity in Every Wise Man* (given a circus-style production at the Proletkult Theatre), or of Meyerhold's *Tarelkin's Death*, would have served to convince the West of the 'barbaric' nature of Bolshevik arts. The Kamerny provided evidence that the revolution had sought to preserve 'culture' in the more traditional sense.

On his return from France and Germany, Tairov embarked on a rather unusual project – a stage version of G.K. Chesterton's detective novel *The Man Who Was Thursday*. One of the most interesting aspects of the production was the setting by Vesnin – a constructivist skeleton, the elements of which combined to suggest a modern urban landscape consisting of skyscrapers, oil derricks, pitheads, moving walkways, ironwork bridges and liftshafts. According to Koonen, Tairov said he wished the production to show the generalised image of a large capitalist city with its usurpatory power, a city which held man in its pincer-like claws, turning him into a machine.[74] This mechanical element was represented by the construction itself, which was in movement throughout – escalators, lifts, along and in which the anarchists/detectives pursued each other. The constantly flickering neon lights of the advertisements combined with the frenzied pace of the production to produce a feeling of nightmare. The characters were turned into mannequins who spoke in a standardised, monotonal fashion. Constant changes of rhythm underlined these mechanical movements and intonations, lending the production 'an expressionistic character'.[75]

It was described as the first 'urbanist' production at the Kamerny at a time when 'urbanism' was all the rage. The movement of people in this environment was one of ceaseless activity, like ants in an antheap, except that the ants wore check suits, mackintoshes, top hats and flat caps. Crime, avarice, poverty, exploitation and hopelessness were said to have been the abstract elements which emerged through the matrix of animate and inanimate objects on stage. Critics detected a certain aesthetic slickness in the setting, which tended to undercut the production's ostensibly political message. There was also a feeling that the formerly predominant scenic artist had simply been replaced by the technician, who had a similarly swamping effect on the action. In essence, Vesnin's 'urbanism' was seen to be all of a piece with the 'excesses' of *Romeo and Juliet* or *Princess Brambilla*. Tairov and Vesnin were also accused of plagiarising from Meyerhold, whose production of Alexei Faiko's *Lake Lyul*, at the Theatre of the Revolution, had set the standards and paved the way for further 'urbanist' productions in that vein. Huntly Carter's account – that of an observer very sympathetic to the Soviet theatre of the day – saw the production as a celebration of collectivism and the urban age.[76]

What was it which drew Tairov who, up until then, had largely ignored the classic Russian repertoire, to Ostrovsky's nineteenth-century drama of provincial life, *The Thunderstorm*, in 1924? Partly it seemed a case of a continuing polemic with Meyerhold, who had staged an 'eccentric' production of *The Forest* earlier that year. It also seems to have been a response to Lunacharsky's call for a return to Ostrovsky, as part of an attempt to curb some of the experimental excesses which flowed from the political extremism of the 'October in the Theatre' movement. However, far from being a 'realist' version of the play, Tairov appears to have conceived the production more in the spirit of the 'grotesque'.

The production also introduced the work of the Stenberg Brothers[77] to the stage of the Kamerny Theatre and marked the beginning of yet another fruitful collaboration. The key to the overall conception lay in the contrast between the setting and the characters. The construction was composed of clean, geometrical lines and balanced, arched forms which spoke of the harmony and proportion of life, of reason and balance. The structure was light and airy, seeming to support itself endlessly. Beneath its central span, the distorted shapes of the characters, clad in black and dark colours, showed themselves to be out of place and somehow crushed beneath it. Here the emphasis was on grotesque distortion, madness and breakdown. The beautifully functional lines of the setting were echoed in the large square tiles of the stage floor so that characters (especially when seen sheltering from the thunderstorm in act 4) seemed like primitive, superstitious elements of an otherwise harmonious, natural world. A series of arched motifs were both geometrically precise and redolent of rainbows in a world where a thunderstorm is an omen of terror, evil and death.

Tairov considered the conventional evaluation of Ostrovsky to be incorrect – that of a straightforward depicter of the manners and mores of the merchant class.

The Thunderstorm, he felt, occupied a special place in Ostrovsky's output (quite apart from its being set in the provinces rather than in the merchant quarter of old Moscow). The play could only properly be understood if compared with Sophocles or Shakespeare. In Katerina, the heroine, he saw the tragic pathos of the age-old struggle against servitude. In her he saw the clash between a *ponizovaya vol'nitsa* (a wilful woman of the lower middle class) and the concept of *domostroi* (the obscurantist stress on traditional domestic values and roles). He felt that the characterisation of the town of Kalinov, where the action is set, took second place to the drama of spirtual torment in Katerina.

The traditional portrayal of Katerina was as a figure in an icon painting – a woman condemned to her fate, enveloped in an aura of religious mystery. Or else she was represented as something of a dreamer in whom love suddenly flared up in hysterical quasi-religious exaltation. Tairov would have none of this and portrayed Katerina as a flesh-and-blood scion of that patriarchal existence which had reared and nurtured her.[78]

With one or two exceptions, critics tended to react with hostility to this controversial interpretation, although the general public were very taken with it. It is worth noting that audience figures for the 1923/24 and 1924/25 seasons fell generally, largely owing to the introduction of free market forces under NEP and the consequent increase in ticket prices. However, despite this, the Kamerny played to 74 per cent capacity in 1923/24 (higher than anybody else) and 78 per cent capacity in 1924/25, which was way above the Moscow average of 61 per cent.[79] Tairov himself was not altogether satisfied with the production and revised it within the year, placing a greater emphasis on lighting effects to provide an even stronger feeling of light and air.

Following this, Tairov turned his attention to another serious play and another female sacrificial victim – Shaw's *St Joan*. The premiere took place, with designs by the Stenberg Brothers, on 21 October 1924. It was not considered a successful production and was strongly criticised for its schematicism and its expressionist elements, which had the effect of reducing the forces opposing Joan to mere caricatures. Defending himself in a speech made in November 1924, Tairov said there was a need to polemicise with Shaw's depiction of the characters as, apparently, decent human beings. He felt that there were certain contradictions between what is said in the Preface and what is portrayed in the play. It was the responsibility of the director to restore the balance, reconcile the contradictions and even 'correct' Shaw's mistakes.[80] Tairov appears to have conceived the production on two contrasting levels – the crude and the farcical on the one hand, set against the elevated and the heroic on the other. These oppositions were staged with great inventiveness in an attempt to highlight elements of irony and sarcasm.

Lunacharsky rejoiced in the production's simplicity, its abandoning of a former, extravagant and conspicuous aestheticism in favour of something more austere. At the same time he felt that the choice of play was itself not a good one. In *St Joan* Shaw had rehabilitated the Middle Ages, praised individual human genius and described Inquisitors as wonderfully intelligent people. As such, the play was totally irrelevant to the needs of the present. In fact, Lunacharsky even went so far as to declare that Repertkom (the repertoire committee)[81] should not have allowed the production to go ahead, although he appreciated that to suggest banning a play by Shaw was something of an insult. In the final analysis he was forced to admit that the director's approach and the actors' performances had been brilliant and that many of the difficulties had been overcome including, in his opinion, the play's basic unstageworthiness.[82]

The principle behind the set design was an abstract sense of the 'gothic,' combined with extreme manoeuvreability and lightness. Tairov wanted a portable setting which would be suitable for club performance. The 'gothic' elements were portrayed by means of a dozen or so thin pillars in 'telescopic' sections with the broadest section at the base, in front of which were arranged a number of levels and bench-like constructions which gave an abstract impression of choir-stalls. The costuming of the characters ran to extreme caricature, with strong emphasis on the grotesque in the depiction of the French court, the church and the military. Against this background, Joan was depicted as a creature of naive beauty and gauche simplicity, dressed in clumsy padded clothing with knee-length boots, or clad in armour and bearing a heavy sword.

Shaw learned of the production through an article and photograph published in the *Daily Sketch* on 21 November 1924. Under a caption: 'This is how the bolshevist theatre interprets *St Joan*', a photograph showed Koonen as St Joan sitting on the Dauphin's knee. Shaw was, naturally, very displeased and showed Tairov the photograph when he visited Moscow in July 1931, at a time when the production was no longer in the theatre's repertoire. He was shown, in his turn, a folder with photographs of scenes from the 1924 production from which Tairov extracted two – one showing the Dauphin sitting on the throne, the other St Joan sitting on a stool. The one had clearly been superimposed on the other in the newspaper reproduction.[83] At the time, it had been rumoured in the British press that the production had been removed from the repertoire because of government pressure but this was denied by Tairov in a letter to *Pravda* on 10 January 1925.

There followed a further tour, this time to Germany and Austria between April and August 1925, during the course of which the theatre was awarded a medal by the University of Cologne. Having returned home, Tairov set to work on a political sketch, entitled *Kukirol*, devised by a quartet of writers and described as 'a satire on American, French and British bourgeois decadence.'[84] It was, in fact, an eccentric clown show with decor by the Stenbergs and with music by L.A. Polovinkin and L.K. Knipper. Tairov claimed it was the first example of a 'revue'-style entertainment to be seen in the Soviet Union[85] and announced that it was to be 'a political pamphlet and satire on contemporary capitalist society in Western Europe'.[86] Writing in *Krasnaya Gazeta* on 27 November Tairov said that *Kukirol* was not a typical native production, where everything tended to be drily schematic, nor was it in the style of Western European revue-sketches which exploited the 'cult of sensual nudity'. He was going to stage a 'revue-play' with a plot and developed action.[87] However, the final result was ambiguous. In trying to turn the

Western revue on its head the production, according to some, managed to contradict the professed aims of the director and took on 'an obviously expressed cosmopolitan and capitalist character'.[88]

The production was generally considered not to have been a success and Tairov was to admit as much in 1931. However, the theatre recovered much of its lost prestige the following year with its productions of two plays by Eugene O'Neill. The first of these, *The Hairy Ape*, opened on 14 January 1926, in a stage setting designed by the Stenberg Brothers which combined, in constructivist form, all the various locations of the play – stokehole, ship's deck, Manhattan sidewalk, prison cell, zoo cages, and so on. The choice of play may, to some extent, have been purely fortuitous but it answered many of Tairov's own interests – in the theme of anarchic individualism, for example. It also silenced those critics, such as Lunacharsky, who implied that almost every play staged at the Kamerny was simply a chosen vehicle for Koonen, irrespective of any other significance it might or might not have. There was also the fact that, in O'Neill's depiction of conditions on board a luxury cruise liner and of the American bourgeoisie, the play offered splendid opportunities for an anti-capitalist critique of the society against which 'Yank' was rebelling. Pessimists considered the play unstageable, but Tairov worked out several ingenious *mise-en-scènes* sometimes altering or adding to the play. For example, he incorporated a dance scene on board ship which anticipated, in its marionette-like movements, the New York street scene of scene 5. The scene which made the strongest impression was the opening one set in the ship's stokehole. This was staged as a pantomime to sound and musical accompaniment and lasted for a full seven minutes. The actors, naked to the waist, hurled imaginary shovels of coal into the blazing maw of a furnace to the accompaniment of cries, oaths and a sound score orchestrated in a single rhythm.[89] Yank was portrayed as a lone individual struggling against his environment and desperate to find in others a trace of decency and fellow-feeling. Despairing of ever finding this quality among people, he finally turns to the world of animals and is crushed to death by the gorilla in the final scene at the zoo.

Lunacharsky wrote an appreciative criticism of the play as well as describing the merits and demerits of the production. The play's main deficiency, he felt, was its expressionist form. The Soviet theatre was already over-familiar with this method through the work of Kaiser, Toller, and others which, in showing the subjectivist inclination of the contemporary European intelligentsia, produced an essentially poor and boring genre consisting for the most part of extended monologues instead of a strong narrative line. However, in Lunacharsky's opinion, Yank made a far more interesting and relevant hero than, say, the cashier in Kaiser's *From Morn to Midnight*. He also felt that the play spoke of the colossal revolutionary potential of the lower proletariat but also of the 'great strength of the walls of America's social boiler'[90] which could contain the force threatening to explode it. Turning to aspects of the production, he suggested that nobody had as yet managed to give such a sculpted and metallic rhythm to sound and movement as Tairov had achieved in the first, third and fourth scenes. He referred to many previous attempts, by Foregger and others, to express the dance of labour, or the 'machine dance'. This was the 'most genuine aesthetic' and the 'most genuine proletarian' art.[91] Lunacharsky found Tairov's depiction of the bourgeoisie no less interesting 'in whose nerves and muscle beats the senseless rhythms of the foxtrot. This is cruel and truthful reality to the point, I would suggest, of genius.'[92] He concluded:

> Whatever the case, we have at the Kamerny Theatre a genuine, great, shattering artistic spectacle, containing an enormous social charge . . . I confirm with joy the success of the theatre. Two or three productions like this and we won't be hearing any more arguments about the place of this theatre in our theatrical system.[93]

Other opinions were cooler, describing the production as a 'political revue' in the *Kukirol* style, staged in a simplistic manner typical of an earlier period based on oppositions between workers and exploiters – 'some work while others foxtrot' etc. In essence, the production was seen by these critics as 'an elegant *agitka*'.[94]

The next premiere to take place at the Kamerny was of A.P. Globa's *Rozita*, a play based on a popular American film of the time with the same title. Its theme was the struggle for civil freedom and the overthrow of the monarchy. It was essentially a melodrama, containing both tragic and comic episodes, set in the Spain of Alfonso XIII, in which the heroine is a street comedienne, Rozita. Her agitational speech after the people have overthrown the monarchy invariably received a rousing reception from the audience. The role provided opportunities for Koonen in the realm of the exotic as a pretty anarchist with whom everyone is in love, including the king. In the finale, she contrives that her lover undergo a mock execution and that the king is poisoned. Koonen grasped these opportunities with both hands and some of her dancing put observers in mind of her earlier role at the Moscow Art Theatre as Anitra in *Peer Gynt*.[95]

1926 was a significant and transitional year in the history of the Soviet theatre and in Soviet political life generally. It marked a point between the first phase of the revolution, personified by Lenin (who had died in 1924) and the second phase to be personified by the emerging figure of Joseph Stalin. 1926 saw the key production at the Moscow Art Theatre of one of Stalin's favourite plays, Bulgakov's *Days of the Turbins*. It saw Meyerhold's theatre reach an important turning point, with his production of Gogol's *The Government Inspector*. As far as the Kamerny was concerned, the highpoint of the year was the theatre's production of a second O'Neill play, *Desire Under the Elms*.

The play was chosen because it seemed to present concrete problems and provided the opportunity to establish the theatre's work on the basis of a new 'concrete realism' (Tairov's term). The play also treated motifs which appealed to Tairov, and which had been interpreted in *The Hairy Ape* as a conflict between class feeling and sexual feeling, between the individual and the collective. Here he sensed the conflict was between genuine love and the desire to possess. In this case, the desire to possess was closely linked with the desire for property. Another important reason for choosing the play lay in its proximity to a classical tragic model, where the passionate love of a woman for a son-in-law brought it close in spirit to *Phaedre*.

Tairov felt it would not be correct to portray Abbie as a mere adventuress but that here was someone who, until this point, had not known the meaning of real love and had therefore been prepared to sell herself to the seventy-year-old Cabot. Her love for Eben was expressed through the child and through its murder which, to that extent, appeared justified (although Eben was guilty of putting her in the position of having to kill the child in order to express her love for him). In the final resort, the murder of the child appeared justified and both Abbie and Eben were exonerated by the strength of their love for each other. Tairov saw Eben as a 'possession maniac' and the farm as a 'fetish object'. The spirit of possessiveness died in Eben with the death of the child. For him, the child was as much an object of possession as was the farm. In this play, Tairov considered O'Neill had scaled the heights of ancient tragedy, where people are led to a new life via a process of cleansing and renewal which involves some monstrous crime.[96]

Explaining the principle which underlay the staging methods of the production, Tairov pointed to the phase of 'concrete realism' which his theatre was going through – an attempt to achieve a balance between the formal methods of constructivism and straightforward naturalism. Either, on their own, was seen to destroy unity through too great a degree of abstraction (in the one) and through the chaotic ramification of everyday, realistic objects in the other. A naturalistic representation of the farm would have concentrated on the importance of cattle, even to the extent of depicting cowsheds, having lowing noises off-stage and people wheeling manure barrows, etc. A constructivist version would have gone to the other extreme in presenting an outline, a mere scheme of a farm, its mere potentiality. The Kamerny took both the general idea of the farm and its particular manifestation in this instance. From the particular they extracted those elements which seemed to them most general. In order to stress that one of the themes of the production was that of private ownership, the theatre adopted the idea of the farm as some indivisible piece of real estate. It needed to be a place which appeared constricted and stubbornly immovable, unable to satisfy the possessive instincts of the protagonists. An attempt to convey this sense of stubborn immobility was made in the representation of the heavy wooden pillars and beams, the cellular structure of the building and the low ceilings. There was no attempt made to fulfil the terms of O'Neill's own description of a building sheltering beneath the protective embrace of the elms, which have a seemingly animate connection with the dead mother.

Koonen decided that Abbie was someone very close to nature. In her, some form of organic, animal-like principle existed cheek by jowl with an almost child-like spontaneity and purity. Abbie, in Koonen's view, was not a calculating evildoer, or a moral monster, but someone with a terrible, tragic fate. A woman who is used to living in the clutches of trivial, everyday calculations, mercenary interests, is suddenly seized by an emotion previously unknown which blinds her with its unusual shining. She is ready to destroy anything which threatens to take it away from her, without being conscious of the horror of the act she commits.[97] The theatre went to the lengths of conducting a mock trial of Abbie and Eben, in which Tairov was witness for the defence and in which well-known psychiatrists

7 Scene from O'Neill's *Desire Under the Elms* (1926)

and legal experts took part. Koonen and Tseretelli (who played Eben) dressed for their roles and defended themselves with great passion from the witness box, Koonen even breaking down in tears at one point. The trial ended at 2 a.m. with the acquittal of the defendants.

The production was a great success,[98] especially for the actor Fenin, who had played Yank and now played Cabot. His drunken dance in part 3 scene 1 was brilliantly choreographed by the ballet master Natasha Glan, whose hand was also evident in the same scene where the dancing guests cast monstrous shadows on the doors and windows in a broken and fantastic rhythm.[99] The production was also another triumph for Koonen, who managed to connect the mercenary Abbie with the great figures of tragic drama. As the critic S. Mokulsky wrote: 'The fact that Koonen has managed to discover the fine borderline between a particular, everyday drama and a general, abstract, "universal" tragedy, is her great achievement.'[100]

True to form, a month later Tairov staged another operetta by Charles Lecocq, *Day and Night*, in a version by V.Z. Mass and, once again, with scenery and costumes by the Stenbergs and with dances arranged by Natasha Glan. In reworking the original, Mass brought it up to date, sharpening the sense of parody and strengthening the socio-satirical base of what Tairov called a 'musical eccentriade'. As well as creating design and costume with a distinctly 'punkish' air to them, the brothers Stenberg tried an experiment in designing the set as a continuation of the auditorium.[101] The production was approved of in *Pravda*, who pointed to the beneficial influence of a visiting black American troupe.

The next two years were not especially productive as far as Tairov was concerned. Of the four productions attempted, only two were adjudged passable and one, of Bulgakov's satire *The Crimson Island*, was subjected to more serious condemnatory criticism than any other production by Tairov staged during the Soviet period to date. Probably the most successful and interesting of the four was the one to be staged first, on 1 October 1927, a production of Walter Hasenclever's pacifist/expressionist version of Sophocles' *Antigone*, reworked by S.M. Gorodetsky and with designs by A. Naumov and music by A. Shenshin. Tairov explained the choice of play as being dictated by the theatre's feeling that it contained those opposing forces and competing interests which could culminate in a world cataclysm. It also contained a protest against 'imperialist war'.[102] It was in order to make this feeling more explicit that the play need to undergo a certain amount of rewriting.

'What ideas did I put into this new *Antigone*?' asked Gorodetsky.

> My aim was to reveal the contemporary political situation in Europe. We live in an epoch in which a polar opposition of forces is concentrated: at one extreme the proletariat is gathered, at the other, fascism. This is the definitive theme of *Antigone*. The emotion of Antigone, as leader of the risen mass, not just a leader but an embodiment of their feelings, her struggle and death under Creon's heel, signifying the temporary defeat of the European proletariat and the folly of weakness, of fascism triumphing over the corpses – this is the definitive theme of *Antigone*.[103]

A suggestion of the part played by the decor and costuming in contributing to the desired effect of the production is contained in the following description:

> The production of *Antigone* raised the tragic genre to heights that the Soviet theatre had never attained before. It turned out to be the last crowning attempt at all the quests for the forms of classical tragedy. There was something prophetic in this 1927 production. Creon's palace rose in cubes above the abyss cut into the stage floor. It was like a 'pillbox' from the cities or 'Atlantic Wall' of the Third Reich. The warriors were heavily armoured from head to foot with iron mesh. The platform of the palace turned menacingly. The power of Creon's dictatorship annihilated everything, marking the peak of coercion and militarism. Such was the theme of this uniquely powerful presentation which showed the European reality of thirteen years later. Tairov's particular skill at moulding sculpted groups and crowd scenes was especially evident in *Antigone*. There were frightening interwoven lines of half-naked people in rags. At times they would come out of their numerous trapdoors and drag themselves up the walls and ladders of Creon's fortress. At other times they were thrown down and cowed by the firm step of the warriors. This was the one presentation of the Kamerny Theatre in which the actors' voices, the noises, the whirlwinds of motion, the rumblings and the sounds of Creon's armoured 'robots' achieved superhuman power.[104]

There was something both timeless and suggestive of the space age about the costuming of Creon's military, with their domed headgear and leather uniforms. There also appeared to be a detectable influence of the costuming for the Art Theatre's 1911 production of *Hamlet* – a hint of something scaled and reptilian. The drawbridge which let down as a flight of steps leading to the palace gave on to a platform above two square bastions pierced by entrances and with projecting levels on which guards, armed with spears, stood in threatening eminence. Stage grouping, both on the steps and across the width of the stage, was charged with an inner dynamism and given sculpturally expressive form. Koonen's stylised facial make-up, reminiscent of Phaedre, with accented eyebrows, nose and mouth lines, was relieved and made more contemporary by her natural hair, either held severely off her face or falling loose about it. The deeply shadowed eyes and mouth held open in a silent scream lent her appearance a strong suggestion of the Attic mask of tragedy itself.

On 8 November 1927 the Kamerny staged a premiere of a play about the French revolution by M. Levidov, entitled *The Conspiracy of Equals*, which was an attempt by Tairov to examine the role of members of the intelligentsia in changed historical circumstances.[105] The fate of this production is hardly touched on in standard Soviet histories as it was removed from the repertoire after a single performance. It was important in so far as, for the first time, it involved Tairov in work with a designer who was to make a significant impact on the work of the Kamerny Theatre and on Soviet theatre generally in the following years – Vadim Ryndin.[106] It was also Tairov's first attempt to stage a serious play by a native Soviet dramatist and it was regrettable that this should have happened just a year before his production of Bulgakov's *The Crimson Island*, merely serving to confirm suspicions (where these existed) that Tairov's main interest was in mounting productions of 'foreign' works unless, as in the case of Bulgakov's play, these could be seen as satirical and 'anti-Soviet'.

The debacle of Levidov's play was followed on 28 January 1928 by the premiere of an operetta by the Soviet composer L.A. Polovinkin, entitled *Sirocco*, with designs by the Stenberg brothers. In this production, Tairov moved away from the eccentric spirit of *Day and Night* and created an attractive, joyous, realistic comedy. Tseretelli played the part of a sham Bolshevik, Kazakov, with whom a young Rumanian princess is madly in love. The use of music was unusual in that it did not accompany the arias but carried on conversations with itself, or underscored the dialogue.[107] According to a contemporary reviewer:

> Tairov's *Sirocco* occupies a notable place among his researches into the sphere of musical comedy on account of its simplicity as well as its unusual scenic resolution, as well as for the joyous lightheartedness which fills the production.[108]

From a satire on Western civilisation, Tairov turned to a satire on revolution and colonialism, with a side-swipe at Glaviskusstvo, the censorship body which had come into existence in July 1928. The premiere of *The Crimson Island* took place on 11 December with designs by Ryndin and music by Metner. It is worth remembering that the attempts to stage plays by Bulgakov which had been made prior to this – *Days of the Turbins* and *Flight* at the Art Theatre and *Zoya's Apartment* at the Vakhtangov Theatre – had all run into trouble for one reason or another. Tairov could hardly have expected an untroubled ride in the present instance – a satirical play which deals with revolution on a Pacific island led by natives who appear to have a thinly disguised relationship to Russian revolutionary leaders. The final scene involves the banning of the play-within-the-play (written by a Soviet dramatist calling himself 'Jules Verne') by a member of the Repertory Committee, who is portrayed unflatteringly and who, having banned the play, then changes his mind and permits it, subject to certain, approved (and rather crude) 'revolutionary' revisions.

All the press reviews had a sharply negative character and Bulgakov was attacked as much as, if not more, than were Tairov and the Kamerny, with doubts being cast on his political loyalty. Despite this, the production remained in the repertory almost until the end of the season. O. Litovsky provides a flavour of the criticism surrounding the reception of Bulgakov's play which had been fuelled by the Art Theatre's attempt to stage *Flight*:

> It would be a mistake if we were to consider the situation on the theatrical front to be favourable. The general intensification of the ideological struggle found its reflection in the theatre. Is it not the case that the struggle around Meyerhold's theatre had to do with the demarcation of ideological lines? Isn't the struggle about staging *Flight* a reflection of the petty-bourgeois attack on the theatre? It was precisely this year that we had the production, which was itself a slander on the October revolution: I am speaking of *The Crimson Island*.[109]

On 21 February 1929, Tairov presented his third production of an O'Neill play – *All God's Chillun Got Wings* (re-titled *The Negro*) and with significant alterations to the original, including a changed ending. According to Koonen, the production sounded a protest against racial discrimination and indifference to people's fate. Tairov composed a veritable symphony of light, sound and imagery in the sad songs of the white and black singers, in the noise of a large city with its crowds and intense emotions.[110] The Stenbergs' designs consisted of two surfaces which joined to form a corner of two streets at a crossroads between the black and white ghettos. The set gave a suggestion of high buildings forming a gloomy canyon where sunlight rarely penetrated.

The scene in which the mad Ella decides to murder Jim was staged with chilling realism. Jim, played by I.N. Alexandrov as a neat, bespectacled image of 'a black whiteman', dressed in buttoned-up jacket and highly polished shoes with a tight white collar and tie, sat at a table working by the light of a lamp. Suddenly, from behind a curtain, Ella glanced into the room. Creeping up behind him, all her concentration focused on the black curly head in front of her, she suddenly took a knife from beneath her dressing gown and made as if to strike at him. But, at that precise moment, the heavy legal tome which Jim had been studying and nodding asleep over, fell to the floor with a thud. This had the effect of bringing Ella to her senses. Gazing about her in bewilderment, she let the knife drop from her hand and there, behind Jim's back, the audience were treated to a schizophrenic glimpse of the 'other' Ella as she embraced Jim tenderly, hugging his shoulders. He responded by kissing her hands and covering them with his tears.[111] Tairov's altered ending consisted in having Ella die of a heart attack in Jim's arms following the episode where she redirects her aggressive feelings for Jim towards the African mask on the wall by stabbing it. O'Neill does not seem to have objected to this new ending and, after seeing the production in Paris during the 1930 tour, said he was happy to have

such a co-author as Tairov. Paul Robeson, who also saw the production, offered to
take on the role of Jim for some guest performances and even went to the lengths of
auditioning for Tairov to prove that his Russian accent was acceptable by reading
some speeches from Pushkin's *Boris Godunov!*[112] Tairov had actually planned to
stage *The Emperor Jones* before *All God's Chillun* and, following two evenings spent
with O'Neill and his wife in Paris, the dramatist also sent Tairov and Koonen a copy
of *Mourning Becomes Electra* in the hope that they would consider staging it.
Unfortunately, nothing came of the idea. In a letter to Tairov dated 2 June 1930,
O'Neill wrote:

> Having seen your production of *Desire Under the Elms* and *All God's Chillun* I am
> amazed and full of heartfelt thanks. I must admit that I went to the theatre with
> hidden misgivings. Not because I doubted that your productions would not be
> magnificent in themselves, artistically conceived and executed. I know the
> reputation of the Kamerny too well as one of the best theatres of Europe. But the fear
> of the author spoke in me, that in the difficult process of translation into another
> language, that which is most essential and dear to an author – this spirit might,
> bearing in mind all the obstacles, be interpreted incorrectly or become lost
> altogether. How great was my excitement and thankfulness when I saw your
> productions which so thrilled me. They completely communicated the inner life of
> my work.[113]

Anxious to fulfil an obligation to stage work by Soviet writers, Tairov next
turned his attention to a dramatised version of a novel by the proletarian author
Sergei Semyonov, whose *Natalya Tarpova*, written in 1928, deals with the personal
and official lives of party functionaries during the NEP period. Semyonov was one
of the best practitioners of 'psychological realism' and his chief skill lay in reporting
the stream of unspoken thoughts and desires which lie behind his characters'
actions. The central theme of the novel, and of the play, is the conflict within a
healthy, full-blooded woman between her natural affection for a non-party
engineer and her strict communist values. The novel has been described as 'a
valuable historical document in that it gives an entirely credible account of the
problems of marriage and morality as they were examined at that time'.[114] In the
history of the Kamerny Theatre it proved to be yet another failed attempt to found a
theatre production on the basis of the available Soviet repertoire.

The premiere took place on 8 December 1929, with designs by the Stenberg
brothers following a rehearsal period during which Tairov worked in close
collaboration with the author.[115] In Tairov's view, the basic problem of the play
and the production was that of the 'social' versus the 'personal' centring on the
question of the relationship between the individual and the collective at a point
where two ideologies were seen to intersect – the proletarian and the bourgeois.
According to Tairov, Natalya had been forced to re-examine her privileged
position in society as a result of the revolution with the result that she confronted
these 'great events' in total bewilderment. However, the end result was that class
instinct won the day and Natalya entered the ranks of the party, became a zealous
worker and ended up as secretary of a factory committee. It was at this point that the
'personal' element came to the fore in the shape of her love for Gabrukh (a non-

party specialist and enemy of the Bolsheviks). This had the effect of exposing the duality and indecisiveness of her personality. Discord then arose between her perception of the world and her actual experience of it, expressed as a struggle between personal and class feeling. Only under the influence of a tragic shock (the death of Lenin) was she able to recover her authentic social instincts and recognise herself as an inseparable part of the collective.[116]

The theatre's Artistic Council examined the play at its meeting on 5 March 1929, and declared in a resolution that certain ideological corrections were needed. The play was discussed at meetings of Glavrepertkom on three separate occasions during 1929 before the premiere on 8 December. The production was adjudged unsuccessful and taken off that month. Tairov blamed himself for being too preoccupied with the notion of staging what he described as a 'production-meeting'. At certain key moments, the actors mounted rostra specially positioned at the front of the stage and addressed the audience directly. 'This directorial idea was introduced into the scenic realisation of the play and prevented me from seeing its ideological weakness', Tairov wrote later.[117] Koonen was much less apologetic:

I very much liked one of the devices which Tairov brought into the action. In moments of internal alarm or reflection, Natalya or Gabrukh would mount a rostrum which rose from the orchestra pit during the course of the action and from which they spoke directly to the audience, as if confessing their feelings and ideas, trying to discover in themselves the answer to questions which excited them.[118]

Pavel Markov clearly believed that the theatre, and Koonen in particular, were not up to understanding or portraying working class people:

When Koonen imitated the typical characteristics of a working girl as she imagined them to be – rolling up her sleeves and walking about the stage with big strides in a careless manner, the spectator believed in neither the actress nor the author . . . this first, unsuccessful, brush with contemporary literature asserted that the essence of character lies less in external imitation than in understanding its core.[119]

How Tairov came to hit on Brecht for his next production is not clear. The play in question, *The Threepenny Opera* (given as *The Beggars' Opera*, Opera Nishchikh), had been very successful in Germany in 1928 and this must have been one of the first (if not *the* first) performance of a Brecht play outside his own country. At the time, Brecht was unpublished in the Soviet Union and did not become more widely known until the mid 1930s, largely through the efforts of Sergei Tretyakov. Koonen says that Tairov got to know Brecht when he visited Germany and met him on several occasions, but this was later that same year and can have had little bearing on the choice of play in the first instance.

The production opened on 24 January 1930. It was staged as a tragi-farce, with interesting decor by the Stenbergs, who provided a central device of screens and doors reminiscent of Meyerhold's setting for *The Government Inspector*. It was used very effectively in the brothel scenes, which were staged on a revolving carousel which revealed a different girl in varying stages of undress behind each door. The impression was one of cynicism, corruption and venality.[120] This first production of Brecht on the Soviet stage was given in a satirically grotesque, pamphleteering style. The exaggerated and eccentric nature of the characters laid bare the core of a hypocritical, mercantile society, despite a certain expressionist colouring in the representation while the fast and furious rhythm of the production engendered a sense of 'phantasmagoria'.[121] Generally speaking, it was felt that the theatre had avoided the pitfalls of 'opera' and had managed to overcome one of the main dangers – which was to render heroic or romanticise the 'bandit-vagrant' and 'lumpen' characters in the play. The grotesquerie and the particular form which the caricature assumed in this production, enabled the theatre 'to circumvent this potential hazard'.[122]

Between this and Tairov's next production, on 6 June 1931, there was more than a year's interval during which the Kamerny embarked on its third and last European tour which, this time, was extended to include the American sub-continent. Forty-seven members of the company set off on 25 March 1930, spending three months in Europe and two in South America. A further two months were spent travelling by boat. They gave 128 performances in nine countries – Germany, Czechoslovakia, Austria, Italy, Switzerland, France, Belgium, Argentina and Uruguay. In the meantime, the theatre building was closed while the auditorium and stage were being reconstructed. On his return, Tairov became involved in a polemical debate with RAPP and advanced his theory of 'structural realism' for the first time during a debate held on 4 January 1931.[123] He also published articles on the 'crisis' of the theatre in Europe and South America.

The two productions he mounted in 1931 were both of serious plays from the new Soviet repertoire – N.N. Nikitin's *Line of Fire* and N.G. Kulish's *Sonata Pathétique*. Before going abroad, Tairov had agreed with Nikitin, a Leningrad-based writer, that the latter should write a play for the Kamerny. Once again, as was the case with *Natalya Tarpova*, Tairov needed to do a considerable amount of the composition work himself, working in collaboration with the author of whom both he and Koonen grew extremely fond. The central character of the play, Murka, is a teenage waif who accidentally finds herself caught up in a building project. The official view of the theatre's Artistic Council was that the play was 'immature' and that the decision to stage it was a sign of the theatre's state of confusion. Koonen, who played Murka, suggests in her memoirs that the production was, in fact, very popular with audiences.[124] Another memorable aspect of the production was the striking 'constructivist' setting provided by the Stenbergs.

More successful was the production, later the same year, of *Sonata Pathétique*, with semi-constructivist decor by Ryndin, which opened on 20 December. The form of the play resembles an expressionist monodrama, with objective reality appearing in a sequence of mental images and lyrical monologues. The central character, Ilko, pursues a mental journey along his 'unenviable, but instructive revolutionary route', through events which take place in an old provincial Ukrainian town in the spring of 1918. According to Kulish, his work was an attempt to present the condensed dramatic image of the world which exists in the hero's mind, divided into three parts, as in the *vertep* (Ukrainian puppet dramas) with Heaven (the poet's garret), Earth (the street) and Hell (the basement) shown in the form of a single apartment block. In his garret, Ilko dreams of Marina, his beloved, and finds the rhythm for his verses in the sounds of a Beethoven sonata (the one of the play's title). The key scene in the play deals with the hero's dream which, when interpreted, means that Ilko has betrayed the common cause by rising above the revolution in wishing to play a solo part in the 'orchestra of humanity'. He finds himself on the side of the counter-revolutionaries and brings about the deaths of many people. In the final scene, Ilko abandons the secluded garret of his fantasies and moves into the street of life to join the great march 'in the name of universal justice, brotherhood and freedom'.[125]

Ryndin's design provided a cross-section of an apartment block, consisting of three levels with a number of cellular playing areas linked by flights of stairs. The angles and perspectives were deliberately distorted and compressed by an upper angle, reminiscent of a roof, but which had the effect of seeming to crush the set in one direction, giving the whole a nightmarish effect not unlike one of the settings for Robert Wiene's film *The Cabinet of Dr Caligari* (although this impression was more apparent in the original design than in the actual stage realisation). The play unfolded on the various levels of the apartment block where people of differing stations and views of life lived. This enabled Tairov to cut from location to location very rapidly, giving a cinematographic effect. According to one critic, the set itself was like a grand piano with the lid raised, while the play was like a sonata played by the winds of revolution blowing across the piano strings.[126]

The finale to the first act caused great critical excitement. It is Easter night. Ilko is in his attic dreaming of eternal love. Next door, Zinka the prostitute sings to her own guitar accompaniment. At the general's they are raising their glasses. Marina, the teacher's daughter, and her father are standing at the window contemplating the vastness of the Ukraine. On the landing, a chain of people descend the stairway bearing lighted candles. A sharp contrast to this was provided by a counter-procession in the foreground of wounded and exhausted soldiers returning from the First World War front accompanied by the echo of wailing shells and a melancholy soldiers' song.

The RAPPists accused Kulish of 'political mistakes', especially in the interpretation of the nationalist counter-revolution (in fact the play depicted the ideological and political defeat of nationalist, counter-revolutionary forces). But according to RAPP, the depiction of *negative* individuals with a degree of psychological concretion and conviction equivalent to that with which positive characters were treated amounted to 'objectivism' and 'compromise with the class enemy'.[127] Tairov was obliged to introduce a whole range of alterations.

Tairov's next production was of another play by a Ukrainian author – L.S. Pervomaisky's *The Unknown Soldiers*. Again, the production was not a critical success but proved important in so far as it prepared the ground for his production of *Optimistic Tragedy*. The premiere took place on May Day 1932, with settings by Ryndin and music by Metner. The play concerns an episode at a Black Sea port during the civil war and focuses on events surrounding a French sailor, Jean, who

8 Setting for *Sonata Pathétique* (1931)

whilst on guard duty on a French cruiser learns of the impending arrest of a revolutionary underground committee and, feeling sympathy with the revolution, warns them in advance. For this betrayal of his military obligations, he is sentenced to death but his fellow sailors turn their weapons against their own officers and, as in Eisenstein's *Battleship Potemkin*,[128] a mutiny breaks out on board ship. Tairov thought of staging the play, which was rather schematic and immature and needed a considerable amount of reworking, in 'agitational' fashion as a 'production-poster'. Ryndin provided him with a setting which could be easily transformed from the deck of a cruiser, with its huge gun muzzles, into a secret hideout for members of the underground cell, then into the headquarters of the counter-espionage unit, and so on. It also provided an excellent space for the staging of mass scenes. Vishnevsky was very interested in the production and attended several of the rehearsals, which served to prepare the ground for work on his play *Optimistic Tragedy*. According to Mikhail Zharov, an actor formerly at the Meyerhold Theatre who transferred for a short time to work with Tairov at the Kamerny, critical response to *The Unknown Soldiers* was fairly scathing. It was considered 'primitive', failing to satisfy even the most elementary stage demands.[129]

Ryndin provided the designs for Tairov's next production, which took place in what was something of an *annus mirabilis* so far as the Kamerny Theatre was concerned. It was in 1933 that Tairov staged the production for which he will always be honoured in his own country – that of *Optimistic Tragedy* by Vsevolod

Vishnevsky. However, it was preceded in that same year, on 2 May, by a production which is also historically valued in the Soviet Union – of *Machinal*, by the little-known American playwright Sophie Treadwell. In many respects the production was a continuation of the O'Neill cycle and was intended to show the ill effects of the capitalist way of life on ordinary, vulnerable people. Tairov had already staged his vision of the mechanisation of human life in the 'Fifth Avenue' scene from *The Hairy Ape*. The model which he had in mind for *Machinal* was a product of his recent visit to South America when, standing on one of the main streets in Buenos Aires, with its rushing traffic and neon advertisements, he was put in mind of a process whereby people were made to seem mere adjuncts of the city, cogs in a machine-oriented environment. In a pre-production exposition, given in 1932, he talked of the 'mechanisation of the human psyche'.[130] It was his belief that, despite its much-heralded faith in individualism, capitalist society in fact destroyed the individual as well as standardising and depersonalising people.[131] In the play he saw two characters – Ellen Jones (the heroine) and 'the city'. The latter was expressed by a whole gallery of types differentiated according to sex, height, degree of fatness, hair colour, temperament – but all, essentially, marionettes. Standardisation had so entered their flesh and blood that they themselves neither noticed nor felt it, naively believing that they lived 'freely', according to their own will.[132] Only Ellen was different, despite being unheroic, neither a real rebel nor a fighter. She had simply been left behind by the pace of the machine and, therefore, the machine had ruthlessly, step by step, stifled each minute appearance of her tiny, living 'self'.

Tairov knew little of the author, except that she was young, Mexican, and a professional journalist. He invited her to Moscow to attend rehearsals. Sophie Treadwell's main impression was that her play, which had been interpreted as a naturalistic tragedy in America,[133] was here raised by Tairov to the level of a 'social tragedy'.[134] Where the emphasis in the American production had been on the personal tragedy of a woman who killed her husband, Tairov placed the emphasis on the generalised image of the capitalist city which killed a woman who was just one of the many victims of a process and a system. Ellen's problem lay in her being out-of-step with the majority in not having become standardised or adapted to the machine – a fact sufficiently criminal in itself. The giant city, with its mechanised psyche, cannot tolerate this and Ellen perishes as a result.

Ryndin's setting and Polovinkin's music combined to create the effect of an overpowering, crushing city of skyscrapers, grilles and tower blocks – the structure of a capitalist city as evoked in *The Negro* by the Stenberg brothers, with music, in this instance, intensifying the effect. Tairov divided the play into three acts with three scenes in each – the Office, the Family, the Honeymoon (act 1), then Maternity, Sobriety, Love (act 2), followed by the Hearth, the Law, the Machine (act 3). There was to be no curtain between the acts and the scenes were to be linked by 'introductions' based on *son et lumière*, each in its own rhythmical plan. The final scene in the prison was terrifying. Identical walls and benches. Iron grilles on all sides with, behind them, as in a mist, the heights of skyscrapers. In the middle of all this sat the tiny, lost figure of Ellen Jones. A hairdresser entered. Boasting about his artistry he cut away a section of hair from Ellen's head whilst she endured this in trance-like bewilderment (she is being prepared for the electric chair). It was only with the entry of two warders that she suddenly grasped the significance of what was happening to her. Whilst they gently tugged at her she kept repeating over and over again 'I won't! I won't!', as a priest tried to administer a blessing. The final scene showed three identically dressed newspaper reporters all scribbling down details of the execution in their notebooks.[135]

The designs for each scene consisted of screens which filled the entire height of the stage and, when lit, gave the impression of skyscrapers in a large city. Panels opened at varying heights affording a view of life inside the apartments. At other points, the stage was illuminated vertically and horizontally by neon advertisements, flashing signs, etc. By means of small truck stages, placed in various parts of the stage, it was possible to move sections of the action on to the forestage and fade out the background, or retain it like a 'looming mirage'.[136] Ellen's difference from her surroundings was suggested in the opening scene. Above each typing table in the office was a symmetrically-arranged, neatly-hung jacket belonging to each identical, fashionably-dressed typist. In contrast, Ellen took off her jacket and simply threw it across the back of a chair. In the trial scene, both the prosecuting counsel and counsel for the defence were of identical height and complexion, wearing identical spectacles and dressed in standard black suits, dark ties and white shirts. Not all criticism of the production was favourable. Once again, Tairov was accused of accentuating the formal elements:

> The mistake made by Tairov in staging this production is at the root of the entire creative method of the Kamerny Theatre, which is far from having overcome its formalist leanings. Until now, the external staging methods of the production have always taken first place. This is also true of *Machinal*, in which the atmosphere of an American city, created by Tairov and Ryndin with great mastery, is conveyed through straight, upward-running lines of skyscrapers and by means of lighting effects. But the people who are mutilated by the capitalist city are non-existent apart from Koonen, and in their name alone was it worthwhile staging Treadwell's play at all.[137]

On 18 December 1933, what might be described as one of the most significant events of Tairov's life, as well as one of the most significant events in the history of the Soviet theatre, took place when Vsevolod Vishnevsky's civil war play, *Optimistic Tragedy*, was staged at the Kamerny. The play itself is a unique work in manner and conception, inextricably linked with the spirit of Russia and the post-revolutionary history of the Soviet Union. In form and substance it appears alien to cultures whose artistic traditions are based more on emotional restraint. In many respects, it is a play unlike any other ever written before. It concerns particular historical events associated with the civil war in the Soviet Union but, more generally, it is an article of faith – in the triumph of Life over Death, of the Collective over the Individual, of faith in the necessary tragedy of revolution, of the necessary destruction of those who oppose revolution, of hostility to the spirit of anarchism, and faith in the leadership of the party. It is a play of epic scale and epic emotion which has served as a rallying cry for a whole generation of theatregoers, dramatists and directors.

It was staged at a difficult time of historical indecision at a point where faith in the revolution needed to be encouraged more than ever. The expected European revolution had not materialised and the rise of fascism was marked by the assumption of the German chancellorship by Hitler in this same year. The international communist movement was weakening and was to be weakened even further by an increasing tendency in the Soviet Union to turn inwards upon itself. It was the end of the first five-year-plan and the phase of forced collectivisation of agriculture. It was also on the eve of an important period of industrial reconstruction when divisions in Soviet society were seen to intensify as class conflict intensified in proportion to the closer attainment of socialist society (or so it was thought at the time). It was the period just prior to the official promulgation of the doctrine of 'socialist realism' following the First Writers' Conference of 1934. Tairov's production of this play was to be cited as a model of what socialist realism in the theatre should be. It was also on the eve of the 'purges' in a country which felt itself threatened from without by a resurgent, rehabilitated, more aggressive capitalism, and from within by disaffected members of the intelligentsia, 'bourgeois nationalists', spies and saboteurs. Indeed, much of the drama of the time deals with these very topics. The fact that a person such as Tairov should place himself at this juncture in the vanguard of socialist affirmation was astonishing to many and the last thing that was expected from this 'aesthete', 'formalist' and 'fellow-traveller.'

The plot of the drama is fairly straightforward. A commissar is sent by the party to impose discipline on a group of sailors in a Baltic seaport who are dominated by a group of anarchists led by the Chief (the play appears to have a direct connection with the sailors' revolt at Kronstadt in 1921 which was put down, on Lenin's orders, by the Red Army which, at the time, was commanded by Leon Trotsky). At the outset, the only person to lend his support to the commissar (who, to everyone's surprise, turns out to be female) is a Finnish communist sailor, Vainonen. One of the commissar's first acts of assertion, in the name of the party, is the unceremonious shooting of one of the sailors who threatens to rape her. The anarchists are shown in an unfavourable light when they exact summary justice on one of their number when an old woman reports having had a purse stolen (which turns out not to have been the case). They are also guilty, later, of conducting a summary court-martial of two officers suspected of being 'Whites'. The commissar's tactic is to win over the mass of the sailors by winning over their leaders where she can and, where she cannot, by turning the men against them. She is also astute enough to exploit the loyalty of the pre-revolutionary officer class where, as in the case of the ship's commander, they are prepared to remain faithful to command and country and, therefore, indirectly loyal to the party despite being hostile to the Bolsheviks in principle. The chief of the anarchists is himself dealt with by his formerly cowed comrades, largely because of the revolt of one Alexei to the commissar's side. However, through the treacherous murder of Vainonen by another unregenerate anarchist, the group of sailors who have been organised to fight the interventionists are captured by foreign forces before being freed by a division of the Red Army. In the course of the fighting, the commissar is killed.

Since the war, the play has been revived by the Berliner Ensemble in East Berlin and by Peter Stein in West Berlin, but it remains a play unlikely to exercise much appeal for a typical British West End audience – a fact recognised at the time by the Soviet ambassador to London, Ivan Maisky, when negotiating with the British authorities for an official tour by the Kamerny to London in 1936.[138] Tairov's conception of the play was based on the conflicts it depicts between life and death, between chaos and harmony, between negation and affirmation. The emotional, plastic and rhythmical line of the production needed to be constructed in a distinctive curve, leading from negation to affirmation and from anarchy to conscious discipline. This curve derived all its growth from roots implanted in the social basis of the play. The essential content was seen to be the process of the crystallisation of new class consciousness in place of the 'chaos of petty-bourgeois, individualist perceptions'.[139] In this lay the origin of the struggle between two forces, two elements – the centrifugal and the centripetal – those striving towards integration and those towards disintegration. The struggle between these forces resulted in a series of collisions which led to the victory and maximum assertion of the centripetal force. This movement required scenic expression through the specific construction of the *mise-en-scène*. Where two currents meet they create whirlpools, which suck in all those who try to swim against the current. It was precisely this notion of a whirlpool which Ryndin sought to incorporate in his setting.[140]

He and Tairov wished to give palpable expression to three elements – Sky, Earth, Humanity. The circular setting with its central vortex, in addition to suggesting the elemental aspects of the struggle, also gave rise to the suggestion of a Greek amphitheatre. It could also, with slight adjustments, take on the appearance of a warship, or become the endless road along which the regiments marched to immortality. Above the set reigned the vast expanses of a troubled sky with constantly moving clouds (an effect achieved by back projection). In this setting, the characters themselves became aspects of nature, which the commissar set out to organise. A young woman of intellectual appearance, with her hair combed back from a fine-featured face, wearing a battered leather jacket and speaking in crisp, precise phrases, she seemed to personify the insight and lucidity of the best revolutionary workers. Koonen won the audience, not by romantic eloquence or gesture, but through power of intellect. However, mingled with this were sparks of humour and the rough leather jacket failed to conceal the fact that she was a delightful person as well as a party functionary.[141]

Tairov divided the play into sections, each with its own culminating point. The first was the anticipated rape of the commissar before she defended herself by shooting the sailor. The second was the scene of the dance on board ship which is demanded by the sailors and is held prior to the regiment's departure for the front. The third culminating point arose when the Chief, attempting to sound out the commissar, asked her which side she is on. (Her answer is 'The regiment's.') The

9 Scene from Vishnevsky's *Optimistic Tragedy* (1933)

fourth culminating point was the victory of the commissar in her power struggle with the Chief (the final stage of the struggle between the centrifugal and centripetal forces). The fifth culminating point occurred at the moment when the commissar instructs Alexei to play his accordion while the foreign troops are advancing, when the sounds of the accordion became an instrument of battle. The appearance of the priest preceded the sixth culmination (when he is rejected by the men) and the seventh, when the commissar calls for new naval regiments and new generations to further the work of the revolution.[142] According to F. Panfyorov: '*Optimistic Tragedy* is a new type of play and a new type of production . . . It is agitational through and through. But if this is propaganda, then it is propaganda raised to the level of art.'[143]

It was a year before another production appeared on the boards of the Kamerny. The fantastic success of *Optimistic Tragedy* was to keep that production in the company's repertoire for a total of 800 performances, not many by London West End standards, but a considerable number in a theatre which already had eight productions in the repertory during the 1931/32 season, prior to the inclusion of *Sonata Pathétique* and *The Unknown Soldiers*.[144] In the meantime, Tairov had been contemplating a production of John dos Passos's *Fortune Heights*, as well as laying plans for a production of Bizet's *Carmen* in Leningrad. Neither of these projects came to fruition. From 8 to 14 October 1934 he attended the Convegno Volta conference in Rome, which was also attended by Pirandello, Yeats and Gordon Craig. Tairov addressed the conference. However, most of that year was spent preparing an unusual production of a play to be called *Egyptian Nights*, consisting of three versions of the Antony and Cleopatra story – Pushkin's *Egyptian Nights* (three short chapters of an unfinished piece of fiction), Shaw's *Caesar and Cleopatra* and Shakespeare's *Antony and Cleopatra*. Once again, Ryndin provided the settings, and music was specially commissioned from Sergei Prokofiev, who had recently returned to live in the Soviet Union.

Tairov adopted a Marxist-cum-sociological approach in his interpretation of the Shakespeare play. He felt that an important fact about the background to its composition was the clash between feudalism and the emerging capitalist order. Tairov's hypothesis was that Shakespeare intended a likeness between the Earl of Essex and Antony and expressed, through him, sympathy with the Essex rebellion. Shakespeare only dared suggest this by donning the mask of Plutarch. Just as Shakespeare's epoch was that of a transition from feudal society to one of mercantile capitalism, so the epoch of Antony was accompanied by the transformation of the Roman Republic into the trading empire of Octavius Caesar. Similar to the way in which, during the reign of Elizabeth, absolute power was concentrated in the monarch who acted in the interests of the emerging class of mercantile bourgeoisie, so, in the interests of the Roman mercantile bourgeoisie, was the great Roman Empire gathered into a single unit by Octavius Caesar. Just as, historically, Essex was bound to lose the unequal contest, so Antony was bound to perish in his struggle with Octavius Caesar. But where did Cleopatra fit in? Tairov believed that Shakespeare intended at first to write a play with a singular title, probably called *Marc Antony*, and linked with the other single-title, Roman plays such as *Coriolanus* and *Julius Caesar*. However, Cleopatra was born as a result of a struggle between Shakespeare's original ideas and the material which he subsequently found in Plutarch. This gripped him to such an extent (thought Tairov) that he was completely conquered by the image of Cleopatra. The political struggle within the triumvirate remained the basic subject of the play, only now rendered more complex by the tragedy of love. The fact is that the world was too narrow a place for Antony and Cleopatra. That which interested the mercantile bourgeoisie, of which Caesar's imperialism was a champion, also demanded the unification of the western and eastern halves of the Roman Empire, the economic interests of which were closely connected with this 'narrow world' and could not be completely satisfied without its unification. From this arose the second subject – the struggle between Egypt and Rome; of Cleopatra for the independence of Egypt and against her country being turned into a Roman colony. The struggle between Antony and Octavius also contained echoes of the present day, according to Tairov:

> Mussolini, Hitler and a whole range of large and small 'Caesars', in the interests (on this occasion) of powerful, imperialist capital, are attempting to repeat, in different historical conditions, and with different means, the experience of Octavius ... Only, this time, a new organised force (the proletariat) has entered the struggle ...[145]

Both the wretchedness and the limitations of the first accumulative period of the mercantile bourgeoisie were personified in Octavius. This fact stood out in greater relief when compared with the self-abnegation from riches of a Julius Caesar, rather than if compared with the impetuous and decadent heroism of an Antony. This was why Tairov chose to broaden the framework of the production by including Shaw's play. Shaw was of interest because he revealed the colonial tendencies of Rome of which he spoke in the Preface. But why bring in Pushkin? In explanation, Tairov pointed to the fact that, between the end of Shaw's play and the beginning of Shakespeare's, there is a gap of approximately seven years. The inclusion of the Pushkin fragments seemed organically necessary as, on the one hand, Pushkin managed in a few strokes to depict the atmosphere of the Alexandrian court and also provided a remarkable illumination of the 'debauched' aspect of the life which, according to legend, was led by Antony and Cleopatra. Gordon Craig considered these ideas dubious, until he saw the production in 1935, when he said he felt that Shaw's play formed a magnificent prologue which helped the spectator to understand Shakespeare's tragedy as well as the complex line of Cleopatra's development.[146]

Only certain sections of Shaw's play were actually used, concluding with Caesar's promise to Cleopatra that he will send her Marc Antony. The seven-year interval was taken up with an interlude set in a harbour in Sicily with Roman guards on duty when a wandering poet appears (this image was borrowed and adapted from the Italian 'improviser' who haunts the salons of Petersburg in Pushkin's story). To the accompaniment of Prokofiev's music he began the six-stanza poem with which Pushkin's fragment concludes:

> The palace glitters; the songs of the choir
> Echo the sounds of the flute and lyre;
> With voice and glance the stately queen
> Gives animation to the festive scene . . .

The final words were overheard by Gallus and Enobarbus as they entered a harbour tavern. Excited by the improviser's words, the soldiers then began to question Enobarbus about Cleopatra. This was the cue for Shakespeare's account of her meeting with Antony on the river Cydnus.

An American observer in Moscow at the time, Norris Houghton, attended rehearsals and was especially struck by Tairov's handling of the crowd scenes:

> The memorable moments are ones like that in which Cleopatra sits at the apex of a pyramid of steps; below her stand or recline her court and attendants, first distinguishable on a dark stage by the points of light which are their glowing torches: like the fleeting scene when two ships are joined in the battle of Actium and the fighting legions overrun the stage – the finest staging of Shakespearean 'alarums and excursions' I have ever seen; or like the moment when Cleopatra's terrified attendants, fleeing from her presence, scurry down long narrow flights of steps in seemingly endless number, and make the whole stage an agitated anthill of movement.[147]

Critical reaction generally, however, was unfavourable. The production 'arouses curiosity only'; it had 'no leading idea' and was 'artistically superficial'. According to one critic,

> the union of Shaw with Shakespeare . . . is one of the weakest aspects of *Egyptian Nights* . . . The Kamerny Theatre has a great advantage over other theatres when it comes to staging Shakespeare in overcoming the naturalism which has become customary for many of our theatres and which gets in the way of creating a sense of

character. From this point of view, *Egyptian Nights* showed to advantage, especially in its Shakespearean section where it appeared a production of great proportion and monumental style . . . However, while completely getting away from naturalism, from trivial characterisation, the production appears . . . declamatory, without a profound emotional basis.[148]

In January 1935, the theatre celebrated its twentieth anniversary with a production consisting of excerpts from *Salomé*, *Giroflé–Girofla* and *Optimistic Tragedy*. On 5 January, Tairov was awarded the title of 'People's Artist'. Between March and May he resumed his acquaintance with Gordon Craig, whom he had met in Rome. While in Moscow, Craig saw the productions of *Egyptian Nights* and *Optimistic Tragedy*. He appears to have marvelled at Ryndin's settings but was actually more impressed by a production of *King Lear*, directed by Sergei Radlov, at the State Jewish Theatre in which Solomon Mikhoels played the title role.[149]

The only new production of Tairov's to be staged in 1935 was of S.A. Semyonov's play *No Surrender*, which was chiefly memorable for the fact that the sets were designed by the artist famous for designing the monument to the Third International, Vladimir Tatlin. The play told of the voyage of the *Chelyushkin* under the command of Otto Yulevich Shmitt. Tatlin's setting for act 1 consisted of a cross-section of a vessel with four acting areas – a cabin on the level of the deck itself, the deck (marked by a rail and lifebelt), and two cabins below deck. Scenes played in the Arctic wastes managed to suggest the polar vastness by means of lighting effects and by having the actors dressed in authentic furs.

At the beginning of 1936, Tairov restaged his production of *Optimistic Tragedy* with the actors of the local theatre in Rostov-on-Don. But a warning of things to come appeared in the form of a series of articles in *Pravda* containing criticisms of the theatre in general and singling out the Kamerny in particular on the grounds of its 'formalist' approach. Matters came to a head in October when Tairov staged a new production of the nineteenth-century 'opera farce' by Alexander Borodin called *Bogatyry* (The Epic Heroes), which had been provided with new words by the peasant poet Demyan Bedny. The opera parodied cliché motifs from opera through borrowings from Meyerbeer, Rossini, Offenbach, as well as from Russian folk songs. The production was condemned as an outrage and virtually signalled the end for the Kamerny Theatre as it had hitherto been known. The reasons for this may require some explanation.

Several important changes had occurred in the Soviet Union between 1934 and 1936 involving, amongst other things, changes in the military and educational structure. These changes appeared to mark a reversion to the past in many respects and to restore patriotism, military ranks, titles, awards and academic degrees to their formerly respectable place. Such was, for example, the title of People's Artist with which Tairov had recently been honoured. Until now, patriotism had been considered a bourgeois prejudice and a denial of internationalism but now the nation's past began to take on a different meaning. Even former sovereigns began to be treated as heroes of a glorious Russian heritage – people like Alexander Nevsky (the subject of a 1938 film by Eisenstein), Peter the Great, General

Suvorov, Fieldmarshal Kutuzov (all of whom had plays written or films made about them during the mid to late 1930s). Even Ivan the Terrible was subjected to historical revaluation. The production of *The Epic Heroes* could not have been more ineptly timed in that, despite the fact that it treated Russia's tenth-century conversion to Christianity satirically, it was seen as an offence to the resurgent nationalism glorifying the nation's past. Bedny had a considerable reputation for his witty political fables, popular songs and couplets written in accessible style, as well as for his satirical attacks on Western capitalists and statesmen. However, in this case, the libretto was considered 'an insolent misrepresentation of the country's history'. A recent Soviet account throws some light on the episode:

> Things became more difficult for Tairov following the production of the 'opera farce' *The Epic Heroes*. The press first reported the production's success with the audience: 'Bedny has created a quite new, original, integrated popular satirical play', but, within a fortnight, the production was being spoken of as a falsification of the history of the people with 'its pseudo-populism, hostility to the people, distortion of the popular epic, and perversion of the history of the people, whilst being false in its political tendencies.'[150]

It was as a result of the hostile opinions directed at the theatre following this production that the Kamerny was merged with the Realistic Theatre, headed by Nikolai Okhlopkov, in August 1937. It may have been intended as a recipe for curing whatever ills it was felt were afflicting either, or both, theatres. In fact, it served as a recipe for disaster as the two diametrically opposed personalities and production styles sought to find some kind of *modus vivendi*. Koonen, in her memoirs, recalls how the news of the merger stunned Moscow and describes the sombre atmosphere of the 'celebratory' meeting held in the foyer of the Kamerny to mark the merger of the two troupes who had gathered to meet each other for the first time. They then proceeded to go their separate ways for a little over a year while continuing to share the same building. Tairov hardly directed anything. The situation could not last and in October 1938 the main half of the Realistic Theatre, headed by Okhlopkov, left the Kamerny for the Theatre of Drama and Tairov returned to the business of running his own theatre.

The first play he tackled was a documentary based on the life of the doctor-biologist Pokrovsky called *Stronger Than Death*, which remained in the repertoire for quite some time and proved very popular with the public on account of its simplicity and sincerity. The times were fraught. Meyerhold's theatre had been closed in January 1938. It was the period of the 'purges'. Tairov's theatre was not regarded with favour, despite *Optimistic Tragedy*. Even the achievement of this production was being revalued, as the account of a British commentator at the time suggests:

> His theatre was a haven of rest from struggle – struggle sublimated into an aesthetic sentimentality. His productions never touched the masses nor expressed the life of the masses. His first attempt at 'realism' came as late as 1932 – Pervomaisky's *Unknown Soldiers* – but that was crude dramatic material. Occasionally, he produced plays with a contemporary content, like Vishnevsky's *Optimistic Tragedy* . . . which

had greater success . . . But the heroism of the woman commissar in that production was the outward heroism of a newspaper headline, a Wagnerian heroism, Racine's monumental Phaedre in a modern uniform.[151]

On 16 March 1939, the theatre premiered a play *Bridge of Devils* by A.N. Tolstoy. It was an anti-fascist satire written in a sharply grotesque style and with much excellent dialogue. Tairov invited the Spanish expressionist artist Alberto, who was then living in Moscow, to design the sets and the latter created a brilliant impression of a huge international fair on stage. However, an anti-fascist play on a prominent Moscow stage became something of an embarrassment following the signing of the ten-year non-aggression pact between the USSR and Germany on 23 August 1939. The result was that the production was removed from the repertory.[152]

In June 1939, Tairov participated in the First All-Union Directors' Conference, although there is no record of his having spoken. Following Meyerhold's arrest on 20 June, the atmosphere for creative work in the theatre, especially in Moscow, became dire. However, Fate intervened kindly as far as Tairov and his theatre were concerned as they were despatched on a ten-month tour of the Far East – about as far away as it was possible to get from the agonisingly fraught and complex artistic life of the capital. It was while in the Far East that the theatre gave the premiere of an adaptation by Koonen of Gustave Flaubert's novel of nineteenth-century French provincial life, *Madame Bovary*, with Koonen herself in the title role and with music especially composed by Dmitri Kabalevsky. Whilst on tour, the theatre also gave a concert performance of Mayakovsky's *The Bedbug*, a play which Tairov valued very highly. The company left Moscow in October 1939 and did not perform there again for a year.

The Kamerny returned to the capital the following August and the production of *Madame Bovary* was staged at its own theatre in October. It was greeted with acclaim as one of the theatre's finest efforts. The Moscow Art Theatre had previously staged, during the 1930s, successful dramatisations of nineteenth-century novels such as Tolstoy's *Resurrection* and *Anna Karenina*. The taste for dramatising great classic works could also be attributed to the poverty of the contemporary repertoire and the fact that dealing with works from the past tended to be less controversial than the handling of work on contemporary themes.

Plans for staging *Madame Bovary* had been laid as early as 1938. The novel was popular in the Soviet Union, where a volume of Flaubert's letters had recently been published. Tairov felt the production would have great social significance and would help the Kamerny to strengthen the realistic basis of its work. The preparation was long and painstaking. On their last visit to France, Koonen and Tairov had undertaken a great deal of research into the background of the novel. Tairov and his designer, Boris Shchuko, collaborated on the development of an appropriate form for staging the play and hit on the idea of three revolves, the movement of which would be closely linked with lighting changes and music. Because of the number of different scenes and the need to move fairly rapidly from one to the other, the arrangement of the sections of the set on the revolves was technically very complicated but managed, nevertheless, to sustain the flow of the action and to give the audience the impression that they were turning over the pages of the novel as they went along. Music played an important part in the production, in particular a waltz which became a leitmotif in Emma's life story connected with the most romantic moments of her life. It sounded during the carnival when she had already sensed her tragic fate and, again, during her fever prior to her death. In fact, the production contained two musical leitmotifs – the waltz and the cynical song of a blind street musician, which also entered Emma's life at critical points. This latter song was accompanied by a barrel organ. The waltz became a personification of her passionate thoughts, the barrel organ music brought her back to earth and the confined space of her actual life. Act 1 concluded with the sounds of Leon's departing carriage, covered by Emma's howls of anguish with which were merged the sounds of the barrel organ and the croaky voice of the blind singer.

The production's final moments were considered especially effective. Tairov felt that Emma's death was described in the novel in excessively naturalistic detail and, as it was undesirable to pursue this effect on stage, the following scenario was conceived. The even beat of a church bell was followed by a sudden, terrible scream. One of the rooms in the Bovary house was lit. Félicité could be seen sitting with the priest, crying whilst being comforted by him. The action moved to the bedroom where Charles knelt at the foot of the bed in which Emma was lying, breathing with difficulty. As the sounds of the waltz entered, Emma seemed to return in a feverish dream to the world of the ball, imagining the gleam of candelabras. Suddenly, she sat bolt upright in bed and cried out: 'The sun! Is there a fair today?' Then, turning to Charles she exclaimed suddenly: 'A mirror! Give me a mirror!' This was brought and placed in her hands. Raising her head with her husband's assistance, Emma gazed at herself in the mirror for a long time before tears welled up and overflowed. Suddenly, her face became distorted by a grimace of horror and revulsion, at which moment the familiar sound of the barrel organ and the nasal voice were heard, seeming to terrify her. Shrieking wildly, 'The blind man!', she dropped the mirror and broke into shrieks of terrible, hoarse laughter. This was cut short by a sensation of ice cold in her throat. She then fell back on the pillow, drew a final breath and lay still.

Slowly, the light faded. Emma's room disappeared. One by one, in the windows of their houses, the characters of the drama appeared – Rodolphe, sitting comfortably by the fire with his pipe; Lhereux, looking through his registers and totting up his accounts; Guillaumin, chuckling vilely to himself. Blackout. Quietly, the music entered and Emma's room was softly illuminated, the light falling on the figure of Justin drooping woefully in the doorway. Finally, it fell on the face of Emma, looking at peace, almost happy. Justin quietly approached the head of the bed, then fell to his knees. With love and pity in his voice he whispered sobbingly: 'Why did you do it, madame? Why . . .?' Then the lights faded slowly to the final sounds of the orchestra.[153]

In order to get as many episodes on to the stage as possible (the original version

10 Scene from Flaubert's *Madame Bovary* (1940)

had more than sixty, which were eventually reduced to a little over forty) Tairov adapted a basic device of his working method and converted the stage area into a structural system consisting of three storeys divided vertically from one another, so that they formed separate, self-contained little cells, in each of which the episodes were played out in succession. The single tone of the novel, which conveys the monotony of provincial life was, by these means, given a more fragmented, impulsive quality designed to accord with the theme of Emma herself. The characters of the town were presented as precisely recreated typological studies, but with a slightly grotesque emphasis, which also extended to include Emma's two lovers, Leon and Rodolphe. Tairov's characterisation went somewhat against

Flaubert's. Where the latter saw Emma as someone whose ideals were tainted by the environment she stemmed from, as a victim of her own false dreams, Tairov presented her as the only sound, complete and feeling person in the world of the play, while all around her – with the exception of her husband, were false and hypocritical. Emma's tragedy lay in the fact that she was someone who counted on the genuineness of others' feelings and received only cruelty and hypocrisy in return. In fact, critics compared Koonen's interpretation of Emma both with Anna Karenina and with Racine's Phaedre. Ilya Ehrenburg wrote: 'There is a sense in which the wife of a gentleman in some out-of-the-way-place in Normandy carries a hint of Phaedre about her', and went on to say that the height of Koonen's acting was the moment of grief among the surroundings of the carnival, when she first saw the insignificant nature of her own dreams. What the Kamerny was presenting was not the life of Emma, but her fate: 'What is fundamental to the fate of Emma Bovary lies in her attempt to assert her own happiness, to find that selfless and limitless love of which she herself is capable, to find her "hero", her "authentic ideal".'[154]

With the outbreak of war following the Nazi invasion of the Soviet Union in June 1941, the theatre was evacuated for a two-year period to Barnaul in western Siberia and, later, to Balkhash, a recently built town on the shores of a lake in the Karaganda steppe. Here the players performed in the club premises of a large copper works, Medzavod, the roof of which was only 3.5 metres from floor level and where they had no props, scenery or costumes and where audiences had little previous acquaintance with the theatre. A month before its departure from Moscow, the Kamerny had premiered a play by G.D. Mdivani, called *The Battalion Heads West* and, during its stay in Barnaul, staged four other war plays with patriotic themes. Probably the best of the four was Konstantin Paustovsky's *Until the Heart Stops Beating*, premiered in Barnaul on 4 April 1943 with music by Sviridov.

At the centre of the play is an actress who finds herself living under German occupation. Her child has been killed by a fascist soldier and, her mind unhinged, she wanders about the town with the dead child in her arms. Coming face to face with the murderer on the town square, she tries to choke him to death. While in prison, she regains her senses and is set free. Meanwhile a German major has fallen in love with her and the actress proceeds to conduct a subtle and dangerous game with him. Having established contact with a group of partisans, she acts in accordance with their instructions and uses her influence on the officer. The high command of the occupying forces are due to attend a performance in which she is appearing and, at this point, the partisans are to storm the town. The plan is successful and the play concludes with the victory of the partisan detachment. One of the strongest moments of the production was the point where the actress, Anna Martynovna, deranged with grief, finds herself surrounded by a group of German officers who link hands and perform a kind of dance around her in their studded boots. In a moment where reality and feverish imagination seemed to merge, the monotonous music sounded a monstrous accompaniment to the dance of 'wildly happy automatons'.[155] The finale took place in the theatre where Anna, dressed in a wide flowing dress with a red scarf in her hand, flourished it like a banner as a summons to revolt. At this point, the partisans burst into the building. Despite the play's moments of sentimentality and the fact that the allegorical/symbolic moments were 'not especially profound',[156] the psychology of fascism was effectively laid bare, although an influential critic declared that 'the devices of the symbolist theatre appear often unsuitable and false in the realistic theatre' and that they were 'out of place in depicting the feelings of contemporary people'.[157]

In October 1943, the Kamerny Theatre returned to its Moscow home and Tairov turned his attention to two classic plays and one modern one. His plans for a production of L. Tolstoy's *Fruits of Enlightenment* did not materialise, but he was more successful with a concert performance of Chekhov's *The Seagull* – the first major revival of this famous play since 1905. Tairov also wanted to stage Evgeni Shvartz's anti-fascist fairy tale *The Dragon*, but that privilege fell to Nikolai Akimov's Comedy Theatre in Leningrad. For the production of *The Seagull* he used Tchaikovsky's music – vocal, instrumental and orchestral – as an almost permanent background to the action. An open stage was hung with grey drapes. The set consisted of a horseshoe-shaped rostrum with armchairs and round tables and, during the second half, a black grand piano with, on it, the effigy of a seagull. Across the grey backdrop passed misty visions of a purplish colour while Nina and Treplev listened to part of a Tchaikovsky symphony. The colour of these visions altered to gold during the performance of the play-within-the-play. The B-Flat piano concerto was brought in at the point where Treplev cast aside his manuscript and sat at the piano, the invisible orchestra taking over from him like the soundtrack to a film. At the end, to the accompaniment of a Tchaikovsky nocturne, after Trigorin has been presented with the effigy of a seagull in flight, a single spotlight picked out the image of this same seagull now hovering above the darkened stage. The actors wore evening-dress throughout to emphasise the concert-performance nature of the production. A contemporary critic recalled the production's mood of 'stern triumphalism' and its tremendous emotional power.[158]

It seemed a logical step, in the circumstances, to move from one play about the world of literature and the theatre to another with a theatrical theme – Ostrovsky's *More Sinned Against Than Sinning*. The play deals with the somewhat melodramatic subject of seduction and abandonment. The central character, Otradina, has an illegitimate son before being abandoned by her seducer. She leaves her home town to return seventeen years later (now a famous actress who is guesting at the local theatre), her name changed to Kruchinina. She meets a bitter and cynical youth, Neznamov, a member of the local theatre company, who has his faith in human nature restored through contact with her. A group of local actors plot to disillusion him and, in a climactic scene in which Neznamov denounces mothers who abandon their children, is recognised by Kruchinina as her own child. The critic Boris Alpers wrote of the production:

> A. Koonen has created an original interpretation of the heroic image of a Russian actress, throwing a challenge to the hypocritical society of dull, bourgeois, callous proprietors and artistic mediocrities. She passes through the events of the

production with head held high among a crowd of greedy, trivial, envious people, proud in her lonely suffering – a living incarnation of the great purifying power of authentic art. Something of the loneliness of the Baudelairean albatross was in this Kruchinina of Koonen's, in her abstracted glances straining towards the distance, over the heads of the surrounding people, and in her movements, involuntarily rapid and precise, out of keeping with the rhythm and tempo of everyone else.[159]

During 1945, Tairov laid plans to stage a dramatised version of Dostoevsky's *Idiot*, Tolstoy's *Fruits of Enlightenment* and Mayakovsky's *Bedbug*. None of these plans came to anything. However, the two productions which he did manage to stage were strangely contrasting. The first, *At The Walls of Leningrad*, by Vishnevsky, continued the tradition begun by *Optimistic Tragedy* in being based on mass scenes involving sailors of the Red Fleet in a production which was realised in the manner of an oratorio. The other production of this year was something of a surprise choice – J.B. Priestley's *An Inspector Calls*. Tairov hoped that the Vishnevsky play would form part of a trilogy (the first part being *Optimistic Tragedy*), the third section of which was to have been a play about the post-war life of the country. He spent a great deal of time and trouble on the production of the Vishnevsky play. Much of the text was reworked and a great deal of superfluous, rhetorical didacticism was removed. In fact, it was cut and altered to such an extent that the posters announced the play as a 'scenic composition' by Tairov. The mass scenes were elaborately worked out with a very small group of actors. The mimed scenes of hand-to-hand fighting were brilliantly staged as was the scene where the sailors read their commander's reply to the fascist ultimatum, where both the dramatist and the director, it was felt, had clearly been influenced by Repin's famous painting of the 'Zaparozhean Cossacks' Reply to the Sultan of Turkey'.[160]

On 28 January 1945, Tairov was presented with one of the country's highest awards, the Order of Lenin. The premiere of *At the Walls of Leningrad* was given on 27 March when the war in Europe was still being fought but where final victory now appeared certain. In the circumstances, it seemed odd that Tairov and his assistant, Lukyanov, should turn their attention to Priestley's play, which opened on 5 July. According to Yuri Golovashenko, the decision to stage the play arose out of Tairov's constant search for the best of the most 'progressive' works of world drama.[161] He saw the subject as connected with the problems of social justice in bourgeois society and with the theme of man's responsibility for man. In a brochure issued to accompany the production, Tairov and Lukyanov commented:

> The originality and freshness of Priestley's talent, the skilful structure of his plays is such that he seems to place at one large dining table almost the entire world. In the fates of the members of a single family, Priestley makes us feel an echo of the fates of entire social stratas.[162]

The characters were interpreted as, psychologically, very real people and the Birlings' dining-room was converted into a form of courtroom. The theatre sought to emphasise the fact that what Priestley had written was not a form of 'whodunnit' but a psychological play about morals and conscience. The title was altered to *He Has Arrived*, to stress the point that the question was not simply one of the arrival of a particular police inspector who was representative of the state's legal authority but concerned his role as an 'Inspector of Consciences'.

The directors and the designer, Kovalenko, emphasised the significance of Inspector Goole with his first entry. In the twilight of the Birlings' room, with only the dining-table area lit, the light was seen to grown progressively brighter as Goole made his entry until it illuminated every corner of the stage. At the same time, special footlights cast a flame-coloured glow over the setting. There was no attempt to be faithful to the period of the play. P. Gaideburov's Inspector Goole wore a 1940s-style jacket despite the fact that the action is set in 1912. The critic Boyadzhiev wrote:

> The statuesque quality of the *mise-en-scène* is full of content. The director has taken the central theme of each scene and sought its most plastically expressive form. This form is static but, from this, the action only gains because this immobility expresses the basic dramatic theme of the incidents to precisely the extent that the inner dynamic of a painted canvas is transmitted by the discovery of authentic pictorial composition. Brilliant compositional mastery has enabled Tairov to broaden the dimensions of Priestley's play and to lend this work the characteristic of social drama. . . . P. Gaideburov, who plays the role of Inspector Goole, does so with such concealed force, of a kind which simultaneously speaks of genuine civic sorrow as well as the fiery political anger of the man. It would have been easy, as well as tempting, to portray the traditional English detective in the manner of the shrewd Sherlock Holmes or the good-natured Father Brown . . . His Goole is a considerable, complex figure who, at the same time, cannot be described as wholly real. At times, it seems as if Priestley himself had entered the house of an ordinary English bourgeois and opened his eyes to the nature of his existence. Gaideburov transmits magnificently the inner struggle which takes place in the soul of Goole, when feelings break out on the surface and willpower smothers them.[163]

On 10 April 1937, Tairov had staged a production of Maxim Gorky's *Children of the Sun*, at a time when the author's recent death had led to his work being more widely staged than ever before. Strangely, compared with others, Tairov's production was largely ignored and has been treated as insignificant within the overall context of his work in the theatre. The production appears to have been 'caviare for the general' and appreciated by a few discriminating critics only. Disagreement with Tairov's interpretation seems to have centred on his reading of the relationship between Protasov, the scientist, and the vengeful locksmith, Yegor. However, undeterred, Tairov returned to Gorky for what was to be his last major production, in collaboration with Lukyanov, of Gorky's 1915 play *The Old Man*. It is a work which explores the nature of guilt and innocence in the context of a Russian provincial town where the merchant and philanthropist, Mastakov, is confronted by a wandering pilgrim who, like himself, is an ex-convict but who, unlike Mastakov, has lived out his sentence in suffering and now wishes to expose Mastakov's past on the grounds that the latter evaded his share of retribution by absconding from the prison camp before his sentence had been completed. Although he protests his innocence of the murder for which he was imprisoned, and despite the fact that the old man does not make any direct blackmailing attempts, nor does he unmask him to the world, Mastakov is driven to take his own life for reasons which are, finally, more complex than the objective facts would seem to suggest.

Tairov treated the play as a study of one aspect of fascism and took as his starting point something which Gorky had said in the preface to the second, American edition of the play:

> In *The Old Man* I attempted to show how repellent a person can be who is weighed down with his own suffering . . . who has come to believe that he has the right to torment others on account of his own suffering. If a man has convinced himself that he has such a right, that he is a chosen instrument of revenge, he loses any right to human respect. It is just as if someone were to burn down houses and entire towns just because he was feeling cold.[164]

The parallel, as Tairov saw it, was with the fascist insistence on the right to *Lebensraum*, in pursuit of which towns and villages had been invaded and destroyed. Moreover, just as fascism had seemingly been defeated on the field of battle it had, in fact, merely 'withdrawn into its shell' (to quote Gorky's remark) like the old man, and lived to fight another day. Tairov felt it had been mistaken of previous interpreters of the play to consider that the old man was a person who stood for some particular ideology (the Proletkultists had even seen him as a positive character who opposed the class represented by Mastakov). In Tairov's view, the old man was a coward and it was in this cowardly sense that one of his key lines needed to be interpreted. 'Look how they've built everything up, the hyenas. Shut out the sky. Trying to cut themselves off from God, the heretics. Hiding their iniquity behind brick and stone.' According to Tairov, the old man was not yearning for heaven. Whilst speaking of heaven he was, in fact, thinking of prison. 'He would smother the earth with prisons and incarcerate everybody so that he could be the warder who gives orders and issues commands. That is his real ideology.'[165]

One of the greatest critical successes of the production was the performance of Pavel Gaideburov as the old man – the same Gaideburov who had given Tairov his first opportunities as a director with the Mobile Theatre before the First World War. The critic V. Ermilov wrote:

> P. Gaideburov creates a figure of broad and generalised significance, and the audience thinks about all the bearers of ignorance who hate mankind because of its aspiration towards goodness and happiness. Some of them cover themselves with their own papal 'infallibility' and teach their flocks to accept humbly any suffering or torment inflicted on them by the executioners of mankind. They say that all people wallow in their sins and need to suffer. Others threaten entire nations with death because those nations do not want to endure torment and oppression. Such 'old men' willingly appear as judges of humanity precisely because they refuse to condemn its enemies and exterminators.[166]

Other critics suggested that Tairov, through Gorky, was arguing against a Dostoevskyan view of 'necessary suffering' as well as opposing the Nietzschean doctrine of 'the will to power'.[167]

Although Tairov was to direct a few more plays before his death in 1950, this production effectively marked the end of his creative life in the theatre and the end of the Kamerny Theatre itself, which was closed in 1949. The Moscow theatrical world was stunned by an announcement in the newspaper *Soviet Art*, on 25 June 1949, that Tairov had been relieved of responsibility for the artistic leadership of the Kamerny Theatre. More humiliating than this was the fact that he had been transferred to the Vakhtangov Theatre in the capacity of assistant director to Reuben Simonov. In his sixty-fifth year, and in Koonen's sixty-first, they were both awarded state pensions for life and Tairov laid plans to write his autobiography. This work was interrupted by illness and his death in a Moscow hospital on 25 September 1950. The previous month, his theatre had been renamed the 'Pushkin' and a new artistic director had been appointed.

An account of the events which followed his death is movingly chronicled by Boris Filippov, director of the Moscow Theatre of Satire and a friend of Tairov's:

On Monday, 25 September 1950, at 10.00 p.m. I was telephoned by N. Sukhotskaya, a producer at the Kamerny Theatre, and told that Alexander Tairov had died an hour ago . . . Tairov no longer had a theatre . . . A new one, the Pushkin Theatre, occupied the building on Tverskoy Boulevard, near Herzen's house. Some of the Kamerny actors had joined the new troupe. They even included Tairov's favourite students. He was particularly upset about this. But what else could they have done? . . . It would have been impossible to hold the civic funeral in a building where everything recalled the sad end not only of Tairov, but of the theatre created by him. Sukhotskaya conveyed to me a request from Koonen that the funeral be held in the Central Art Workers' Club . . . Around midnight I telephoned the Arts Committee, where they used to work late at that time. Nobody there knew about Tairov's sudden death and they seemed confused, trying to assess the event . . . The civic funeral was scheduled for 28 September in the Central Club and the burial in the Novodevichy Cemetery. Tairov had once expressed the desire not to be cremated. On that sad day I arrived at the Central Club at 7 o'clock in the morning. Tairov's friends and theatre colleagues had assembled very early. Shortly afterwards, the coffin with the body was carried into the Large Hall of the Central Club, which had been emptied of chairs and placed on a catafalque. Alisa Koonen arrived at 10 o'clock. Her outer control emphasised even more her inner emotions. Together with Tairov's sister Alexandra and N. Sukhotskaya she made her way towards the coffin. It was not until the last moment that her strength failed . . . Musicians from the former Kamerny Theatre played for the last time the funeral march from *Adrienne Lecouvreur*. At 1.00 p.m. those great Russian actresses, Alexandra Yablochkina and Yevdoksia Turchaninova, took their places at the head of the coffin. The guard of honour was completed by Ivan Kozlovsky and Ilya Ehrenburg. The hall was packed, restless and full of wreaths. Then came the sad rite of farewell. And at the end a sincere, impassioned speech by Ehrenburg . . . The writer said what was in everyone's minds but was not spoken aloud – a great artist had died, who had experienced both success and failure in his time, but in whom the flame of art had never been quenched.

Koonen asked that the funeral procession should stop in Bolshaya Bronnaya Street by the house where she had spent the best years of her life with Tairov, but this turned out to be impossible. The transport authorities objected. They went to the Novodevichy Cemetery by the shortest route.[168]

In his autobiography, Ilya Ehrenburg noted grimly: 'Tairov travelled a long and tortuous road, but when he was lying in his coffin, some producer at the memorial service still recalled his past errors – reading them out from a little piece of paper.' Of Tairov himself, he wrote: 'Whenever I think of Alexander Yakovlevich Tairov I am reminded of Pushkin's lines: "Once there lived a poor knight, taciturn and simple, dark and pale in looks, bold and straight in spirit".' And, describing Koonen's performance as Phaedre, he recalled: 'I recognised that fullness of art which makes one feel light and a little afraid. (The first men who leave earth's gravitational field may feel something of the same sort).' Of them both, he had this to say: 'I must confess that I am not a theatre man. But there are many Kamerny productions I cannot forget, from the early *Princess Brambilla* to *Madame Bovary* . . . I am grateful for these to Tairov and Koonen: their art has often helped me. Their friendship helped me too . . . Every injury one suffered was softened by their sympathy and affection.'[169]

Koonen, who had been transferred to the Vakhtangov Theatre at the same time as Tairov, continued her acting career after his death and gave a memorable performance as Mrs Alving in Ibsen's *Ghosts* at the Moscow Literary Theatre in 1958 (directed by M.E. Lishin). Chapters from her memoirs were published in the theatre magazine *Teatr* during the late 1960s and were issued in book form as *Stranitsy zhizni* (Life's Pages) in 1975. She died in 1974.[170]

2

Evgeni Vakhtangov, 1883–1922

The canonical figures of post-revolutionary Russian theatre are Stanislavsky and his disciple, Evgeni Vakhtangov, neither of whom worked extensively in the theatre after 1917 – Stanislavsky because of age and ill health, Vakhtangov because of his premature death from cancer less than five years after the events of October. They are the only two major directors to have theatres in Moscow named after them – what was the Art Theatre's Third Studio being renamed the Vakhtangov Theatre in 1926, in honour of the great director whose studio stood on the site at no. 26 Arbat Street. It is pointless to speculate as to what Vakhtangov's creative history might have been had he lived on into the 1960s and 1970s, as many of his own disciples and pupils were to do, but interesting to consider why his reputation should stand so high in the annals of Soviet theatre history when the scale of his actual contribution appears slight in comparison with, say, Meyerhold, Tairov or even Alexei Popov.

The accounts left by those who knew him both as man and artist bear witness to the fact that he was a remarkable and charismatic individual who left the mark of his personality permanently on anyone who came into contact with him. It is also a commonplace in Soviet criticism of Vakhtangov to say that he represents an important point of intersection between two artistic extremes which have always been at odds with each other, represented by the 'realism' of Stanislavsky at one end of the scale and the 'conventionalised theatre' represented by Meyerhold at the other. In actual fact, whilst being critical both of the methods of Stanislavsky and Meyerhold at various stages of his life, his development as an artist brought Vakhtangov closer to Meyerhold of whom he was much quoted as saying: 'Meyerhold provided the roots for the theatre of the future. So shall the future honour him.'[1] At the same time as his artistic disagreements with Stanislavsky and the methods of the Art Theatre intensified towards the end of his life, so his personal love and veneration for the man himself increased. He spoke of him in March 1919, and continued to speak of him, in the following terms: 'There is no one and nothing higher than you for me. In art I love only the Truth of which you spoke and which you teach.'[2]

Vakhtangov's artistic career may be described, in one sense, as a journey away

11 Evgeni Vakhtangov, c. 1920

from Stanislavsky towards Meyerhold. In 1911, the year he entered the Art Theatre after graduating from the Adashev School, he spoke of the need to 'take the theatre out of the theatre and the actor out of the play',[3] of the need to study the Stanislavsky method intensively so as to produce the kind of performance in which the actors immersed themselves in a role to such an extent that 'they . . . forget about the audience and create for themselves'. By 1920 and 1921 he had moved away from this position and was talking in terms much more reminiscent of Meyerhold: 'Theatre is theatre. A play is a performance. The art of performing is acting skill . . . the actor – a skilled master possessing internal and external technique . . .'[4]

He was also developing a theory of 'the grotesque' under the influence of Meyerhold's productions, which he much admired, such as *The Puppet Show*, *The Female Stranger*, *Columbine's Scarf* and *Harlequin the Marriage Broker*, the influence of the last being clearly visible in Vakhtangov's final, and finest production, of

Gozzi's fairy tale *Princess Turandot*. In March 1921, he wrote: 'The slice-of-life theatre must die' and that 'everyone capable of being a character actor . . . must learn to express themselves grotesquely'.[5] In August the same year he described the road which he had previously followed (that of the Art Theatre) as the road to a 'luxurious cemetery',[6] and a notebook entry for 26 March 1921, which contains critical remarks addressed at both Meyerhold and Stanislavsky ('Meyerhold knows nothing about the actor . . . Stanislavsky . . . has very little knowledge of psychology'), also stresses that 'All theatre in the near future will be built along the main lines that Meyerhold long ago foresaw.'[7] In his final conversations, held during April 1922, with his students Boris Zakhava and Ksenia Kotlubai, Vakhtangov spoke for the first time of his theory of 'imaginative realism' where 'form and content harmonise like a musical chord'.[8]

The sense that Vakhtangov provides the means of synthesising the various methods adopted by other great directors is well conveyed by Michael Chekhov in his appreciation of Vakhtangov's talent:

> If Vakhtangov had accomplished nothing else, he still would have won his place among those early 'greats' by proving that the seeming irreconcilables of the theatre can be reconciled – that the diverse techniques of Stanislavsky, Nemirovich, Meyerhold and Tairov could be brought together, amalgamated and metamorphosed into a new wonderful product without doing violence to any of them. For each of Vakhtangov's productions was a harmonious blend of the very beautiful, very deep, very light, very mathematically clever and humanly true. He believed . . . that for the imaginative craftsman of the theatre, there were no artistic boundaries that could not be crossed without some benefit to the adventurer.[9]

There were times, especially during the troubled 1930s, when Vakhtangov's contribution to Soviet theatre – especially his stylised productions of Strindberg's *Erik XIV* and Ansky's *The Dybbuk*, were being reassessed and downgraded within terms which characterised their formalist excesses. Even a life-enhancing and affirmative production such as *Princess Turandot* did not entirely escape formalist strictures during this period. However, the true importance of Vakhtangov's historical position as a 'reconciler' of extremes has come into its own since the rehabilitation of Meyerhold, in 1955, and the reopening of the debate surrounding the formal methods which are available and/or tolerable within the parameters of 'socialist realism'.

It has become increasingly common, when comparing the differences between Stanislavsky and Meyerhold throughout their artistic careers, to point to the fact that, as Meyerhold himself believed, their principles and methods were merging towards the end of the 1930s, like two people who began digging separate tunnels but discovered, finally, that all the while they had been tunnelling towards each other and had finally met.[10] According to Brecht, Vakhtangov was this 'meeting point' between Stanislavsky and Meyerhold – someone who embraced the other two as contradictory elements but who was, himself, at the same time the freest.[11] This proximity was certainly not officially recognised at the time but, instead, was defined as an irreconcilable opposition between 'realism' and 'formalism' which had terrible consequences for both Stanislavsky and Meyerhold. On the one hand it led to an empty, unadventurous truth-to-life naturalism accompanied by an equally, empty, optimistic emphasis. On the other hand, where sterile formalist experimentation had led to what Meyerhold himself described as 'Meyerholditis' (the formal equivalent of 'MATitis'[12] in the realist sphere), it had also, far more seriously and tragically, led to the forceful suppression of the tendency in the person of Meyerhold himself, as well as others like him.

Since the 1960s, the figure of Vakhtangov has served to symbolise the historical closeness between the apparently divergent principles of Stanislavsky and Meyerhold although again, according to Brecht, 'Vakhtangov is the Stanislavsky–Meyerhold complex *before* the split, rather than its reconciliation later.'[13] In addition, Vakhtangov has also served to evince the flexibility of the bounds of a socialist realism which could embrace methods of production, like those inherent within *Princess Turandot*, which were lightyears away from 'realism' in any conventionally accepted sense. Vakhtangov's symbolic, historical position as a reconciler of formerly irreconcilable opposites is actually more important than this role as a father-figure whose legacy has been taken up and extended by his pupils. The history of the Vakhtangov Theatre itself would appear to have a marginal connection with Vakhtangov's own history and theatrical practice from the mid 1920s onwards. The work of Vakhtangov's senior pupils, especially the more significant ones such as Boris Zakhava[14] and Yuri Zavadsky, was always much closer to mainstream realism than it was to the adventurous spirit of their mentor's post-revolutionary productions.

The main bearers of the Vakhtangov inheritance, in so far as the physical management of the affairs of the Vakhtangov Theatre is concerned, have been Reuben Simonov and his son Evgeni. It has to be said that there has been little in the work of either of them which can stand comparison with the achievement of Vakhtangov himself. Reuben Simonov's most significant contribution has been an influential book about his teacher (rather than a production in his spirit). The revival of *Princess Turandot* which Simonov undertook in 1963, whilst true to the formal methods of the original, had little in common with its original spirit and was even considered vulgar by comparison. Similarly, since his father's death, Evgeni Simonov has staged little to convince observers that the spirit of Vakhtangov is alive again and moving among us.

Perhaps the closest in spirit has been Alexei Popov, who joined the Moscow Art Theatre a year later than Vakhtangov (in 1912), acted with him in a production of Leonid Andreyev's *Thought*, alternated the role of Daantje with Vakhtangov in Richard Boleslavsky's[15] production of Herman Heijerman's *The Wreck of 'The Hope'* at the Art Theatre's First Studio and staged his first production (of Alexander Blok's *Female Stranger*) at Vakhtangov's Mansurov Studio in 1916 before going on to found his own 'Vakhtangov Studio' in Kostroma. There he staged versions of productions which Vakhtangov had previously staged, such as Henning Berger's *The Deluge* and a version of Dickens's *The Cricket on the Hearth*, in which Vakhtangov had acted Tackleton at the Art Theatre First Studio. Popov also staged an evening of Chekhov 'miniatures', just as Vakhtangov had done between 1915 and 1917.

Popov returned to Moscow in 1923 and became a director at what had formerly been Vakhtangov's Studio and which had now become incorporated within the Art Theatre as its Third Studio. He remained at the Third Studio (which became the Vakhtangov Theatre in 1926) until 1930, when he moved to the Theatre of the Revolution. The Vakhtangov spirit was very much alive in his productions of three plays by Prosper Mérimée (1924) and in _Virineya_ by Lidya Seifullina (a very significant production in Soviet histories because of its contemporary subject matter and the fact that the play was by a Soviet dramatist). Popov's productions of Bulgakov's _Zoya's Apartment_, of Boris Lavrenyov's _The Break-up_ (Razlom) and of Olesha's _Conspiracy of Feelings_ were among the most significant of the 1920s and he continued to invoke the marvellously inventive and life-celebratory mood of his mentor in fine productions of Shakespeare during the 1930s, especially _Romeo and Juliet_ (1935), and _The Taming of the Shrew_ (1937). One cannot help feeling that Vakhtangov would have approved of his productions of plays by Pogodin in the 1930s[16] and of the lyrical production of Alexander Gladkov's comedy _Long, Long Ago_ staged in 1942 at the Theatre of the Red Army, which Popov headed from 1935 until his death in 1961. Seen in these terms, the Vakhtangov legacy has been a comparatively small but significant one. The wealth from which it is drawn is vast and remains to be tapped.

Evgeni Bagrationovich Vakhtangov was born on the 1 February (old style) in what is now the Soviet Republic of Armenia, in the town of Vladikavkaz (since renamed Ordzhonikidze). His father was a wealthy tobacco manufacturer with whom his son was on consistently bad terms from a very early age. Nevertheless, he seemed to inherit some of his father's characteristics including an enormous capacity for work and a very active nature. He also appears to have inherited some traits from his grandfather, a minor artist who enjoyed folk poetry and folk music. The story of Vakhtangov's childhood is one of paternal oppression and dissension. It is hardly surprising that his first independent work as a director was on the chosen topic of family strife in S.A. Naidyonov's _Vanyushin's Children_, which was closely followed by his production of another domestic tragic drama, _Sick People_ (Vakhtangov's version of Gerhard Hauptmann's _The Festival of Peace_). Both plays deal with complicated family relationships and portray the bourgeois family as a hell which affects anyone who comes into contact with it.

He attended school in Tiflis and Vladikavkaz and gave his first stage performance in 1900 – a domestic production, put on with some of his classmates, of Gogol's comedy _Marriage_, in which he played the part of the much solicited Agafya Tikhonovna. He graduated from High School three years later and, having failed his entry examinations to Riga Polytechnic, was accepted by Moscow University to study physics and maths. He retained his interest in the amateur stage and mounted his first production, of Hauptmann's _Sick People_, in August 1904, with a group calling itself the Vladikavkaz Students' Workshop. Relationships between the 21-year-old Vakhtangov and his father were more strained than ever. Not only did his father not approve of his son's artistic activities but it was apparent that the son had no intention of following in his father's footsteps and becoming a tobacco baron. He asked his father for 25 roubles to stage his production of *Sick People* and, when this was refused him, Vakhtangov deliberately staged the play at a circus which had pitched its tent opposite his father's factory and, in an ostentatious gesture, distributed more than a hundred tickets free to the workers. He also staged cabaret performances in the town, much to his father's anger, as the theatrical profession was distinctly lacking in respectability amongst the professional classes. Vakhtangov made no attempt to disguise his family name and protect his father from scandal, as Konstantin Alekseyev had done in adopting the stage-name of 'Stanislavsky'. The final break with his father came in 1905 when, on 9 October, Vakhtangov married Nadezhda Mikhailovna Baitsurova, which put paid to any notions his parents may have had of an alliance between their son and the daughter of a rich factory owner.

During 1905, Vakhtangov staged plays with a student group at Moscow University and, in the meantime, transferred to the Law Faculty. The following summer he organised the Vladikavkaz Student Society, staging productions in various towns and, in October, he created the 'Drama Circle' at the university where he first met Boris Sushkevich,[17] with whom he later became closely connected in his work for the First Studio. It was with the Moscow Students' Drama Circle that Vakhtangov staged a production of Gorky's *Summerfolk* in December 1906, in which he also played the role of Vlas. He was to stage a production of *The Lower Depths* two years later for the Vladikavkaz Music and Drama Circle in which he performed the role of the Baron and, in July 1909, he also directed a production of Chekhov's *Uncle Vanya* in which he played the role of Astrov.

In August 1909, he became a student at the School of Drama organised by A.I. Adashev, who was an actor at the Moscow Art Theatre. Vakhtangov was immediately taken into the second year and, within six months, was transferred to the third-year course. He was identified as an outstandingly gifted student by one of the school's teachers who was to have a profound influence on Vakhtangov's career during its initial stages. This was Leopold Sulerzhitsky, an outstanding educator, a fierce propagandist of Stanislavsky's 'system' and a disciple of the moral teachings of Lev Tolstoy. At the end of his life, Stanislavsky was to declare that there were only two people who ever understood his views on theatre – Sulerzhitsky and Vakhtangov; but whereas Vakhtangov only ever understood one half, Sulerzhitsky grasped and understood at least three-quarters. The tragically premature deaths of both men were bitter blows to Stanislavsky from which, according to some commentators, he never fully recovered.

Sulerzhitsky (1872–1916) was the son of a bookbinder who developed artistic talents at an early age and when only thirteen acted as assistant to the painter Vasnetsov on ten frescoes for Kiev cathedral. He studied fine art at the University of Moscow at the end of the 1880s, when he came under the influence of the teachings of Leo Tolstoy. Following expulsion from art school in 1894 for anti-government activities, he became a merchant seaman and spent time in prison from 1896 to 1898 for refusing to take the oath of allegiance when called up for military service. On his release he was commissioned by Tolstoy to organise the evacuation to Canada from the Caucasus of a persecuted religious sect known as the Dukhobors (Wrestlers with God), which he accomplished successfully. He spent some time in exile before returning to Russia and, through his friendship with Gorky and Chekhov, established close ties with the Moscow Art Theatre where he began work as a director in 1906, participating in the productions of Hamsun's *The Drama of Life*, Andreyev's *The Life of Man*, Maeterlinck's *The Blue Bird* and the Craig–Stanislavsky *Hamlet*. He also took an active part in organising 'fringe' work with the Art Theatre such as the 'cabbage parties' described by Stanislavsky in *My Life in Art*. He also staged cabaret performances at Baliev's theatre The Bat.[18] The final period of his life was spent organising and directing plays at the First Studio of the Art Theatre where his Tolstoyan ideas were put at the service of a heightened and intensified, intimate stage naturalism. His influence was strongly evident in the Studio's first productions such as *The Wreck of 'The Hope'*, *The Cricket on the Hearth* (directed by Boris Sushkevich) as well as in Vakhtangov's production of Berger's *The Deluge*. Sulerzhitsky was an idealist with high aesthetic and moral aims who sought truth and inspiration through communion with nature, simplicity of living, and active love. It was this Rousseauistic element in him which led to his establishing an artistic 'back to nature' movement every summer, in which Vakhtangov was a regular participant, when Sulerzhitsky and a group of Studio actors lived rough in the wilds under aboriginal conditions, whilst seeking to convert their lives into art for the duration of the 'holiday', by adopting new persona and acting out fictional situations.[19]

Sulerzhitsky was so impressed with Vakhtangov's abilities that he twice invited him to accompany him as assistant to direct productions abroad. The first occasion was in 1910 when, together, they travelled to Paris where Vakhtangov assisted Sulerzhitsky in mounting a production of *The Blue Bird*, based on the Art Theatre original, at the Théâtre Réjane. The second occasion was in 1912 when Vakhtangov was invited to accompany his teacher to London where they had been asked to stage a production of Maurice Baring's *Double Game*. Unfortunately, this visit did not take place.

Having completed his training at the Adashev School in 1911, Vakhtangov applied to be taken on at the Art Theatre and was interviewed by Nemirovich-Danchenko on 4 March. The serious-minded applicant kept a detailed record of the interview, which was short and to the point, concluding with an offer of an appointment for 40 roubles a month (which was ten roubles less than Richard Boleslavsky was being paid). He was introduced to Stanislavsky for the first time on 11 March the latter declaring that 'he had heard a lot' about him. By August, Stanislavsky was already approaching Vakhtangov with a view to organising classes on the basis of his 'system', but fearing gossip and intrigue within the theatre which might be disruptive, asked Vakhtangov to keep his own (i.e. Stanislavsky's) involvement secret. At the same time he offered Vakhtangov a salary increase of 20 roubles.

In that same year, Vakhtangov, together with a group of actors who had also completed their training at the Adashev School staged a repertoire of plays in the town of Novgorod-Seversk, all of them directed by Vakhtangov and including Ibsen's *An Enemy of the People* and Hamsun's *At the Gates of the Kingdom*, both of which had already been successfully staged by the Art Theatre. He also staged a production of a play called *The Tin Soldiers* at The Bat cabaret where he also took part in a production parodying the Art Theatre version of *Hamlet*, in which he apparently gave a superb impression of Kachalov in the title role. In 1912 he began holding classes in the Stanislavsky Method with a group of actors at the Art Theatre and also began teaching at the Khalyutina Drama School, a post which he retained until 1915. On 23 September, he was cast in his first role in an Art Theatre production – as one of a trio of gypsies in Tolstoy's *A Living Corpse*.

He went on to play a number of minor roles at the Art Theatre which, together, form a poor contrast with his performance of some fifty major roles prior to his entering the Adashev School. Vakhtangov was later to muse ironically on the way in which the Art Theatre valued his talents as an actor:

In the course of ten years' theatrical activity you have played the following roles:
(1) A guitarist in *The Living Corpse* (an unforgettable character)
(2) A beggar in *Tsar Fyodr Ioannovich* (an invisible character)
(3) An officer in *Woe From Wit* (a brilliant character)
(4) A gourmand in *The Possessed* (a trenchant character)
(5) A Jew in *The Cherry Orchard* (an outstanding character)
(6) A Messenger in *In The Grip of Life* (a colourful character)
(7) A Courtier in *Hamlet* (a bright character)
(8) The Player Queen in *Hamlet* (a tender character)
(9) Sugar in *The Blue Bird* (a well-defined character)
(10) Kraft in *Thought* (a sharply psychological character)
(11) A Doctor in *The Imaginary Invalid* (a stylish character)
(12) Tackleton in *The Cricket on the Hearth* (a unique character)
(13) Frazer in *The Deluge* (a character with Michael Chekhov's distinction)
(14) Daantje in *The Wreck of 'The Hope'*
(15) Nordling in *The Deluge*
(16) The Fool in *Twelfth Night* (an elegant character)
(17) The shepherd Filon in *Balladyna* (a poetic character)[20]

Vakhtangov omitted to include in this list a fop in the trial scene of *The Brothers Karamazov* and a flunkey in Turgenev's *Where It's Thin – There It Breaks*.

In May 1912, Vakhtangov received an invitation from the poet and playwright Alexander Blok of the Fellowship of Actors, Artists, Writers and Musicians, who had established themselves, under Meyerhold's artistic directorship, in the town of Terioki, Finland, inviting him to participate in the staging of plays by, mainly, Western European dramatists, including Cervantes, Goldoni, Strindberg, Shaw, Calderon and others. Vakhtangov turned down the offer and went, instead, on a European tour, spending the summer in Sweden before returning home via Denmark and Norway. That same spring (of 1912) there had arisen within the Art Theatre the notion of establishing a separate studio, affiliated to the main theatre, which would serve as a training ground in Stanislavsky's 'system' for a new generation of Art Theatre actors. A group emerged under the tutelage of Stanislavsky and Sulerzhitsky, which was then entrusted to the care of Vakhtangov. Rehearsals began on a play by the Dutch playwright, Herman Heijermans, called *The Wreck of 'The Hope'*, a naturalistic drama in four acts about a hypocritical ship owner whose cupidity destroys an entire family. The appointed director was the young Richard Boleslavsky.

The ideological platform of the First Studio (as it was called) was that of the psychological, intimate theatre pioneered by the likes of Strindberg in Sweden and Reinhardt in Germany. Something of the same sort appeared necessary to Stanislavsky and Sulerzhitsky who were both dissatisfied with the excessively 'external' naturalism of earlier Art Theatre productions and also felt that the attempts made at a symbolist theatre had not borne fruit. What was needed was further experimental work on the, hitherto, unsystematically elaborated and unpublished 'system' and the training of a new breed of actor capable of filling the stage with 'the life of the human soul'. The first two years of the First Studio's existence were devoted to teaching and restricted to improvisational work, the staging of excerpts, etc. The tiny dimensions of the building in which the Studio was housed (on the corner of Tverskoi Boulevard and Gnezdikovski Lane in what had formerly been the premises of the Lux cinema) permitted the actors to speak in low tones, encouraged them not to exaggerate gesture or coarsen feeling and to transmit subtle psychological nuances through their acting without overt theatrical emphasis or stage affectation. The actors performed at floor level, without footlights, and this had the effect of bringing the actor close to the spectator and making the latter an emotional participant in the circumstances of the action. Stage decor tended to consist of basic materials with a simple canvas curtain dividing 'the stage' from the auditorium. This 'keyhole' realism (against which the likes of Meyerhold and Tairov rebelled so strongly), or 'spiritual naturalism', derived its philosophical strength from Tolstoy. It set itself against the horrors of the contemporary world, proposing the ideal of an unspoiled civilisation of simple and naive people. Thus was developed the notion of the 'ideal' human being, freed from the distorting effects of civilisation and creating, through simplicity and closeness to nature, the strength and clarity of spontaneous human feeling. As mentioned earlier the group paid summer trips to the countryside and tried to live the life of unspoilt people without personal possessions. The first of these trips took place in the summer of 1913, to Kanevo, in the Kievski province. Here, under Sulerzhitsky's leadership, life was turned into an improvised play-cum-drama which lasted the entire summer. All the participants became sailors, with Sulerzhitsky assuming the role of captain whose word was law. His regime was strict and he insisted on iron discipline. However, physical labour was carried out in an atmosphere of happy play and all returned to Moscow strengthened and refreshed by the experience, which was to be repeated in subsequent years.

Much of this same spirit had been evident in the production of *The Wreck of 'The Hope'*, where the accent had been on showing simple and uncomplicated people,

Dutch fishermen, living in an aboriginal state, and on 'the revelation of the human soul' of those who live in close proximity to nature, free from the influence of urban culture.[21] Meanwhile, Vakhtangov had been rehearsing what was to be his first production at the Studio of a new version of Hauptmann's *The Festival of Peace*, which he had staged nine years earlier in Vladikavkaz.

Where his earlier production had dwelled on proximity to his own domestic experiences – a poisonous family atmosphere, a despotic father and a bourgeois family – on this second occasion, in retaining the play's original title, Vakhtangov did everything possible to ameliorate the work's pessimism and to stage it as an exercise in wish-fulfillment. In his desire to show people as being better than they actually were, he softened the conflicts and introduced conversion states into the hellish relationships. The 'festival of peace' which the mother in the play seeks at Christmas time is a failure. Despite this, Vakhtangov sought to interpret this failure in the light of a reconciliatory joy, as part of an attempt to portray the triumph of goodness in the human heart. He seemed to be saying that, despite the fact that the play's resolution was unsuccessful, people needed nevertheless to try and seek some sort of accommodation with reality and in their own personal relationships. The emphasis, throughout, was on the personal rather than on the social – the willingness to undergo a Dickensian 'change of heart'. The production became a search for this 'good' in people. During rehearsals, Sulerzhitsky emphasised the point that the family did not quarrel amongst themselves because they were wicked people, and made up their differences afterwards because they were essentially decent:

> Give all the warmth you have in your hearts. Find support in each other's eyes, tenderly encourage each other to open your souls . . . There's no need for hysterics, chase them away. Don't be carried away by nervous effects; go to the heart.[22]

Work on the production began in January 1913 and concluded in November. The role which Vakhtangov had previously played (that of Wilhelm) was on this occasion assigned to Boleslavsky. He acted the part of a sardonic intellectual, a member of a disintegrating family who attempts a reconciliation with his father but suffers from morbid indecision, fearful of carrying within himself the hidden traces of future insanity and afraid to marry for fear of passing this stigma on to his children. Vakhtangov's notes on the director's copy of the play provide a clue to his interpretative scheme as well as giving a poignant sense of the frustrations which accompany any rehearsal period. On this occasion a major problem was the attitude and behaviour of Boleslavsky. Entries in Vakhtangov's diary for 26 February (the twenty-second rehearsal) and 2 March (the twenty-fifth rehearsal) indicate that Boleslavsky was apt to fool around, paid little attention to his work, was narcissistic and was, generally, poisoning the working atmosphere. In a letter to Sulerzhitsky on 27 March, Vakhtangov asked him to inform Stanislavsky of Boleslavsky's 'careless, frivolous and superficial' attitude and of his disrespect towards his fellow actors. He had missed six rehearsals without informing anyone and 'turned our joy in work into sheer torment'. Following this, he noted that Boleslavsky's attitude improved and rehearsals began to proceed with greater harmony.

In the production, Vakhtangov tried to universalise the domestic events and make them express more complex, more extreme situations, where each monologue became like a confession emanating from some tragic source. He tried to construct the production as a 'polyphonic vision . . . the sum of disconnected, multifarious, disassociated voices and consciousnesses'.[23] The characters were presented as if at the point of death, with a passion for analysis as if the present day were their last. They conducted this analysis with a busy feverishness, as if trying to understand everything before the inevitable darkness fell. Vakhtangov worked strictly according to the 'system' but the only actor who achieved anything like what he was seeking was Michael Chekhov as the unconstrained drunkard, Friebe, who paradoxically, seemed the only healthy individual in the house, reflecting the imperfections of the world like a crooked mirror and, believing not the slightest in a festival of 'reconciliation'. Gorky, who saw the production, took Friebe to be the hero – someone with greater insight than the rest, the servant who was, at the same time, the 'shabby chronicler of the House of Sholtz'.[24]

A critic described the production as 'a sharp psychological experiment' but that the psychological detail tended to be taken to extremes, turning 'a difficult and perhaps tedious play . . . into some kind of piece by Dostoevsky'.[25] Another critic described the decor in the following terms:

> Almost no setting. Three walls and a ceiling of grey canvas. Two doors and a window with snow on it. An iron stove, a divan, a table and a few chairs. Stags' antlers above the door and window. A table lamp. That is all it seems. Only the absolutely essential.[26]

This impression of rather Spartan aestheticism was also heightened by the ambience of the new premises in to which the First Studio had recently moved. The stage had been modelled along the lines of the previous one at the Lux but was larger. According to Boris Zakhava it was reminiscent of a Protestant church with its small auditorium, smooth white walls and plain wicker chairs raked steeply to accommodate about 300 people.[27]

Another critic described his impression of the production as follows:

> Before us we have a nest of people from a corrupt life, with overstrained, sick nerves: people in whom everything human, tender and warmhearted has been deeply hidden away somewhere while on the surface of their souls there remains only pain, irritation and nervous spite ready to break out at any minute in the most frightful and monstrous forms.[28]

There is little doubt that this emphasis on exposed nerves and hysterical suffering was both intense and difficult for audiences to take. Vakhtangov's own comments alongside Hauptmann's text in act 1 provide some idea of those naturalistic excesses to which he was prone during this period of his career and from which the advocates of a 'stylised theatre of convention' (uslovny teatr) recoiled in horror:

Hauptmann's dialogue	*Vakhtangov's notes*
	Wilhelm can arrive at any minute. Tension.
Suddenly Auguste *runs in. Frightened. Enters hurriedly. Slams the door behind herself and leans against it. Frau Sholtz runs quickly up to her:* 'My God . . .'	Ghosts. The Sholtzes have – 'paralysis'. A family (*pathological*).
Frau Büchner: What is it? . . .	
Auguste: Oh, my God . . . Somebody was chasing after me.	Babble. Doesn't know what she is saying. Only *don't explain. Ghosts.*
Frau Büchner: (*taking out a watch*). Perhaps Wilhelm is here already. But the train can't be in yet. (*goes to open the door*)	*Bared nerves, don't touch me.*
Auguste: Don't. Don't!	*Painful.* (bright). *Scream.*[29]

Sulerzhitsky's injunction that there was 'no need for hysterics' was ignored and where he placed emphasis on the notion of reconciliation, Vakhtangov appears, despite his intentions, to have strengthened the pessimistic side of the play, focusing on the 'family catastrophe' and on the revelation of the psychology of the bourgeois family, their suffering reactions to their surroundings.

It was said of the production afterwards that it produced, through the actors' performances, an unusual and powerful impression of truthfulness and a merging of the actor with the character. Such giving of themselves to the events on stage, was unknown even in the Art Theatre. The feeling of inner communication between the actors was thought striking as was the general feeling of ensemble. According to Serafima Birman,[30] who played Auguste, the production as a whole was, unfortunately marred by the actors' tendency to forget completely about the audience and to act entirely for themselves.[31]

During the autumn of 1913 Vakhtangov was approached by a group of young students, who had been much impressed by his production of *The Festival of Peace*, with a request that he help them establish a Drama Studio dedicated to serious work in the vein established by that production. The group had found small premises in a first-floor room on Mansurov Lane off Ostezhenka Street. The auditorium could seat about forty people and the stage area measured a mere 5 by 3 metres. Thus, in November, Vakhtangov's own studio was born, first referred to as the Student Drama Studio and later, in 1917, as the Vakhtangov Moscow Drama Studio, but more frequently called the Mansurov Studio. The group held its first meeting on 23 December and decided, somewhat against Vakhtangov's own preferences, that it wished to work on a new play by a young dramatist, Boris Zaitsev, called *The Lanin Estate*.

It was during rehearsals of *The Lanin Estate* that Vakhtangov began to put Stanislavsky's theories into practice with even greater rigour. A statement which he made on 18 January 1914 already employs the terminology of the emerging 'system':

In each role the author has placed a sequence of 'tasks', which the actor must determine and execute; the creativity of the actor consists in the beautiful and precise performance of these tasks. Each task consists of three elements: action, desire (purpose) and the form of execution (the means). Each action of the actor is determined by a specific desire; living in the role, he actively wishes something at every moment and from this desiring, action is born and, finally, feeling appears. Feeling is thus determined by two elements of the task: by desire (purpose) and action . . . The feelings which are summoned up by a whole range of tasks constitute the 'gamut' of feelings of the role. The execution of the tasks is the fact of acting on stage. The feelings which have been aroused need to be expressed externally. This expression is called the means; the character of the means depends on the talent of the performer, the more talented the actor the more varied his means, the more varied his resolution of the tasks. A bad actor has a limited means with which to resolve the various tasks . . . and acts, as we say, in clichés.[32]

The actors threw themselves into performing the 'tasks', which Vakhtangov called *études*, watched with great interest by Zaitsev, who attended several of the rehearsals looking, as an observer remarked 'like Christ in an icon painting'.[33]

Quite apart from expressing disappointment with the actual play itself – a Chekhovian piece set in the Russian countryside and dealing with the idle intelligentsia – Vakhtangov's interpretation was also at odds with that of the students and of the author himself. According to Vakhtangov, the finale was 'a juxtaposition of the indifferent grandeur of the natural world set against the ulcers and sores of human life on the estate'.[34] Consequently, he viewed the estate as something abnormal, temporal, from which there arose a desire to depart to another, healthier life. In the rainbow which appears at the end, Vakhtangov detected 'something cosmic, pitiless and cold standing above the sufferings of people'.[35] It was soon apparent that nobody agreed with this interpretation. It was pointed out to Vakhtangov that the fourth act was couched in an appeasing mood and, in the end, Vakhtangov was forced to concede that the appearance of the rainbow was intended as 'a symbol of peace'. Zaitsev explained:

> Life is a fabric, at several points of which occur events of one sort or another which grow, reverberate, destroy and raise themselves again – and so on, endlessly. One of these 'points' is the estate. In it, life completes its cycles; thus, for centuries, a drunken Spring repeats itself, thus people circle in a whirlpool of love, laughter and tears, enjoy themselves and suffer. After a while, peace and tranquillity replace passion and people rest from what they have lived through and a new generation once again begins to take the same path which their fathers and forefathers took before them.[36]

In this way, according to Zaitsev, men's lives have neither sense nor real movement. Life moves on the spot, repeating itself. The production, which was given on 26 March 1914, was staged with great difficulty but with the conviction that what the group was doing was important. Little money had been available for sets or costumes so the group had to make do with what was available on the premises of the Hunting Club on Vozdvizhenye Street, where the production was finally given. According to B. Vershilov, rehearsals were a major headache. Of a total of forty-five, thirty-three were held in various locations, often late at night when Vakhtangov had completed his normal day's work. These sometimes began between 11 pm and midnight and ended at 5 or 6 am.[37] The group rejected the standard pieces of setting which the Club possessed – the usual pavilions and wooden arches – and opted instead for plain drapes. Having tried, unsuccessfully, to borrow these from the Nezlobin Theatre, they eventually managed to acquire some grey-green hessian, against which they set some benches, painted white, a white statue, a white balustrade, some columns and a few items of furniture. Critics took offence at this and were ironic about the way in which the beauty of the Turgenev-like estate with its resplendent gardens, was relayed through 'dirty, crumpled rags'. What is more, the director had had the bright idea of making 'a gap in one of the dirty rags' through which he forced the actors to look and 'exclaim on the beauties of nature'.[38] Other reviews described the production as 'weak', 'childishly incompetent', 'excusable only as a first attempt'.[39] According to Zakhava, after the production, all the actors gathered in one of the dressing rooms. 'Well, we've flopped', said Vakhtangov happily and 'strangely enough, nobody was miserable, nobody was angry and everyone's face shone with joy and happiness as if they had just experienced a victory.'[40] Stanislavsky thought the failure owed something to the fact that Vakhtangov was taking on too much work as well as to the production's excessively naturalistic mood of morbid neurasthenia. The result was that Vakhtangov's Studio did not go public again until 1918. In order to appease Stanislavsky, Vakhtangov began to turn his attention more to the First Studio but continued to work secretly with his own Mansurov students.

The outbreak of the First World War had little obvious impact on Vakhtangov who simply immersed himself further in the warm haven of security which was the First Studio. He conducted work simultaneously at the Mansurov Studio where he tried to combine theatrical with general ethical training. There arose a special understanding among the group of what was *studiny* behaviour (i.e. conduct worthy of a Studio member) and what was *nestudiny*. Vakhtangov defined the 'Studio spirit' in a message to members and associates in November 1918, the essence of which needed to be reflected in each Studio member's artistic, ethical, moral, psychological and public life, as well as in his comradely relations with others. Above all it meant discipline. As for what was hostile to the Studio spirit, Vakhtangov mentioned the following: 'Lateness for classes, skipping classes, carelessness towards studio property, the tone in which students address each other, frivolous behaviour in class . . . disorder backstage . . . rudeness to outsiders, criticism of senior Studio members by their juniors . . . the way in which cigarettes are held[41] . . . the way students sit during lessons . . . the attitude towards the Studio's finances . . .'[42] There is little doubt that any breach of Studio ethics was a source of intense pain to Vakhtangov.

On 24 November 1914 the First Studio had held the premiere of a production by Vakhtangov's friend, Boris Sushkevich, of a stage adaptation of Charles Dickens's *The Cricket on the Hearth* in which Vakhtangov acted a significant role, in so far as it would appear to have affected the future development of his acting theories – that of the toy manufacturer Tackleton. The description which Nikolai

Volkov offered of Vakhtangov's performance suggests an intriguing blend of the stylised and the naturalistic as the, at first, inhuman Tackleton, in a typically Dickensian transformation, turns from a mechanical doll into a living, breathing, warm-hearted human being:

> Jerky intonations. Squeaky voice. A croaking laugh. Clicking heels. One eye half closed. His mouth in a permanent expression of disgust. A striped waistcoat . . . You look at him and wonder whether what you see before you is a human being or a wound-up doll made by the skilled hand of Caleb Plummer. Hardly any movement. Gesticulation kept to a minimum. Just as the mechanism winds down, this comical and unpleasant gentleman freezes on a half-word or a half-gesture . . . But at the end . . . The same movement, as if with hinged joints. The same frock coat. But despite this something has happened to Tackleton. His intonation is warmer. His voice has softened. There is anguish and loneliness in his glance. It is as if the unfeeling piece of wood has had its day. There is no longer a coiled spring inside him but a human heart which is beating and the audience fully accepts Tackleton the human being as it had, formerly, Tackleton the marionette.[43]

As a coda to this, it is interesting to note that Vakhtangov had begun to note, during improvisatory sessions held with his students in December 1914, that the relationships between the characters took on some of the archetypal features of the relationships between types of the *commedia dell'arte*. The question arose as to whether or not a production should be stylised. At this stage, the decision had been to reject the idea in the interests of a felt need to concentrate on the demands of an 'intimate-psychological' and 'subjective-naturalist' theatre.[44]

The first evening of public performances given at the Mansurov Studio itself was devoted to a series of short one-acters, which Vakhtangov had prepared with his students as an example of 'work in progress' rather than a fully-fledged production. These consisted of a dramatisation of Chekhov's short story *The Huntsman*, I. Shcheglov's *Feminine Nonsense*, *A Page of Romance* by Marcel Prevost and the vaudevilles, *A Match Between Two Flames* and *The Salt of Marriage*. Even in his staging of the vaudevilles, Vakhtangov attempted to put his ethical credo into practice: 'A vaudeville must be acted with a pure heart . . . Let it be as children say – I am kind, I am good . . . Everything in the world is fine. If people are wicked, this is because they don't know that their actions are wicked.'[45] The second public evening was given the following December 1916, retaining only Prevost's *A Page of Romance* and Chekhov's *The Huntsman*. The group added a dramatisation of Maupassant's *The Port* and two of Alfred Sutro's 'miniatures' – *A Marriage Has Been Arranged* . . . and *The Open Door*. Vakhtangov had devoted the whole year to the precise working-out of every phrase, word and gesture, declaring: 'Until now we have given the external appearance of feeling, its imitation . . . Now I want genuine feeling from you. To live through something means to repeat again on stage that with which we are familiar in life.' In this respect, the revival of *The Huntsman* provided opportunities for the actress playing the slighted wife to express feelings of insult, jealousy and tenderness. Sutro's plays called for refined, psychological portraiture with attention focused on the intimacies of relationship, on the revelation of psychological situation achieved through close eye contact between the actors and an awareness of sub-text. Intimacy of mood was sustained by the environment which, in *The Open Door*, consisted of a tiger-skin rug and two armchairs in which the protagonists – the lonely eccentric Lord Geoffrey and the woman he loves, Lady Torminster – sat facing each other with hardly any movement. The screens which framed the action served to concentrate the audience's attention on the slightest 'soul movement' of the characters.[46]

The autumn of 1915 brought with it some response to the European war when the students, under Vakhtangov's guidance, began work on an adaptation by Michael Chekhov of Tolstoy's story with an anti-militarist theme, *Ivan the Fool*. Unfortunately, like many of the Studio's projects, it was not brought to fruition and Vakhtangov returned to it later, at the Second Studio, in 1919. Meanwhile there were beginning to be murmurs of discontent within the Mansurov brought on by lack of success with a series of improvisatory sketches and the failure to bring about a production of the Tolstoy play. The students complained of never completing anything, of never performing before a wider public. In addition, they were becoming increasingly dissatisfied with their 'illegal', underground status.

The 1916 season commenced with the premiere of Vakhtangov's second production for the First Studio – of Berger's allegorical play *The Deluge*, which was given its premiere on 14 December 1915, with Michael Chekhov in the part of Frazer, an unsuccessful Jewish stock exchange speculator, Richard Boleslavsky as the barrister, O'Neill, and O.V. Baklanova as the prostitute, Lizzie. At the same time as he was working on *The Deluge*, Vakhtangov also began work on Jacinto Benavente's *The Bonds of Interest*, but only got as far as the eighth rehearsal because the actors did not have sufficient time in between rehearsing *The Deluge* and acting in the Art Theatre's main house. However, what is notable about this abortive attempt is that the play was based on the typical characters of *commedia dell'arte* in which Stanislavsky himself was currently showing an interest – viz. his production, with Alexandre Benois, of Goldoni's *La Locandiera* (translated as *Mistress of the Inn*) in 1914.

Vakhtangov made many cuts in the text of *The Deluge*, as well as altering details of the characterisation. He also sought to emphasise the connection with the biblical story of the Flood, so that the strange figure of Frazer should seem like a prophet instead of a petty corn-dealer on the stock exchange. The action of the play, written by the Swedish writer Johann Henning Berger in 1906, is set in a town in North America and takes place in a local bar on a day of intense heat. An argument takes place between Frazer and a man called Beer, a wealthy capitalist and chairman of a company which has built a dam which stands above the town. If the heatwave comes to an end and is followed by a deluge, will the dam hold? Frazer says it will not and openly accuses the businessman of building a defective dam. The fierce row is followed by a sudden downpour. People rush in with the news that the water level is rising and the dam bursts at the end of the act. In act 2, the same scene has become a kind of 'Noah's Ark', as the water is said to be rising inch by inch and everyone is convinced that they are going to drown. The belief brings about a profound change

12 Scene from act 2 of Berger's *The Deluge*, Moscow Art Theatre First Studio (1915)

in them. Enmity turns to friendship. There are mutual confessions. The chairman admits that his company built a defective dam for dividends and profit. A young man and a woman who have just met again after a long separation, renew their love in spite of the woman's confession that she is a prostitute. The miserly bar-owner, Stratton, distributes free champagne and at the end of the act they all link hands in a dance, led by Frazer, and vow to die together. The water has continued to rise during the act and, as it does so, means of contact with the outside world are lost, one by one – first the telephone and, finally, the electric light. The scene is lit by a candle as all sit waiting for the end. Act 3 opens in darkness with the characters asleep. It becomes clear that the alarm was exaggerated and that the danger is past. There is an instantaneous change of mood. Previous antagonisms revive, old quarrels are resumed. The young man repudiates the prostitute. The chairman repudiates his promise of reform. The bar-owner produces a bill for the champagne. The electricity and telephone are restored. The scene returns to the one on which the curtain first rose. The sun bursts in.[47]

Vakhtangov formulated the objectives of the first two acts as follows:

> In the first all are wolves to each other. Not a drop of compassion. Not a shred of attention. Each has his own concerns. They grab things from each other. Everyone is isolated . . . The whole of the second act is repentance. Joy and tenderness. All are purified. All are righteous. The human element has emerged. The crabs, octopi and sea monsters come adrift from the bodies of men. Man is cleansed through love of his fellow man. We shall die together, taking each other by the hand and opening up our hearts.[48]

According to Alexei Diky, Sulerzhitsky especially valued the significance of act 2, with the result that he almost ignored act 3, where everything reverts to 'normal'. Sulerzhitsky saw the production as continuing the line begun by *The Wreck of 'The Hope'* and liked the 'Noah's Ark' idea of the second act: 'Oh, what strange people;

all of them kind and sincere, each has the beautiful possibility of being good . . . Reveal this kind-heartedness and they will be ecstatic in the delirium which new feelings reveal to them.'[49]

Vakhtangov sought a rhythmically 'finished' quality, emphasising the characters' external expressive aspects. One critic noted that the production was staged as if on a chess board, with a kind of cruel precision and with pedantic measure.[50] It was very much an ensemble production in which the very idea of 'togetherness' was shown to be sacrificed. Vakhtangov also looked for other sharply expressive means in the costuming and staging. Beer the businessman was like a god with gold teeth worshipped by the others and there was a good deal of gold colouring incorporated in the setting. A minor role, that of the Second Client was interpreted like a personification of stock exchange 'gold fever'. He appeared for a second during the first act and then at the very end of the play. A permanent visitor to the bar, who regularly drinks his cocktail at ten every evening, he was intended as the personification of respect for punctuality and mechanical living. His appearance for his ritual drink at the end was as if nothing had happened in the interim:

> He burst into the bar like a water spout, sweeping away napkins, trays and chairs in his path. He was the personification of the stock exchange with its yellow fever, an image of bourgeois practicality – even the cocktail entered the business-like time-table of his day.[51]

There occurred a striking moment during the second act, which became known in criticism of the production of 'The Chain'. It began with the bar in total darkness except for the light of a few candles which flickeringly lit the faces of the people in a last sign of life and hope. Suddenly, a voice of almost primeval resonance emerged from the gloom: 'A-ra-ra-ra-ram! Arar-rar-ra-ra . .!!' This was the voice of Frazer, who continued to emit hair-raising sounds as he passed from one to another of the group, linking their hands together before crying out in a kind of ecstasy: 'We . . . are a single chain! We are all linked together! We must all be together!' The 'conversion' device of the second act was also incorporated into the way the furniture was used. In act 1 Vakhtangov had sought to tone down the decor and make the bar appear a run-down sort of place with ordinary chairs and tables which could be used as part of the quarrelling and fighting among the protagonists. In act 2, this same furniture became a means to raise everyone above floor level as a metaphorical equivalent of the spiritual elevation which all had undergone. A critic stressed the allegorical aspect of the production's conception:

> A simple story of ordinary Americans[52] gradually grew into a wild, horrific story about the struggle for existence, the threat of death . . . Vakhtangov removed the action from the level of everyday life to a more general abstract level . . . The acting style was marked by a more clear-cut and graphic quality – the rhythm of American luxury and violence in hyperbolical, exaggerated images. It was a struggle between the spirit of the Studio and the emerging 'spirit of theatre'.[53]

One of the most interesting aspects of the production was the performance of the role of Frazer by Chekhov (the first of his three versions of the role) and by

Vakhtangov himself. According to Zakhava,[54] Chekhov's interpretation had an improvisational lightness where Vakhtangov's had depth of feeling and precision of outline. Chekhov played the third act, following the false alarm, as if the events of act 2 had left no mark on him whatsoever. Not only that, Chekhov went even further in stressing a previous preoccupation with his personal affairs and a sense of social enmity towards others. Vakhtangov thought this view of the role 'cynical'. His Frazer was more thoughtful in the final act, both ironic and mournful. The character abandoned his illusion of human decency with greater difficulty, as well as the feelings of unity and love which had been experienced. There was a sense in Vakhtangov's performance, during act 3, that the events of the previous night had left a profound trace on him and that the sadness with which he left the stage would accompany him for a long time. Vakhtangov's interpretation was much closer to Sulerzhitsky's belief in the fundamentally decent instincts of the protagonists.

According to Marc Slonim, Vakhtangov acted Frazer as a man at the end of his tether where Chekhov portrayed someone agitated by 'a sort of inner tremor and while drowning, never lost his fighting spirit and the hope to float again to the surface.'[55] Others saw a mean and maniacal streak in Chekhov's Frazer. He hated Beer and those like him because, to date, it is they who had drawn the lucky number in life's lottery while Frazer desperately wanted to be in their place. The Wheel of Fortune had turned and, at the moment, he was in the pit beneath but, tomorrow, it might be his turn to fly to the top. It was this hope which sustained Frazer, a mean spirit, full of destructive passion. His whole being shrieked with a sense of helpless disillusionment at what the great world of business had done to him. Nevertheless, it was Frazer who, when the flood warning was given and iron shutters were placed at the doors and windows and the lights went out, preached to others, in the new circumstances, a new sense of reality.[56] Other critics pointed to the humour with which Chekhov, especially, invested the role. When first entering the bar he stood on the threshold and gave a little skip as he changed his stride before entering. Chekhov explained this as part of the unsuccessful speculator's superstitious nature. He always came into a room with his left foot first.[57]

When the production was almost complete, Stanislavsky turned up to a rehearsal and, dismayed by the excessive naturalism (as he had been by the previous production of *The Lanin Estate*), set about restaging three-quarters of the play in an attempt to make it more sharply 'theatrical'. Vakhtangov protested, and hinted in his diaries that 'others' came along at the last minute and 'spoilt' his production. At this historical point, Vakhtangov was still a vehement disciple of a Stanislavsky who had moved on creatively from the point where Vakhtangov thought him to be. He was later to accuse Stanislavsky of betraying his own principles in the way that he staged *Twelfth Night* at the First Studio (1917) where, again, the emphasis was on a more overt, external theatricality. As B. Sushkevich pointed out: 'We all believed in the Stanislavsky system to the limit, to the point of fanaticism. Vakhtangov most of all of us . . . He considered that Suler[58] should fight with Konstantin Sergeievich[59] to defend the new laws which Stanislavsky himself had created.'[60]

However, Vakhtangov's own ideas were not always as uniformly Stanislavskyan as this would seem to suggest. In March 1915, Vakhtangov had jotted in his diary a scenario for a doll pantomime on the theme of life and art. He had also been very taken with Meyerhold's productions of Blok's *The Female Stranger* and Schnitzler/Dohnanyi's *Columbine's Scarf*, which had toured Moscow in the autumn of 1911. He actually began to work at the Mansurov Studio on a version of the Blok play, which he invited Alexei Popov to direct. When this project came to nothing, another arose in its place equally revealing of Vakhtangov's interests. A student of the Studio, P.G. Antokolsky, later well known as a poet and theatre director, had written a short dramatic fairy tale called *The Doll of the Infanta* the subject of which was a little princess whose doll had broken – the winding mechanism has come to grief. The princess is in great distress and turns for help to a moorish magician who, by means of a magic spell, makes the doll work again and returns 'the joy of youth and liveliness of step' to the little girl. The director's task was given to Yuri Zavadsky, who was to base his work on preliminary sketches by Vakhtangov, who wanted to stage the play as a puppet show with each actor playing the part of a doll. 'If you proceed from the notion of the doll you will find the form and feeling' declared Vakhtangov. 'These feelings are extremely simple. A human being's emotions are complex and subtle. A toy cannot experience subtilised feeling. At each moment of the production, only one person should be in active movement – the one who happens to be speaking. All the rest listen motionlessly.' Vakhtangov insisted that, not only should the actors move and talk like dolls but that each should also feel, think and suffer in a doll-like fashion. When objections were raised to this on the grounds that dolls do not actually live and feel, Vakhtangov agreed that this was true in nature but false in imagination. Everything which existed in the imaginative fantasy of the actor could and should be embodied on stage.[61] This account is important, not so much because of the actual production of *The Doll of the Infanta*, but because some of the ideas which Vakhtangov was elaborating at this stage are useful for understanding his later development and the forms which his post-revolutionary productions took.

The 1916/17 season was heralded by a speech from Vakhtangov in which he spoke of embarking on a new phase in the life of the Studio where a completed production would be the target. For this purpose, he had chosen Maeterlinck's *The Miracle of St Anthony*, the first version of which was performed in September 1918. 'We could act this play as a satire on human relationships', declared Vakhtangov, 'but that would be terrible. Every character must have within it something which can be loved – some pleasant qualities. One must discover in all these people that which amuses, that which makes our peace with them. The actor must be above the character he portrays.'[62] If this smacks of that Tolstoyanism which is echoed in Stanislavsky's apothegm that 'When playing an evil person one should seek out the good in him', then the second version of the Maeterlinck play, performed in 1921, represented a complete abandonment of a former, uncritically 'humanist' outlook.

The revolution of February 1917 was followed by another public evening of performances at the Mansurov Studio of dramatised short stories by Chekhov, consisting of *The Huntsman, The Story of Miss N., Enemies, Ivan Matveyich, Long-Tongue, Verochka* and *The Malefactor*. That spring, Vakhtangov also received an invitation from the Jewish 'Habimah' Studio to work there as a teacher and director. He accepted and, the following October, opened the studio officially with a production of one-act Jewish plays. However, between that event and his next important production – of Ibsen's *Rosmersholm* – lay the broad gulf of the October revolution which, in Vakhtangov's own words written in March 1919, had 'drawn a red line between the "old" world and the "new"'.[63] However, there is little doubt that Vakhtangov met the October revolution in the same spirit of indecision and fear which characterised the majority of members of the Art Theatre, most of whom were in no sense politically committed or politically active, the older generation, especially, tending to be conservative. The shooting in the streets outside the theatre, the hunger and the cold which accompanied the circumstances of civil war gripped everyone in a disgruntled and apprehensive equality. It was a brave man who anticipated the outcome of the struggle by coming down on the side of the Bolsheviks, but this is essentially what Vakhtangov did. He underwent a kind of revolutionary conversion, much to the horror of some members of his Studio, and there is little doubt that the revolution was responsible for the split which was to open up the formerly unbroken ranks of this army of serious theatre artists. The moment of Vakhtangov's conversion may be apocryphal but is said to have occurred while observing a worker mend a broken overhead tram wire. There was something about the way in which the man handled his tools, bent with absorbed concentration over his work, that suggested to Vakhtangov in a flash of insight that here was someone no longer engaged on somebody else's work, but who was doing it for himself and on behalf of others.[64]

According to Pavel Novitsky, Vakhtangov was almost totally unfamiliar with Marxist literature. As a high school student he apparently read and studied volume 1 of *Das Kapital*, but his library contained only two Marxist books – Charles Andler's *Introduction and Commentary to the Communist Manifesto* and a copy of Karl Kautsky's *Erfurt Programme*. In the Andler brochure only forty-eight pages had been cut. The other book contained no signs of having been read. His library was also devoid of books on philosophy. His copy of Chelpanov's *Introduction to Philosophy* remained uncut. On the other hand, several books on the theatre – Romain Rolland's *The People's Theatre*, Meyerhold's *On the Theatre*, Craig's *On the Art of the Theatre*, Georg Fuchs's *The Revolution of the Theatre*, Kerzhentsev's *Revolution and the Theatre*, plus all the theatre books of Evreinov and Komissarzhevsky showed every sign of careful reading and prolonged examination.[65] In a recent article, A.S. Matskin quotes a hitherto unpublished extract from the reminiscences of Michael Chekhov, which explains Vakhtangov's approach to the revolution in an interesting manner:

> Being comparatively young, living constantly in a creatively emotional state, surrounded by the images of his imagination, Vakhtangov was naturally inclined towards romanticism. His intelligence was never abstract or dry. His ideas flowed from the heart. His life was full and he long remained indifferent to that which the

October revolution brought with it. But soon, his sensibility began to suggest to him that he, despite living a full life, was somewhat isolated and apart from reality. He began to get more used to it, to read and to observe and to feel that, behind everything that happened around him there was, or at least there ought to be, something whole and harmonious. And there, before his mind, there unfolded a strong and logically welded materialist world view. He saw how those who made the revolution systematically inculcated this world view in the consciousness of the Russian people and that this was, in fact, the reality of the present day. With the gifts which were natural to him, Vakhtangov began to poeticise this reality.[66]

The immediate consequence of the revolution was a crisis within the Studio and a creative crisis in Vakhtangov's own mind. The Mansurov Studio fell apart during 1918 and 1919 while the production of *Rosmersholm*, which Vakhtangov had been working on since August 1916, turned out a failure. Matters were complicated by a worsening of his own health and the need to undergo two serious operations between October and December 1918. During his absence, discipline at the Studio collapsed, the artistic level of performances declined, differences of opinion came out into the open, internal conflicts broke out and administrative work became disorganised. In the meantime, Vakhtangov, through his production of *Rosmersholm*, was mounting a last ditch attempt to save the precious, unsullied, monastic values of the 'Studio idea'.

In Vakhtangov's production of *Rosmersholm*, it would be no exaggeration to say that he carried certain principles of the psychological theatre to extremes, almost to absurd lengths, in an attempt to create a situation where theatre ceased to be 'theatre' and became truth itself. As early as 1911 he had resolved to chase the 'theatrical' out of the theatre and now, almost a year and a half after the revolution, here he was trying to put this slogan into practice. It was almost like a last desperate attempt to stem the tide flowing in from the outside world. In a letter, Vakhtangov compared Stanislavsky's production of *Twelfth Night* unfavourably with his own *Rosmersholm*. What was needed at this juncture was 'a pure art of the highest sort and a step towards the 'mystery'.[67] Interestingly, his preoccupation with the 'mystery' was something he shared with many other artists of the period, although each tended to interpret the 'mystery' in his own way.

Although Vakhtangov commenced work on *Rosmersholm* in 1916, the ideas behind the production reached back to 1908 and the production which Nemirovich-Danchenko had staged at the Art theatre, with settings by Yegorov. Vakhtangov even went to the lengths of employing members of the original cast, including Olga Knipper, who repeated her performance as Rebecca West. G. Khmara was cast as Rosmer with Vakhtangov himself and L.M. Leonidov alternating the role of Brendel. Nemirovich's production had draped the stage of the Art Theatre in a green, stylised cloth and had rejected everyday details and ethnographic features. Although Vakhtangov never actually saw the earlier production, he too adopted the method of using drapes and invited Nemirovich to deliver a talk to the cast and other members of the First Studio about *Rosmersholm* and to make suggestions as to how the play should be interpreted.[68]

Like Nemirovich, Vakhtangov rejected the symbolism of Ibsen's play, interpreting it as 'a poetic work dealing with people and their destinies', and quoting Ibsen's own authority for this emphasis.[69] He wanted a performance in which the actors were not seen to be playacting but were transformed through living the feelings of the characters as if they were their very own. Just as Stanislavsky had attempted in his production of Turgenev's *A Month in the Country* (1909), Vakhtangov wanted his actors to convey the subtlest nuances of thought and feeling and for their acting to have a 'lofty, spiritual quality'. As Sophia Giatsintova recalled:

> In *Rosmersholm*, he was totally carried away with the possibility of conveying thought. He wanted the actors to stand still, not to move about, and only to disclose their thoughts on stage. Performing as Brendel, Vakhtangov achieved an inner transformation. Brendel had the eyes of a fanatic, of a believer, burning and dreadful – totally transfigured by his inner passion.[70]

Giatsintova also mentions that Vakhtangov succeeded in accomplishing the incredibly difficult task of fusing both dramatic and satirical elements in his acting.

Vakhtangov took as his starting point Lessing's words taken from his 'Dissertations Concerning the Fable', which Hauptmann had borrowed as an epigraph to *The Festival of Peace* – '. . . every inner conflict of passions, every consequence of diverging thoughts, where one annuls the others – is action too'.[71] In leading the characters to physical extinction (the leap into the mill-race) Vakhtangov simultaneously insisted on the triumph of their consciousness. The physical triumph of the 'House of Dead' (the spirit of Rosmersholm) had the simultaneous effect of exposing the rotting, corpse-like nature of its existence. The white horses (of death) had carried off Rebecca and Rosmer but this was only incidental. The genuine thing was the life of their spirit and its triumph. The 'House of the Dead' had freed itself from these revolutionaries of the spirit but this was only an apparent freedom. Vakhtangov stressed two key elements in the actors' approach to the play. The first was that each performance should be played in an improvisatory spirit (every performance being a completely new performance); the second was that, despite the play's gloomy mood, that of the actors should be one of 'holiday' (*prazdnik*). In this, too, lay the play's proximity to the 'mystery'. The actors should love the play and feel that the day of its performance was a celebration. The actors should await the play's next performance expectantly, 'as Easter Sunday is awaited on Good Friday'.[72] Another sense of the 'mystery', with connotations of the 'mysterious' bordering on a kind of expressionism, was contained in Vakhtangov's own description of the setting, properties and *mise-en-scène*.

He imagined a room of huge proportions with heavy, sombre drapes and felt that the austere style of Gordon Craig would best approximate to this rather than the more elaborate, decorative style of a Benois or Dobuzhinsky. The furniture was to consist of heavy sofas, tables and armchairs – massive, ancient and silent but which then took on a kind of animated life of their own. 'Then the sofas and armchairs squeak something in their own language and the folds of the age-old drapes rustle and whisper among themselves.'[73] This element of mystery was intensified by the use of lighting. As Pavel Markov remembered: 'Vakhtangov used lighting as one of the main stage devices: the stage was either submerged in darkness, or flooded with light, or effectively lit by glimpses of light ... with ghosts walking near it.'[74]

Vakhtangov wanted the lighting to intensify the effect of the eyes, both the eyes of the portraits on the walls and those of the characters. He refers to the portraits' 'severe, unwavering eyes' which pierce the darkness and the need for the lamplight to blur the outlines of the furniture and highlight people's faces 'especially their eyes'. The effect of the lamps was actually meant to increase the sense of surrounding darkness but, when the room was flooded with daylight 'the drapes, furniture and portraits shudder' (a very expressionist effect). It was a world in which ordinary actions took on an aura of mystery. Rebecca is described as knitting her own shroud (at the opening of act 1) and watering the flowers which are to be 'her funeral wreath'. She is a 'sorceress', an 'alien and sinister woman' and both she and Rosmer are trapped by the spirits of the house which Vakhtangov ventriloquises, as if the ghosts of the past are speaking: 'Let these pathetic creatures, these apostates, learn what it means to forget us ... they don't know that they will meet the white horses. We already feel the tremulous shadow of their wings. We already sense the impending chill of their approach.'

Rosmer and Rebecca, in Vakhtangov's interpretation, constituted a counter-movement to everything represented by Rosmersholm. The motivating action behind the play was 'the striving towards a new life' which is 'like a hurricane which blows everything away in its path, including Rosmer'. Rebecca was possessed of a 'revolutionary spirit' which inflamed Rosmer while the idea which animated him was that 'everybody in the country must be happy'. The advent of Rebecca, a passionate, uninhibited woman, into Rosmer's life had the effect of a mutual transformation. He changed from someone 'fixed numbly in his own nobility', childless, with no life-giving force (a true product of the Rosmer line) unable to respond sexually to a morbidly passionate wife (Beata), into someone suddenly quickened into intellectual life by the arrival of another passionate woman, whom he initiates into the world of ideas. Rebecca is conquered and her personal desires vanish as Rosmer's lofty spirit enobles her. For Rebecca, Beata had stood in the way of Rosmer coming to grips with life so she drove her to suicide in order to save the situation before the spiritual child, born of their spiritual union, perished.[75] Thus characterised, the action of the play is a perverse one, but that was not the kind of construction which the actual production put on it. It needs to be remembered that Vakhtangov's remarks were written in 1918, long after work had begun and, as such, did not constitute preparatory notes or amount to a 'directorial plan'. The production was a fascinating experiment and an unforgettable experience for the actors but, despite the play's positive ending – 'Rosmer and Rebecca triumph by their deaths' – the production was not a popular success and was taken off after only nineteen performances.

Vakhtangov spent part of the summer of 1918 in hospital and underwent two operations the following year, in January and again in March when part of his stomach was removed. Despite these constant periods of hospitalisation and the extreme pain which he suffered, especially towards the end of his life, Vakhtangov's involvement in the theatrical life of his country actually increased henceforth and it was during these years that he came to full maturity as a major artist. He returned from the sanatorium in Grebnovo in the summer of 1918 to discover that the directorial committee of his Studio had concluded an agreement with the Theatre and Music section of the Moscow Soviet, according to which the Studio was obliged to serve as one of the theatres belonging to the section. They were offered new premises on Kamenny Bridge (in a building which later became the Red October Club) and which was much better appointed than the cramped Mansurov Studio, and which contained seating for about 520 people. It was also proposed that, apart from Vakhtangov's own group, the Art Theatre's First and Second Studios would also play at this venue. The Vakhtangov Studio took upon itself responsibility for operating and servicing the building as a whole, controlling the administrative and financial side of things and bearing responsibility for the upkeep of the premises. At Vakhtangov's suggestion, the theatre was to call itself the People's Art Theatre. However, because of objections made by the Moscow Art Theatre directorate, the word 'Art' was dropped from the title. The People's Theatre opened on 17 December 1918, with a programme of one-act plays performed by members of the Vakhtangov Studio and consisting of Maupassant's *The Port*, Octave Mirbeau's *The Thief* and Lady Gregory's *The Rising of the Moon*. Apart from these, the People's Theatre later presented the Second Studio's production of Zinaida Gippius's *The Green Ring* and an evening of excerpts from *The Brothers Karamazov* staged by members of the Art Theatre.[76] Vakhtangov's ideas for the People's Theatre, which he elaborated in March 1919, were very ambitious.

In February, he had received an invitation from the Theatrical Department of the People's Commissariat for Education to take over management of its Directors' Section. He agreed to do so but was later compelled to turn down the work on grounds of ill health. However, the plans he laid for the future of the People's Theatre came under what he saw as his responsibilities as Head of the Directors' Section. These plans imagined daily performances of a single play – Verhaeren's *The Dawns* – performed by different companies, the Kamerny, the Maly, the Art Theatre, Proletkult etc. In his view, the performances of the People's Theatre needed to be heroic and large-scale with mass scenes (difficult to imagine in so small a theatre). Quite apart from this work, Vakhtangov was also involved in teaching at the Drama Studio of Anatoli Gunst. He was reading Romain Rolland's book *The People's Theatre* with great enthusiasm, responding to requests from Nemirovich-Danchenko and Stanislavsky to organise an opera studio and conduct classes with members of the Bolshoi. Another group of students asked him to stage a production of Tchaikovsky's opera *Eugene Onegin* and he was invited to work in an Armenian Drama Studio, which had just been established in Moscow. However, it was Rolland's ideas, coupled with those of Vyacheslav Ivanov, which attracted him most. He was also quoting Wagner with approval: 'Only on the shoulders of a great social movement can an authentic art raise itself from its conditions of civilised barbarism to a height worthy of it.'[77] He believed, with Rolland, referring to the French revolution, that 'a free and happy people needs festivals more than theatres', and that creative work needed to be conducted in the open air with the spectator transformed into an actor. He began to feel the need to get away from the theatre of psychological intimacy, of small forms, and began dreaming of productions on a grand scale. Apart from the Verhaeren play, he thought of staging Byron's *Cain* and a dramatised version of *The Bible*. He wanted to explore the nature of leadership by building a play around the life of Moses. He wanted to take over the Bolshoi and convert it into a People's Theatre. His characteristic mode of thought during this period strove towards the realms of myth and legend. He contemplated staging Pushkin, Lope de Vega, Sophocles. Of all these plans, none saw the light of day, although there are records of some work accomplished on Sophocles' *Electra* and a more detailed account of work done on Pushkin's *Feast in Time of Plague*. This latter production appears to have taken the form of a polemic with the Art Theatre's approach to the same play. For the first time, Vakhtangov worked on new ways of verse speaking and on the principle of sculpted theatrical form in which allegorical/symbolic motifs were to the fore:

> On stage are a table and a street lamp. At the rear are the lights of the town and houses silhouetted against a background of black velvet. At the table are a group of people, dispositioned as if sculpted in space by means of a huge grey covering with slits cut in it for heads and hands. The cloth covers all the actors and the table simultaneously and the actors' heads and hands poke through the slits.[78] Torches burn on the table. Extraordinary economy of movement. Every shift of the head constitutes a scene change. A hand reaches for a goblet, covers a face, grasps another, gives a gesture of refusal, and every detail becomes immensely significant. With these means, Vakhtangov conveyed the feeling of the tragic spirit of the plague.[79]

The People's Theatre continued to exist throughout the 1918/19 season but it never achieved its hoped-for popularity, playing at best to only 46.5 per cent capacity.[80] Matters were further complicated by Vakhtangov's having to spend two months on a health farm prior to his operation at the beginning of 1919 (he was away from 27 October to 29 December 1918). His work for the theatre's celebration of the first anniversary of the revolution was undertaken by Sushkevich and Boleslavsky. There was also his work at the Habimah Studio to consider and there were additional complications threatening the survival of the People's Theatre. The First Studio, which had begun by agreeing to the merger, subsequently backed down. The Second Studio stayed for only a few productions, as did the Art Theatre. In order to try and heal the breach between those who, like himself, offered general support to the new political order, and those who were plainly hostile to it, Vakhtangov dreamed up the impossible idea of establishing a kind of 'theatrical monastery', without any reference to politics or the kind of external pressures which were contributing to the break up of his own Studio.

Five members of the Mansurov Studio's council decided to resign and form a new one, threatening to leave if their authority was not recognised. Thus, the Studio was effectively split in two, although the majority of members leaned towards the new council who, however, incorporated in their own rules a veto to be operated by Vakhtangov, thus effectively tying their own hands. Vakhtangov decided that the best way to save the Studio was to recognise the new council and to persuade those who remained loyal to him to follow his example. The upshot was that the rebel members of the new council eventually left the Studio, taking with them most of the talented members of the group and leaving Vakhtangov with a rump of supporters. Those who left included Zavadsky and Antokolsky, the latter angered by the fact that Vakhtangov had initially agreed to a production of his Tieck-inspired play *Puss In Boots*, but had then sought to change the title of the play and, when this met with resistance, barred the production. Vakhtangov also quarrelled with Zavadsky, who was to direct, over the general conception of the production. Vakhtangov suggested that the play, which contained characters such as a Cat, Pierrot, Doctor Brahm the paradoxist, and Estrella the circus star as well as magic transformation scenes, be rendered more 'realistic' and that it be acted as if it were a dream of the heroine. The play should be re-titled *The Dream Betrothal*. The consequence was that twelve trained and accomplished actors left the Studio, leaving behind five of the 'old guard', who included Boris Zakhava, and a small group of, as yet, untrained newcomers.[81]

When he was not in hospital undergoing surgery or recuperating, a typical daily schedule for Vakhtangov must have been similar to the one described in October 1918:

> 12.00 – 3.00 Habimah; 3 – 5.30 a lesson, 6 – 10 p.m. *Festival of Peace* 10.30 – 1.00 a.m. rehearsal of plays to be performed for the November holidays.[82]

He then went on to enumerate the studios which were making claims on his time: 'First Studio, Second Studio, My Studio, Habimah, Gunst, People's Theatre, Proletkult, Art Theatre, Lessons, Performance for November celebrations . . . just ten of the organisations making demands on my waking hours.' He was also touring, appearing in *The Deluge* in Simbirsk and playing roles with the Art Theatre in Leningrad. In June 1920, he went on tour with the First Studio to Kharkov and, in September, staged the first version of his production of Chekhov's *The Wedding* at his Studio. On 13 September, the Vakhtangov Studio was included in the Art Theatre group and was given the title of Third Studio and on 29 January 1921, the first of Vakhtangov's major post-revolutionary productions was staged at the Third Studio – the second version of Maeterlinck's *The Miracle of St Anthony* which included Zavadsky in the title role who, after a year's absence in the provinces, had reconsidered his earlier decision to leave Vakhtangov and had been accepted back into the fold with open arms.

Immediately prior to the break-up which involved the departure of Zavadsky, Vakhtangov had received a request to stage some work for the Second Studio – a request which had been supported by Stanislavsky. Vakhtangov agreed, on condition that the Second Studio admit some of his own students – that is, those who had remained with him following the collapse of the Mansurov. Vakhtangov decided to stage the version of Tolstoy's *Ivan the Fool* which he had originally planned for his own Studio and spent the summer of 1919 in the countryside around

Penza working on the play with the actors. When he returned in the autumn, he was taken ill and was forced to abandon the work, which was eventually completed by the author of the scenario, Michael Chekhov. It was during the following, 1919/20 season, that the idea of resurrecting the Mansurov Studio was mooted. A group of the old guard taken into the Second Studio had never abandoned the notion of recreating their own Studio under Vakhtangov's leadership and this ambition was aided by the existence, within the Mansurov prior to its dissolution, of a self-contained group consisting of members of the former Mamonovsky Studio (so-called because of its situation on Mamonovsky Lane). By merging the Mamonovsky group and the remaining loyal members of the Mansurov, a new collective was created, who were then supplemented by orphaned students from the Gunst Studio (Anatoli Gunst having recently died). Although Vakhtangov was, in principle, against the resurrection of a 'Mansurov' Studio (perhaps fearing a repetition of the past) nevertheless, this is what the students insisted on calling themselves and Vakhtangov grew to accept this *fait accompli*. When the directorate of the Art Theatre announced, on 13 September 1920, that this new collective would be incorporated within the Art Theatre as the Third Studio and be given its own premises, this set the seal on the direction of Vakhtangov's remaining theatre work which was to take place in these new premises with this, essentially, new group. However, whilst the new building was being fitted out, the first production of Chekhov's *The Wedding* was given in two rooms of the building which had formerly housed the Mansurov Studio, which were converted into a small auditorium with a capacity of fifty, using some of the existing furniture as decor, such as a tiled stove set in the corner of one of the rooms and which provided a suitable decorative background for the second-rate restaurant in which the action of the play is set.

Vakhtangov's original idea was to stage *The Wedding* in a double-bill with Pushkin's *Feast in Time of Plague*, incorporating some of the production devices of the latter: 'A large table, behind which, facing the auditorium sit the participants of the grim feast . . . The entire scenic action lends itself to sculpted groups of guests sitting at a table. The attention of the spectators must be concentrated, past the words, on the faces of the people.'[83] This was difficult to achieve in the circumstances as there was not enough space for the wedding table in one room so they were forced to use two, smaller tables, and extend one of them into an adjoining room. In the event, the production of *The Wedding* was staged in a double-bill with *The Miracle of St Anthony*, but the connection with Pushkin's play remained a relevant one for understanding Vakhtangov's interpretation. As he explained in notes written in the Vsekhsvyatski Sanatorium in March 1921:

> I want to stage *Feast in Time of Plague* and Chekhov's *The Wedding* in one programme. *The Wedding* contains elements of the other play. Those infested by the plague do not know that the plague has passed by, that mankind has been freed, and that one does not have to invite generals to weddings. Chekhov is tragical, not lyrical.[84]

Zakhava compared Vakhtangov's work on this production with his ideas on how *The Doll of the Infanta* should be staged. If, on that occasion, he wished the actors to perform as 'live dolls', in this instance he wanted to disclose the 'dead essence' in the living individual. In the former case, the marionette acted like a human being: in this instance, the human being assumed the characteristics of the marionette. As a result, the comic proceedings were turned upside down. The audience still laughed but the laughter froze on its lips as the comic was transformed into the tragic and what was funny became frightening:

> Not the living in the dead, but the dead in the living was what Vakhtangov revealed in *The Wedding*, so that the 'general's' cry, 'Chelovek!' [meaning both 'Waiter' and 'Man' in the abstract] seemed the hopeless howl of an insulted old man, transformed into a symbolic idea whose echo reverberated in the hearts of the audience.[85]

A recent Soviet critic has characterised Vakhtangov's developing philosophy and method in these terms:

> The theme of death is at the centre of each of his productions. The problem of the 'living and the dying' is also at the heart of his creativity. He carefully seeks out the forms of scenic expression of that inner ossification, that death-like aspect of the soul (spiritual deadness) and incapacity to be creative, which makes nominally living beings into actual corpses. In his productions, this 'deadness' is not only in terrifying activity, in a dynamic of moral decomposition, but in a real struggle with the 'living' creative consciousness. And this struggle is brought to an apotheosis. Hence the tragic origin of his productions, the authentic grotesqueness of form – not the tragic and comic alongside each other in conflict, but the comic raised in its development to the authentically tragic, and the tragic turned into the comic. The grotesque depiction of reality intensifies in his work as maturity approaches and is especially sharply expressed in the post-revolutionary period.[86]

The most detailed and extended treatment of Vakhtangov's production of *The Wedding* is contained in Reuben Simonov's book about his teacher. Simonov played Dymba, the Greek with a shaky command of Russian. Simonov states that the fact of the revolution demanded a reinterpretation of Chekhov who could no longer be viewed in the light of a sentimental, compassionate relation to 'Man' in general. It was necessary to express 'a forthright repudiation, an active denunciation of the philistinism, the narrow-mindedness, the devouring banality of the old petty-bourgeois class'.[87] What was it that induced Vakhtangov to combine the idea of producing this play in the context of his thoughts on Pushkin's *Feast in Time of Plague*? 'It was the contrast between the tragedy of the commonplace round and the tragedy that is heroic. He discovered a high theatricality in both genres in which the form and content are equally important . . . The idea is the triumph of the free human spirit over the Black Death, over the infection of the habitual and everyday.'[88]

Authentic bottles of madeira, vodka and other beverages were placed on the 'restaurant' table bearing the labels of famous old brewing firms, such as Shustov, Smirnov and others. Everything was authentic, including the candelabra. The bentwood chairs were old and worn. Costumes looked second-hand or shabby and tasteless. Some looked as if they had been borrowed for the occasion. Father wore an old-fashioned, double-breasted frock-coat; Dymba had a large red scarf tied in a bow round his neck. The women wore dresses in strikingly bright colours which looked as if they had been stitched together by cheap labour at the seediest of dressmakers. Great stress was laid on accoutrements and exaggerated make-up. The mother's lace handkerchief covering her hair was fastened with a monstrously ornate pin. Hair styles and moustaches were also of exaggerated proportions. Much attention was paid to the way the lighting was arranged so as to give the impression of being shed by kerosene lamps. Everything was conducted in strict tempo with strong acoustical effects, whether it was the voice of the Master of Ceremonies barking his commands, or Aplombov's monotonous, hollow voice 'dripping on the audience like water on a stone' or, when raised in anger, sounding like a dentist's drill. A lackey arranged wine and hors d'oeuvres to the opening rhythm of the music as Aplombov pounded the back of a chair while conducting an argument with the mother, both in time to the music and in accompaniment to his own words. The dialogue between the romantic Zmeyukhina and the telegraphist, Yat, was accompanied by a rattling waltz on the piano whilst she fanned herself in a rapid, nervous tempo. When her voice broke on a high note while singing a romance, Yat took over the fanning, with broad majestic sweeps, his stylish pince-nez vibrating on his nose in time to his movements.[89]

The production opened at a brisk tempo with a rousing quadrille. The group danced to the commands of the MC (a motif taken up later in the naval commands shouted by the 'general'). Vakhtangov suggested that each actor perform some simple, initial action like moving a chair, adjusting something on the table so as to produce the necessary auditory effect. The shouting of the MC was accompanied by the sound of an out-of-tune piano, the guests then seating themselves at table to the accompaniment of a bravura march. The 'command' theme was continued as Aplombov quarrelled with his mother-in-law and threw a menacing command to Yat. This was interpreted by the pianist as an order addressed to him and he promptly struck the keys with a powerful flourish. Aplombov and Yat then set about each other. The women shrieked while the men tried to separate them. Thunderous music accompanied the general bustle while a single figure sat motionless – the phlegmatic bride remained at the table, munching imperturbably, observing the fracas with dull impassivity.[90]

The production built to a climax with the entry of the sea-captain, played with warmth and simplicity and a great deal of charm. His arrival seemed to fulfil the dreams of those present about the possibilities of a more beautiful life – 'A real live general at the same wedding as us!' His presence had a salutory effect on all present. 'How long since you retired?' asked Aplombov with a newly acquired dignity in keeping with his name. In response to the 'general's' question 'You a sailor?', Mozgovoi leaped from his seat and stood to attention with exaggerated, hackneyed militariness. When demonstrating how to issue commands at sea in order to bring a ship around in a force-10 gale, the captain became so carried away that he rose from his seat and started to move forwards, leaning over the table which, hitherto, had appeared to be solid. As he continued to issue commands and move forward, the table divided in the middle and advanced on the audience like the prow of a ship held together by the tablecloth. Knives, forks, dirty plates and glasses crashed to the floor as the 'ship' sailed towards the auditorium under the command of the grey-haired captain in the bow. Only the bride and groom continued to sit motionless, like stone idols, amidst the chaos. The stage was an array of mouths – round, wide-open, senseless, some dumbly yelling 'Hurrah!', others compressed with outrage as they contemplated the behaviour of the 'general'. It was like looking at an etching by Goya, one of Vakhtangov's favourite artists, according to B. Vershilov.[91]

Finally, when asked to leave, the captain seemed to address the whole of mankind with his call for a 'chelovek!' to come to his assistance. The miserable old man gazed about him in humiliation, as if seeking support or compassion among these people. Nobody moved. After a moment, he groped his way from the table, crossed the room as though in pain and exited into what seemed like oblivion. At the finale, the musicians were told to play the quadrille with which the play opened but now in a sad, slow tempo. Zmeyukhina repeated the phrases she had used earlier: 'I'm suffocating! Give me air!', but this time the words were delivered in melancholy fashion. The characters stood with their backs to the audience gazing after the departed figure of the captain as the sounds of the sad quadrille played more and more softly.[92]

If, previously, Vakhtangov had insisted on 'temperament from the essence', now the actor was answerable for every gesture, for the slightest movement, for each intonation. If, formerly, Vakhtangov had demanded improvisation of the 'means' (scenic colour, gesture, intonation) so that everything was fresh, new and true-to-life, he now required that everything be precisely fixed. He wanted definite outlines and unaltered repetition at every performance of everything that had been discovered during a series of careful rehearsals. But he still wished the actor to utilise these discoveries 'as if' they were being improvised by the actors before the eyes of the audience. Through these means, he achieved a combination of 'improvised feeling' combined with precise external form and presentation. The time had come to return 'the theatre' to the theatre. As Zakhava has suggested: 'The initial work of this later period began with *The Wedding*, which became a tragic mask of *poshlost* in the style of Sukhovo-Kobylin or Gogol. The human ciphers became carnival masks, animated Toby Jugs, set in motion by the sounds of the quadrille.'[93]

The first production on the stage of the new Third Studio was given on 29 January 1921. This was the second version of *The Miracle of St Anthony*. Work on the first version, in a translation by A. Vorotnikov, had begun in September 1916 and ended in 1918. This earlier production had significance for Vakhtangov's Studio, as it was the first fully-fledged production they had mounted and, as such, was quite different from the 'training' work with which they were normally preoccupied. Maeterlinck's teaching about the 'inner life' played an important role in the moral and ethical education of the Studio and his work had especial appeal in Russia, particularly among the symbolists. Meyerhold's production of *The Miracle of St Anthony* (1906) had been in terms of a puppet-show in which Fate was seen to pull the strings, the world of marionettes being seen as an ironic reflection of the actual world. The style of a production by Gaideburov, in 1916, had been more mystical and other-worldly. Vakhtangov's approach to his first version of the play had been rather different from his predecessors in that he wished his actors to serve the Studio's desire to assist the cause of human decency and reflect the reconciliation and betterment of humankind.[94] The focus had been on an attempt to discover natural simplicity and this led to emphasis being placed on the role of the serving maid, Virginie. In the manner of a morality play, each of the characters was to represent a human frailty. The actors were also called upon to love the characters they were asked to impersonate and discover 'a gentle smile' at the expense of their creation, rather than 'a satirical grimace'. Only thus would there be 'creative joy'. The actor needed to be 'above' the character represented and had to act in 'a triumphal, holiday mood'. If the actor adopted this kind of attitude to the character, there was no possibility of grotesque caricature. Genuine comedy consisted in simple-heartedness and goodness. 'We always laugh a little at ourselves when we make fun of the characters', said Vakhtangov. 'After this production, I want people to feel touched and slightly ashamed.'[95]

Vakhtangov stressed the fact that Maeterlinck was a universal artist and it was the presence of this universal element in the play which made it a great work of art: 'The content of this production is a smile – Maeterlinck's smile at our expense.'[96] He asked his actors to imagine a situation in which Christ Himself arrived at an ordinary fifth-floor apartment:

> It can't be true. It's impossible; or so it seems to everyone, except Virginie. We may think it curious and smile to ourselves when she makes the saint bring her water in a bucket or when she insists he wipe his feet before entering. However, for the simple believer, Virginie's behaviour is not strange in the slightest. For her, prayer is as serious a business as cleaning a room is. For her, a saint is, by definition a thoroughly good person so why not ask him to help by carrying a bucket and not tracking up the floor with his dirty feet when it's just been washed. As soon as we seriously contemplate the possibility of a genuine relationship with God, we immediately cease to believe. In this production, we must act so that there is no overacting. You remember how, in *Cricket*, a spiritual warmth embraced the spectator from start to finish? Here must be added the smile. For this, each performer must find in his role something amusing, some basic characteristic which softens him[97] . . . From whence does Maeterlinck's smile arise? It is similar to that of Gulliver when confronted by the Lilliputians. In fact, imagine yourself to be a little person who could drown in an ashtray. If you say of a drowning man 'Let's save him', this isn't comic; but to say this of a Lilliputian drowning in an ashtray full of water is comic. Or imagine a tiny cow from the kingdom of Lilliput, small enough to place in your hand, and say to yourself, 'Right, let's milk it.' This, again, is comic.[98]

What could an actor find loveable in a character like Achille?

> We feel for him because he sincerely wants to give the saint something but does not know what. A tie-pin? A cigarette-case? Wine? Achille has a problem and we find ourselves in sympathy with him. What about the priest? He has a comical unctuousness. His professional work consists in talking to God and this fact has given him certain professional mannerisms. When he sees Anthony, he is not altogether convinced that this is a saint but, just in case, he addresses him as if he were.[99]

The priest was made up to look naively surprised and bore his hands across his chest in a stupid, sheep-like manner. The doctor was portrayed as a professional who understood next to nothing about his profession. Achille was good-natured, fat and immobile. He had one overwhelming desire – to get back to the table and finish tucking in to the partridge. The servant, Joseph, was played as all fire – a dandy with a black moustache and flying coat-tails. Gustave, who led the onslaught against the saint, wore an expression of arrogance, emphasised by his pince-nez and jutting beard. When the guests emerged from the funeral supper to gaze at the saint, they were like beetles with moustaches poking their heads out from their shells. Vakhtangov also brought in a whole row of women in black – relatives of the deceased – who sat like motionless statues with expressions of hostility and disdain directed at St Anthony. The saint himself was a combination of submissiveness and extreme attentiveness. He examined people as if they were under a microscope, in the manner of a very intelligent and very good old man. There was no need for any facile 'ecstasy' or theatrical 'saintliness', according to Vakhtangov. The actor simply needed to play him with conviction. The servant, likewise was a naive, simple-hearted girl who believed in St Anthony from the moment he entered the house.

The set was drenched with pine essence to make it smell like a real funeral parlour and the first scene was constructed as a symmetrical bas-relief, without any depth. In the middle of the backcloth was a glass door and symmetrically arranged hangers. In the scene between the doctor and Anthony, they were both placed stage centre while the guests were displaced in a line along the front of the stage, half-turned towards the central characters in a completely symmetrical pattern. The second scene was constructed on the diagonal, with Hortense's bed in a niche stage centre. A table in the right half of the stage divided the stage area into two separate sections. The spiritual world of the bourgeoisie was emphasised through details of the setting which consisted of a plain backcloth, heavy plush tablecloths, portraits with fringes, carpets, a large wooden bed with a mountain of soft pillows. The mirrors and portraits were meant to be indicative of the status of the deceased.

In 1920, Vakhtangov worked on the production again. On this occasion, he began from a starting point which focused on the disclosure of the crowd of relations as, in some sense, personifying the spirit of the bourgeois world, with the inheritors fearful of losing the legacy as a consequence of the miracle of resurrection. In this later version, hyperbole bordered on the fantastic, with sudden shifts between the tragic and the comic. The only element which was retained from the earlier production was the relationship between St Anthony and Virginie – the latter now played by K.I. Kotlubai, instead of E.A. Aleyeva, as a little old woman who, at the outset, does not believe in the saint but, having become convinced of his saintliness, bends all her energies to save him. The world of the 'profane' and 'the banal' was sharply contrasted with the 'sacred' world of the naive and pure in heart. Again, there arose the Vakhtangovian contrast between the living and the dead.

The production opened in the Third Studio's new premises on the Arbat on 29 January 1921, and, according to *Ekran* 'was a clear artistic achievement and showed outstandingly the great value of the Studio's work'.[100] The same review referred to the spirit of Goya, the style of the grotesque in Leonardo da Vinci and tones of 'Grand Guignol'. The earlier lyrical – ironic tone had been given a satirical twist. The characters who had previously been viewed through the prism of 'the smile', now seemed like terrifying figures out of Hoffmann or the grotesques in a Goya etching. The specific world of the grotesque was perceived, not only as if through a 'distorting mirror', but as if seen through the peculiar consciousness of Virginie and of Anthony himself, who both lived in another dimension. Vakhtangov described the production as a manifestation of 'imaginative realism' (fantasticheskii realizm).

The emaciated, barefooted saint appeared in the house like a wanderer, or tramp, dressed in a long sack-like garment, patched in places, which looked something like a cross between the traditional garment of a saint (as seen in Renaissance paintings) and an old dressing gown. His face bore no determining social or individual characteristics. He appeared simply, with a single justification, to 'resurrect' as if it were a matter of fixing the parquet floor or repainting the walls. His appearance was the realisation of a dream, the prayer and ecstatic wish of Virginie. Everything that happened was real but, at the same time, as if it were the play of Virginie's imagination, the movement of her consciousness. However, this was no ordinary stream of consciousness, but a conflicting one – a collision between belief in a higher spirituality and her realistic knowledge of life; hope in a 'good and all-powerful God', contrasted with the spiritless world which surrounded her. Virginie had learned the nature of the bourgeois world through experience. She was the only one who wanted Madame Hortense to be brought back to life, as she was the only one who valued life. She is appalled by the way the saint is treated and this fact took on the objective status of nightmare in Virginie's consciousness.[101]

During rehearsal, the actors were asked to erase all 'everyday' devices from their arsenal of gestures, every inconsequential movement, in fact everything considered life-like and natural. The images were constructed on the schematic basis of limited, but complex and strongly defined movements and poses which were deliberately rendered inflexible, redolent of automatons and marionettes. Hortense was made to seem like a doll with her arms extended woodenly in front of her, dressed in a nightcap and gown festooned with frills and flounces. From under the nightcap there appeared a lifeless, wooden face marked with deep wrinkles. Her head lay thrust back and the actress was not permitted even a half-turn to the audience, so as to intensify the marionette effect.[102]

Vakhtangov strove for sharp, mathematical precision in the external design and to sculptural expressiveness of form. He worked out a complicated design for the mass scenes. Deprived of individual, psychological characteristics, the crowd represented a single mass and was presented in sharply grotesque fashion. At the moment of resurrection (performed with total seriousness and with deep emotion by Zavadsky) the saint called out twice and, on each occasion, raised his arm in the air, a figure of colossal and fanatical power, possessed of tremendous inner strength. The actual moment of resurrection was then followed by moments of

13 Scene from Maeterlinck's *The Miracle of St Anthony* (second version), Moscow Art Theatre Third Studio (1921)

stark terror as the guests attempted to hide behind chairs, crawled under the table or else collapsed helplessly on the floor. There was a jam in the door with the women shouting hysterically while the men gasped for breath. They stumbled into each other, overturning chairs and scattering wreaths (the latter were ordinary lifebelts wound with black crepe). Some crawled out of the room while others moved senselessly in circles. The panic scene was played with absolute precision, although the means were totally improvised. Vakhtangov asked the actors, in rehearsal, to fix and codify the scene so as to remember the precise nature of the disorder, which objects had been stumbled over, who had collided with whom, so as to be able to perform the scene successfully with each repetition.[103] Whilst the scene of panic was being played out, it was noticeable that the saint had relapsed from his extraordinary state into static ordinariness as he quietly contemplated the chaos of terror. With his high forehead and long, swept-back hair, the saint created an impression of superhuman power and great intelligence, 'to whom all laws and desires were known and from whom no secrets were hid'.[104]

During rehearsal, Vakhtangov tried to teach his actors to live and breathe rhythmically on stage. He invented practical exercises involving the moving of furniture, laying the table, cleaning the room, etc., to music. It was necessary to learn, not only to move in a certain rhythm, but to live in it. He taught that every individual, every nation, every phenomenon of nature, every event of human existence, possessed its own especial rhythm.[105] To discover the rhythm of the play was the key to the success of the production. In *The Miracle of St Anthony*, Vakhtangov aimed at total concentration by the actors on the significance of each movement, gesture or word. Nobody moved on stage when someone else was speaking. This would not seem artificial and lifeless to the spectator if each frozen movement and gesture was justified, organically, from within. External immobility must never become inner lifelessness and the internal dynamic needed to be strongly felt through the externally static form. Bodily composition in the mass scenes was expressively sculptural and provided a background against which the performing actor spoke and moved. Vakhtangov also demanded from his actors maximum simplicity and sincerity as well as the correct physical actions – for example the way in which the saint fetched and carried a bucket of water was rehearsed exhaustively.[106]

Boris Shchukin's priest was broad-shouldered, stocky and typically Russian in this, otherwise, Gallic environment. He used heavy padding to emphasise his corpulence and widened his cheekbones by means of make-up to give the appearance of bulging eyes. He created the prototype of a Gargantuan, life-loving, healthy glutton who indulged in the joys of living. He also gave the impression of a priest who was fond of women. Despite his stoutness, he attempted to be graceful and in this there was something coquettish and almost feminine. He talked in a high-pitched, thin tenor sing-song voice. Beginning in melodic, mellifluous tones, Shchukin would imperceptibly reinforce the sound, altering it to church recitative until, by the end of a phrase, he would be singing rather than speaking.[107]

Boris Zakhava's doctor had carefully arranged strands of hair plastered across his cranium and wore a walrus moustache. Dressed in a black frock-coat, he carried his hands in front of him, palms upwards, like a surgeon who, after washing his hands, waits for a towel to be brought. As the guests came into the entrance hall from the funeral supper, with their napkins tucked into their collars, still clutching knives and forks and half-filled glasses of wine, Zakhava entered chewing a dainty morsel of trout, his napkin hanging loosely about his neck like a bib. Fixing the saint with a professional stare, he began scrutinising the 'patient', conducting his medical examination in the tempo-rhythm of a Frenchman (which, according to Vakhtangov, was approximately twice as fast as a Russian). Despite this, it took him a whole two minutes to carry out a thorough, professional diagnosis. With an ear trumpet he examined neck, heart and lungs, then felt the patient's head and took his pulse before pronouncing him to be mad and suggesting that nothing would be lost by allowing him to enter the dead woman's room.[108] Vakhtangov devoted enormous attention to the dynamic design of the scene, the tempo-rhythm of each actor, increase and decrease of movement, the culminating point of a scene. He made the participants in group scenes behave as a single unit so that the group expressed the conformity of philistine morality. Each actor was given a concrete, sculptural moulding for his body which best expressed his feelings in movement and in a precise rhythm. The twenty people on stage had to express feelings of anger, displeasure, grief, impatience, curiosity, etc., in definite poses, positive gestures and by means of their entire bodies. It was important, not only to feel this or that emotion, but to express it in a defined form which cohered compositionally with the adjacent person and which blended harmoniously with the group. This was achieved through improvising the most intricate group combinations in which great attention was paid to the hands. It was most important to use the French manner of gesticulation, for example.

'Maeterlinck loved to observe bees', said Vakhtangov. 'What if an alien creature were allowed to enter the bee's work-loving hive? Can you imagine what would happen? The same thing occurs among the guests and relatives of Mlle Hortense when St Anthony arrives.'[109] He is not regarded as a saint but as an expropriator who has come to rob them of their newly-acquired riches. In search of an appropriate form, Vakhtangov turned to Daumier's political caricatures. He also wanted to create a gamut of light and shade in the decor reminiscent of Daumier. This was achieved by using white walls as a background and by dressing the relatives in black and having a line of black coats and hats against the rear wall. In the resurrection scene, the decor had a simple browny-yellow uniformity with all the furnishing arranged symmetrically. The life-like details of the first version were replaced by unnaturally large, grotesque wall-lamps with matching outsize candles, as well as the lifebelt wreaths. In the final scene, the frightened guests returned to the room to find the aunt sitting up in bed scratching spots of candlewax off her nightgown. She then behaved as she had in life by demanding to know who had allowed a beggar to enter her house. The police commissioner was sent for, and recognises the saint as a local madman, who has already spent some time in hospital. He needed to be removed to prevent embarrassment. Joseph and Gustave between them, having rolled up their sleeves before attempting to remove the saint in a well-bred manner befitting the circumstances, discovered to their astonishment that the saint appeared to be immovable, like a rock. They then attempted to shift him as furniture removers might remove a bureau full of books, busily and seriously.[110] Virginie, meanwhile, tied a scarf of her own around the saint's head and gave him a pair of her wooden clogs. As the 'madman' was hustled out with Virginie holding an umbrella over his head, the rear doors opened on to blackness and the sounds of wind and lashing rain. With his removal, the aunt promptly lay down and died again. The guests rapidly assumed appropriate poses of sorrow whilst failing to conceal their delight at this fortunate turn of events. Peals of thunder sounded as the curtain finally fell.[111]

During the course of the next year, Vakhtangov was to stage three major productions, all of which reflected the important changes which had overtaken his view of the world and which were reflected in his artistic methods. The first to be staged was a production of Strindberg's historical play, *Erik XIV*. This production was given at the First Studio of the Art Theatre with Michael Chekhov in the leading role of the divided and tortured monarch. Strindberg's play had already been noted as a possible production by the First Studio before the revolution but the play had been affected by censorship and had only recently been permitted for performance. It belongs to the Vasa Trilogy and concerns Erik, the son of Gustav Vasa, who lives with his devoted lower-class mistress, Karin Mansdotter, but who dreams at the same time of becoming the husband of Elizabeth I of England. His eccentricities drive him into opposition with his

14 Setting by I. Nivinsky for Vakhtangov's production of Strindberg's *Erik XIV*, Moscow Art
Theatre First Studio (1921)

hardheaded, ambitious nobles and his throne is usurped by one of his dukes. The
play itself is not always faithful to historical facts and Vakhtangov's version took
further liberties. Instead of concluding with the capture of Erik and the declaration
of the reign of John III, Vakhtangov ended the play with Erik's suicide. (His actual
death took place some time later during his captivity.) The theme of madness on the
throne was interpreted as a consequence of the mania of spying and suspicion – the
historical legacy of an atmosphere thick with lies, flattery and envy which tended to
surround the throne irrespective of its occupant. The production did not focus on
the struggle against feudalism, or on the situation of the people, but on the
psychological drama of Erik. This led to its being structured along the lines of a
'monodrama' with stylistic elements of expressionism.[112]

   According to Boris Sushkevich, when Vakhtangov first mentioned the
possibility of staging *Erik XIV* in the spring of 1920, he talked of it as if the same
principles which informed the production of *The Cricket on the Hearth* would apply.
It was only in the autumn of that year that his ideas began to change when he began
referring to the ossification of the Stanislavsky 'system' and the need for a new kind
of art which jettisoned the notion that there must be nothing 'of' the theatre 'in' the
theatre. Instead, a special form needed to be discovered for every play. This
particular production was fraught with difficulties, largely because Vakhtangov
found himself working with a strong cast who had already been raised within the
Art Theatre Studios and the Art Theatre itself, with the result that each actor
needed to be convinced of the correctness of Vakhtangov's new methods. Half the

cast simply did not accept them while the other half tended to make mock.[113] From his convalescent home Vakhtangov had written of his great respect for his mentor and spoke of Stanislavsky's intimate understanding of the actor. In his next breath, however, Stanislavsky was being compared unfavourably with Meyerhold as a director: 'Stanislavsky is faceless. All his productions are banal . . . Stanislavsky's theatre is dead and will never be reborn.'[114] In addition, he accused Stanislavsky of rendering the theatre 'boorish'. Vakhtangov's health continued to fail. He was under constant medical supervision, swallowed bicarbonate of soda in increasing quantities during rehearsals so as to ease his stomach pains, lost weight, took cures, and returned from periods of convalesence to a heavy workload which involved him in having to give lessons in the 'system' while staging productions which had less and less connection with it. Stanislavsky saw only caricature in Vakhtangov's production of *Erik XIV*. He did not feel 'the life of the human spirit' emanating from 'the black silhouettes which jerked neurasthenically around the First Studio's small stage.'[115] N. Zograf suggests that Vakhtangov's work on a production of J. Slowacki's play *Balladyna* at the First Studio was influential in his approach to *Erik XIV*. This had, essentially, been Richard Boleslavsky's production but Vakhtangov attended some of the rehearsals and took notes.[116]

There is little doubt that the entire production was dominated by Michael Chekhov's central performance, which embodied a schizophrenic dualism at the heart of the production. Vakhtangov described the character of the disturbed monarch in an article published in *Theatrical Culture*:

> Erik . . . Poor Erik. He is an ardent heart, a keen mathematician, a sensitive artist, an unrestrained dreamer doomed to be king . . . He brings charges against the aristocracy and pardons them . . . creates in order to destroy . . . dashes between the fossilised world of the pale-faced courtiers and the world of lively, simple people . . . By turns angry, gentle, arrogant, simple, protesting, submissive, believing in God and Satan . . . alternately displaying genius and intelligence, smilingly helpless, instantly decisive, hesitating and doubtful. Heaven and Hell, fire and water, master and slave – he is a man of contrast hemmed in between life and death, and he inevitably must destroy himself.[117]

In Vakhtangov's interpretation, Erik was not simply the historical King of Sweden, but a generalised figure of royal power harnessed to a tragic personal life. The contrast between the living and the dead was embodied in the production as part of a contradiction between 'figures of stone' and 'figures of flesh and blood' – weighty robes and restrained dialogue on the one hand set against earthy speech and peasant costume on the other. He used an expressionist style to denote the one and, for the other, he turned to something more like everyday naturalism, while insisting that the audience remain aware that this was a theatrical performance. The production advanced the idea that 'the people' were the only living force but that they had also been degraded to the status of a depersonalised, faceless mob by the feudal elite who were, themselves, mere corpses clothed in rich tissue. Between the worlds of the living and the dead there was meant to be eternal, relentless, struggle. Sometimes the dead triumphed, and at other times the living. It was those who belonged to both worlds, lacking the strength to overcome their dual natures, who perished first – victims of their own inner conflict.

Zavadsky described the production as a 'life-asserting and tragic view of the world' and spoke of its 'grotesque theatricality'. He felt that Mikhail Bakhtin's description of the grotesque applied very appropriately to Vakhtangov in this particular instance, where the former refers to the fact that 'the grotesque is more often peculiar to those works which reflect essentially profound, great turning points in the epochs of world history and applies to those writers who have to do with the uncompleted reconstruction of a world replete with the corruption of the past and the still unformed future'.[118] Vakhtangov placed primary emphasis on the philosophy of history. Erik was seen to perish from the hatred and corpse-like coldness of his stepmother (the widowed queen), from the cruel cunning of Duke John and from the arrogant contempt of the aristocracy, headed by the Strure family, and from the courtiers. According to Hallie Flanagan:

> the essence of Strindberg's *Erik XIV* is conceived to be a broken world with the dead forces of imperialism on one side and the living forces of peasants on the other, while between them wanders the doomed figure of the mad king. This broken world is presented scenically by fragmentary columns, pillars and steps, not of flat grey, but of chaotic design shot through by irregular lightning flashes. The characters which are spiritually dead are also dead as to voice, costume and make-up; Birman, as the widow, skeletonic and sinister, brings on to the stage the chill of the grave. The acting of the dead is peculiarly cold and rigid, the gestures all intaken, indrawing, lifeless, the voices flat and savourless, the eyes unseeing. Even in scenes of violent action the dead forms move with bloated, purplish weight of decay . . .[119]

The general feeling of fracture in the palace scenes was conveyed, not only through the hacked lines and alarmingly uneven combinations of gold, black, white and fleeting tones of grey, but by the sumptuousness of the gothic architectural forms. There was a stairway towards the rear of the stage and one near the front with, between them, huge architectural blocks. Almost in the centre, literally hemmed in by these huge forms, extended a narrow arch. Through it was a view of isolated towers projecting against a background of bright sky and a bell tower. All these forms seemed to clasp themselves together in torment.[120] Everything about the palace setting spoke of the impending tragedy. Somewhere near the roof, at a break in a wall, were depicted little white cupids, serene witnesses of better days. Directly above them, a streak of lightning seemed to split the golden column in two. Disorder and decomposition wafted from the fractured pillars and the odd, broken circular gold columns which seemed about to collapse on the bases which supported them. The black and white chequered flooring was irregular and displaced, seeming to have no beginning and no end.[121]

The world was presented as seen through the consciousness of the central character. Allegorical figures such as the stepmother, the executioner, Duke John appeared schematic and abstract, their reality perceived by Erik as antipodes of his own personality, like immovable statues, deprived of inner development. As King John III mounted the throne at the end, to the accompaniment of a funeral march, he approached the figure of an executioner, clad entirely in blood-red, who stood immediately behind the throne.[122] The production was 'barbed' with arrow motifs, which appeared on the crowns, on the swords, on walls, on the costumes and even on the faces of the characters.

The setting seemed a labyrinth of passages, stairs and platforms which created a deceptive, distorted perspective where courtiers scurried, exchanging glances, meeting briefly, whispering together and going their separate ways. The stairs, squares, steps and cubes all gave rise to an impression of endless obstacles as if forewarning of those pitfalls into which Erik might stumble. In creating this cubist, abstract setting, Ignati Nivinsky was undoubtedly influenced by the work of the Kamerny Theatre and, in particular, by Alexandra Exter. The bronze and rust colours gave a feeling of sunset and spoke of Erik's impending fate. The scenes outside the palace took on an altogether different character, whilst retaining the cubist features and the sloping set. Persson's room, for example, consisted of three acting levels but was full of characteristically true-to-life detail, with its washbowl, barrel, jug, crock and plates on a shelf above a window.[123]

On the reverse side of one of Nivinsky's designs, a sketch by Michael Chekhov suggested a wish to portray the world of the court as one of animals (something which he carried over into his own production of *Hamlet* later). Vakhtangov himself planned a production of *Tarelkin's Death*, which was based on the idea of a company of wolves in a dog-eat-dog world. In this production, the queen mother was rather like a bat trailing through the palace rooms. Her face was deathly pale and lifeless. Her half-closed eyes, with huge, swollen lids and eyebrows of unusual thickness, stood out sharply against her pale face with tightly compressed lips. One eyebrow was raked sharply upwards. Clutching her cross and prayer book, she appeared grotesque – a fact emphasised by details of her costume with its huge, deformed collar. Duke John (Johann Redbeard), Erik's successor, was presented in monumentally motionless fashion, his glances full of cunning threat and evil suspicion. His brother, Duke Charles, was dressed in black velvet and spoke in a soft, gentle voice through thin lips above a black, jutting beard, while his eyes seemed constantly alert. Karin was dressed in typical national costume, emphasising her liveliness and openness – a white cap, green bodice, brightly coloured skirt and shoes with buckle clasps. The members of the crowd were given coarse, heavy clothing in grey and brown tones. Dark, heavy capes rendered their figures massive and terrestrial, clumsy and subjugated.[124]

In the last act, Vakhtangov wanted to depict 'alarm in the palace' as the army of Erik's enemies approached. In the distance, an ominous roar could be heard. Erik and Persson stood centre stage. A courtier appeared stealthily, as if gliding along, failing to halt at the king's command. Revolt was evident in this single moment. At the same time, an alarmed courtier emerged from the opposite wing. Three courtiers then gathered, whispering together on the central square, as a fourth crossed the stage purposefully, as if his mind were resolved on some action. Instantly, the three central figures separated on the diagonal towards the other three corners of the stage. Vakhtangov managed to create the impression of an abandoned palace by these very simple means.[125]

15 Serafima Birman as Katarina Stenbok, Erik's stepmother

Chekhov's Erik was like a man between two worlds, sensing the fateful outcome and desperately trying to find a way out. Thin arms and legs poked from the folds of his silver raiment and he spoke in a voice which veered between gentleness and harshness. His movements consisted of sudden flights and bursts punctuated by momentary relapses before being succeeded by further bursts of strength. This was a portrait of a man who had lost himself, who was subordinate to an alien power with which it was vain to struggle and against which it was pointless to cry out. He was a plaything in the hands of elemental forces which confronted him at every turn in the walks and corridors of the palace and even within himself. This sense of being a plaything of Fate was especially poignant in the scene where Chekhov played with his daughter, Sigurd's, doll at the end of act 3 when he thinks he has been abandoned. Chekhov's performance was marked by a form of inner hysteria which was peculiar to the actor. The bloody arrows on his clothing symbolised the blood which was on his conscience. The mark of insanity lay on his brow in the exaggerated zig-zag shape of his eyebrows. His first entry was like a dart of lightning. 'Never spare yourself!', declared Chekhov 'From your first entrance try and 'shoot' the audience inwardly . . . and don't consider where you're going to get the strength from to develop the role further . . .'[126]

Criticism of Chekhov's performance was fairly hostile. He was accused of possessing the *emploi* of a neurasthenic in a 'poor, noisy story of a provincial king recounted from a standpoint of a clinical case history'. Another critic called the production 'Ward 6 for the spiritually ill' and Erik was seen as a compound of Tsar Fyodr and Paul I. V. Rapoport, in an article headed 'Degeneratio Psychica', wrote:

> but one trick of M.A. Chekhov's . . . opened my eyes. You remember that authoritative vertical raising of the arm with an extended index finger, which Chekhov uses every time a cruel order is given? You recall that, passing on to other thoughts, he still retains this gesture forgetting to order his arm to adopt a correspondingly fresh psychic condition? This is a typical symptom of spiritual illness which in psychiatry is called catatonia. Twice, during the course of the play, Goran forcibly lowers Erik's arm, frozen in an upwards gesture . . . I have a clear picture of the doctor's prescription according to which the role was prepared:
> Degeneratio Psychica – 6%
> Neurasthenia – 3%
> Hebephrenia (infantilism) – 30%
> Abulia (lack of will) – 60%
> Catatonia – 1%
> The third symptom was accompanied by 'wide open eyes and kneeling to your partner' and the fourth consisted of 'the repetition several times of the partner's name while busily extending both arms wide'.[127]

Another critic registered that

> Chekhov's acting was not art in the ordinary sense. The palpitating human body, with its bared nerves and muscles, its open and pulsating heart, the thoughts running through the convolutions of the brain, beat convulsively before the astonished auditorium . . . The next step must be to eliminate art, to remove the actor from the stage as a conscious creator and master, to change him into a maenad with a shattered conscience and to draw the crowd into a circle of ecstasy.[128]

The final image of the production was of an empty stage and a throne in darkness with, barely visible, children's playthings scattered about it in disarray.[129]

A celebration to mark the tenth anniversary of Vakhtangov's work in the Art Theatre was held on 7 April 1921 and, on 13 November, the Third Studio was officially opened, marked by a performance of *The Miracle of St Anthony* and a recital

16 Michael Chekhov as Erik XIV

given by, amongst others, Stanislavsky, Vakhtangov, Michael Chekhov and A.I. Yuzhin of the Maly Theatre. His next important production was staged at the Habimah Studio on 31 January 1922 and was subsequently to travel the world and bring Vakhtangov's work before a much wider audience. This was his production of Ansky's *The Dybbuk*. As Zakhava pointed out, the choice of play was not an indication that Vakhtangov shared the 'Zionist' outlook of the Habimah Studio's leaders, but he was simply attracted by the musicality of Old Hebrew and by the possibility of contact with the ancient sources of Hebrew culture.[130] The authenticity of the production even led some commentators to assume that Vakhtangov was Jewish, like his great compatriots Meyerhold and Tairov.[131]

The opening of the Habimah (Stage) Studio on 8 October 1918 was an important event in post-revolutionary theatrical life. The original Studio had been formed between 1911 and 1914, when a group of young people tried to organise an amateur Jewish theatre to perform productions in ancient Hebrew. The revolution had brought about a shift in the group's hitherto nationalist – Zionist character and, in difficult circumstances, they had turned to Stanislavsky for help. He, in turn, had recommended Vakhtangov to them. When the new Studio opened with a production of four plays directed by Vakhtangov – *The Elder Sister* by Sholem Asch, *The Fire* by J.L. Peretz, *The Sun! The Sun!* by Yitzhak Katznelson and *The Nuisance* by J.D. Berkowitz, this had largely been made possible by the efforts of Nahum Zemach, who obtained premises and a government grant in face of criticism from Bolshevik Jews who felt that the existence of such an institution, which had been associated with strongly Zionist elements and which played in a language considered 'bourgeois' and 'clerical', was counter-revolutionary. Ironically, it was Stalin's rejection of the protest of the Jewish section in the Department of National Minorities which led to the granting of a subsidy to the Habimah. The theatre was established in a house on Lower Kiselovka in the former residence of Count Kornilov who, through another ironic twist, had been an active anti-Semite who fled the country at the outbreak of revolution. What used to be the reception room was fitted out with a small stage and raked benches to accommodate an audience of about 120. A white-and-blue sign with the word 'Habimah', in Hebrew, hung at the entrance. Present in the audience on the opening night were members of the 'Yevsektsia', the Jewish section of the Bolshevik Party who, for months, had fought to outlaw the Studio.[132]

The success of the evening of one-acters was followed by a successful production of David Pinsky's *The Eternal Jew*, which came to be considered one of the Studio's great achievements, but this was far outshone by their production of *The Dybbuk*. The play concerns demonic possession and exorcism and deals with the themes of power and money as well as Jewish law and traditional rites. Leah and Chonon, the two lovers, are offered as the only authentically living elements amidst a grotesquely depicted dead mass. They both perish, being too weak to overcome the repression and spiritless atmosphere of Jewish bourgeois existence.

The material for the play had been gathered by Ansky while travelling with his friend, Yoel Engel, through Russia collecting stories and melodies of the Hasidic Jews. The period of the play was the early nineteenth century, when Polish Jews were manifesting a form of religious faith called Hasidism, which originated in the eighteenth century. The Hasidists were a new religious sect, composed mainly of clergymen, who opposed the orthodox belief of the Rabbis. Hasidism embraced a sort of religious ecstasy to be attained by methods similar to the practice of yoga, which Vakhtangov is recorded as having recommended to an actress of his acquaintance for her health, especially the exercises on breathing and *prahna*.[133] In Miropol, Ansky had come across the story of the great Tzaddik (wonder Rabbi) who had exorcised a *dybbuk* (a cleavage of an evil spirit to the body). This possession by a transmigrated soul of another living body arose from the belief that the soul of a dead person who had suffered injustice could not find peace except by crying out in the body of another being until that wrong was righted. Ansky wrote the play in 1914 and described it as 'a realistic play about mystic people'. According to a recent commentator, he highlighted this mysticism on the advice of Stanislavsky by adding a 'Meshulach', or 'Messenger', like a Greek Chorus, a character who represented the link between the ghetto and the outside world.[134] Stanislavsky sent the play to the Habimah and Nahum Zemach persuaded the poet Chaim Nachman Bialik to translate it into Ancient Hebrew. Stanislavsky then recommended Vakhtangov to the Studio as a director, despite the fact that the latter did not understand a word of the language and had to work from the original Russian script. However, he was extremely interested in the background to the play and loved the sound of Ancient Hebrew. While in hospital he read several books on Jewish religion, folklore and the Hasidic movement.

Music and design played an extremely important part in the production and were the responsibilities of, respectively, Yoel Engel and Nathan Altman. Engel had previously been better known as a music critic but, under Ansky's influence, he became interested in Jewish folk music. Altman was an expressionist painter who collaborated closely with Vakhtangov in working out designs for the setting and costume. Vakhtangov had originally asked Marc Chagall, then still resident in Russia, to supply designs but the latter had refused, fearing the Studio's connection with the Moscow Art Theatre would result in a naturalistic production. According to Huntly Carter, who attended rehearsals,

> the scenery for this effective production . . . was . . . broken up to express rhythm of form and colour. And the chairs and tables were placed at different angles and levels . . . The last scene was very telling, with its long white table, at which the trial took place, sharply inclined towards the audience. An effective use was made of concealed lights, placed behind various stage objects, for instance, behind a pile of books on the table at which four figures were seated, thus carving them into Rembrandtesque masses of light and shade.[135]

Make-up and gesture were extremely stylised, as Zavadsky's memoir suggests:

> It was a genuine philosophical poem for which Vakhtangov found unique means of stage expressiveness . . . I adapted the range of make-up at my disposal, which consisted of primary colours, and painted the actors' faces as if painting on paper or canvas. My work as make-up artist gave me the opportunity to attend Vakhtangov's rehearsals. I recall how he found an amazing touch for the role of the Passer-By (the Messenger), played by Alexander Karev. The character is the embodiment of folk wisdom, a man eternally striving towards something, perpetually in motion, eternally searching for the truth. Vakhtangov searched hard for a means by which to convey perpetual motion on stage. In the action, the Passer-By conducts a dialogue with someone on stage, stops and stands, and immediately something important was lost – the sense of perpetual motion. Then suddenly Vakhtangov discovered what was needed. He showed Karev how to halt in mid-movement. He seemed to stop for a second, but had not ceased his movement forward. It seemed as if he was already moving on – one leg, his outstretched hand holding a staff, and his entire body strained ahead, while his other leg was bent in mid-step . . . This frozen motion made it possible for the actor to carry on a dialogue without halting his movement forward.[136]

The play tells the story of the doomed love of the beautiful Leah (played by Hanna Rovina) and of the youth who loves her, Chonon (played by an actress in

Vakhtangov's production). Despite the fact that Leah and Chonon have been betrothed to each other since birth, Leah's father does not keep his word and decides to marry his daughter to a rich man. This is where the most complicated part of the legend occurs. Chonon dies and his spirit enters into Leah, who becomes 'possessed'. The Tsaddik is summoned to exorcise the devil and forces Chonon's spirit to leave Leah. Leah then crosses out of the magic circle which the Tsaddik has placed around her and dies. The souls of the two lovers, separated on earth, are joined together in eternity. Vakhtangov condensed and rewrote the play, collapsing the third and fourth acts together and expanding the scene of the beggars' dance in act 2. He also superimposed the significance of the Russian revolution on to his interpretation of the play. The result was a version in which the revolution was seen in microcosm. For Vakhtangov, the beggars represented the opposition to the bourgeoisie, whilst Chonon and Leah represented a break with established law – the one in his quest for forbidden knowledge, the other in her rejection of the husband who had been chosen for her on the basis of wealth. As the critic M. Zagorsky discovered to his surprise:

> What would you say, please, if you found the mythos of the Soviet revolution revealed in ancient folk legend created by the genius of a people? Wouldn't your heart be moved to see the spirit of the revolution revealed in its internal, essential meaning and the victory of a great love? On the surface of it, there is nothing in common between the Russian revolution and *The Dybbuk*. So why did this show give me a sudden illumination of the magic and splendour of the thunderous days? Why is it that thanks to *The Dybbuk* I recognised the deep meaning of the mythos now being created? Because this production reveals the meaning of building and destruction, of abandoning historic tradition for the sake of victory of love . . . In a sea of powerful human emotions – of love stronger than death – a centuries-old social system disintegrates.[137]

The play was attractive to Vakhtangov because of its grounding in myth. In fact, the play contains two myths – the first, typical for all eastern legends, concerns the transmigration of the soul from a dead person into the soul of a near one; the second, borrowed from European legend, is the traditional subject of the lovers whose bodies cannot be united in life because of social obstacles (e.g. Romeo and Juliet). The play contains many motifs of ancient Hebrew literature. It begins with the words which run like a thread throughout the text: 'For what cause, for what cause does the soul fall from the heights to the abyss, oh so deep, from the heights to a deep abyss? The soul falls that it may rise again, fall only to rise again.' The struggle of good with evil, as it exists in the play is one of the motifs of Zoroastrism, which manifests itself in the Jewish religion as messianism and a dualism of the spirit. However, the basic poetic source is the Song of Songs, an ancient Hebrew epic which found its way into the Bible as a kind of collection of wedding lyrics.

Vakhtangov and his translator reworked the four-act play into three sections which represented three worlds – Chonon's world of complex spiritual search; the spiritless world of Sender (Leah's father); and the basically human world, although one deprived of search and movement, of the Tsaddik. Through these Dantesque circles, Chonon and Leah were led, causing their living, authentic feeling to collide with the logic and inertia of the mundane and everyday. Every attribute of the stage, every movement, every gesture had a symbolic connotation. The kerchief of the Messenger was a symbol of death, his book a symbol of apostasy, the door to the Ark was the gate to the world of bigotry and traditionalism. Dances and pantomime scenes occupied a central place in the production, while the second act was staged like a Feast of Fools, where the despised and downtrodden took on the role of kings. The production was greeted enthusiastically by Lunacharsky, Stanislavsky and Nemirovich-Danchenko. It was appreciated by one group of critics, not understood by another and ridiculed by the rest.

Act 1 opened in the synagogue and was preceded by a musical motif before the curtain was raised. The set revealed was painted in grey, black and dark brown with touches of yellow. A grey stove stood stage right, next to the table and benches of the Batlanim (men with no occupation who devote their time to religious study). Their costumes were theatrical versions of traditional Hasidic clothing in differing shades of grey, underscored on the lapels with white paint. The Bimah (prayer platform) was stage left and below it was a brown bench. The study lectern of Chonon, a student of the Kabbalah (books of mysticism), was down left and the triangular Aron Kodesh (Holy Ark), painted brown, stood upstage centre. Next to it was the grey-and-brown lectern of Chonon's friend, Hennoch. Stage right, four grey-and-brown flats overlapped at different angles. Steps led to the stove, to the raised Bimah and to the Ark. Pools of light and shadow lent the place a sombre mood. A candle, covered by a standing book on the table, cast the shadows of the hands of the Batlanim on to the wall.

The production began with a silence which lasted several seconds. In the gloom there arose the melody of a violin as if approaching from a distance. A spotlight picked out the hands of Leah and Chonon slowly moving towards each other, twining around a wooden pillar decorated with a carved pattern. They approached and, with a final shudder, knit together. Then the light extinguished and the audience was led, through the sound of the violin, into the interior of the synagogue. All the Hasidic sect were dressed alike in dark-coloured *lapserdaki*, tied with girdles and specked with 'grease spots'. All illustrated, through movement, a single general theme but, if the first held his arms bent at the elbow, with palms open and with head and body inclined to the right, then the second stood erect, with arms closed and pressed to his chest and with the palms held open. A third stood turned to the left, with arms extended forward and with palms open; the arms of a fourth were extended forward with palms raised and with the upper half of the body bent. The backs of open prayer books on separate tables served to mask the candle lighting. The dwarf-like Tsaddik appeared with a skipping gait holding a sacred book, his face painted in a blue-and-white mask. He behaved like a decent, but weak, old man who did not quite believe in his own saintly status.

In the involved discussion of talmudic problems and the mysteries of the kabbalah with which *The Dybbuk* opens there was a complete symphonic score of gestures augmenting the argument:

> Logic is underscored, made visual and more powerful with the help of the thumb. The thumb punctuates the air, and sketches arabesques, as if signatures under what was said. When high points of the arguments are reached, when talk stops after a

thought has been expressed, the open-palmed hand remains hanging against the background of the white wall in peaceful bliss, looking down from its heights on the surroundings.[138]

M.A. Elias, who played Chonon, was especially effective during the sung moments of act 1, where she managed to create the impression that the only realities were love and death. Another powerful moment was Gnessia's emotional chant for the cure of her only child, performed in front of the Ark with its Holy Scrolls. The moment reminded critics of the sound of David's harp:

> This is ritual weeping; it has a specific melody, and yet is most sincere and genuine... It was something that cannot be expressed in words, something monumental, psalm-like. It is with such tears that the Prophet Jeremiah must have lamented in his days; with such tears the prophet of destruction fled to Egypt. It was this weeping that was heard on the banks of the rivers of Babylon.[139]

The second act opened in the courtyard of Sender's house, where Leah's wedding is to take place. The upstage area representing the house was pink and purple with a green window. A green fence stood stage right. Three 'puppet' women relatives dressed in purple, pink and green were perched on a bench upstage and stood erect for most of the act. Grey flats and beams hung askew from the ceiling and a translucent, red wedding canopy hung above the stage left. The Hebrew banner for act 2 'Kol chatan v'kol kallah' (The voice of the bridegroom and the voice of the bride) was taken from the wedding blessings and also presaged the moment when Leah, possessed by Chonon's soul, spoke in his voice. The act began with the beggars' dance, which continued throughout, building to a frenzied pace.

The *chef d'oeuvres* of Vakhtangov's production were the mass scenes and, in particular, the beggars' dance at the wedding staged against this background of dolled-up, daubed, bourgeois bigots, presented like statues or smart mannequins. Vakhtangov increased the number of beggars from seven to twelve and presented them in grotesque form, in the state to which social inequality and class oppression had reduced them. Bent, crooked, some without noses, others suffering from dropsy, some idiotic, some consumptive or blind – they were like creatures from a nightmare – inhabitants of the 'Brown Wooden Bar' in scene 13 of Brecht's *Baal*, or like the beggars who parody the Last Supper in Luis Bunuel's film, *Viridiana*. Their make-up and movement were animal-like: frog, monkey, fox, hyena, ape. One, an idiot, seemed to be rotting alive; another, an old woman in a sheepskin coat, looked like a pig. Some were one-armed, others hunch-backed and their dance was a dynamic protest which combined greed with threat and malice, concluding with a prolonged cry (added by Vakhtangov) and with clenched fists raised in the direction of the rich man, Sender.

> In them were personified neither class demands nor the idea of social inequality. In this general theatrical metaphor was its own kind of philosophical lyricism . . . coloured with feelings of man's shame, observing the self-abasement of the people, constricted by misfortune, centuries of poverty, inequality, violence, lacking the strength to overcome it. The sources of this imagery lay in a famous poem by the play's translator about the pogroms, which Vakhtangov had read in hospital some time before.[140]

17 Scene from Vakhtangov's production of *The Dybbuk* (1922)

The dance was interrupted by the sound of violin and bells as, under a baldachin, the bride, in an old-fashioned, white silk dress, entered on the arm of the groom with the figures in the background looking like a *lubok* frieze.[141] According to one account:

> Vakhtangov stared penetratingly, with fierce curiosity into the swarming clump of human fragments which he had summoned to life. He increased still further the tempo of this whirlpool of grey tatters. And then, suddenly, the white ray of Leah cuts through – a white lily, a light Ariel among this crowd of Calibans. Her dance in the chimerical procession of human monsters is extraordinary in its power. Vakhtangov does not pity the whiteness, he spots it with the paws of a toad, with ape-like points of contact. The scent of the first rose is mixed with that of the plague.[142]

As a climax to the dance, the beggars lifted the exhausted Leah above their heads (the point at which the *dybbuk* invades her body, according to Vakhtangov). On a raised level above her, the fateful Messenger materialised to announce the fact. The bride seemed to float in mid-air (an effect achieved with the help of steps covered in black velvet). One critic felt that this act deviated from the spirit of the original play – the beggars, cripples and monsters belonging rather to the world of E.T.A. Hoffmann, Edgar Allan Poe or Leonid Andreyev . . . 'the accent on the grotesque folklore . . . is not in keeping with the spirit of Judaism'.[143]

The third act was set in the house of the Tsaddik, Rabbi Azriel. The back wall was blue mixed with white, like his facial make-up. A doorway was cut out of the rear curtain and three steps led down to the stage, while another three led up to an elongated table covered with a white cloth. The table stood on a raked platform and extended downwards, from the rear of the stage, towards the audience. At the upstage head was the Tsaddik's blue-and-white chair. Brown benches lined the table. A three-sided Ark in dark brown and yellow with blue-and-white curtains stood stage left and three white wooden flats stood stage right. Painted on the backdrop was the phrase, written in Hebrew script 'Zeh haha'ar l'Adonai' (this is the Gate of God). As preparations were made for the exorcism, Leah sang the Song of Songs. The Hasidim entered and removed the Torah scrolls from the Ark. Black candles were lit and the Ark was covered with a black curtain while the Hasidim covered themselves with black-and-white shawls. As a ram's horn was blown, Leah struggled and, finally, collapsed on the bench, weeping in her own voice. Following the moment of exorcism, Leah's recitative flowed in an extended song, containing the synchronised sources of all folk melody, the song of a free individual going into the expanses of endless space. The Hasidim joyfully removed their shawls and replaced the candles and scrolls. The Tsaddik then drew a magic circle round Leah to protect her. A crescendo of music accompanied Leah's violent efforts to break out of the circle. Crossing its symbolic limits, Leah slowly began to fall and as her body fell, her black-sleeved arms extended along the long white table and grew still. From the street there suddenly burst a bravura march announcing the arrival of the bridegroom. At that point the Messenger appeared, a poor simple Jew, wandering from synagogue to synagogue, but transformed by Vakhtangov into a personification of the Higher Justice, a Messenger of Asmodeus. 'Too late', he pronounced, and covered Leah with a black cloth while chanting the blessing for the dead. The rest of the candles suddenly toppled, simultaneously, from the chapel shelf and total darkness fell. The wedding march ceased and, once again, the opening melody was heard: 'For what cause . . .'

An English version of the production was given at the Neighbourhood Playhouse, New York, in 1925, directed in Vakhtangov's style by David Vardi and Henry G. Alsberg a year before the actual Habimah group performed it in the original at the Mansfield Theatre. It was again seen in New York during a later visit by the Habimah in 1948. George Gershwin contemplated turning it into an opera in 1928. Stark Young saw the production at the Mansfield Theatre in 1926:

> . . . the dim, clay-coloured walls, the naked, drab, architectural shapes, and above all the extraordinary use of light are completely one with the whole idea. The very stylised make-ups, carried to the point of violent mask patterns at times – noses painted white on one side, black on the other, triangles in blue or green or black on the foreheads and so on – are of a piece, as a whole, with this effect of a dream dreamed by a race for a thousand years and fiercely and tenderly kept. The acting is throughout admirable, every role and every ensemble and dance movement is served with devotion . . . This Habimah production is the only instance of extreme stylisation that I have encountered in which the whole of it seemed inevitable. Here in it we get both the extreme stylisation that ritual can go to and at the same time the truth that worshippers bring to ritual.[144]

It was elsewhere described as a 'strange, burning shaman production'[145] and, in the words of another 'the work of the Habimah was permeated with religious lyricism . . . which dissolves everything that falls into it and turns even slag into gold . . . The words give forth light and joy as upon the day when they were issued on Mount Sinai.' But let the last word on this remarkable production be with Nikolai Evreinov:

> I am happy to testify under oath that such an achievement is possible in the present-day theatre ... To take this folklore, all this humour of Jewish life, and make of it an integrally, deeply moving, organic part of a mystery play, calls not for ability, but – and I say this without hesitation – genius.[146]

During the 1921/22 season, Vakhtangov rehearsed the role of Master Pierre in Nadezhda Bromley's play *The Archangel Michael* at the First Studio, as well as rehearsing his last production, Gozzi's *Princess Turandot* at the Third studio. In addition to throwing himself heart and soul into the role of Pierre, he was preparing to double as Erik in the Strindberg play. He was also planning a production of *Hamlet* to be staged at both the First and Third Studios. His work on the leading role in Bromley's 'tragi-farce', got as far as the public dress rehearsal in May 1922. It was at this point that Stanislavsky asked him to help revise his work on the role of Salieri in the production of Pushkin's *Mozart and Salieri*, which he had staged in 1915 and which had been a source of traumatic failure for him. A letter dated January 1922 reads: '2 – 4.30 *Archangel Michael*, 5 – 7.30 or 8.00 work with K.S., 8.00 either the Third Studio or the Habimah, or acting. After the show, rehearsal. Bed every day 6 to 7 a.m.. Sleep till 1.00 p.m.'[147] Following the premiere of *The Dybbuk*, Vakhtangov departed for the sanatorium the following day, where he spent ten days before returning to the theatre feeling more ill than before. Despite this, he set to work on preparing *Turandot*. The Third Studio, worried about his condition, decided to summon a council of doctors, who established that Vakhtangov was suffering from cancer. The diagnosis was kept strictly secret, although it was evident that Vakhtangov knew of the seriousness of his condition. Rehearsal continued with Vakhtangov in constant pain, having to medicate himself with soda, or take breaks during which he retired to his own room and lay doubled up on a couch in a way he had discovered alleviated pain after a while. The final rehearsal took place on the night of 23–24 February and, after this, Vakhtangov took permanently to his bed. The dress rehearsal took place on 27 February and was attended by Stanislavsky and members of the Art Theatre. A speech from Vakhtangov was read out at the start by Zavadsky, explaining what the production set out to achieve.

Nowhere was Vakhtangov's concept of the 'festive spirit' of theatre, the idea that a theatrical performance is a celebration conducted in a holiday mood, more apparent than in his legendary production of Gozzi's *Princess Turandot* which[148] not only lingers in the folk memory of Soviet theatre, but can still be seen to this day at the Vakhtangov Theatre in a revived version staged on 21 April 1963, by Reuben Simonov, who acted the part of Truffaldino in the original. The production was a celebration of the creative, improvisatory art of the actor, a manifestation of tremendous optimism in a revolutionary world where starvation, hunger, cold and the threat of war were the norm. It answered a need for a feeling of social uplift and corresponded to the imaginative perspectives of a land on the brink of something

18 Setting by I. Nivinsky for Vakhtangov's production of Carlo Gozzi's *Princess Turandot*, Moscow Art Theatre Third Studio (1922)

exciting, new and, at the same time, uncertain and mysterious. It was the kind of production which had even someone like Vladimir Mayakovsky applauding wildly. Everything about it was thrilling and nowhere was this more apparent than during rehearsals, conducted with inspirational vigour, unerring inventiveness and physical energy by a dying man. The production became a poignant synthesis in itself of the eternal conflicts which are registered in Vakhtangov's work between the living and the dead. Vakhtangov had an extraordinary ability to inspire his actors with his own creative mood and was not afraid to discard what had been painstakingly discovered in favour of something else which he felt might express the essence of a play more vividly.

The search for a suitable play had begun with Vakhtangov turning his attention to the version of the legend written by Schiller, a scene from which had been staged by a young student at the Third Studio in 1920. Vakhtangov found the work interesting and included it in the theatre's repertoire, entrusting Zavadsky and Ksenia Kotlubai with the preparatory work. As part of the rehearsals, the cast recalled plays and ballets with fairy-tale backgrounds and employed the traditional masks of *commedia dell'arte* to represent chancellor, minister, chief eunuch and chief of police. When Vakhtangov took over rehearsals on his return from the sanatorium, he expressed dissatisfaction with aspects of the approach and began to look around for something else. In doing so, he hit upon the Gozzi version of the legend. It seemed to him to correspond to an audience's dream of the future – something which answered to the optimistic love of life which Russians shared with the Italians but which was not reflected in the Russian climate. The idea became one of acting a contemporary attitude towards the fable of the cruel Princess Turandot, an irony addressed at its 'tragic' content.

First notions concerning the production imagined the theatre decorated in a Chinese style, so that the spectator would be surrounded with atmosphere as soon as he entered the foyer. It was also intended that the action be dispersed in separate areas of the auditorium so that, unexpectedly, the spectator would suddenly find himself assailed by the fantastic world of Old China (this was when the plan had been to stage Schiller's version). Vakhtangov's own plans were, initially, reminiscent of pre-revolutionary productions of the play staged by Fyodor Komissarzhevsky at the Nezlobin Theatre in 1912 and Max Reinhardt's production at the Deutsches Theater in 1911. Komissarzhevsky speaks of having employed the devices of *commedia dell'arte*, as the characters 'improvised their parts, talked to the audience, sang and danced, produced acrobatic tricks, and played, to use the latest term of Meyerhold, in the "biomechanical" manner'.[149]

Mention of Meyerhold suggests what was probably the most important influence on Vakhtangov's production. He had certainly read Meyerhold's publication called *The Love of Three Oranges* (named after Gozzi's work) which had been published in Petrograd before the revolution, in which Meyerhold, Solovyov, Bondi[150] and others expounded on their experimental work in acting classes based on the comedy of masks. But an even more direct influence is traceable to Meyerhold's production of V.N. Solovyov's *Harlequin the Marriage Broker*, which Meyerhold had staged in Petersburg and Terioki in 1911 and 1912. According to N. Volkov, when a performance was staged in the house of F. Sologub, all the participants wore dinner jackets, dresscoats and ball gowns, to which certain items had been added, such as a mask, bells, Harlequin's baton, etc., almost exactly as Vakhtangov employed in this later instance. Simonov suggests that another important influence was Stanislavsky, with whom Vakhtangov had some important conversations around this time on the nature of 'the grotesque' in theatrical art.

The great appeal of the Gozzi play for Vakhtangov lay in the fact that he saw it as belonging to a folk tradition, the 'theatre of improvisation', which had been born on the streets of Italy. He wondered whether it would be possible to recreate the fierce passion which inspired those actors of bygone days in the circumstances of the present. Brilliant colours would need to predominate, great zest, the joy of life and, most important of all, the improvisational state. In order to achieve this, Vakhtangov wanted his actors to behave like members of an imaginary Italian troupe and to find an *emploi* which suited each of them. For example, working with the actress Orochko, who played Adelma, Vakhtangov asked her to think of herself as having a dual role in life and in art – to play the tragic actress of a particular Italian company and the tragic character in the play, someone who was in love with the hero, not only as the character, but in life (i.e. she is actually in love with the leading man). She had to live the tragedy of unrequited love. Vakhtangov felt that this would appeal to the minds of naive and unsophisticated theatregoers who tended to identify the role with the portrayer, thinking the actor and the character to be one and the same person. He spoke of the travelling companies of the *commedia* and of their ability to capture the hearts of their audiences.

He wanted to create an atmosphere of sunshine and orange trees in a freezing cold Moscow. How could this be done? What did the spectator want?

> 'They want their future', said Vakhtangov 'and are dreaming of what playwrights have not yet written. But they still have "fairy tales" which depict what people might become when they have overcome the forces of evil. So, let there be blue sky over the whole stage, over the entire auditorium. And let China be as the Italian playwrights imagined it. Scenery should be light and airy, bright coloured and even transparent, like a balloon.'

Vakhtangov even imagined houses, palaces and temples made of bright coloured rubber which could be filled with air, like balloons. When a scene ended, the actors could kick the temple or palace into the wings, while the next scene floated into place.[151] An entire scene might be staged in which actors played football with the scenery. The actors who were not involved in the production but who attended rehearsals were asked to imagine that they were a typical Italian audience and to respond accordingly, cheering and applauding if those on stage performed well, whistling and pelting them with orange peel if they did not. Vakhtangov urged his actors to imagine themselves travelling from town to town in covered carts and, when performing, to be so in control of their temperament, that they could pass from passion to contemplation in an instant:

> Imagine an actor coming out on stage. He is the hero. His eyes blaze with passion. He delivers a monologue. Sincere suffering is felt in every word. Tears run down his cheeks. He does not hide them from the audience. He smiles at them through his tears and catches an orange tossed to him from the audience. He blows a kiss to a beautiful girl sitting in the fifth row. Finally, he sits on the edge of the stage, his legs dangling into the arena, and calmly eats the orange while the next scene is acted out in front of him. When his cue comes, he again enters the action and grips the audience with his passion, his sincerity, his superb technique. Then he goes back-stage, where his real wife – the troupe's leading actress – makes a scene over the kiss he blew to the girl in the audience.[152]

During the final scenes, Vakhtangov suggested that Orochko, in addition to imagining herself the wife of the director of the troupe and fancying herself mistress of the male lead, should also imagine she wore slippers too large for her causing her to stumble and slither on stage. As well as this, she was to be a tragic actress with a capital 'T', who always carried a dagger in her hand. The actress playing Zelima was asked to imagine herself a lazy member of the troupe who did not want to act, a fact which she was not to attempt to conceal from the public (constantly showing signs of wanting to lie down). All these devices were employed to achieve the correct, ironic approach and to create an improvisatory impression. There needed to be a constant sense of risk, especially the risk of failure, the preparedness to tell ten jokes badly in order to win an audience with the eleventh. The actors also needed to lose a 'sense of shame', to feel confidence in themselves and attain complete inner calm, allied with a sense of excitement and the boldness which is born of this.

This improvisatory spirit had then to be carried over into costumes and properties. Beards were made of towels and clothes brushes, hats out of wicker baskets, soup spoons, serviettes and odd bits of material. Altoum wore a hat which consisted of an electric lamp shade; a football became an orb, and a tennis racquet a sceptre. An improvised orchestra consisting of mandolins, balalaikas, castanets, flutes, drums and cymbals was supplemented by a comb and paper band which played waltzes and polkas. A fringed towel served as a long beard, black wool became a maiden's raven tresses, bits of rag and odd scarves were filched from the costume department – a cloak for a prince thrown over ordinary evening dress, fantastic masks of painted paper. The audience was to be let into the secret, and observe the conversion of rags and oddments into 'glittering satin' and 'rich velvet', by witnessing the actors don them before their eyes as if it were a game of charades. The audience was to be encouraged to 'dream' the scenery into existence, so that a twisted pole and a curving arch could serve as a palace, a semi-circle of muslin rising behind a couch strewn with brilliant cushions could be accepted as a princess's boudoir. Nearly all the properties were made of paper or odds and ends of cardboard.

Vakhtangov's original idea was to have a large window at the rear of the set through which could be seen a reproduction of the street outside, covered in snow. The actual scenic design which Ignati Nivinsky produced was reminiscent of a tumbledown ancestral home with broken stairways, cracked columns and plaster falling from the ceilings, to which were to be added aesthetically abstract elements in the manner of the Kamerny Theatre. The stage servants were to hang the set with brightly-coloured curtains with locations indicated by notices – PEKING –, or to set the stage with simple objects, such as a bright yellow sun or a plain white chair. The curtains were to be suspended from the grid on brand new ropes with visible counterweights in the shape of small vari-coloured sandbags. The visual aspect of the setting was to be characterised by selective detail taken from Chinese painting – for example, a line of roofs and pagodas that looked like slippers with the toes turned up. Landscapes were cut out of silk and placed on the curtains in the form of 'appliqué' hangings. Proscenium servants were to change and hang these, as well as raise and lower the sun and moon when required.

Central to the success of the production was the role of the *commedia* 'masks'. Initially, there were problems in improvisational inventiveness but gradually, the 'masks' began to assume certain characteristics – Tartaglia's traditional stutter, a Pantalone who spoke in the accents of a Russian provincial, a Brighella, who was a tremulous and simple-minded glutton. Truffaldino was a joker and prankster. The 'masks' gained considerable help from the Italian conductor of the orchestra of the Moscow Circus, who helped them to master the humour and temperament of Italian actors. They were to provide the 'bridge' between the actors, who play serious roles, and the audience. Like the masks of Italian comedy, they needed to possess the qualities of a fairly good acrobat, be something of a tightrope walker and able to juggle. They had to vie with each other in capturing the audience's attention by talking, dancing, singing and performing acrobatic stunts. They needed to be able to perform improvised *lazzi* (there was one where a 'dentist' extracted teeth through the ears, nose and other orifices of the body, in addition to the mouth, concluding with the extraction of hair because it, too, possesses 'roots').

19 Sketch by Mironov of Yuri Zavadsky as Kalaf

Another *lazzi* consisted of Tartaglia eating the buttons on his clothing as if each were a delicacy. Everything had to be light and beautiful as well as profound in content. At one point, Truffaldino clapped his hands and ordered the proscenium servants to change the 'street' into a 'meeting hall'. Brighella rushed on screaming 'Bring down the curtain!' whilst frantically trying to screen the 'theatrical' proceedings from the public. While the curtain was closed, they performed a series of *lazzi*. Brighella entered the auditorium and sat among the spectators as the others anxiously looked for him. They insulted late-comers and exchanged puns and 'sage saws'. They assessed Kalaf's preparedness for the riddle by asking some of their own:

What has two sticker-outers, four hanger-downers, a swisher and, generally speaking, is a domestic animal?

'A cow', answered Pantalone and then manifested extreme embarrassment at having given the game away. Tartaglia then crept forward, imitating a cat:

> *Tartaglia*: What has four legs. A tail. A nice fluffy tail, catches mice and miaows?
> *Pantalone*: I know that. (*Profound pause*) A cat!
> *Tartaglia*: No, that's what I thought at first. In fact, it's a kitten.[153]

Alongside the 'masks', the *zanni* (or stage servants) also fulfilled an important role in the production. They were cast early on in rehearsal but only began to perform when the final structure of the play had been decided on. The trick was that the *zanni* were meant to be 'invisible' whenever they did anything on stage. They had to learn to perform as if they were 'absent' without 'acting' or seeming to pay any attention to what was happening around them. When handing Kalaf a portrait of Turandot, or giving Adelma a dagger with which to kill herself, these actions needed to be performed without any emotion. Whether taking off Kalaf's shoes, changing the scenery, bearing the severed heads of the hapless suitors or wiping away Barach's tears when he was being tortured, everything had to be done in the same unemotional style. Their actions were co-ordinated with specially written music. At the same time, whilst not revealing any emotion, Vakhtangov wanted the sense of a group of people in love with the theatre and their work. Like Adelma, they also needed to be secretly in love with members of the cast so that it became the height of bliss to hand the hero or heroine a looking glass or to straighten a fold in a cape. But these actions had to be performed without a shred of sentiment, without the trace of a smile. Their love for the theatre and for the actors was a matter both serious and passionate.

The *zanni* were given their own pantomime sequence following act 2, when they acted out in mime the course of events to come. However, this pantomime was staged in such a manner as to deliberately mislead the audience into anticipating a tragic outcome involving the deaths of Kalaf, Adelma and Zelima together with the triumph of the 'wicked' Turandot. The audience was thus led 'up the garden path' of tragedy only to be confronted by the 'peripeteia' of a comic denouement as the play concluded with the happy marriage of Kalaf and Turandot.

The play began with a 'parade' of the cast before the curtain preceded by the four 'masks' in traditional Italian costume, who bowed to the audience and announced the start of the play. Tartaglia, as High Chancellor, introduced Pantalone (the Emperor of China's minister) to the audience, Truffaldino (Chief Eunuch) and Brighella (Captain of the Guard). The scene developed into a parade of all the participants. This was first conceived as a musical march with the actors approaching the stage from the auditorium, where they had been sitting alongside members of the public. However, this was rejected in favour of having the actors appear in an extended line before the curtain, the purpose being to establish the festive character of the performance and to reveal the secrets of the performers' art as they effected transformations before the eyes of the audience. Tartaglia shouted

'Parade!' and, with Pantalone, parted the curtain in an inverted V-shape through which the actors appeared – ladies to the left, gentlemen to the right. All advanced to the front of the apron. Then, slowly, to the strains of the Turandot waltz (a variation on a melody used in *The Deluge*), the curtain parted to reveal the stage in carefully arranged disorder, littered with vividly coloured pieces of material. On a circus command from Truffaldino 'Alee-oop!', the actors dispersed over the stage and, to a second command, lifted the coloured strips of material, gracefully tossing them in the air to the rhythm of the music before adding the bits and pieces to their costume. They then lined up again and sang a song. Vakhtangov wanted everyone to finish dressing at the same time and for the actors to perform some rhythmic movement with the piece of cloth, hat or sword. He wanted a firework display of multi-coloured cloths fluttering in the air followed by the resumption of the formal line-up and the song:

The simple song/We sing today/Shall waft you off/To Old Cathay.

Then everyone left the stage and the 'masks' began to indulge in buffoonery. This was followed by a short pause and then the sounds of a polka. On came the *zanni*, young girls in blue theatrical overalls with numbers on the backs like members of a football team. They changed the set to music, transforming the empty, sloping platform into a street in Peking. Three wide drop-curtains were hung on poles and the ropes with the coloured counterweights were let down. On the curtains was an appliqué representation of a Chinese city. A sign in large letters, informed the audience that we were in 'PEKING'.

Barach, Kalaf's tutor then entered, humming a variation on a tune from Rimsky-Korsakov's *Sadko*, which was suddenly interrupted by a chord of alarm, a warning of something mysterious. Then Prince Kalaf made his entry. The text of this first expository scene was cut to assist the dynamic of the action, whilst the lights in the auditorium remained fully on. As well as recounting tales of woe and suffering, both Barach and Kalaf were permitted elements of *buffo* as they played the fool or behaved in an ironic fashion. Having appeared on stage, Barach bowed politely to the audience, then proceeded to play an imitation stringed instrument which, to his consternation, emitted the sound of a kettledrum. He reacted in scared fashion, rolling his eyes whilst making great play of listening concentratedly. With his entry, Kalaf bowed several times to the audience then, at moments of high tension (when debating whether to run away with the woman he loves or die) proceeded to remove his shoe and wave it about to emphasise his gestures. Whilst recounting their joint adventures and depicting their woes, Barach rolled on the ground weeping, accompanied by the genuine tears of Kalaf who was so overcome at one point that a *zanni* brought on a bentwood chair for him to sit on. Tartaglia rushed on clutching a shaving bowl in which he collected Barach's tears and then ran forward to the front of the stage to demonstrate their genuineness. At the mention of Turandot's name there was a jingling of silver bells made with spoons struck against glasses. Guards entered with cushions on the tops of spears, representing the heads of the suitors who had been executed for failing to answer the riddles. A circus drum-roll. Kalaf and Barach fell to the ground in terror. Then

Ismaele entered, mourning the loss of his friend who had also been unable to answer the princess's riddles. His leitmotif was a constant self-castigation for failing to prevent each of his charge's unconsidered and potentially tragic moves. This was built on two elements – plaintive melodic intonations and traditional gestures of woe and despair (hands and arms akimbo, hands clasped to the sides of his head, or pathetically clasped on top of it). Having gazed at Turandot's portrait – a crude sketch done on a piece of cardboard – Ismaele threw it to the ground and trampled on it before exiting to music which sounded like a continuation of his lament. Kalaf promptly snatched up the portrait, which he proceeded to contemplate and admire as if it were an exquisite work of art.

The stage servants then changed the set to the Palace of the Emperor Altoum. The 'masks' meanwhile, indulged in chit-chat on topics of the day, made satirical remarks about political figures or commented on the shortcomings of life in the Soviet Union. They then announced the 'divan' scene – the council of the sages. The procession of the sages began with a march resembling Chinese national music performed on flutes and percussion. The sages strutted ceremoniously, expressing their concern for the misfortunes of their country with stylised sighs and much spreading of the hands whilst greeting each other. Vakhtangov suggested that each sage look at his partner and think a naive thought while feeling sorry for the fact that his opposite number did not appreciate the wise thing he was thinking about. He suggested that the sages read the second part of *Gulliver's Travels* in search of thoughts typical of wise men. He referred to the philosophers of Laputa and himself made some sage suggestions as to the kind of profound problem which might be exercising their minds, such as: 'How ought one to feed a fly so as to make it as big as an elephant?' 'How useful would it be to have six ears and where might the other four best be located?' The sages needed to be able to gibber wisely, all at the same time, each on his own particular theme, while swaying slightly to the music and with fingers pressed to foreheads. Their first entry was performed with their heads nodding in time to the music as they drifted across the stage with expressions of concentrated thoughtfulness, pencils pressed against their foreheads and writing slates hanging at their sides. Their capes were brightly ornamented and covered with numbers, stars, chemical formulae and geometrical shapes. Their caps were shaped like coxcombs and they wore long ribbon-moustaches flowing from nose to waist. Finally, they sat in a row with their backs to the audience.

Following them, nodding his head to the music like a dummy, appeared the emperor walking fast, out of breath and hobbling like an old man. He scrambled up the steps and settled on his throne with difficulty. He was apt to shed tears at the slightest provocation and held a handkerchief in his hand with which he wiped his eyes as he spoke, each phrase being punctuated by music and the ritual bows of the sages and ministers. A comic scene then ensued between Tartaglia and Pantalone, before Kalaf was introduced and Altoum summoned Turandot. She entered, preceded by her slave girls, who performed a floating dance based on a parody of Isadora Duncan. They were followed by Adelma and Zelima. Finally, Turandot herself appeared, her face covered with a light veil. The text of the riddle was spoken by Turandot in rhythmically measured fashion and then repeated in the same intonations by everyone present. There was a clash of cymbals, followed by deep silence. When Kalaf came up with the first answer, the sages opened a sealed envelope to check its accuracy. They then repeated the answer happily three times and showed the audience the piece of cardboard on which the word was written. Following Kalaf's successful answer to all three riddles, Turandot fainted, Kalaf himself having previously fainted at the sight of her beauty when she half unveiled. Truffaldino then announced the interval.

The second act began with Adelma's declaration of her love for Kalaf. Tartaglia and Pantalone then attempted, unsubtly, to discover Kalaf's name by asking for his autograph. Kalaf's father, Timur, then entered – an old man in rags with a towel beard. Barach explained to the confused old man why his son's name needed to remain secret by throwing himself at him like a tiger, clapping a hand across his mouth and threatening him with a dagger. There followed the arrest of Barach and his wife Schirina, followed by a scene in which Timur and Barach were tortured in an attempt to discover Kalaf's name. Below Turandot's balcony there was a dip in the stage, supposedly leading to a dungeon. This 'well' was filled by four executioners. The scene was lit with lamplight which shone on a heap of gold with which the torturers sought to bribe Timur and Barach. Timur's torture consisted of his being beheaded several times in quick succession. The executioners wore sacks with holes cut in them for arms and legs. Two wore fencing masks, one of them with a rag of dark ribbon around the mask to suggest that he had an eye missing, while the faces of the others were covered with black paper. All had bare arms and each had a distinguishing mark – one had been stung on the nose by a bee, one had toothache and one wore boxing gloves. Turandot's order from the balcony was followed by fifteen-second bouts of torture, then casual conversation between the women, then another fifteen seconds of torture. This was accompanied by a cacophony of cries, noises and savage yells of pain, as Barach performed a *dance macabre* when his turn came. After each beheading, Timur waited calmly for the next one. The yelling was accompanied by sound effects – the striking of pots and pans, then, when everything stopped, Timur took a piece of bread out of his pocket and chewed it thoughtfully. Barach was tortured in every possible way, including being suspended from the balcony by a rope which ran under his armpits, supporting him during moments of torture and permitting him to run on the spot after each decapitation, before relaxing. The worst moments were those during which the executioners rested from their frightful labours in a mood of casual indifference.

The *zanni* then performed their witty pantomime before the curtain, based on a condensed version of the play. They re-enacted the 'parade', the meeting between Barach and Kalaf, the riddle scene, then a pantomimic prophecy of how the play would end. The servant girl impersonating Turandot delivered a wrathful speech, with a veil over her face, so that her extreme emotional state was indicated by the inhalation of the veil with every breath taken, performed in time to music. Then each of the *zanni* stabbed herself.

The night scene which followed was considered an atmospheric masterpiece. The setting consisted of a couch, centre stage in front of a low white circle with greenish-silver curtains. The only other decoration was a moon which hung from a pulley. Spotlighting was in varying intensities of blue. On the white couch lay Kalaf with Brighella standing guard on the balcony at the rear, looking like a chimney sweep with a lantern in one hand and a stepladder in the other. At the beginning of the scene soft chimes were heard and the yawning Brighella crossed the stage carrying a Chinese lantern. Having told Kalaf not to be frightened of ghosts, instantly pandemonium broke loose. On orchestral cue the *zanni* ran on carrying household gadgets, banging pots, ringing bells, beating drums, clashing cymbals and swinging rattles whilst rushing about the stage for a whole minute, appearing and disappearing, frightening themselves as much as others. The orchestra thundered discordant music while the *zanni* rushed about uttering exclamations in gibberish, waving their fantastic weapons. Another wild chord and they disappeared. Turandot's women then glided on and stood, secluded, in the stage corners. Altoum covered himself with a piece of cloth like a draped Buddha. Adelma, dressed in black, ran in seeming to glide over the surface of the floor. Schirina, dressed as a soldier, materialised at the bedside of the sleeping prince. The stage seemed to be full of ghosts. 'You didn't see anything did you?' asked Brighella. 'No, no, not a thing', answered Kalaf. Then another apparition materialised. This time it was Zelima, who manifested terror at being in the same room as a man and pattered her lines like a recitative compounded of lyricism and embarrassment. Then came the meeting between Adelma and Kalaf, both dramatic and tragic, with Adelma shedding real, bitter tears as she cried for revenge for the death of her brother and the suicide of her sisters. The scene covered a whole gamut of emotions expressed through silence, moonlight and deep darkness, the alternation of hushed conversation with excited shouts, all of which the audience experienced as if it were a musical composition in which thought, music and feeling merged into one.

The final act, which lasted about twenty minutes, took place in the Hall of Meetings. Turandot, whose love for Kalaf has been conveyed to him in the night scene by Zelima, guesses the prince's name. He is about to kill himself (with a paper-knife) when Turandot confesses her love for him. At this point Adelma gave vent to a magnificent tragic monologue. Vakhtangov managed to get a superb performance from Orochko by deliberately provoking her, during a memorable rehearsal, to tears of bitter rage. This intensely dramatic moment was then undercut by having Adelma threaten to commit suicide with the very same paper-knife. There followed the final wedding scene. According to Vakhtangov, the ending needed to be reminiscent of a fairy tale. A Chinese dragon motif would be lowered from the flies, the emperor placed before it and crowned with golden wreaths. After this, the troupe was to line up, bid farewell to the audience and leave the stage to music. The actual *mise-en-scène* began with Adelma going off into voluntary exile. As she disappeared, Altoum sighed heavily and wiped his eyes with Timur's towel-beard. Someone announced – 'To the temple!'. Spreading out in a fan-shape, the

20 Scene from act 1 of *Princess Turandot*

wise men, the 'masks' and the slave girls marched towards a door in the centre rear. As they reached it, a curtain embroidered with a huge golden dragon suddenly descended from above. The high priest raised his arms to bless the bride and groom. Kalaf and Turandot knelt and the others crowded round them. The courtiers, wise men and slave girls went down on their knees, holding their hands together on top of their heads in an eccentric gesture of prayer for the happiness of Kalaf and Turandot. A mournful blessing was hummed to the tune of a 'galop', played softly. Then the tempo grew faster and faster until everyone broke out into 'la-la-ing'. The result was an extremely naive scene filled with pathos in which the courtiers hummed their good wishes with the utmost sincerity and the singing sounded warm, moving and heartfelt – a recognition of the trials Kalaf had gone through and of how much he had suffered. Turandot then addressed the male spectators in the audience, telling them how much she loved them and how she really regretted the crimes she had committed in sending so many suitors to their deaths. These final words were spoken with total sincerity. The actors then stood in a line before the curtain as they had for the opening 'parade', bowed to the audience and filed off. The 'masks' then announced that 'our presentation of Carlo Gozzi's fairy tale, *Princess Turandot* is over'.

On the evening of that first dress rehearsal, Stanislavsky had been wildly excited. Barely able to contain himself, he left the theatre at the interval and rushed round to Vakhtangov's apartment to convey his personal congratulations on his pupil's outstanding achievement. Following a brief and moving conversation at the sick man's bedside, Stanislavsky returned to the theatre and joined in the wild applause at the end.

Vakhtangov's final months were spent confined to his bed. Nevertheless, he found time to write a letter in pencil to Nemirovich-Danchenko (he could not use ink as he could only write lying down) thanking him for an inscribed photograph the latter had sent him. In April, he talked at some length on the 10th and 11th of the month with Boris Zakhava and Ksenia Kotlubai about some of his theatrical ideas and influences. In response to Zakhava's opening remark on the second day about 'genuine theatricality', Vakhtangov talked of naturalism, realism and 'imaginative realism', concluding as follows:

> The theatre should not contain naturalism or realism, but it should have imaginative realism. The appropriate theatrical means give the author a true life on stage. Means can be learned, but form must be created, it must be a product of the imagination. That is why I call this imaginative realism. Imaginative realism exists and should be in every form of art now.[154]

This was his last public statement. He died at 9.55 on the evening of 29 May 1922, and was buried in the Novodevichy cemetery on 31 May.

3

Nikolai Okhlopkov, 1900–67

When the first substantial volume of memoirs dedicated to Meyerhold was published in the Soviet Union in 1967,[1] the name of one obvious contributor was missing, that of Nikolai Pavlovich Okhlopkov, who had died, following a long illness, in January of that year. Meyerhold had many pupils who went on to make a name for themselves as actors, theatre directors and film directors. Among them are Sergei Eisenstein, Igor Ilinsky, Mikhail Tsaryov, Erast Garin, Sergei Martinson, Valentin Pluchek, Boris Ravenskikh and many others.[2] But there is little doubt that the greatest claim to be considered the true heir of Meyerhold belongs to Nikolai Okhlopkov. Like his teacher, he was a genuine 'Renaissance man' of the performing arts – an outstanding actor and director who worked successfully in both theatre and film. In no one else did Meyerhold's own universal genius show itself more distinctly than in Okhlopkov.

Having said that, however, it is important to stress Okhlopkov's own uniqueness as an artist. He was no pale imitation of Meyerhold, but someone who made his own individually unique contribution to the history of Soviet theatre. His uniqueness stems from a deeply rooted Russianness – a quality which speaks through Okhlopkov's productions in ways which cannot be found in the work of other great directors. When Eisenstein was looking to cast the role of Vasili Buslay, the thatch-haired peasant *bogatyr*,[3] who personifies the epic scale of the Russian spirit, its broad expansiveness, optimistic boldness in the face of mighty odds, it seemed almost automatic for him to cast Okhlopkov in the role. In an article published in August 1939, Okhlopkov described how he arrived on the film set, was given a costume and sword and simply told to 'act'.[4] The results suggest that he took to the 'epic' style like a duck to water. As he said of himself: 'If it is true that one's childhood and youth determine the course of one's life, then mine had been determined for ever by the festival on the public squares.'[5]

Can there have been any other person in the history of modern theatre whose very first production was a mass spectacle performed before 30,000 spectators in the town square of a major city?[6] It was also apt and fitting that one of Okhlopkov's final productions should have been an open-air performance of Euripides' *Medea*.[7] How many actors have there been who, in order to portray events truthfully, went

21 Nikolai Okhlopkov in the 1930s

to the lengths of starving themselves so as to be able to faint convincingly? Okhlopkov did so when acting in Mikhail Romm's film *Lenin in 1918* (1939). Okhlopkov was larger than life and his vision corresponded to this. He possessed what one critic has described as 'telescopic eyes', gigantically intensified vision which enlarged subjects a hundredfold.[8] The same critic described the singular moments of a typical Okhlopkov production, where the grand emotion and the grand gesture were gathered up into a moment of intensity which was both intimate and universal, as if the feeling generated in Art Theatre Studio work were raised to the power of 'x' and transferred to a vast amphitheatre, causing 30,000 rather than just 30, to respond with sympathy, even to the point of tears:

> Can one forget those soul-piercing moments of Okhlopkovian discovery . . . which have entered the creative history of the theatre: Katerina whipped by the winds on the peak of a huge Volgan precipice; Hamlet's first perturbed entrance 'like a startled fawn from a mountain forest' . . . cutting through the ranked order of the throne

room; the journalist Tryan leaping across almost the entire stage to clasp his resurrected friend Konovalov and suddenly, in a passionate whisper, beginning to sing the anthem of Republican Spain: the lonely sobbing of Valya in the silent crowd before being herded off to Germany; the desperate dance of Victor as if it were a matter of life and death? These are moments of art for which the theatre exists.[9]

'I dream of a theatre', said Okhlopkov on one occasion, 'of a theatre, from which someone passing by hears a howling roar and wonders "What is this? A football stadium?" No, it is a theatre performing *Othello* and at that moment, the Moor is suffocating Desdemona.'[10]

Like Edward Gordon Craig, Okhlopkov's notions of the highest kind of art found expression in a work such as Bach's St Matthew Passion and he often dreamed of staging an oratorio-like stage work of equivalent emotional power. Music was always inextricably woven into the fabric of his theatre productions – Rachmaninov's First Piano Concerto was an intrinsic element of his production of *The Young Guard* as was Tchaikovsky's music in his production of *Hamlet*. He also used the music of Scriabin, Liszt and many others, including modern Soviet composers such as Taneyev. 'Write me a play', he once asked Isidor Shtok, 'a play which can be performed to organ accompaniment. And with a choir. No, not one, two choirs! Like an oratorio. But let it be a drama as well . . .'[11]

In a general sense, Okhlopkov, whilst acknowledging a debt to Meyerhold and Stanislavsky, did not work according to any particular system. He appeared to master the laws of the stage intuitively and his working methods were uneven, chaotic and tempestuous. He constructed an entire dramatic action in his mind, rather than on paper, as he seemed uniquely capable of conceiving ideas in images and pictures as a chain of associations and visual-emotional impressions. He loved the art of *mise-en-scène* like an artist loves colour or a musician loves melody. As he said: 'By staging something in a certain way a director can express the character of the protagonist, his psychology and the line of action; his place and significance in the play. *Mise-en-scène* can assist the actor to disclose what is going on in the soul of a person. *Mise-en-scène* can become a dramatic force, can strengthen the action.'[12] He might also have added that *mise-en-scène* can turn a mediocre work into a work of art.

At the same time, he was prepared to acknowledge the importance and significance of Stanislavsky and found it 'difficult to imagine serious creative people in our age who ignored Stanislavsky's system in their theatre work'.[13] However, he did not think the latter's ideas were recipes or dogmas. 'Some of them have to be subjected to critical analysis, to further development.'[14] During his later life, he was a teacher at the GITIS Institute[15] as well as head of the Mayakovsky Theatre and it is somehow typical of Okhlopkov's attitude to Stanislavsky that, after giving a lecture on the 'system', he asked one of his students to dramatise *An Actor's Work on Himself* in the manner of a film-strip which demonstrated the living quality of 'the system'.[16] As far as his own methods in rehearsal are concerned, he felt the most important role of the director was to create the circumstances in which actors could relate directly and immediately to each other. There needed to be warmth from the start, followed by the 'heat' of relationship. He had no time for technical, 'cold' rehearsals and, for this reason, felt that improvisation was a good thing, especially for actors who tended to be either withdrawn or who lacked faith in themselves: 'And when the spark of relationship is born, when the actors begin organically and truly to live, whilst relating to one another, then the author's text won't get in their way but, on the contrary, will release their creative potential towards improvisation based on the "materials", on the "sub-text", on the "outer elements", and so on.'[17]

Okhlopkov's theatrical credo can be summarised as a passionate love of life, which he learned from his favourite poets – Mayakovsky and Walt Whitman. There is a strongly pantheistic element in his work and a desire, which he shared with Stanislavsky, to restore the word 'nature' to 'human nature', to achieve an organic merging of mind and body, heart and head – a unity of being in the actor, an integral unity in the work of art which reflected a communal unity in the theatre audience, which was itself a microcosm of the new communal, post-revolutionary society. It was for this reason that he sought an appropriate form in the 'mass spectacle'. The atmosphere he was seeking could not be found in enclosed buildings, but only on the streets and open platforms: 'From the first, I turned to the tradition of the popular shows.'[18]

It is ironic that only on one occasion did Okhlopkov work under the ideal conditions which he dreamed of all his life and that this occasion was when, as a raw youth of twenty-one, he staged a mass spectacle in his home town of Irkutsk. For the rest of his life, his practice as a theatre artist was conducted indoors, often in buildings of small proportions (the Realistic Theatre could barely hold 325 people) or else in rather old-fashioned traditional theatre buildings such as the former Theatre of the Revolution (the Mayakovsky Theatre on Herzen Street) or the Vakhtangov Theatre on the Arbat. As an actor, most of his work was performed in another ancient building, the former Sohn (later the Meyerhold Theatre) on what is now Mayakovsky Square. Towards the end of his life he worked on a project for a circular amphitheatre which contained echoes of what Barkhin and Sergei Vakhtangov had projected for Meyerhold and which also contained aspects of the 'universal' theatre, or 'total' theatre imagined by Walter Gropius.[19] The ideas which lay at the back of Okhlopkov's mind at this time (c. 1950) were derived from the theatres of ancient Greece, mediaeval performance conditions, a production of *Goetz von Berlichingen* which he had seen performed in Frankfurt-am-Main in 1932, a production of *A Midsummer Night's Dream* which he heard had been staged in a Californian valley, as well as Reinhardt's production of *The Miracle*, staged in a circus arena.[20]

Since his untimely death in 1967, the Mayakovsky Theatre, which he headed for a number of years, has been under the quite different leadership of Andrei Goncharov and it is difficult to trace a distinctively Okhlopkovian legacy in the Soviet theatre. His reputation in the West, and in English-speaking countries, rests mainly on what was reported, (by Norris Houghton, André van Gyseghem and others), of his experimentally 'formalist' productions at the Realistic Theatre during the early 1930s.[21] What seems clear from his work is its ideological commitment which remained overt and unwavering. Okhlopkov took up the theme of commitment at a point where, it might be argued, that of others was becoming more faint under pressure from the political and artistic demands being imposed in the 1930s. Okhlopkov chose to stage dramatised versions of politically committed fiction, such as Serafimovich's *The Iron Flood* and Gorky's *Mother*, or plays such as Pogodin's *Aristocrats*, which someone like Meyerhold noticeably refrained from staging. It is also fair to say that Okhlopkov's 'formalist' experiments in a world where 'socialist realism' was promulgated as normative, always sought to stress the ideological content of the work he was dealing with. The 'formalist' means were never the primary concern but often seemed necessary to disguise a fundamental weakness in the dramatic material – a problem which confronted both Tairov and Meyerhold. Whilst Okhlopkov's stylised version of *The Iron Flood* was criticised, it was never actually forbidden, as was Meyerhold's version of Ostrovsky's *How the Steel Was Tempered*[22] and although, like Meyerhold, Okhlopkov suffered the indignity of having his theatre closed down (his company was merged briefly with Tairov's in 1937) he seems to have accepted the way he was treated as the lot of any talented artist and certainly never appears to have kicked against bureaucratic insensitivity with any degree of permanent hostility.

There is little doubt that official Soviet criticism places as high, if not a higher value on Okhlopkov's work after he left the Realistic Theatre and would probably single out his productions of a dramatised version of Fadeyev's novel *The Young Guard* as his major claim to fame. At the same time, from a Western point of view, his most interesting work remains that which he staged at the Realistic Theatre in the 1930s, which is not to say that the later work lacks interest in comparison. Okhlopkov never became a less significant artist by virtue of his adaptation to changing times and varying demands. His later work remains a unique record of a major artist's response to the desperately serious, occasionally traumatic events of an epoch to which his emotional range and theatrical style seemed uniquely adjusted.

Some remarks recorded by Lee Strasberg in an interview with Okhlopkov in 1934 remain relevant to an understanding of his work throughout his life. Explaining the difference between himself and Stanislavsky, Okhlopkov described it as the difference between a priest and an engineer:

> We took from Stanislavsky his sincerity and his realism. But we don't believe in intuition . . . We believe that you cannot *invent* life. We prepare a theme and its structure, we make a plan for it, we make an ideological–political analysis of the plan, and only then do we begin our work. We give our work a broad, sound, class viewpoint, and the details come later. Stanislavsky also has a plan, but his is more that of a trusting priest, while our plan with its base firmly set upon class-consciousness, is the plan of an engineer.[23]

Nikolai Pavlovich Okhlopkov was born on 15 May 1900, in the Siberian town of Irkutsk, the son of an army colonel. He attended an army training school in his teens but, instead of following in his father's footsteps, he abandoned a military career for art school. He also commenced studying the violin at a local conservatoire. One of his reasons for changing course at this period of his life was his enthusiasm for the work and lifestyle of Vladimir Mayakovsky,[24] a leading futurist poet before the revolution who, after 1917, became a staunchly pro-Bolshevik artist who placed his talents as a poet and publicist at the service of the new Soviet government. Okhlopkov even took to wearing a flamboyant yellow peasant blouse like Mayakovsky when, in 1917, he joined the local theatre company in Irkutsk as resident furniture-maker and scene designer. Within a year he had graduated to becoming an actor.

It was in the spirit of Mayakovsky that, dressed in his yellow blouse, the brash young man approached Comrade Rzhanov, secretary of the regional party committee, with a plan for the May Day celebrations in 1921. At that point in his life Okhlopkov had staged nothing at all in the theatre. Despite this, he was given permission and, within thirty days, had written his own scenario for a mass entertainment entitled *The Struggle of Labour and Capital*, which was to involve thousands of people, including foot and mounted military units, artillery, enthusiastic amateurs and the local citizenry. 'It was difficult for us', recalled Okhlopkov at a later date, 'as this was the period of the establishment of the new Soviet society. In Irkutsk, this process was held back as the town had, until quite recently, been in the hands of the Kolchak forces and the Japanese.'[25] He had noted a lack of enthusiasm within the theatre to stage something for the May Day festivities and it can be imagined that, as it was only a year since the arrival of the Red Army, there was still a number of people who were none too keen to celebrate a workers' festival. Okhlopkov decided to stage the show on Tikhvinski Square, in front of the cathedral. The theme of the scenario was the struggle of a tyrant with the proletariat. Okhlopkov played the tyrant, borrowing the character's physical image from Kachalov's portrayal of Anathema, the devil, in Leonid Andreyev's play which had been staged at the Moscow Art Theatre in 1909. Attempts were made to sabotage the production by a local Ataman, who had a reputation for executing his opponents, and who sent his agents around Irkutsk to paste up notices warning anyone who took part in the entertainment, or who watched it, of the likely consequences. Just before the performance was due to commence, someone managed to get into the cathedral belfry and tried drowning the performance by ringing bells. Okhlopkov placed agitators among the crowd to try and involve the more passive spectators in the action.[26]

His next production took place at the Irkutsk Youth Theatre and, again, involved his strong admiration for the work of Mayakovsky, when he mounted a production of the latter's 'Heroic, Epic and Satirical Portrayal of our Epoch', *Mystery-Bouffe*, for the May Day Festival of 1922. There he attempted to out-do Meyerhold himself, whose production of the second version of the play Okhlopkov had seen at the RSFSR Theatre No. 1 in Moscow the previous year. The production had seemed to the young director-initiate to 'lack boldness'.[27] Following the success of this venture, he was despatched by the local party committee to GITIS in Moscow, to train as a director in the Department of Mass Spectacles.

GITIS began its first year of operation on 17 September 1922, with a total of about 500 students and lecturers. At the opening session speeches were made by Meyerhold, who had a semi-autonomous workshop within GITIS, N.M. Foregger, B.A. Ferdinandov and S.M. Mikhoels. Among members of the first year's acting course were future members of Meyerhold's troupe, N.I. Serebryannikova, N.I. Bogolyubov and L.N. Sverdlin. The first-year students of direction included, apart from Okhlopkov, two others who were to have important associations both with him and Meyerhold – A.V. Fevralsky and P.V. Tsetnerovich.[28] One of the first productions to be mounted at the GITIS Theatre, on 24 November 1922, was Meyerhold's version of Sukhovo-Kobylin's nineteenth-century tragi-farce, *Tarelkin's Death*, with Eisenstein as assistant director and with Okhlopkov cast in the role of a police thug, Kachala. One of the most successful scenes involved Mikhail Zharov, cast in the role of the laundress Brandakhlyustova, who, having been 'arrested' and flung into a constructivist 'cell' (a contraption of slatted wood, painted white), then proceeded to indulge in an outrageous piece of flirtation with Kachala. According to Nina Velekhova, Okhlopkov was first and foremost an improviser, with the result that his fellow actors felt the need to request Meyerhold to curb their colleague's tendency to indulge in *lazzi* during the course of the performance.[29]

Okhlopkov followed this up with his first apprentice work as a director at the GITIS Workshop. In February 1923, Meyerhold's student directors were preparing a number of productions, consisting mainly of excerpts from plays. All were second-year students with the exception of Okhlopkov. It therefore demanded a particular kind of boldness of this young, first-year student to choose to stage an excerpt from the very same play in which he had appeared under Meyerhold's direction. According to Fevralsky, Meyerhold, far from being offended, considered that Okhlopkov had discovered an interesting and original approach to the staging of *Tarelkin's Death*.[30]

As a student of the directors' course, Okhlopkov's opportunities for acting were not so great as others, but he seems to have been cast, albeit in fairly minor roles, in almost every one of Meyerhold's productions between 1922 and 1926, before he graduated from GITIS and parted company with Meyerhold. Among the roles he played were those of a soldier in *Earth Rampant*, a Russian sailor in *Give Us Europe!*, General Berkovets in Faiko's *Bubus the Teacher* and an old Chinese boatman in *Roar, China!* by Sergei Tretyakov. Of them all, his performance as the general was probably his finest. He acted the part of the commander of a unit of troops who have been sent to deal with striking demonstrators. Before rehearsals started, Meyerhold had asked Okhlopkov to develop the image of the role by studying the caricatures of George Grosz. After searching in various libraries, he discovered several caricatures of barrel-shaped military types and tried to make himself up as a fat man. Finding that this did not seem to work, he started to research in the opposite direction, exploring the possibilities of his own elongated physique. Luckily he found just what he was looking for among Grosz's caricatures. Okhlopkov intensified the thinness and exaggerated the height through the lines of his uniform and by wearing very high topboots. He knew he was taking a risk in developing something which was precisely the opposite of what Meyerhold had requested but, as it turned out, the latter was well pleased with the results. Everyone remarked on the quality of Okhlopkov's stage movement in a production which was remarkable for the introduction by Meyerhold of the concept of 'pre-acting', which involved a slowing-down of the entire pace of the production. Meyerhold proposed that the role of Berkovets be based on pauses and silences, played in counterpoint to musical accompaniment. The critics Gauzner and Gabrilovich devoted an entire chapter of the volume *Theatrical October* to an analysis of Okhlopkov's acting, describing how he played in a special tempo-rhythm, based on consecutive time fragments, microscopically exaggerated rises and descents and uninterrupted play of time segments of greater or lesser length, which united to form one extended whole. He created a remarkable image of a polished and slow-witted martinet, managing to convey consecutive impressions of alarm, joy, despair and lust in rapid succession. At moments he moved about the stage like a shadow or a lithe panther. In the final act, he performed a complicated mime sequence of a dying man, after the general has been shot from a window by one of the demonstrators. Despite being wounded, the character did not fall down but walked, it seemed interminably, the entire width of the stage, keeping close to the rear wall, stumbling and seeking support, before collapsing on to a divan.[31]

His role as one of the soldier rebels in *Earth Rampant* was that of a man of the mountains, who had seemingly sprung from nowhere, invulnerable like a mythological creature, an emanation of nature, who could only be destroyed by stealth and cunning. His other great popular success as an actor was the role of the Chinese boatman in *Roar, China!* In this case, the production was accompanied by a background of subdued eastern music which Okhlopkov made into his personal leitmotif – the 'inner sound of an agonised song of suffering'.[32] He acted the part with great strength and simplicity, especially at the moment where he went to his death for the sake of his compatriots. However, of all the roles which he played during his period with Meyerhold, Okhlopkov thought his own crowning achievement, despite its comparatively minor nature, was that of Kachala in *Tarelkin's Death*, which enabled him to exploit the improvisatory qualities of *commedia dell'arte* and cope with the physical demands of the complicated constructivist stage furniture.

Like Eisenstein who, having achieved independent status as an artist under Meyerhold's guidance, subsequently 'fell out of the theatre into the cinema'[33] so, on completing the directors' course at GITIS, did Okhlopkov. There is no reason to believe that there was any fundamental rift between the two men although, usually, when a student of Meyerhold's left his theatre it was on account of some personal difference with the 'Master'. Okhlopkov appears merely to have felt his increasing independence as an artist and that at this stage, his true path appeared to lie in the cinema, rather than in the theatre. Evidence that Meyerhold retained a high regard for Okhlopkov is apparent in the fact that, when the former was considering making a film of Turgenev's *Fathers and Sons*, in 1928, his first choice for the central role of Bazarov was Okhlopkov.[34]

Okhlopkov's entry into films was made indirectly via the theatre in that his first film role (that of a sailor in *Death Bay*, 1926) was directed by Abram Room,[35] who had earlier worked with Meyerhold as assistant director on the production of *Lake Lyul* at the Theatre of the Revolution.[36] The film was a straightforward melodrama and had sub-titles written by Victor Shklovsky.[37] It was the latter who, together with Lev Nikulin, provided the script for Room's next film *Traitor*, in which Okhlopkov also acted. The film traced the exposure of a Tsarist police provocateur who has been responsible for wiping out a pre-revolutionary circle of Bolshevik sailors.

Okhlopkov's first independent work as a film-maker occurred the following year, 1927. The film was *Mitya*, about a telephone mechanic, in which he also starred. The film is of additional interest because of its script, commissioned from the playwright Nikolai Erdman,[38] who had had tremendous success with his comedy, *The Mandate*, both in Leningrad and at Meyerhold's theatre. The film is a domestic satire involving a case of mistaken identity, which Erdman invested with 'tragic overtones', according to Okhlopkov.[39] His next independent work was a film version of a story-fable by Paul Laforgue – *Un Appetit Vendu* (The Sold Appetite) – about a young worker who cannot support the healthy appetites of his family on his own income and so sells his appetite to a rich man who cannot enjoy the wondrous foods his wealth can buy. The ironies of this tale were again developed in a scenario by Erdman, working in conjunction with Anatoli Mariengof. The film was a broad burlesque on capitalist contradictions and filmed by Okhlopkov 'in a strikingly uninhibited style'.[40] This film was produced and released by the Ukrainian film studio Vufku.

Okhlopkov wrote his own scenario for his next, and probably his best film, *Way of the Enthusiasts*, on which he worked with the remarkable Alexander Medvedkin,[41] who acted as assistant director. The film, which concerned the popular strength of soldiers and peasants in their battle against foreign interventionists, attempted to supply some of Eisenstein's 'intellectual' solutions to the problems of making a comedy. It also dealt with the mutual suspicions between peasants and city workers. The film was produced by Sovkino, instead of Vufku, and was never released. Okhlopkov's peculiar dynamic earthiness was everywhere apparent in this film, which was subjected to stringent criticism by the influential Platon Kerzhentsev, who then held a leading position in the Association of Proletarian Writers. Typically, the film was strongly defended by Mayakovsky, who was also coming under criticism from RAPP. The film was subjected to drastic modifications, so much so that it lost much of its original force. Writing in the 1950s, Victor Shklovsky declared it would have been a great film had it not been subjected to remaking and re-editing.[42] M.G. Lifshitz recalled a remarkable sequence involving a bearded peasant standing in the middle of a river, up to his waist in water, wearing a battledress shirt, when, all of a sudden, medals descended like stars and affixed themselves to his chest one after the other.[43] Following his experience with this film, Okhlopkov turned his attention permanently to the theatre, with only the occasional foray into screen acting. In 1932, he played the part of the worker Zakharov in Alexander Macheret's film *Jobs and Men*, on which the assistant director was Mikhail Romm, who later cast Okhlopkov in two of his films about Lenin. However, Okhlopkov's major change of direction was to join the Realistic Theatre as its artistic head during the second half of 1931.

The Realistic Theatre had been formed in 1927, on the basis of the Art Theatre's Fourth Studio, and was headed by a triumvirate. Owing to financial problems, the theatre had been taken over by a regional committee to help them pay off the theatre's debts and to conduct a refurbishment of the building. This occurred in August 1931, shortly before Okhlopkov took over. When he arrived he brought with him some of the actors from the Meyerhold company. The theatre's existing repertoire at this juncture included a version of Hasek's *The Good Soldier Schweik*, Somerset Maugham's *The Land of Promise*, and a dramatised version of Fyodor Gladkov's novel *Cement*. The theatre was renamed the Krasnaya Presnaya Theatre in 1931 (after the workers' district in which it was located) and then reverted to its former name, Realistic, in 1934. Okhlopkov's first production, on 30 March 1932, was of V.P. Stavsky's play about collectivisation, *Razbeg* (Running Start).

In one of his first interviews, Okhlopkov declared that his first production would tackle the subject of class war in the countryside.[44] The play itself was based on sketches and notes made by Stavsky which were put into dramatic form by G.I. Pavluchenko, who had co-authored the scenario of Okhlopkov's film, *Way of the Enthusiasts*. The production dealt with the struggle for collectivisation in the Kuban region in 1929. The theme appealed to Okhlopkov because it 'resounded with heroism', and a feeling of *Sturm und Drang*. He envisaged a ten-fold enlargement of life with people marching ever onwards with a view to attaining new heights – just like images in the lithographs of Käthe Kollwitz. The production was to be about 'the front-line struggle for bread' in which the principal reporters had been Panfyorov and Sholokhov.[45] 'And everywhere you hear of the heroism of the people, and by no means isolated cases only. Collectivisation is proceeding . . . root and branch changes are taking place. A terrible struggle is ensuing . . . I do not want to stand aside from events' declared Okhlopkov.[46] In order to achieve this, he wanted his own 'root and branch' transformation of the Realistic Theatre's interior, although he recognised that 'fate' seemed to be laughing at him:

> After my 'spectacle' on a city square, after the scope of *Mystery-Bouffe*, after directing in the movies where almost nothing limited me, I acquired, for the realisation of my dreams, a tiny stage and a small auditorium with a capacity of 325 persons![47]

He wanted to disposition the audience in a new way to help the spectators be other than mere observers of what happened on stage; to promote an active involvement of the audience in the maelstrom of the action.

> I wanted to make the action 'his own' for the spectator, to propel the spectator into the action, and make the action itself more graphic, more vivid, more three-dimensional. I wanted to do everything I could to make the audience creatively share the characters' life, feelings, thought and hopes . . . We are trying to create an intimacy with the audience . . . the kind . . . that a soldier marching to the battlefield feels towards the soldier marching beside him. Our ambition is to achieve a

'fraternisation' between the audience from all sides . . . above him, and even under him. The audience in our theatre must become an active part of the performance. . .[48]

What he wanted was something like the atmosphere which the Art Theatre had achieved but without naturalism being evident in either the direction or the setting – a situation where the stage 'disappeared' and the member of the audience stopped being a 'spectator' and became, instead, an invisible participant in the action on stage. 'The theatre must do everything to make the spectator believe in what goes on in the play, let him laugh till he cries, let him hold back his tears only with great effort. One should not fear the burning grief, the deep suffering of the spectator in the theatre, because these must be creative emotions, not naturalistic ones . . .'[49] He decided, as he put it, to use the small theatre to make 'directorial sketches' for future large-scale productions. It was to be 'a theatre of large passions and one of experiment'.[50]

It was around this time that Meyerhold was having a new theatre built on Triumfalnaya Square, not so far away from the Realistic Theatre. Okhlopkov's own project was quite different from that of his teacher and, despite being unrealised in practice, throws light on what he was trying to achieve. Okhlopkov wished to exploit scenic technology and stage architecture to solve two basic theatrical problems – the need for large auditoria and the existence of a theatre art based on laboratory conditions, both of which demanded differing acting styles. A socialist theatre could be nothing other than a mass theatre so how could the problem be resolved? Okhlopkov considered the best plan was to divide the theatre into sections and to dismember the theatrical action. Thus, a few groups of spectators, dispersed in different parts of the auditorium (approximately thirty-five to fifty in each section) would watch several variants of one and the same episode. Then, when scenes of a more general, mass character were shown, the spectators of each 'laboratory'[51] would become united in one auditorium with each group relating to the mass action through the particular quality which characterised the laboratory performances. Intervals and transfers from the 'laboratory' to the 'auditorium' and back could be included as part of the production. Moving from one part of the theatre to another during the interval the spectator would be confronted by pictures, sculptures, photo-montages and music which continued to develop the theme of the play in the languages of the other arts. If, for example, photographs displayed during the first interval developed the situation of the first act, they would then be replaced in the second interval by different ones.

Okhlopkov thought it might be possible to fulfil these imaginings within the context of the old theatre building. For the 'auditorium' episodes, the stage would be used, together with the auditorium itself, the foyer and even the street outside (in winter, the spectators would watch through windows and, in summer, from special balconies). The action of the 'laboratory' episodes could be performed in the dressing rooms, administrative offices, on the stairways, and so on. The small building of the Realistic Theatre would permit a production episode to be played in ten variants. In each of the ten locations would be found differing means of disposing the actors and the audience. This 'montage' effect, which Okhlopkov

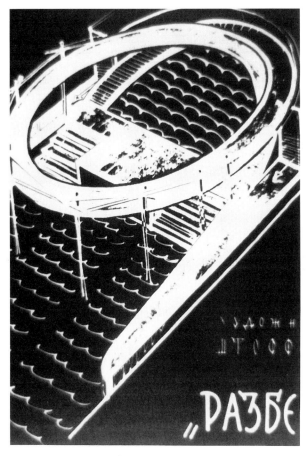

22 Sketch by Ya. Shtoffer of set for *Running Start* (1932)

inherited from Eisenstein, lent itself very well to the dramatisation of works of fiction, which is why, of the seven productions staged by Okhlopkov at the Realistic Theatre, four were dramatisations of prose works. The theatre wished to retain and carry over on to the stage the complex and rapidly shifting appearances of life. Okhlopkov built *mise-en-scènes* in separate 'blocks', showing events occurring in different places and involving different characters, which both supplemented and acted in counterpoint to each other. These sections were then assembled into one whole. In the printed copy of the play *Running Start*, for example, there were eighty-three such 'montage' elements.[52]

For this production, Okhlopkov completely reorganised the auditorium. A section of the audience was placed where the stage had previously been and a wide transverse passage ran between it and the audience sitting in the old auditorium (with a small stage in the centre). Around both parts of the audience stretched another, narrower aisle which circled three-quarters of the hall and then raked upwards over the spectators' heads to form an upper walkway. Main scenes were staged in the central aisle, while other moments of action occurred in different places simultaneously, or moved rapidly from one spot to another. The designer, Yakov Shtoffer, managed to combine naturalism and 'conventionalism' in decorating the construction with apple trees, pear trees, willows, sunflowers, poppies and maize, giving a striking impression of the sunshine, gardens and fields of the Kuban region. Shtoffer said he got his ideas from the Elizabethan theatre and from El Lissitsky's designs for Tretyakov's *I Want a Child*.[53] The critic, Boris Alpers, commented:

> Just as in life events usually occur simultaneously in different parts of the globe and, even in different places you find one and the same cossack village, one and the same apartment, so, on this stage the theatre attempts to convey action simultaneously on different points of the scenic platform, wedging one episode into the other and occasionally conducting them in parallel. This naive notion is especially evident in one place in the production where a peasant who has been wounded by kulaks crawls for ten minutes along a walkway while the action in other parts of the setting takes its ordered course . . .[54]

Even hostile critics had to admit that the setting was perfectly adapted to the ideas of the play, that the audience was captivated by the carnival spirit of the costumes and decor, and that the bright colours and the way lighting was used elicited applause. The audience seemed to find themselves in the middle of a fruit orchard, or in the yard of a collective farm. The actors strolled among the audience and acted in their very midst. The spectators frequently had to turn in their seats to discover where a voice was coming from, or where new episodes were commencing. The transitions between scenes were sometimes so sharp that an actor would break off in mid-phrase and the scene would shift, or revert, to another group, before rapidly moving on to another part of the construction.

A strong poetic mood made itself felt throughout the production, a meditative lyricism and a powerful feeling for nature such as had been apparent in *Way of the Enthusiasts* – a pantheistic quality, accompanied by an intuitive grasp of the characteristics of the particular region: 'it was as if *Running Start* contained not only people, but beautiful horses, cows, birds, goats . . . from the world of nature there flowed some kind of connection with the man of the countryside, the peasant'.[55] The style of the production was reminiscent of the nature poetry of Kornilov and Zabolotsky[56] and there was a subtle use of real objects which served to bring the imaginary world to life – real nets cast into 'water' awakened the world of water, just as the blow of a knife seemed to alter something in nature: 'The air hummed with mosquitoes, cicadas, grasshoppers – this was a conversation, the voices of the earth, a symphony of the unknown, concealed life of nature . . .'

Okhlopkov caused the action to unfold, in the sounds of the night, in darkness, in chaos, in immobility. (The central stage seeming to be a still centre of immobility, like an oasis.) It was the sort of production, according to Nina Velekhova, where you could almost imagine hearing Zabolotsky's monologue of a horse – 'a fantastic, anthropomorphic element'.[57]

Some critics felt that the production was over-burdened with movement and bustle, with too many 'biologically' crude, naturalistic moments – belching, snoring etc., as well as there being too much preoccupation with ethnographic detail.[58] Okhlopkov was also accused of combining excessive theatricality with naturalism, escapism and 'sociologism', with expressionism and impressionism, with aestheticism and plain bad taste. In attempting to overcome old-fashioned styles of production, he had fallen into the trap of 'formalism'. His 'crude' feeling for life was dubbed naturalism and the abundance of popular humour was described as a *balagan* (a clown show).[59]

Most of the criticism of the production occurred during the course of a three-day debate which took place at the premises of the All-Russian Drama Committee in April 1932. Critics accused Okhlopkov of being carried away with false preoccupations, although most admitted that his approach was far more revolutionary than that of the Art Theatre's to Kirshon's *Bread* (1931) or Afinogenev's *Fear* (1931). One of the most hostile was V. Zalessky, a theatre critic and then deputy editor of *Literaturnaya Gazeta*, who defended the socialist realist principle of *ideinost*[60] which, in his view, Okhlopkov had sought to destroy. He detected in the brightness and theatricality, aspects of (heaven forbid!) entertainment, external attractiveness, and a dubious 'scenic' quality which sought a formal resolution to the problems of reworking literary texts as drama. 'Does an artist have the right to lower the ideological-artistic level of a work as part of an attempt to embody it in stage terms?' he asked. He especially disliked the mixing of serious ideological matters with episodes of comedy and farce. In po-faced disapproval he asked:

> Can it be the case that the opportunistic essence of Bakhno[61] is revealed by the fact that he belches in a disgraceful fashion, eats raw eggs or performs natural functions? All these 'devices' . . . make the audience laugh and entertains them as much as does the artful Charlie Chaplin but, regrettably, this laughter causes the spectator to lose that feeling of alertness, the capacity to be mobilised, that *partinost* which Bakhno arouses in them in the real *Running Start* . . . In the play version, Bakhno loses these traits of *tipichnost*, which here acquire a general character and which become politically devalued.'[62]

Okhlopkov defended himself by casting doubt on Zalessky's competence as a theatre critic and insisting on the ideological value of the 'entertainment'. He was supported in the pages of Zalessky's own paper by I.I. Chicherov, who declared the production to be 'the most powerful event of our theatrical season'.[63] However, the main spokesman for the defence was the playwright Vsevolod Vishnevsky who devoted a special article to the production in *Sovetskoe Iskusstvo* and spoke out in favour of it on the third day of the debate. He accused critics of merely trying to settle accounts with Okhlopkov. He pointed out that, on the opening night, the audience had been composed mainly of party members and that their response had been to greet the first act with an ovation. 'Applause', he added ironically, 'serves, as is well known, as an expression of approval.' He went on to argue in favour of the production methods adopted by Okhlopkov for the portrayal of such 'momentous events' as collectivisation, as opposed to the more traditional means of the Moscow Art Theatre. He then made comparison with Zarkhi's *Joy Street*[64] which, like *Running Start*, contained 'the most marvellous device borrowed from the cinema'. Vishnevsky pointed out that an audience accustomed to boldness of montage, close-up technique and episodic structure in the cinema, was still afraid of this in the theatre. 'You still cling to the smoothness of sequential "acts". Everything has to be concrete; three or four acts, nine scenes.' But Okhlopkov and Pavluchenko had gone further than someone like Zarkhi, who inserted an episodic structure into a conventional four-act scheme. This production was 'groping towards devices of great expressiveness, both monumental and lyrical'. The production sought to do away with decorative deadness of the Art Theatre kind whilst managing to convey the theatrical sense and feeling of a village; of water (the bathing episode); of wide expanses of steppe (travelling along the upper walk-way). It also succeeded in interweaving, in a complex fashion, devices of Japanese theatre, the theatre of Meyerhold, of film, and various other means. Vishnevsky concluded: 'Yet the critics rebuke him for formalism. But you should rejoice that people are searching! You should congratulate them! Beat the drums of joy! Demand that each master write in his own hand and say something new...' He conceded that there were a few unnecessary tricks, such as the 'superfluous shouting' of the young Komsomols, too much dancing and excessive 'business' with a dagger at one point. But these did not constitute the principal elements of the production, which lay in bold, innovatory exploration: 'Just take the device of constructing each *mise-en-scène* in profile and based on circular movement, bearing in mind that the actor is observed from all sides. Here lies an entire problem concerning a new approach to the art of the actor bearing on the influence of the arena stage.' Vishnevsky also approved of the design. Where critics saw only the search for formal novelty, he declared the entire structure to be the fruit of an ideological concept 'to give the production and the movement in it a quality of dynamic class warfare; to provide an organic unity between actor and spectator; to convey the close-knit feeling of the collective; to convey feeling itself'. Winding up the discussion, general secretary of the Association of Proletarian Writers, Leopold Averbakh, suggested a black mark be put against Okhlopkov's name for future reference.[65]

In 1933, Okhlopkov was joined by another refugee from Meyerhold's theatre, Pavel Tsetnerovich, who had worked there for ten years as a director's assistant and who was a friend of Okhlopkov's from his Irkutsk days. Together they embarked on a joint production of a dramatised version of Gorky's novel, *Mother*. Here again the inspiration may well have sprung from the cinema and the powerful film based on the novel which Pudovkin had made in 1926. In fact, the decision to try and stage a version of the novel may have been tempting providence, as comparisons with a classic of Soviet cinema were inevitable.

Some of the most telling accounts of Okhlopkov's work during this period were emerging in the reports of British and American theatre historians, practitioners and researchers who found themselves in Russia during the early 1930s and who, like Shaw, Brecht, Piscator and others, who also visited the Soviet

Union during the early and mid 1930s, were either communists themselves or well-disposed towards the Soviet system and, especially, towards the Soviet theatre. Brecht was interested in Okhlopkov's work and Norris Houghton recalls Tretyakov, Brecht's Russian translator, stating that Brecht envisioned 'a future mass theatre which Okhlopkov will create, where this energetic style of his will have room for proper expression before thousands of spectators . . .' Houghton concluded: 'Okhlopkov is an ardent communist . . . one of the most striking examples of the new social artist in the Moscow theatre.'[66] André van Gyseghem described Okhlopkov's mind as being 'as ruthless as Meyerhold's whilst his authority over his actors was not exercised autocratically'. Again, according to van Gyseghem, Okhlopkov used 'the classic conventions of the Kabuki theatre reinterpreted in modern forms' and pointed to the importance of music, 'adjusted to the atmosphere of the play, revealing its pulse, its respiration'[67] This was a factor which Houghton also noted, as well as the fact that Okhlopkov's productions were studies in 'perpetuum mobile':

> From early in his rehearsals Okhlopkov works, like Meyerhold, with music. His score . . . is written and is played in its final form from the start. Music is here . . . an integral part of the production, and since it serves as an accompaniment to action, it must be carefully rehearsed with. For regular rehearsals, the piano alone is used, but full orchestra is used at full run-through even those of a single act which may take place a month or two before the opening.[68]

In addition, Houghton noted Okhlopkov's 'dynamic personality' and his 'talent for the stage' which made his theatre so interesting. But he also felt the need for a sense of humour 'to lighten his ferocity'.[69]

Lee Strasberg, who was in Moscow in 1934, interviewed Tsetnerovich and confirms the impression that the production of *The Mother* was more his than Okhlopkov's (the latter having been responsible for the dramatisation). The aim, according to Tsetnerovich, had been to maximise pathos without resorting to grand gestures or hysteria. Even the absence of furniture sprang from this desire for pathos and provided the opportunity to exploit comic effects for tragic purposes. There was a scene in which the mother entered in an emotional state – took off her coat and went round looking for a place to hang it, before simply letting it drop on the floor. According to Strasberg, this was a variation of the old clown's trick of removing a coat, dusting it carefully, hanging it on an imaginary nail, then deliberately turning away and letting it fall to the floor.[70]

According to Fevralsky, Okhlopkov realised he could not convey the total ideological density of Gorky's work and so wrote 'Fragments of Gorky's Novel' on the poster. The theme of the 'fragments' was 'socialist morality'.[71] As in *Running Start*, the division of the theatre building into stage and auditorium was broken down. The action unfolded on a main circular platform placed in the centre of the auditorium, on a low gallery surrounding the main seating area and on three promontories which led from this gallery to the central platform. The effect was to divide the audience in three. The entire structure was encircled by bollards, linked by sagging chains, on which was the initial 'N', evocative of the era of Nicholas II.

23 Sketch by Ya. Shtoffer of set for Gorky's *Mother* (1933)

The play was broken down into dozens of episodes marked off from one another by switching the lighting to change the location. The platforms were devoid of furniture and there were few hand props. Circular plaques, bearing the arms of Imperial Russia, were hung at intervals around the walls. André van Gyseghem described the action as follows:

> The central platform is the mother's home – here we first see her going about her chores . . . Illiterate, religious, deeply intuitive, she is completely unaware of her own capacity for sacrifice, heroism, and selfless devotion. She is Mother.
> Suddenly, the lights spring up at the end of the auditorium and on the steps leading from the balcony we see her husband . . . a great brute-peasant, flushed with drink, brandishing a whip . . . Transfixed, arms outstretched to ward off the familiar blow, the mother stares at him . . . Then slowly he moves down towards her – the lights follow him . . . until he reaches her . . . Like a flail it descends . . . again, and again. Pavel her son dashes on . . . wrenches the whip away and sends his father reeling to the floor. The lights black out – to come on again at a point on the balcony where men are talking, factory workers. It fades on them and goes back to the

mother's home – goes back to another spot which is the factory gates where a meeting is being held – and so on . . . Finally comes the day when Pavel is to be let out of prison. This scene builds to a tremendous climax. We see him at one end of the theatre on the narrow balcony. In front of him blocking his way, is an iron barred door. The gaoler unlocks it slowly . . . But there is another door to halt his impetuous rush forwards – and this is unlocked while he shakes the iron bars impatiently – only to find, as he slams it behind him, yet another in front of him. So it goes on, the whole length of the theatre, music accompanying him all the way. At last he bursts through the ultimate door, rushes down the centre aisle to his home. Mother is standing in the beam of light, arms outstretched, saying nothing, tears streaming down her face. He flings himself into her arms . . .[72]

The critic Yuri Yuzovsky responded to the close sense of intimate contact between actor and audience which the production generated:

There arose the impulse to move towards Nilovna [the mother] and Pavel Vlasov [the son], even to enter into conversation with them . . . Nilovna . . . came down the steps into the auditorium and, having done so, spontaneously turned to one of the audience with a few words . . . similar to the way in which, for example, someone turns to you in the tram with a request to pass your fare down the car for a ticket and you simply do it without thinking. And at precisely that moment, the whole audience felt itself in the position of that individual spectator, and there arose, so to speak, a supreme contact between both sides.[73]

Van Gyseghem referred to this quality of contact during the scene in which the mother is preparing a meal on the day she hears of her son's imminent release from prison. She is so full of her feelings of the moment that they boil over into conversation with members of the audience about what a wonderful lad Pavel is. She discovers, in mid conversation, that her hands are full and so passes a loaf of bread to a member of the audience to hold, while another helps her spread a table cloth. 'She has played a whole scene alone, yet we feel she had told all her neighbours about it. We share her delight and envy her happiness – those members of the audience that have been actually included in the scene have in some way stretched the veil of illusion to include us all.'[74]

Critical response appears to have been fairly muted. Fevralsky referred to E.P. Melnikova's creation of a touching and powerful image as the mother and to N.S. Plotnikov, who acted the role of the proletarian activist, Nakhidka, with tenderness and conviction. The production also included the great Georgian actress Veriko Andzhaparidze in the small role of Sofia Vasilyevna, who 'charmed the audience with the excited lyricism which she brought to bear on the portrayal of the brave woman revolutionary, although the critics contrived to ignore the remarkable mastery of the artist'.[75]

Okhlopkov's next production, which took place the following year, was another dramatisation of a novel – A. Serafimovich's *The Iron Flood* based on the 1918 campaign of the Taman army which, finding itself surrounded by anti-Bolshevik forces, retreated from the Kuban and set out across the Caucasus Mountain range to link up with the Red Army led by Kozhukh, an almost superhuman leader who had risen from a peasant background to officer rank during World War I. The novel deals with both the sufferings and privations of the group of men, women and children and the attempts of Kozhukh to mould a heterogenous mixture of unruly and bloodthirsty deserters, mutinous sailors and Bolsheviks into a collective unit. This is all done with implacable optimism, using the techniques of the *bylina* (Russian folk epic) and engaging the reader's sympathetic and suspenseful interest in the journey of a filthy and ragged mob through terrors both man-made and natural until they reach the Promised Land of the Soviet state. Throughout, Serafimovich is concerned to show 'the guiding and directing role of the Communist Party'.[76] The mass is shown without individual, differentiating characteristics, with no separate personalities, the only individual portrait being that of a Menshevik traitor.

Accounts of Okhlopkov's dramatised version of the novel suggest that he strove for something quite different from this. He managed to make his twenty actors seem a veritable army but one in which the depiction of the mass was qualitatively different from the norm:

> It is this qualitative difference which Okhlopkov conveys. There is not one person who is like another . . . Each has his or her own colour – one holds his rifle in a peculiar fashion, the other has an idiosyncratic way of wearing his clothes; a variant kind of humour, a special means of expressing sadness. The monumental Garpina is placed alongside the lyrical Anka, the bearded man in the German forage cap and bare chest is placed alongside the bowed soldier with his cap pulled tightly on his head and with his coat buttoned to the neck. And Okhlopkov clashes these contrasting characters together just as he juxtaposes the events, love and death, and the contrast between tragic and comic emotions.[77]

The strongest impression the critics recorded was the way in which Okhlopkov sought to involve the audience in the life of this group of people, whether marching or camping out under the stars, performing everyday activities such as washing linen, lighting campfires, cooking and eating. This attempt to involve the audience began outside the auditorium when the people queueing in the foyer were suddenly startled by the auditorium doors bursting open and two of the cast rushing through the crowd. Through the entrance doors could be seen a mound extending the length of the auditorium over which stretched the blue dome of the sky. One end of the raised hillside was screened with bushes. As they entered, the audience was greeted by the cracking of whips, the grinding of cart wheels and the sound of singing. As they made their way to their seats, they had to step over soldiers lying round a campfire, duck under washing lines, avoid a soldier's rifle muzzle as he cleaned it, remove a frying pan from the seat in order to sit down. As described by van Gyseghem, 'The whole of one side of this rectangular-shaped auditorium had been built up into a bank, rising to about five feet at its highest point. It is rocky, uneven, a sort of semi-mountainous terrain, and long tongues of it jut right out into the centre of the hall and curl round at the ends. In between these jutting tongues the audience sits.'[78] Women were shouting at each other, babies crying, men yelling orders, lovers quarrelling, a group singing to the accompaniment of an harmonica and, overall, hung the smell of cooking. Okhlopkov bent every sinew of the production to involve the spectator totally in the experience so that, by the end, he emerged exhausted. As Norris Houghton recalled: 'That night was one of the most exciting I spent in Moscow . . . I came out trembling on the surface and profoundly moved within. Here was theatre that was life.'[79]

The two soldiers who had, earlier, dashed through the crowd in the foyer, returned with the water they had been sent to fetch as people gathered round a campfire in the half-light. The audience could see the night sky, the stars and the clouds scudding over the Black Sea. During the course of the action wounded soldiers crawled in pain across the feet of members of the audience; children died and mothers mourned agonisingly; a boy was killed and died in the arms of the partisans; another woman went mad and threw her child from a cliff. The characters openly 'made love', swore and 'defecated'. Life was depicted in 'its earthy crudity, its greedy carnality'. There were suggestions that there might be cynicism and even pornography in some of the scenes. 'But', says Okhlopkov, 'here are my cossacks. I am not ashamed to show them at their most disgusting and most beautiful. From them, real people will grow.'[80]

Most successful of all the scenes was that of the camp by night, where Okhlopkov managed to suffuse the whole with an intense lyrical poetry, in which Shtoffer's design played a large part:

> Night. Stars, waggons, quiet conversation, an old cossack sings a song. A woman feeds a child, a cossack kisses a girl – in various parts of the camp a little scene sparks up then dies down, and over everything, over the audience, over the people of Taman, reigns the high sky full of stars. This is poetry! And the spectator, carried away by the picture, can already sense the crackle of the fires, the neighing of tethered horses and the scent of grass . . . In this density, carnality, passion, black-earthiness, things palpably visual and full of weight – devoid of any beautification or aestheticism – lies the truth of this production.[81]

The finale, when the tired and ragged army joined up with the main body of the Red Army, sealed the bond between stage and audience:

> Finally . . . the main body is sighted. The excitement mounts as the news spreads, the whole company pours on to the rocky steppe, shading its eyes, peering into the distance. Yes! – it is our friends, our comrades – and crying and laughing they rush forward to greet – US! . . . the iron flood breaks over us, our hands are clasped by the gnarled hands of bearded peasants, woman greets woman with a warm embrace and the children dart in among the seats throwing themselves at us with cries of delight.[82]

Moments such as these seek comparison with the festivals organised by Jean-Louis David during the French revolution, the published scenarios of which Okhlopkov found 'among the most fascinating documents of art'.[83]

Critics accused the production of 'anarchism' and 'naturalism'. There was also what was described as a lack of dramatic amplitude and development in the characters, so that it became difficult to sympathise with them. The most telling critical points were made by the, otherwise enthusiastic, Yuri Yuzovsky, who suggested that, if the average artist is pleased when his painting 'speaks', Okhlopkov wanted his canvas to shriek out loud. If the average artist was satisfied with one colour, Okhlopkov wanted three and painted them on so thickly that the colour positively dripped from the canvas.[84] At crucial moments, such as the panegyric over the dead soldier, despite the weeping of the women, the speeches, the flag waving, the solemn procession and the singing, the spectators felt little or nothing, 'even the dirty war-tattered Red Flag made no difference to them'.[85] This was because there had been no psychological character development of the dead soldier. Nobody knew who he was or anything about him, so why should any audience feel moved by his death? It was impossible to generate genuine feeling simply by laying emotion on with a trowel. The production was guilty of excess on several counts. The women not only wiped away tears but declaimed their sobbing to the entire building for a whole minute. If corpses appeared, they did so with 'their heads thick with blood, glassy eyed'. This, according to Yuzovsky, was both false naturalism and hyperbole:

> We meet it with him too often: Kozhukh's wife laughs with the terrible laughter of a mad woman again and again – so as to physically subjugate the spectator. Tired people walk in a circle along the highway, and then once more in an even more exhausted fashion, then again and again in order, so to speak, to work hypnotically on the spectator so that he himself experiences the exhaustion.[86]

The production was most true, emotionally, when it was not striving for effect – as at the end of the funeral scene, when a woman sang a sad song, followed by a pause and the melancholy sigh of a cossack, which was followed by another pause. This was worth far more than all the funeral rhetoric and the processing with the corpse. The fallaciousness of the latter lay in the fact that the audience was presented with a result but not with the process leading up to the result. No matter how well Melnikova acted when she threw the child from the cliff, for the audience the 'child' remained an inert bundle of rags. If, on the other hand, the story of her relationship with the child had been told beforehand, then the audience would have been able to respond. Similarly, with the scene where Kozhukh's wife has lost her reason and laughs and cries clutching the child to her breast. This was rendered powerful by the fact that the actual scene of the woman, alone in the camp, surrounded by the sounds of cannon-fire, had been prepared for by an intimate scene between the mother and child (powerfully acted by the actress Ekk) in which the father also participated and which won the sympathy of the audience. The truth of this was apparent, without the director having to double or treble the 'colouring' of madness.[87]

Even the conclusion seemed false, because there had been no real drama in the way in which dangers and obstacles had been overcome, leading to the final victory. The character of Kozhukh was also something of a disappointment. He was shown to be just like everyone else when he needed to be shown as exceptional. Why, after all, was he the leader? There was insufficient that was epic and legendary about him. Nevertheless, the production had its positive moments – the 'beautiful scene' with the scouts and the plundering and costume changing, the scene of the dancing and the altogether more unified second act, the scene of the night camp and, throughout, the simple accompanying music of Golubentsev. Yuzovsky's conclusion was that the theatre desperately needed a dramatist and also needed to give freedom to the actor to create character. 'The mass yes, but the individual character as well.'[88]

Fevralsky, summarising the general tone of the criticism some years later, was more damning: 'The production turned out to be miniaturised, innumerable everyday trivialities in which genre scenes were thrust to the fore. Every scene was worked out in detail, but in a naturalistic fashion . . .'[89] There was too much emphasis on 'biology' and 'pathology' and there was a number of scenes which were 'risqué', even crude. Okhlopkov confessed to his 'mistakes' when, writing in 1959, he said he had produced a mixture of naturalism with romanticism and conventionality: 'Where but a small hint would have sufficed, Shtoffer and I tried to produce "real" roads winding between "real" hills and even mountains . . . But all the spectators had to do was stretch out a hand and they could touch the "road" and convince themselves that the "bumps" in the road were stage props.'[90]

For his next production Okhlopkov turned, significantly, to a play rather than to a dramatised version of a novel and, after the earlier drama about collectivisation, chose a play with a Five-Year Plan theme about the building of the White Sea Canal, which had the incidental theme of social rehabilitation and moral reclamation. The play in question was Nikolai Pogodin's *Aristocrats* and the highly original setting was designed by a triumvirate, referred to on the poster as Ka-Ge-Ka (KGK) – Boris Knoblok, Vera Gitsevich and Victor Koretsky. Despite his use of conventions borrowed from Chinese and Japanese theatre and despite his obvious debt to Meyerhold, the production (after some initial hostility) proved to be Okhlopkov's greatest critical success during his Realistic Theatre period. He felt there was a strong, popular element in Pogodin's writing and sought to capture its spirit in a 'production-carnival'. This prompted some critics to describe the production as a 'holiday' possessing the kind of significance for Soviet theatre in the 1930s as had Vakhtangov's production of *Princess Turandot* in the early 1920s. In it 'theatricality had been rehabilitated in expressing the pathos of life'.[91] As such, Okhlopkov's production was a direct challenge to the realistic style adopted by Boris Zakhava in his production of the same play at the Vakhtangov Theatre, also in 1935. Here the focus was on the psychological experience of one of the criminals and failed to come to grips with the humour of the play, a humour which has caused someone like Pogodin to be described as 'a city joker, the intelligent scholar, the François Villon of our day'.[92]

The play is set in a prison camp somewhere in the Baltic region and concerns the use of inmates in the construction of the Baltic – White Sea Canal. The inmates of the camp are both criminal and political prisoners, who first oppose any co-operation with the project and, through it, with the Soviet regime. The two central characters are a Cheka (Security Police) official, Gromov (the camp administrator) and Kostya Dorokhov, a thief, who emerges as the leader of the criminal faction and who shifts the balance of forces from rejection to acceptance as he responds to the challenge and experiences a kind of moral and spiritual rebirth. This has prompted some commentators to describe the work as a modern miracle play.[93]

Once again, Okhlopkov and his designers completely reorganised the

24 Sketch by Ya. Shtoffer of set for Pogodin's *Aristocrats* (1935)

auditorium space and the audience's relationship to the events. Two large oblong platforms, rounded at one end and each measuring 5 metres by 3.5 metres, were placed corner to corner in the centre of the auditorium and raised about a metre from the ground, providing a playing length, wall to wall, of 14.6 metres. Both platforms were covered with canvas and the audience was placed around three sides of it. Because of the way the platform and the seating was arranged, there was great intimacy between actor and spectator, the furthest distance between them in any part of the auditorium being 5 metres. The only decor consisted of three large panels along one side of the theatre which were painted with designs symbolic of the seasons and were changed for each act. In act 1, for example, the panels were yellowy-grey and pearly-lilac in tone with conventionalised illustrations of the kind of animals which frequent the *taiga* regions of Russia. The panels of act 2 were coloured spring green and decorated with various kinds of plant. Act 3 consisted of red-painted panels with flying seagulls in white depicted on them. Additional elements were a pine tree which 'grew' next to one of the platforms, up which a toy squirrel climbed in one scene, with astonishing, life-like effect. At another moment, 'an owl on a snowy pine bough against a grey-blue sky indicated that it was winter; apple blossoms against a lemon-yellow background suggested that spring had come . . . Or when a table was required two . . . men would enter with a piece of green baize which, squatting on the floor, they would hold taut between them to suggest the table top.'[94]

This last detail gives an indication of the importance of the *zanni* in this production. In the Russian theatre, the use of conventionalised 'proscenium servants' went back at least as far as Meyerhold's 1910 production of *Don Juan* at the Alexandrinsky Theatre in Petersburg. Probably the other most famous variant of their use was in Vakhtangov's 1922 production of *Princess Turandot*, where they were more obviously connected with the traditions of *commedia dell'arte*. In Okhlopkov's case the use of 'stage servants' was similar to that of the *kurogo*, or black-hooded attendants who assist the actors on stage in Japanese *Kabuki* drama. Apart from their use in the manner just instanced, the scenes in which they were involved to most striking effect were the opening one, in which prisoners arrived at the camp in a 'snowstorm' created by the *zanni*, who scattered white confetti over the actors and the audience; during a 'skiing' scene, in which they created a sensation of movement by running, bearing branches, past a stationary skier; and in an escape scene, during which Kostya engaged in a knife fight with an escapee in the canal, where the effect of water was created by the *zanni* who unfolded a large piece of green satin, which they waved in the air to catch the light, thus producing an impression of moving water. At other points – whenever Gromov used the telephone, for example – a masked figure, dressed in pale-blue dungarees would spring lightly to his side with the implement and then disappear with it when Gromov had finished his conversation.

The performance began with the sound of a gong. Immediately, the lights dimmed before flaring up again on a dozen figures clad in blue scattered about the stage. Music sounded, like a snowstorm, as the figures began to rush about the platform throwing clouds of white confetti at the audience and at each other. Soon the air was full of whirling flakes as the figures rushed about faster and faster so that, eventually, the air was so thick that little was visible. On the platform, figures appeared, seeming to be caught by the wind, huddled together against the cold, the actors leaning forward, as if into a tempest. Then everything calmed down and the entire auditorium was seen to be covered with a mantle of snow with flakes even clinging to the spectators' eyelashes. The attendants then left the stage without having uttered a word.

Comparable devices were employed in the skiing scene. A gong sounded. The lights came up on an actress dressed in a tracksuit and wearing skis, a lock of hair sticking out from under her ski-hat. She stood on a piece of thick white rug in a pool of light, pulling on her gloves, tightening the straps of her skis, while music played quietly in the background. The music then began to increase in tempo and the girl started to move her legs on the spot while, past her, ran those same figures clad in blue. One was bent double and carried a branch of fir, another bore a pine branch, a third caused her hat to be knocked off, then came the branch of a shrub, then a fourth and a fifth, still more, constantly faster and faster. The skier bent to dodge the branches, body bent supply, eyes glowing with exhilaration. Then she suddenly registered panic as a 'rock' loomed ahead of her, threw up her arms and went over on her face as the music crashed to silence and the lights faded.

In the scene of the knife fight in the canal, the satin cloth was stretched over the entire surface of one of the platforms with holes cut in it at irregular intervals. It was secured at two of the corners, while the other two were held by the masked attendants who raised it and lowered it causing the surface to billow and tremble. The dimly-lit scene was again accompanied by music. The renegade escapee emerged out of the shadows with a knife in his hand and plunged under the cloth, which was then agitated by the attendants as the music grew wilder. Kostya appeared and plunged in after him and both their humped forms could be seen under the cloth, which was waved agitatedly to indicate their underwater struggle. The renegade's arm, clutching the knife, emerged through one of the holes as if about to strike but was then arrested by Kostya's arm emerging, clutching it and dragging it down under the surface again. The struggle continued as they both came to the surface and then disappeared again before, finally, Kostya's arm appeared bearing the knife which was then struck downwards. The music grew quieter as a shape could be seen making for the shore. A figure emerged from under the edge of the cloth and lay 'washed up' without any strength left. Meanwhile, in the middle of the canal, the huddled shape of the dead renegade could be seen as 'gently, idly, the "waves" flopped' over Kostya, whose exhausted body lay half in, half out of the water.[95]

A single masked figure was used to great emotional effect in a spring scene in which a violinist attempted a moral seduction of the prostitute, Sonya, following an interview with Gromov, who has attempted to woo her away from her past life. Large artificial flowers were strewn about the platform to suggest a field in spring as Sonya strolled about the sun-soaked meadow with the sounds and smells mingling in her thoughts and feelings together with the words of Gromov. All this was suggested by a masked violinist in blue, who stepped on to the stage playing 'the sweet thrilling tale of a new life'. There then followed a cat and mouse game as Sonya first fled from the seductive sounds of the violin which continued to pursue her, reappearing suddenly out of the shadows into the pool of light which followed her about the platform. Finally the 'musician is playing as though his soul were in his bow, close up to her, pouring the rich sounds into her being. She laughs, with joy this time, and flings herself on the ground, touching the flowers, stretching her body against the earth as though for the first time, exulting. The music rises to a triumphant climax – the lights fade.'[96]

According to Yuzovsky, theatricality in this production was not just a tendency to present stylish and effective spectacle for its own sake, but a striving to express theatrically the very essence of facts, events, people, and 'to express them *positively*'.[97] He was especially impressed by the portrayal of the camp officers, the

'Chekists'. There was none of the saccharine falseness which usually accompanied the portrayal of a communist and which usually denoted a hypocritical author's or director's desire to fawn and flatter. Neither was there an aspect of that tendency to create 'lifelikeness' by introducing artificial 'deficiencies' to counter the complaint that all 'positive' heroes were schematic and lifeless because they were unblemished and innocent. Adding a little bit of criminality here, a touch of drunkenness there, just a hint of corruption and a percentage of opportunism did not add up to a more realistic 'positive' hero. In this instance, according to Yuzovsky, you had the real thing: 'How strongly, simply, manfully, lovingly the Chekists are portrayed . . . Not a trace of falseness . . . Chekist Gromov is alive . . . The very activity of these people is the source of their living quality. It is shown to us.'[98]

This was especially apparent in a scene during which Gromov converted two criminals by demonstrating that he trusted them:

> He throws each a rifle and, having done so, freezes for a moment looking them in the face with a smile, broadly spreading wide his arms before them as if opening up his breast . . . Is he giving himself up to a firing squad, this person dressed in white with a crimson star on his white helmet standing, smiling, in the blue light of a spotlamp?[99]

Gromov was, in fact, indicating to former Red Army men Petipa and Pyzhov that he trusted them enough to send them, armed, on guard duty. Here everything 'transports the episode into the metaphorical plane of the parable', as the men caught the rifles and held them to their faces, 'to hide a tearful grimace'.[100]

There was a grotesque scene in the bathhouse where half-naked prisoners stood under the 'showers' chattering and laughing or beating themselves with *veniki*.[101] It was like 'a comic version of Dante's Hell', a mass of bare legs, naked backs and shoulders, bearded faces, long-haired, dishevelled heads; here a cynical joker, there an obliging scoundrel; two former priests like souls in purgatory; an independent bandit – an 'original', who has a cold and therefore entered the shower fully clothed. The remainder were just 'strong muscles, prehensile hands and crudely fashioned legs designed to stamp the earth flat and all human life with it'.[102]

The following is an effective evocation of a love scene:

> A gong sounds. Light strikes part of the set. Two large boxes. A storehouse. Kostya Kapitan and Margarita are sitting on boxes. He has an accordion. She a cigarette. The bellows of the accordion breathe fragments of song. The cigarette which the woman is smoking is removed from her mouth by Kostya. The accordion breathes a bit more then the hand puts aside the cigarette. Its path, divided into minute sections marks out the inner suspension of the lovers from all that surrounds them. The land of the taiga with its cold savagery flies from them, like a comet. The weight of existence also. The cigarette traces a path like a tiny comet. The music divides its track into sections. The sections render this track long. The sighs of the accordion and the movement of the hand with the cigarette on the parabola – a last chord – and a kiss.[103]

The apotheosis of the process of spiritual 'reforging' was reached at the moment when Kostya and Sonya challenged each other to a contest. This episode took place in the camp eating quarters. 'Overfulfil the plan by 120 per cent!' shouted Kostya, throwing an aluminium plate the length of a long table into

Sonya's hands. '130 per cent' she answered, sending the plate flying back. '140 per cent! . . . 150!!!' The duel of the plates was conducted with great excitement with a sense that unexpected energy was suddenly bursting out along fresh channels.'[104]

The discussion of the production which took place was chaired by Andrei Vyshinsky,[105] who had just been appointed procurator of the USSR. He questioned the play's educational value and accused the theatre of romanticising the criminal world. Okhlopkov and Pogodin countered the arguments energetically, Okhlopkov working himself up into such a state that, at one point, he had to leave the hall to recover.[106] Shortly after this, *Pravda* and other newspapers published favourable reviews. Konstantin Trenyov described it as 'a brilliant production'.[107] Brecht saw it and was very impressed, suggesting to Okhlopkov, during the 1950s, that he revive it. 'Young people must see what genuine theatricality is like.'[108] Unfortunately, the version which Okhlopkov staged at the Mayakovsky Theatre in 1956 was a pale copy of the original which had so impressed one critic that he described it as a production which 'poses the most serious questions and obliges us to behave towards the Okhlopkov collective with great attentiveness and care'.[109] The fact that nobody treated this sound advice with the same 'attentiveness and care' was demonstrated when, within two years the theatre was closed.[110]

Okhlopkov never abandoned his idea of a large-scale, popular theatre for the masses and his interest in this possibility was always linked with folk art, popular performance of one kind or another, including amateur performance, which he sought to encourage at every possible opportunity. In 1926, the first Theatre of Folk Art was established in Moscow in the premises of a former music hall and Okhlopkov was invited to become artistic director, with Igor Moiseyev in charge of choreography. The main purpose of the enterprise was to stage theatrical concerts by amateur groups. In preparing the theatre's first programme, Okhlopkov was at pains to stress the creative links between professional and amateur art. He combined choirs, orchestras and dance ensembles, preceded by a carnival procession through the auditorium in which the actors (who included workers constructing the Moscow underground) took part. In the event, Okhlopkov's association with this theatre was short-lived, but Igor Moiseyev acquired the idea for his famous Folk Dance Company from work conducted with amateurs during his period at the Theatre of Folk Art.[111]

Okhlopkov's next production at the Realistic Theatre in 1936, of Shakespeare's *Othello*, was a critical failure, despite the fact that he approached it from an angle based on the study of 'the folk culture of the epoch', which enthralled him, and elements of which he felt he detected in the play. He wanted to stage it as a piece of street theatre, involving something reminiscent of pageant-waggons processing from station to station. In addition to this, he reintroduced versions of the stage servants from *Aristocrats* and even brought in an Italian choir which accompanied Othello's 'Farewell . . .' speech in act 3, scene 3. Okhlopkov did not appear to have any clear philosophical conception of the play but, typically, tended to imagine it in terms of striking imagery – Othello sitting in the pose of Rodin's 'Thinker', with a naked Desdemona spread-eagled before him on the grass. He also tended towards an interpretation of the play along Russian literary lines. He saw Othello's killing of Desdemona as being reminiscent of Leskov's *The Enchanted Wanderer* and Dostoesvky's *The Idiot*, where men seek to spare women the unbearable pain of life by killing them.[112]

If the principle behind *Aristocrats* had been that of a 'production-carnival', as the poster advertising it declared, then the principle adopted in the case of *Othello* was that of the 'production-procession'. Okhlopkov and his designer, Boris Knoblok, hit on the central image of a gondola as a symbol of Venice, split into two sections fore and aft and jutting through the centre of the auditorium, almost dividing it in two. In the middle, between the two halves of the gondola was a raised acting area which could be reached from entrances up four ramps which cut diagonally across the entire auditorium and along which the actors 'processed' in palanquins and on 'stretchers' carried by black-clad stage servants. The fore and aft sections of the gondola contained seating space for a women's choir, members of the senate, Othello's army, etc. One end wall was covered with a drape with the symbol of the lion of St Mark emblazoned at its centre, while above the acting area there hung a huge boom with an ensign and furled sail, which could be lowered to convert the gondola into an ocean-going galleon. The walls of the theatre were hung with black silk and the black rostra were polished to a high sheen. The stage servants wore black leotards and the specially scented palanquins which they bore were also painted black on the outside. This device lent itself to some remarkable transformation scenes. When, for example, a palanquin was carried in, all the audience could see were the brightly costumed characters inside, apparently being borne weightlessly through thin air. When the palanquins were placed on the central acting area their four sides were let down to reveal the most ornate interiors which had been hand-sewn in gold thread by a brigade of seamstresses who had worked on them for three months. In fact all the costumes and properties were fashioned with extraordinary lavishness and care.

The costumes were worked out in detail to quattrocento designs and showed up brilliantly against the black background. All the elements of the setting were portable. For example, in the scene of the arrival on Cyprus, the prow of Othello's 'flagship' approached the central rostrum, consisting of a painted device carried on stretcher rails upon which stood Iago. This was followed by the 'boat' itself, painted in separate sections like shields, and carried past by the stage servants, some of whom also carried the masts and sails. This was followed by the stern of the vessel (once again carried stretcher fashion, shoulder high) bearing Othello and Desdemona still in their wedding finery. The 'flagship' was accompanied by a squadron of miniature model galleons, like a flock of escorting seagulls, all with snowy-white sails carried past by the *zanni*.

The latter had their counterparts in the *maîtresses de scènes*, clothed in black and wearing white masks, placed on low eight-sided rostra, together with all the necessary properties, which they handed to the actors as required (the fatal handkerchief, a sword, etc.) As action also took place on side rostra, the original idea had been to install swivel seats so that the audience could turn to face the action. When this proposal was abandoned because of the expense involved, it was suggested that all the seats be taken out and that the audience be encouraged to 'process' with the action. In the event, the production retained its more conventional seating arrangements and restricted its experimentation to the setting alone.[113]

Okhlopkov next planned the production of a mass spectacle in the Central Park of Culture and Rest, using an existing theatre, the lake, outside stages and open squares. His idea was to stage a version of Alexei Tolstoy's novel *Bread* and to introduce documentary film sequences. Shostakovich agreed to supply the music and Betty Glan, a movement specialist, was to assist with the mass scenes. Unfortunately, the project never materialised. Okhlopkov was also employed in a consultative capacity by the Kiev soviet in connection with a grandiose project for the construction of a mass theatre on the banks of the river Dnieper. The plan was to use a natural slope overlooking the river as an amphitheatre for 30 to 40 thousand people and install three acting areas at the foot, including one on the water dispersed on different types of flotation which could be adapted for water sports, and another on the sandy slope of Trukhanov Island – the latter to be used mainly for pyrotechnic displays. This project also failed to come to fruition.[114] Okhlopkov spoke, at this time, of walking the streets of Moscow in company with Sergei Eisenstein, both dreaming of expropriating different buildings or spaces for some spectacular entertainment or other. Later, Okhlopkov was to contemplate staging Pushkin's *Boris Godunov* in the Kremlin itself.[115]

In 1937, Okhlopkov appeared in the first of two films made by Mikhail Romm about Lenin in which Boris Shchukin[116] played the part of the Soviet leader. He planned a production of his friend Bertolt Brecht's play, *St Joan of the Stockyards*, retitled *The Saintly Fool*, but, instead, embarked on a dramatisation of Romain Rolland's novel of Burgundian life, *Colas Breugnon* which contained for Okhlopkov, as it did for Rolland, that 'spirit of festive mood' which the former felt was so important in the theatre. Okhlopkov conceived the production as 'a poem of light' filling the theatre with the atmosphere of sunny Burgundy. He was struck by the musicality of Rolland's folk speech and imagined the unique language and bright colouring of the original in terms of a 'folk ballad' about a people's poet, Colas, a legendary character of epic proportions.[117]

The pantheistic spirit which breathed through Okhlopkov's production of *Running Start* could be felt in *Colas Breugnon*, which was filled with the nature poetry which Okhlopkov also felt flowing through Rolland's *roman-fleuve, Jean-Christophe*, from which he was fond of quoting the following:

> Everything is music for a musical spirit. Everything which wavers and moves, trembles and breathes, – sunny summer days and the whistle of the night wind, streaming light and flickering stars, storm, the chirping of birds, the humming of insects, the rustling of leaves, the voices of those we love or hate, all the usual domestic noises, the creaking of doors, the noise of blood in the ears in the stillness of the night, – everything which exists is music; you only have to hear it.[118]

Breugnon himself was testimony to the power of imagination and the stimulating power of great literature as when, following an accident, he is forced to take to his bed with a volume of Plutarch, 'the enchanted eyes of the old Burgundian saw between the lines vanished battles, destroyed cities, Roman orators and severe warriors, heroes with beauties leading them by the nose, wide windy plains, the sparkling sea with the gleam of eastern skies and a world which has vanished'. What appealed to Okhlopkov about Breugnon was that he, too, knew how to dream, how to fantasise. This was contrasted with his son-in-law, Florimand who, whilst Breugnon's imagination was full of the blare of trumpets, the sound of chariot wheels and the noise of battle, looked out of the window, yawned, and said: 'If only there was so much as a cat about on the street today!'[119]

The central image of the production was a soft green lawn shaded by a Burgundian oak under which the acting rostrum was placed in the centre of the auditorium. The rostrum itself was made of freshly cut wooden boards, stacked in a square, which pervaded the auditorium with the sweet smell of the new wood, from which Breugnon carved his sculptures. Other scenic details consisted of the Duke's tower, with a raised drawbridge, placed against the wooden wall where the original Realistic Theatre stage had been. The walls of the auditorium were hung with tapestries showing panoramas of Burgundy, including hunting scenes, castles and people on horseback. Other playing areas were placed around the walls and these were hung with grape vines. At one point a real live donkey made its appearance as the curé rode through, blessing the audience. The play opened with a bucolic scene set at the 'island' of timber in the centre, around which the characters sat feasting from the piles of real food and fruit. To increase the sense of realism, Okhlopkov had his actors toss oranges and apples to the audience and a specific quantity of fruit was part of the theatre's budget for each evening of the production's run.[120]

The general feeling of the critics was that the formal conception suffered as a result of the attempt to create a 'holiday mood' at all costs. This led to a lack of unity between form and content and to the inclusion of a good deal which was superfluous. The one bright spot was the performance of V. Belenkaya in the role of Lasochka. V. Novikov was considered rather lightweight for the role of Breugnon. Because public response to his work at the Realistic Theatre had not been especially favourable and because his critical reception had not stimulated public interest, Okhlopkov's best actors, including the wife of the German director Erwin Piscator, Vera Yanukova, began to leave the theatre. Okhlopkov's future plans included a production of Goldoni's *Mistress of the Inn, Ugryum River* by V. Shishkov, a version of *The Lay of Igor's Campaign* and works by Gogol, Ostrovsky, Dostoevsky and Tolstoy. However, in the event, the Realistic Theatre company was dissolved 'by some bureaucrat' who 'in the strength of his intelligent non-comprehension'[121] merged the remnants with Tairov's company at the Kamerny, in August 1937. Okhlopkov's theatre was handed over to the puppet master, Sergei Obraztsov. During the unsettled year which Okhlopkov spent with Tairov, he directed one production, at Tairov's suggestion, of a play by the little-known Arkadi Perventsev, who adapted a play from his own novel *Kochubey*, about the legendary cossack leader, Ivan Kochubey, who sacrificed his life when coming to the aid of Stalin at Tsaritsyn, during the civil war.

Reviewing the production, Pavel Markov felt that the adaptation of the novel had resulted in a mechanical compression of scenes and the consequent loss of much of the richness of the novel, including the subtle and convincing portrait of Kochubey himself – the 'bright and charming' commander of the cavalry brigade who was 'an authentic popular hero'. Okhlopkov had tried to compensate for some of the deficiencies of the scenario by resorting to his usual theatrical means, but this had not been done in his customary 'mischievous' directorial style and the means were neither 'deliberately harsh nor carelessly awkward'. The general atmosphere of the novel had been finely achieved and intelligently felt, in particular 'the peculiar tenderness and charm' of Perventsev's authorial style. The central characters were shown with a serious, thoughtful and exciting simplicity of a kind unusual with Okhlopkov (according to Markov) and unusual in the treatment of civil war themes generally. It was precisely this simplicity and charm which constituted the positive value of the Kamerny Theatre's new production.[122]

Unfortunately, when the production was almost ready, Tairov and Okhlopkov had disagreements about the interpretation of the central character. Okhlopkov would not re-examine his conception, nor would he agree to take the production off. Following the unsuccessful premiere, Okhlopkov and a section of the former Realistic Theatre company left the Kamerny in October 1938 and transferred to the Theatre of Drama. The merger had lasted thirteen months.

In 1939, Okhlopkov made his second appearance in Mikhail Romm's series of films about Lenin with the legendary Boris Shchukin whom Okhlopkov had long admired as an actor and whom he recalled performing in a nineteenth-century vaudeville, *Lev Gurich Sinichkin*, at the Vakhtangov Theatre in 1925, when he acted 'with such depth of soul, with such rich multifarious art, that all the spectators, myself included, frequently wiped away tears'.[123] It was also during this theatrically 'fallow' period that Okhlopkov made his own memorable acting contribution, as Vasili Buslay, in Eisenstein's film *Alexander Nevsky* in 1938. In 1940, he created the role of the great Russian bass singer Chaliapin in Sergei Yutkevich's film, *Yakov Sverdlov*.

Towards the end of the 1930s, the Soviet theatre was becoming increasingly dominated by an unadventurous 'realism' which sought to justify itself in terms which derived their authority from the officially sanctioned pre-eminence of the Moscow Art Theatre. At a meeting in the House of the Actor, devoted to the theme 'Tradition and Innovation', Okhlopkov scandalised the audience by publicly criticising the Art Theatre production of *Tartuffe*, in which Kedrov and Toporkov[124] had carefully followed Stanislavsky's instructions during their long and painstaking work. 'The Art Theatre has captured everything', declared Okhlopkov scathingly in terms which were meant deliberately to recall the revolution, 'GITIS, VTO[125]. . . The only place MKhAT has not captured is the Post Office and the Telegraph Agency . . .'[126]

Okhlopkov's stay at the Theatre of Drama was short-lived but it was not long before the head of the Vakhtangov Theatre, V.V. Kuza, invited him to supplement the directors' staff and join the incumbent Reuben Simonov, Alexei Diky, Boris Zakhava and Iosif Rapoport.[127] This was a formidable quartet by any standards and Okhlopkov's incorporation into the network was bound to provoke difficulties. There was an immediate personality clash between himself and Diky, who expressed ironic amusement when Okhlopkov enthused about a possible production based on Gogol's *Taras Bulba*. In his conversation with the actors, Okhlopkov described his vision of the production as 'Mighty like the music of Mussorgsky; full of national distinctiveness, sappy, strong and sharply etched, like images from a canvas by Surikov; depicted with such "bursting inner energy", breadth and scope, like the Repin portrait of the Zaparozhean cossacks!'[128] The production was never realised and, in consonance with the somewhat nationalistic spirit of the times, which had led to a revaluation of Russia's historical past, Okhlopkov turned to a play by Vladimir Solovyov about the legendary, real-life Fieldmarshal Kutuzov, conqueror of Napoleon in 1812.

The play was written in verse and exploited certain devices of the historical chronicle-drama tradition such as soliloquies, a large cast and several changes of scene. As Harold Segel has pointed out,[129] the play contained elements which were symptomatic of the times, such as the spirit of Russian nationalism, which intensified the more imminent war became. Other elements included the exaltation of 'Russianness' – the people (*narod*) are shown to be the backbone of the campaign against the enemy and Kutuzov emerges as the extension of the people's will. Another aspect of the play was the shadow cast over the loyalty of non-Russian or people of non-Russian origin within the borders of the state, especially Germans.

Okhlopkov felt that Solovyov's play, far from being a play about the *narod*, was, in fact, what he called a 'general's play', in that it seemed to attribute the success of the campaign against Napoleon to the genius of one man, rather than to the genius of the Russian people. He therefore set out to correct this imbalance. Working with the designers Vladimir Dmitriev and Boris Erdman,[130] he decided to construct the stage in the form of a triptych, so that three separate streams of action could be synchronised and staged simultaneously. The idea was to dispense with the logic of sequential development so that what the spectator saw was not the sum of the episodes but the effect produced by their simultaneous juxtaposition. He wanted to counterpose scenes involving Napoleon with those involving Kutuzov. He also wanted to show a contrast between the death of a French soldier in the frozen wastes of Russia and a scene, somewhere in France, of the soldier's family seen preparing for Christmas and moving closer to a fire. It was the juxtaposition between heat and cold which he wanted to stress. Okhlopkov had been contemplating a stage version of *War and Peace* at around this time and had been attracted by the possibility of cross-cutting between the epic and the domestic, between scenes of war and Hélène's décolleté neck, encircled with diamonds.[131]

Audiences were impressed by the intense patriotic feeling of the production and moments when an unknown soldier, a drummer, refused to abandon his post; or others such as the prolonged and agonising death of the Russian general, Bagration, played by former actor of the Meyerhold theatre, Lev Sverdlin. Critics, on the other hand, felt that these moments were overloaded with theatricality and false pathos. Bagration's death was staged as a ballet-pantomime. The injured commander raced out on to an empty stage and proceeded to convert into artistic poses the movements of someone undergoing the agonies of death – falling, staggering to his feet, seeming to collapse across a fallen branch, before reviving and rushing about the stage again. The movements, according to one critic, instead of being highly dramatic, were like 'warlike variations on a dance macabre', turning the tragic episode into a clumsy ballet number. Critics were equally dubious about the final moments of the production when Kutuzov, contemplating whether or not to abandon Moscow to the enemy, heard 'the voice of the people' in the form of an oratorio, which began to offer advice as to how he should proceed. This succeeded in merely drowning M. Derzhavin's otherwise fine performance of the role.[132]

The repertoire of the Vakhtangov Theatre at this point was something of a study in contrasts, as the premiere of *Fieldmarshal Kutuzov* on 16 March 1940 was followed, on 1 June, by the premiere of J.B. Priestley's *Dangerous Corner* (directed by A. Goryunov and A. Remizova) Okhlopkov's own work and that of the Vakhtangov Theatre, was interrupted by the outbreak of war, when they found themselves evacuated for a time to Omsk. It was here that Okhlopkov mounted a production of Edmond Rostand's *Cyrano de Bergerac*, with designs by Vadim Ryndin. There seems to have been a quality about Rostand's play which linked it, in the history of Okhlopkov's productions with that of *Colas Breugnon*, although a standard history of the Vakhtangov Theatre links the choice of play with the theatre's first war-time production, *Oleko Dundich*, about a civil war hero who was a commander of the First Cavalry Army. In *Cyrano* there was the same 'romantic uplift, the indefatigably bold hero, an individual of exceptional qualities with an exceptional destiny'.[133] This description does not quite square with what seems to have been the mood of Okhlopkov's production of *Cyrano*, which was compared unfavourably with the production of the same play by Serafima Birman at the Lenin Komsomol Theatre in 1943. Ivan Bersenev, as Cyrano, was compared with the rather light-weight Reuben Simonov in Okhlopkov's production, who was not only overpowered by elements of the setting but possessed comic gifts which lent themselves more naturally to a note of 'poetic irony' and 'comic bravado', which conferred an air of 'light entertainment' on the production.[134] This aspect was also noted by a contemporary critic, who assessed it more positively. For her, Simonov's interpretation was both 'brilliant and comic . . . revealing more of the thinker than the lover, more of the comedian than the romantic . . . Cyrano felt the internal isolation of a very intelligent and lonely person.[135]

One of the most controversial aspects of the production was the setting, which consisted of huge sculpted puppets, designed variously for each section of the play. In the scene of the night serenade in the garden, the stage was dominated by an image of Roxane herself. It was of monumental proportions, made of wood and had a large red rose on one shoulder. The hands held a massive guitar and the live Roxane then made her appearance on the 'balcony' in the hole of the sounding board, leaning on the 'strings' as if they were balcony rails, whilst Cyrano cavorted and emoted at the foot of this plinth (something which struck some observers as absurd and tasteless).[136] At the scene in the Rotisserie de Ragueneau, a gargantuan

25 Setting by V. Ryndin for balcony scene of Rostand's *Cyrano de Bergerac*, Vakhtangov Theatre (1942)

figure loomed in the background bearing aloft a cluster of grapes to symbolise the bacchanalian life of a Parisian gallant and, in the final scene, an allegorical figure of Grief towered mutely above Cyrano.

The stage floor was constructed like an oval ramp, which was used very effectively in crowd scenes, such as the scene at the Hotel de Bourgogne, where the colours and movement took on a positively Rubens-like extravagance as the figures swirled in a cascade over the set, crowding and jostling around the isolated figure of Cyrano, the one genuine person in this Parisian social babel. In the first act, the silent observers of the action were the figures of giant musketeers who stood like ironic observers of the passing passions and high-sounding moralising, whilst seeming to embody some eternal, lofty principle. Similarly, in the scene at the rotisserie, the huge figure holding the bunch of grapes aloft in his fist appeared to embody the presence of the elemental Dionysus, presiding over the mock-feasting below. In the scene of the duel between Cyrano and the Marquis de Valvert, the stage was dominated by the images of two warriors with their swords raised at each other while the duel below seemed a metaphor for the assault of intellect against banality, of spirit against puffy flesh, mind against ignorance and talent opposed to the lack of it. In the final scene, the statue like an obelisk, in a grey cape which swathed the figure from head to foot, stood like an allegory of Woe above the events. According to Velekhova, the giant images 'were silent witnesses, sympathisers of the action, helping to break down the barrier between audience and actor, mute commentators, or silent participants in the production – a sounding board for the spectator's feelings . . . They also stood above the action . . . expressing another measure of time (like gods) . . . The spectator was forced to regard two epochs simultaneously.'[137] This description would seem to suggest that this double measure of time, the present and the eternal, was expressed as part of the conflicts registered in the play between the spirit and the flesh, between physical and divine love. In this sense, Cyrano's speech about eternity, was given special emphasis:

> Can you hear how endlessness breathes?
> How the flow of words in orderly fashion moves?
> Do you understand what eternity means?
> Can you hear its implacable call?

Velekhova notes that there was something essentially theatrical and impromptu about Simonov's performance – an exhibition of 'theatre' in the theatre, which chimed with his role as 'prompter' in the love scene in the garden. Cyrano, in this production, was a strange hybrid, neither a person of the salon, nor of the military barracks, He was a 'Polchinella from the Land of Nowhere', who has understood this world and seen that it is only a fit subject for laughter, but behind whose monstrous appearance lay hidden greatness of feeling. The critic concluded: 'We have underestimated, to the point of insult, this work of Okhlopkov's, which was full of profound ideas and unexpected means of artistic expression.'[138]

At the time, Okhlopkov was accused of 'eclecticism' and of lacking an overall conception of the play. He was also advised to remove the allegorical figures. This was done in late 1944, after Okhlopkov had left the theatre to become head of the Theatre of Drama. Instead of appearing on her strange balcony in act 2, Roxane was shown, instead, walking along a garden path between rose bushes.

While the Vakhtangov Theatre had been evacuated to Omsk, the Theatre of the Revolution had spent the war years in Tashkent and, on returning to Moscow, the company members discovered that they had lost their former name and been merged with the Theatre of Drama. Senior members of the company – Marya Babanova, Maxim Shtraukh and Yudif Glizer[139] – approached Okhlopkov with a request that he become head of the new company. Babanova was a friend from their days at the Meyerhold Theatre whilst Shtraukh and Okhlopkov were mutual friends of Eisenstein. The decision to merge the Theatre of Drama with the Theatre of the Revolution and to adopt the name of the former had been taken in September 1943, a month before the company of the Theatre of the Revolution returned from Tashkent. Okhlopkov handled the merger very tactfully and even managed to introduce new members into the company, including Lev Sverdlin with whom he had worked at the Vakhtangov Theatre, and the young Evgeni Samoilov, who had been at Meyerhold's theatre when it closed in 1938.

Okhlopkov presented his proposed repertoire to the company in the autumn of 1943. The first production was to be of Victor Gusev's contemporary verse drama, *Sons of Three Rivers*, a play which dealt with the war in the form of allegorical characters representing the rivers of the warring nations – the Volga, the Elbe, and the Seine – and with real-life characters also symbolising entire nations – Alexei, André and Friedrich. Describing his work on the production, Okhlopkov wrote:

Two starting points should determine the style of the theatre in most things: a striving to reveal the character of our human and simple hero and a bright theatrical romanticising of his lofty human qualities. From this comes a unity . . . of psychologism and theatrical spectacle.[140]

There was far less 'psychologism' than 'theatrical spectacle' in this production for which Okhlopkov returned to the stylised images and types of the mass spectacle of his youth, in which character types were depicted with poster-like simplicity and where models of the world, or the universe, revolved on devices mounted on the backs of lorries in street processions. There was also a clear influence behind the designs, which Ryndin provided, of Meyerhold's productions of *Mystery-Bouffe* in 1918 and 1921. A majestic poly-sphere dominated the stage in the form of a cross section of the globe which rotated to present 'man against a background of the universe'.[141] Against a cyclorama depicting the vastness of the sky, the stage represented part of the Earth with towns and rivers shown in relief and with playing areas located within the gigantic globe. Encircling the globe, like an endless ribbon of road, was the scenic revolve itself. Against this background, three women, symbolising three rivers, stood covered with long veils and ceremoniously declaimed Victor Gusev's verse as they grieved over their sons who suffered or died in war.[142]

Everything was staged with poster-like simplicity and expressiveness. The first act consisted of three scenes – on the Volga, on the Elbe, and on the Seine. In the first scene, a young couple stood on a high bank above the broad expanses of the Volga, flooded with sunlight against a bright blue sky. In the second, against a low, oppressive browny-black sky, images of a bourgeois paradise were schematically parodied in the shape of a well-fed German couple tucked up in a double bed with a wooden cross hanging over it. The third showed the banks of the Seine, the lights of a large town and a pair of young lovers carelessly disporting themselves. At the end of the act, the Parisian couple froze with fright as the air became filled with swirling leaflets announcing the outbreak of war.[143] Searchlights cut the sky as the world turned and Berlin came into view. The audience saw the gleam of helmets, heard the malignant beat of drums, the blare of trumpets and the sound of marching soldiers. The revolve continued to turn and the banks of the Volga appeared. The young lad seen earlier was off to the war. A brief, wordless farewell, then the girl stood for a long time high on the bank as she waved a handkerchief in the wake of her departing lover. In an escape scene, the revolve carried the escaping prisoner back towards his German captors as he simultaneously strove forwards, scrambling through barbed wire, crossing frontiers, crawling and dragging himself along by clutching at the miniature models of houses and cathedrals which formed part of the landscape.[144]

Critics were surprised by the settings, the likes of which had not been seen since the early 1920s. The apparent return to these innovations seemed startlingly original to a contemporary audience preoccupied with war and concerned with their daily bread.[145] Because of the curfew, the production had to be cut by one-third of its inordinate length, otherwise, the public risked having to spend the entire night in the theatre. At a run-through a lace curtain caught fire and rumours circulated that the play had been prohibited. It was known that Okhlopkov himself had had to do some of the rewriting, the author having died in January. The production aroused mixed criticism, some being thrilled by its scope and sweep, the colour and the broad generalisations; others being more critical of the production's tendency towards 'abstract conventionality of character'.[146] Others considered Okhlopkov had discovered a 'major and powerful artistic form' in mounting what was 'perhaps the most powerful of all the presentations about the war'.[147]

Okhlopkov's next production, which opened on 31 August 1944, with a setting by Pyotr Vilyams,[148] was a 'remembrance of things past', as well as another play devoted to the sufferings of the Russian people in wartime. It represented a return to the drama of Pogodin, whom Okhlopkov had neglected since staging *Aristocrats*, but the choice of play, *The Ferry Girl*, was not a happy one. Okhlopkov appreciated the defects of the work but seemed determined to stage a 'show on water'.[149] In this case, his memory undoubtedly went back to his own performance as the old boatman in the production of *Roar, China!*, where part of the stage had been flooded. However, in this case, Okhlopkov went much further than Meyerhold. Not only did he flood the stage and use lighting to great effect but he also positioned four grand pianos along the sides of the set at which pianists sat playing the music of Tchaikovsky. Babanova, who played the part of a Chinese boy in *Roar, China!*, was offered the role of the ferry girl but she turned it down, much to Okhlopkov's annoyance. She considered the play a 'paper prop' and the public reading had not impressed the company, despite the play's tragic subject matter.[150] The ferry girl in question was one of those who worked across the river from what was then Stalingrad (now Volgograd) during the days of the siege, taking refugees night after night, hour after hour to the eastern bank and safety, whilst transporting goods and materials in the opposite direction for the use of Russian troops. Okhlopkov saw the play less as the personal story of Shura, the ferry girl, than the story of all Soviet people at war.

Boris Filippov, who was general manager of the theatre at the time, refers to the vast sums which had been spent in satisfying the demanding requirements of the director and designer, but was forced to agree that the use of light on its own could never have achieved the astonishing effects which the play of light on water managed to do. The theatre went to the lengths of installing a reservoir in the main stage, across which the actress Orlova plied her ferry boat. The effect corresponded precisely to Okhlopkov's attempts to find an image which would exemplify the breadth and boundlessness of the Volga terrain.[151]

The first night, on 31 August 1944, provoked dispute, so much so that Okhlopkov thought the production ought to be taken off. Filippov disagreed because of the expense which had been involved. Two years later, on 26 August 1946, a party directive appeared in the magazine *Culture and Life*, under the heading 'On the Repertoire of the Drama Theatres and Measures for Their Improvement',[152] which singled out the Moscow Drama Theatre for criticism and, in particular, its productions of *The Ferry Girl* and Somerset Maugham's *The Circle*, the latter directed by F.N. Kaverin and which had been premiered in December 1945.

In April 1946, Okhlopkov approached the secretary of the Soviet Writers' Union, Konstantin Fadeyev, with a request that he be allowed to dramatise the latter's novel *The Young Guard* about an heroic group of Young Communist League members. Permission was granted and Okhlopkov, together with his wife, Yelena Zotova, set about staging the production which was premiered on 8 February 1947. It proved to be a triumphant success and remained in the theatre's repertoire for the next ten years. Fadeyev had originally been requested by the Central Committee of the Komsomol to write a novel about the resistance in the mining town of Krasnodon during the German occupation of late 1942 to 1943. The novel was published in the magazine *Molodaya Gvardiya* (Young Guard) in 1945. A second version, 'revised and enlarged', was published in 1951. The central roles in both narratives are based on real people – the commissar of the Krasnodon Komsomol, Oleg Koshevoy, and his comrades Ulyana Gromova, Ivan Zemnukhov, Sergei Tyulenin, Lyubov Shevtsova and others. These were young people who organised an underground resistance group, were betrayed to the occupying forces, and executed.

It was an intensely patriotic production,[153] in which Okhlopkov and his designer, Vadim Ryndin, sought to capture a sense of the conflict between the major forces which seemed to be at large in the contemporary world – those of communism and fascism. The symbol for everything which stood between humanity and a descent into barbarism became a huge red drape, or valence, which was something more significant than the Soviet 'red flag'; rather a symbol of protection, of solidarity, of spiritual uplift, of defiance. The production was unique in the extent to which an item of the stage setting played such a crucial role in determining the mood of each episode as, stirred by the wind, or fluttered by a breeze, the massive drape now rose, now fell, billowed, mounted majestically, looped, traversed the stage, fell in protective folds, raced aloft in alarm or fluttered in trepidation, signalling changes of mood and feeling as the action progressed. Once again, great use was made of the stage revolve, together with music, derived mainly from Rachmaninov's First Piano Concerto played on two grand pianos.

The production opened with the chords of the concerto, echoed by the high sound of trumpets (the production score was the work of I.M. Meyerovich) as the badge of the Komsomol glowed above the stage in the spotlight. In the half-light, a huge red cloth was extended across the wide expanse of the stage and was then raised slowly, 'with grandeur and a special kind of sadness', before looping itself in folds above the empty stage. Then the stage began to revolve and from behind a central screen, a small set emerged consisting of a small pond, backed by trees, and consisting of a grassy mound and a flat, water-lily pond in the form of a mirror tilted towards the audience. The light glanced off its surface, flecking the faces of two young girls, Valya and Ulya, one with her head thrown back, combing her mass of hair. In a very simple manner, the themes of joy, youth and nature had been stated. Suddenly, their excited talk was interrupted by a droning sound overhead which prompted a naive dispute between the two as they attempted to identify the aircraft type. Their innocent vulnerability was further emphasised by their breaking into a rousing folk song which was harshly interrupted by the sound of bursting bombs, which had the effect of sending the red drape soaring and whirling in terrified alarm. Then the set swung slowly out of sight and a garden gate glided into view with sycamores by it. In the scene which followed, Lyubov Shevtsova was shown attempting to calm the panic among the local people. Then the location shifted to a pithead and the silhouette of coal mines appeared. Mineworkers and staff entered, unable to speak except in broken phrases, having just sabotaged their own pit. The drape descended at the end of the scene, as if in mourning for a loss.

A broken wheel and a log next revolved into view with two girls seated on it reminiscing about their childhood. The valence hung to the right. Then an air-raid warning sounded, followed by people running for cover. Then a park seat under a tree appeared, against a shadowy background of houses, a church and bell tower, with a young man in glasses engaged in shy conversation with his girlfriend. The red drape spilled and looped itself to the other side of the stage. The appearance of a coal trolley indicated the pithead, where miners were preparing for resistance. The scene then shifted to a bunker in a garden. Sergei Tyulenin entered, his body slung with automatic rifles, bandoliers and grenades, his hat cocked on one side, his face set, an altogether ungainly and ludicrous figure and greeted with proper laughter by the audience until silenced by the grimness of his soliloquy. As he buried his cache of arms, a sinister red glow began to illuminate the sky and clouds of black smoke could be seen drifting ominously.

The entry of the familiar figure of Oleg Koshevoy, dressed as he was in life, and speaking with his slight stutter, was greeted by the audience with the applause of recognition. A scene then followed in which the invading tanks advanced towards a group of frightened women, caterpillar tracks clanking, their lights glaring directly, blindingly, at the audience. Above the crowd a youthful voice rang out, strong and clear: 'Hold together!', whereupon, people ran towards each other, linking arms, welding themselves into a solid mass as the red drape was lowered above the group like a protective curtain.

Throughout, there was an absence of 'actorish' pathos and reliance on external gesture. This was especially evident in the scene where Valko, the resistance leader with whom Koshevoy has earlier established contact, came to the Shevtsov house to announce the death of a friend, his wife and daughter. The entire scene was conducted in restrained tones and the only external signs of feeling were the shaking hands of the mother as she picked up a pair of large tan-leather boots, which could just be seen to tremble in her grasp. This scene was followed by one of 'fraternisation' with the enemy, during which Lyubov Shevtsova pretended to make overtures to one of the Nazis in order to gain information of use to the resistance. The scene was acted with a mixture of defiance, cheek, intense joy and hatred. At an especially tense moment, she flung from herself a forage cap which had been placed on her head then froze, momentarily, for fear her 'mask' had been seen through, before assuming her bold front again.

This was followed by a harrowing scene of farewell between the two girls whom the audience had met at the outset, as they were now led off under cover of darkness, accompanied by the dull throb of drums, to a concentration camp. As they performed their appalling traverse of the stage the audience was able, for the first time, to see the numbers on their backs. Then, as Sergei Tyulenin told of how the fascists had killed all the wounded soldiers who could not be evacuated in time, the banner was lowered funerially. Next, followed a homely scene of 'everyday' fascism as the occupiers invaded Koshevoy's house and proceeded, in jolly, workmanlike fashion, to cut down the flowers and jasmine bushes outside. Meanwhile, the banner had disappeared, like a conspirator, only to emerge in the form of several bright-coloured flags hung about the town by the Young Guard to celebrate the anniversary of the revolution.

Several more of the forty-two episodes into which the production was divided followed, including those in which the Komsomol group plans to burn down the Nazi registry and open a club for illegal activities in the schoolhouse. Their plans are overheard by a old *babushka* and debate ensues as to whether she is to be trusted. It turns out that she has held a party card for many years and, what is more, owns a radio. On the twenty-fifth anniversary of the revolution, the group gathers around the set to listen to a speech by Stalin.

There then followed the scenes of the group's betrayal as, one by one, they were rounded up before being interrogated and tortured. A stage fight ensued between torturers and victims, during which items of furniture flew about the stage, accompanied by the thunderous laughter of Valko and Shulga, standing aloft on tables like Russian knights of old beating off their midget tormentors as the latter attempted to drag them down and tie them with ropes. Scores of the enemy eventually, with much puffing and panting, managed to secure the two Russians who continued to roar with infectious laughter which continued to resound as they sat, bound, bloodied and beaten in a prison cell, while the Nazis tried to silence the laughter by blowing whistles.

The scene changed and, against a background of the fire-red, fluttering banner, a young Komsomol entered running and, breathlessly, with despair in his voice, on the verge of tears, reported that Valko and Shulga had been buried alive. From the distance rose the strains of the 'International' sung by a group of miners who were at that moment being led away by a firing squad. After those on stage had stood and joined in the anthem, Oleg Koshevoy swore an oath of commitment, to the sounds of which the red banner began to flutter as if the feelings of the group had been transmitted to the colour-cloth, which trembled at the opening words, 'I, Oleg Koshevoy, do solemnly swear . . .' before it soared aloft and, undulating in huge waves, lodged itself triumphantly in the heights.

The impression of the finale was especially powerful. Where the actual deaths of the Young Guard by firing squad had only been seen in silhouette, the group suddenly appeared in a statuesque pose, as if immortalised in marble, their eyes

26 Final scene of Fadeyev's *The Young Guard*, Theatre of Drama (1947)

eternally blank, their clothing flowing in sculpted waves against a background of the rippling red drape. The following description of the finale is that of a sympathetic British commentator:

> The last act is grim . . . One by one, or in groups, the young people are rounded up, imprisoned, tortured. They behave in a manner at which we, whose country was never invaded, can only marvel from a distance and protect from stupid detraction. We are not being harrowed merely to have a good cry. But certainly our emotions are wrung, if we are human at all. We suffer, hope, endure, defy, with each one of them. And, like them, we are shot. Shot as shadows; and when the echoes die away, for the last time the red valence descends, comes to rest, now streaming with indescribable and affecting life, while in front of it, as out of the grave, rise all the brave young people in whose lives we have been taking part; their eyes closed, their heads held high, awaiting their apotheosis in the final liberation.[154]

There followed something of a lull in Okhlopkov's productive output which was not properly resumed until 1953. In the meantime, there had been a revival of his production of *The Mother*, staged by F.N. Kaverin in 1948, and a production by Okhlopkov, in February 1950, of a play by V.D. Pushkov entitled *Sampans of the Skyblue River*, which was little more than a token gesture towards Sino-Soviet friendship. His next, substantial, work was a production of Ostrovsky's *The Thunderstorm*, undertaken in company with A.V. Kashkin, which was premiered on 10 July 1953. This was Okhlopkov's final production at the Theatre of Drama before it was renamed the Mayakovsky Theatre.

Okhlopkov described *The Thunderstorm* as a 'mystery play' and singled out the poetic symbol of the thunderstorm – a redeeming thunderstorm which cleared the suffocating air of the provincial backwater in which the heroine Katerina is incarcerated and which symbolised her revolt against 'the kingdom of darkness' of old Russia. As well as aspects of the mystery play, Okhlopkov saw links with Greek tragedy and introduced a backstage chorus to underscore the spiritual confusion in the heroine, while the thunderstorm itself seemed to rage like a call for justice.[155] In this production, in which an ambience of 'storminess' was present throughout, Katerina did not die for love, or for fear of the community, but for the right of everyone to live in a human fashion. She threw herself from the precipice at the end like a human sacrifice, designed to bring an end to the reign of the power of darkness, spreading her white headscarf like a sail and seeming to take wing like a seagull as she launched herself into space.[156]

The set depicted a soaring rocky cliff overlooking the wide expanses of the Volga: 'Its sharp verticality was set against characteristically circular lines: the whirling force of the storm was expressed in a stage that turned, as well as in the circles formed by the actors throughout the performance.'[157] The ruins of a church, lit by flashes of lightning, created a terrifying picture of hell and the rocky incline was crowned by a tiny birch tree buffeted by the wind. During Katerina's moment of confession, the cliffs behind her suddenly began to move, evoking primeval fears of the powers of natural phenomena. Her tormented soul was stressed by the dynamics and agitated rhythms of the *mise-en-scène*, by the sudden shift of the revolve and by flickering bursts of lightning.[158]

Critics complained about the technical/mechanical aspect of the production, which included the overuse of the revolve. They thought that insufficient piety had been shown to the existing canons of Ostrovskyan interpretation, especially in moments such as the one where Okhlopkov brought on the half-mad old woman dressed in a fashionable travelling costume accompanied by two lackeys wearing white gloves. He had imagined her as a universal figure rushing along the road to catastrophe accompanied by her acolytes. 'The theatre is not a museum and the director is not an archivist',[159] declared Okhlopkov angrily, answering his critics in a spirit which already anticipated a reaction against the years dominated by Stalin, who had died in March. Critics reserved their greatest indignation for the finale when, following Katerina's suicide, Okhlopkov had the figure of a very simple girl appear on the pinnacle of the rock as a reminder to the populace who had gathered of the meaning of Katerina's action. She was intended as a poetic expression of the development of Katerina's character. Okhlopkov also defended his interpretation of the *raisonneur*, Kuligin, who dreams of solar clocks and lightning conductors and has a vague hope that education and science will cure the ills of the town. Instead of the usual dreamer, Okhlopkov stressed his role as an angry and convinced accuser in whom a Promethean fire still burned.[160] An article in *Pravda* headed 'The Right and Duty of the Theatre' defended Okhlopkov and his production and insisted on the theatre's right to creative experiment.[161]

Okhlopkov began work on his production of *Hamlet* in January 1945, at a time when he had hoped to involve Grigori Kozintsev. However, the latter was prevented by his commitment to the Lenfilm Studios, for whom he eventually produced a film version of Shakespeare's tragedy.[162] There is little doubt that Okhlopkov's eventual production, which received its premiere on 16 December 1954, was a retrospective comment on the Stalinist years. This much is suggested in the official history of the Mayakovsky Theatre, which specifically refers to the 'social atmosphere of Leninist norms of life'. It goes on:

> Passionate civil temperament summoned Okhlopkov to the resolution of acute problems of contemporary life. The artist communist always walked in step with his times, lived its concerns. Therefore, in the days when Leninist norms were being properly and undeviatingly re-established, the theme of faith in man was of social significance.[163]

For this production, Okhlopkov collaborated once again with Vadim Ryndin and used the music of Bach, Beethoven and Tchaikovsky.

In an article published in *Teatr* in January 1955,[164] Okhlopkov described his view of the play. He saw Hamlet as a humanist who takes up arms against despotism, rebels against Denmark as a prison and recognises that a tragic fate awaits those prisoners who keep aloof from the struggle and bide their time while an army of murderers is growing. The fate of those who answer blow for blow either too early or too late is also tragic. Claudius's terrorist methods are seen to be the same as those used against Giordano Bruno or Jan Hus, but the future belongs to Hamlet, 'who is aflame with the fire of new ideas which cannot be extinguished by the forces of reaction. Beyond his death, beyond his personal defeat, lies the historic victory of humanism.'[165] Hamlet seeks a way out of the prison in *Weltschmerz*, bitterness and scepticism, irony and sarcasm. He hesitates, not because he is devoured by nervous reflexes and apathy, but because he is afraid of taking a false step which might go against his humanist ideals. He has to disguise his love as vulgar importunity and transform it into cynical coarseness. The very air of Denmark is poisoned by hypocrisy and cant. People are cast into its crucible and melted down to produce convenient miniatures of small moral stature with no scruples. Thought is caught on a thread of falsehood stronger than an iron chain. This is the world which Bacon compared with a labyrinth. 'The castle of Elsinore reflects as in a mirror, all the bubbling irreconcilable contradictions of the world where the remnants of feudalism and the Middle Ages, hand in hand with the development of England as a bourgeois power, were preparing to attack the rights and principles of Renaissance humanism which, in its turn, was seeking to establish its right to natural development.'[166]

The basic principle of the setting derived from Okhlopkov's desire to emphasise the sense of Denmark as a prison. Ryndin's design was a vertical, cellular structure which had its basis in the iconostasis, as well as borrowing ideas from Boris Knoblok's designs for Okhlopkov's unrealised production of *Ugryum River* in 1937. A front drop in the shape of a vast iron grille constituted the central metaphor of the production. This grille could advance and recede, or form a transparent wall through which events could be viewed. It could also open, centrally, like a huge gate. At one point, for example, the mad Ophelia ran across

27 Scene from *Hamlet* (1954)

the stage while the gates first opened then closed behind her as if to stress the tragic helplessness of her situation. For the 'Murder of Gonzago', the stage was divided into twelve small acting boxes, ranged horizontally and vertically with actors stationed in each of these cellular units, observing the 'Mousetrap' scene performed at stage level. In the closet scene, giant columns filled the stage, capped with huge hands from which flames flared upwards (strips of red cloth blown by concealed fans). In another scene, a large statue of the Madonna and Child stood in the background. When Hamlet set sail for England, a huge ship drifted across the stage, while evening clouds floated in the sky as it disappeared. Laertes' return from France, following his father's death, was played as a popular revolt against an incumbent despot. The angry populace stormed the stage from the rear while the portcullis was lowered across the proscenium arch. They then proceeded to clamber up the portcullis as if storming the castle, thus transforming the audience into the cowering courtiers of the effete Danish court.

In the 'Get thee to a nunnery . . .' episode Samoilov, as Hamlet, played the scene as if he knew he was being overheard, declaiming aloud the lines he wished the king and Polonius to hear, whilst whispering soft words of love to Ophelia. The scene was effectively split in two, alternating sanity and 'madness'. In the final duel scene, the protagonists were initially hidden from the audience by a ring of courtiers. This was part of a recurring motif of partial visibility. Hamlet's 'To be, or not to be . . .' soliloquy, for example, was delivered from behind a door with only his hand visible, holding a dagger which, at one point, was raised as if to strike himself before the fingers were seen slowly to open and the dagger fell to the floor. In Claudius' prayer scene, the king seemed to be lost in the swathes of his own cloak, and appeared transformed into an unearthly, almost allegorical figure, as he sank to his knees before a huge image of the crucifixion set against a stained glass background. This motif was evoked again during the final scene when Claudius enveloped himself in stage drapes in an attempt to hide himself from the avenging figure of Hamlet.[167]

The American commentator, Faubion Bowers, found the production lavish and impressive, if not always tasteful, feeling that there was, generally, too much fussy movement:

> The underlying principle of the production . . . is that everybody must be doing something . . . Hamlet constantly kisses the hem of Ophelia's skirt . . . Sabres are rattled in the background; goblets are tossed in the air and caught deftly by waiting retainers. Everywhere people are moving, filling the air with action – sometimes purposeful, sometimes decorative, sometimes lunatic.[168]

Nina Velekhova's description of the 'Mousetrap' scene conveys an air of this constant movement:

> The rhythm is established immediately like a storm force 10 or 12 – in the movement of the courtiers, in the lighting, in the music: the stage is blindingly lit, people in a state of alarmed and intensified excitement, everything redoubled, whipped up. But this isn't all. Into the cauldron of general spiritual fever Hamlet tosses his jokes, full of bitter cynicism. And each time, in response to his remarks, laughter breaks out as Claudius, with a sweep of his arm calls on his menials to 'humour the sad prince' . . . Suddenly, it is as if all the laughter, whistling and so on have receded into the background; Hamlet and Ophelia come forward, the light dimming behind them and Hamlet, bending on one knee, holds her scarf to his lips in complete silence . . .
>
> On stage, the king's brother prepares to murder, pouring poison into the ear of the sleeping king. The rhythms of the music accompanying the action carry you on without pause for breath . . . 'Give me some light. Away!' And already the sober, all-revealing light flares from which the courtiers run like mice . . .

Hamlet's 'Why let the stricken deer go weep . . .' was preceded by his kicking over the throne.[169]

Criticism was, generally, approving, and spoke of a new reading of *Hamlet*, in which Evgeni Samoilov was outstanding, more like a medical student or some humanist world-wanderer than a prince. The music was also effective, seething 'in the soil of the production, in an underground key, like a phenomenon of the action's dynamic'.[170] One major aberration was the casting of Marya Babanova in the role of Ophelia. Okhlopkov must have held an image of her in his mind from more youthful days. She was fifty-four at the time and records her confusion and embarrassment at being cast in a role for which she was completely unsuited, but which Okhlopkov managed to convince her she could play. The critics seem to have brought him up to his senses and, to Babanova's relief, she was replaced by a younger actress after a fortnight.[171] Samoilov was himself forty-two and already slightly old for the part and was soon replaced by the younger Edvard Martsevich, who became the idol of Moscow's theatregoing teenagers.

Okhlopkov continued to settle accounts with the past in his next production, of Alexander Shtein's *Hotel Astoria*, which focused on the tragedy of a pilot,

Konovalov, a Spanish civil war veteran who had become a victim of the purges in the late 1930s, is condemned, and discharged from the service. Despite being imprisoned as a 'fascist', he never loses faith and, once allowed to fly again, comes to the aid of Leningrad during the blockade. This was the second of Shtein's plays to be staged at the Mayakovsky Theatre, the first having been *A Personal Affair*, which Okhlopkov's wife had staged under Okhlopkov's supervision in March 1955. The hero of this earlier play had been the experienced engineer and communist, Alexei Khlebnikov, who had become the sacrificial victim of a careerist, subjected to unjust accusations and excluded from the party. *Hotel Astoria* is set in the hotel on St Isaac's Square in Leningrad, which was the Russian military command post during the siege of that city. The play is a psychological drama, which attempts to illustrate the heroic through concentrating on the everyday. Okhlopkov and his assistant, V.F. Dudin, sought to extend the range of the play and to alter its predominantly 'realistic' form.

Behind the emotional conception of the production lay an incident which Okhlopkov described to Norris Houghton in the 1930s relating to an encounter he had witnessed, during the Soviet civil war, between two old comrades whom the war had separated. It had its counterpart in act 1 of *Hotel Astoria* when Major Konovalov meets a journalist whom he has fought alongside in Spain. This meeting had become a symbol, for Okhlopkov, of the kind of theatre he was aiming for:

> One day during the Civil War I stood on a railway station platform. From one direction a troop train drew in and stopped. In a moment, another troop train arrived from the opposite direction and halted across the platform. Soldiers poured out to refill their tea-kettles, buy a bun, or stretch their legs. Near me one man alighted. From the other train came another soldier. They saw each other, ran foward and embraced, unable to speak for emotion. They were old comrades, dearest friends, whom the war had separated. There on a station platform, as one went one way and the other another, they met for a moment, clasped hands, and parted. In that instant I knew what I wanted my theatre to be ... In my theatre actor and spectator must clasp hands in fraternity.[172]

Okhlopkov staged the play as a 'production-concert', complete with grand piano and symphony orchestra. On the stage there towered a huge circular platform – representing a hotel room – on which stood a grand piano, a few armchairs and a divan. The background to this consisted of a panoramic view of Leningrad executed in the style of an old engraving. On two sides of the forestage a symphony orchestra was placed and, during the more intense moments of the action, the giant shadow of the conductor was thrown against the background, lit by intense spotlights. The entire production was accompanied by the music of Liszt and Scriabin, interspersed with the wailing of shells, sirens and the sound of bursting bombs. Extending from the centre of the stage, a wooden walkway cut through the centre of the auditorium like a Japanese 'flower path'.

Okhlopkov declared that his basic aim in staging *Hotel Astoria* was to reveal 'the spiritual world of a rank-and-file communist devoted to the party and the people'.[173] Faubion Bowers was impressed:

As dramatic structure *Hotel Astoria* has little to offer. As a piece of theatre, however, it is absorbing, moving and often beautiful. The characters are not black and white in the old pattern of so many Soviet characters. They are shades of grey – right sometimes, wrong sometimes; strong sometimes weak at other times. They are human and real . . . Its frankness about the Communist Party and its criticism of the conduct of the war is courageous. The only entirely unsympathetic character in the whole play is the Party bureaucrat who figures in several scenes.[174]

The production was frank in its depiction of people 'in flashy clothes who listened to jazz' who seemed to be 'waiting for the Germans to take over'. A professor of philology described how he deserted from his unit at the front and, whilst preparing to die, dug his own grave but buried his party card and identity documents separately: 'Can you blame me? What has the party ever done for me?' In addition to these bold strokes, the production also contained certain conventional features such as the apparently feather-brained evacuee, Linda, who in fact takes photographs of German military positions and turns out to be a heroine. Okhlopkov managed to make her role dramatically more interesting through his use of the stage. At one point, when dancing and singing during the bombardment of Leningrad, she is asked by Konovalov's wife: 'Aren't you ashamed of yourself?', Okhlopkov directed the actress playing Linda to turn and make an extended exit in total silence along the line of the longest curve leading to the door, stepping very precisely on her heels. On reaching the door she was told to clutch the handle, halt and fixedly, very slowly, turn to Konovalova and pronounce bitterly, but quietly, the next line: 'And you?' (the point being that in her husband's absence, Konovalova had assumed him to be dead and has remarried his best friend). The cross to the door was designed to be expressive of the girl's dignity, with the idea transmitted through the use of stage space rather than with words alone.[175]

The production resulted in a considerable amount of critical debate in the pages of *Teatr*. Among those who took up the cudgels against Okhlopkov were the directors Georgi Tovstonogov and Anatoli Efros,[176] who then went on to imitate much of what they criticised in his work at the time. Tovstonogov objected to the fact that Okhlopkov had chosen to stage a play about the Leningrad blockade which was not actually about the blockade but was, instead, a straightforward psychological drama which happened to be set in a hotel room in Leningrad. Okhlopkov had merely requisitioned the play for his own purposes and had also dragged in a flower path, an orchestra and so on. 'Does it not alarm you?' asked Tovstonogov in terms reminiscent of those who attacked Meyerhold for his formalist influence on others in the 1930s, 'that, apparently leaning on the example of your *Astoria*, the director M. Gersht in his production of *Intervention*, also hung up a map, also constructed a bridge through the middle of the auditorium . . . Similarly, in his production of Goncharov's *In the Ravine*, he brings a piano on stage at which they play Rachmaninov, Glière and other composers who have a doubtful relevance to Goncharov . . .'[177]

Okhlopkov staged another play by Shtein in 1961, *The Ocean*, in which the protagonists were all naval personnel and the action took place on board ship. At one point during the production, against a poetic background of the raging elements, Okhlopkov had the sailors enter by sliding down ropes from a gantry above the stage, while one of their number remarked jokingly to the audience: 'I bet you've seen nothing like this here before!'[178]

Okhlopkov returned to the theme of the war in his next production of Leonid Leonov's *The Orchards of Polovchansk*, a 'Chekhovian' drama written in 1938 and full of premonitions of imminent war. The sound of tanks, artillery and rocket fire reverberate through the play, highlighting the fragility of the calm which reigns at Polovchansk. There is direct mention of the Germans and the Japanese and, as in Chekhov, there is a powerful sense of an external, malignant force encroaching on an erstwhile peaceful and orderly way of life.[179]

The play was staged by A.V. Kashkin, under Okhlopkov's supervision, and was retitled *The Gardener and the Shadow*. The shadow in question was the treacherous parasite Pylyaev and the play was interpreted as a straightforward conflict between him and Makkaveyev, a monumental figure who defends the Soviet Union with arms, rears children and tends his orchards – a symbol of the light which the dark shadow of Pylyaev seeks to occlude. The action was played out on a small circular platform surrounded by the audience, above which hung a branch weighed down with fruit.[180] There were echoes here of the earlier designs by Knoblok for *Colas Breugnon* and *Othello*. The design team in this instance were Kovalenko and Krivoshein and the musical score was adapted from the works of Rimsky-Korsakov by I.M. Meyerovich.

As part of a general reaction against the spirit of the Stalin years, the late 1950s saw a resurgence of a variety of Soviet play which concerned itself with the importance of human relationships and personal feelings, as opposed to the rather hackneyed and impersonal relationships of the orthodox 'boy meets tractor' school, as the socialist-realist genre has been dismissively described. A dramatist who led the way in this respect, who had already established a reputation for himself before the war, was Alexei Arbuzov,[181] whose *Irkutsk Story* and *My Poor Marat* (The Promise) were among the most popular plays of the post-war period. Several theatres staged *Irkutsk Story* almost simultaneously, but undoubtedly the most significant productions of the play were those given at the Vakhtangov Theatre, directed by Evgeni Simonov in December 1959, and the production by Okhlopkov at the Mayakovsky Theatre, with settings by K.F. Kuleshov and music by Scriabin, which was given its premiere on 25 February 1960.

The play lent itself admirably to Okhlopkov's methods for, as well as dealing with ordinary working people in recognisable circumstances, it did so within the framework of a play which married the realistic with the 'conventional', through devices such as a chorus and through the utilisation of mime and the raising of an everyday romance to the level of universal epic. The play is set in Siberia, near the construction site of a hydro-electric power station, and concerns the love of two construction workers, Victor and Sergei for Valya, a local shop girl with a reputation for easy virtue. Courted initially by Victor, whom she prefers, she eventually marries Sergei who loves her. She gives birth to twins. Sergei is subsequently drowned while trying to rescue others and Victor's interest in Valya is rekindled although, since Sergei's death, she seems to have lost interest in everything except her children. Victor manages to get her a job as part of the construction site team and, gradually, Valya begins to come to terms with her tragedy and discover happiness in life. The chorus holds out hope to Victor at the end that Valya may eventually consent to marry him.

Norris Houghton has described the play as a version of Thornton Wilder's *Our Town*, but with the added ingredient of 'the joy of work and of the comradeship that goes with work . . . an attempt at a lyrical expression of human life as it is lived in Russia today . . .'[182] In order to avoid a naturalistic approach, Arbuzov leaves matters of setting deliberately unspecific. Okhlopkov employed the whole broad sweep of the stage, utilising the revolve in such a way as to bring the actors forward beyond the line of the proscenium arch in a manner which seemed to bring them into focus, before swinging them away into the distance. This effect 'enhanced the strongly retrospective passing-in-review tone of the drama', turning the 'tale of simple workers into a sort of twentieth-century epic, in which the rumbling undertone of drums, the swelling choral singing, and the slowly revolving stage combined to make the heart beat faster and the tears flow more readily'.[183]

Something of this effect can be seen in the way in which the opening moments were staged. The play is written in the form of a flashback framed between the opening and closing scenes, elements of which are identical. Scene 1 opens with the Chorus who, in Arbuzov's play, is a single character who introduces the others and has a choric relationship with the audience. Okhlopkov increased the Chorus total to twenty and dressed them so that they looked indistinguishable from the audience, as if they might have stepped straight from the auditorium on to the stage. They entered from the wings in twos and threes, dressed in street clothes and took up their places before the performance started, sitting on the steps leading to the stage. At the outset, the lines of the original Chorus were split up between them but, as the play progressed they became, at the finale, a musical choir assisted by two pianos and rolls on a kettle drum. Typical of Okhlopkov's treatment of the opening was the expansion of the theatrical and dramatic element of the play in keeping with the epic scale of the treatment. Thus, a simple question and answer exchange consisting of two lines:

Chorus: Tell me how it began, that morning.
Valya: I remember. I got up early . . .

was followed by a short pause, shattered by the blows of a kettle drum, its persistent and alarming throb seeming to alter the rhythm of time flowing past.[184] (At this point of the action, Valya has already lived through the life of the play, which includes Sergei's death, and so in remembering the past, seeks to avoid the pain of memory.) Alarm erupted as the light on the stage thickened and the actress ran towards the stage along a 'flower path' which, like the one in *Hotel Astoria*, cut right through the centre of the auditorium. On reaching the stage, the actress first ran with a sense of alarm and urgency towards the right then, as if finding no exit, ran equally strenuously towards the left. Both these movements were performed as if to the point of exhaustion in a manner which was more suggestive of ballet than conventional theatre. Then, following this conventionalised expression of the avoidance of spiritual pain, the need to confront the past was suggested by a very simple gesture of the actress's hand raised to grasp the lobe of her coat collar which she pressed to her neck in a manner expressive both of tension and the need to remember and suffer through everything again.[185]

Once again, in his overall conception of the production, Okhlopkov's feeling for nature played an important part, expressed in images of fire and water and especially marked by his use of lighting. The wedding procession was a case in point, with its subtle play of light and shade creating a feeling that nature 'set off' the joys and grief of people (in the text, a kiss is followed by a thunderclap and the remark: 'Look, rain and sunshine together. What strange company!').[186] The darkness of Valya's room was exchanged for the blinding white light of the wedding procession, rain was replaced by the rays of dawn, the gloomy forest murk was obliterated by the sparkling flames of a fire, the tongues of flame lengthening the shadow of the tall figure of the dancing Victor or, as in the episode 'Children', when Valya returned from the maternity home, the air was suffused with the whiteness of branches of apple blossom.[187]

Another telling example of the way in which Okhlopkov, taking a suggestion from the play, would amplify its significance to epic proportions was contained in the scene which he staged of the celebrations which followed the wedding. This was part of Okhlopkov's attempt to sharply accentuate and enlarge those events which mark stages in the life of man – birth, marriage and death. The marriage celebrations took place, in Okhlopkov's imagination, at night in a forest on the banks of the Angar River, against the background of a blazing fire and a passionate dance performed by Victor. Fire may be said to have constituted the dominant metaphor of the production as the specific Scriabin music which Meyerovich orchestrated was taken from *Prometheus: A poem of Fire*. In the text, Arbuzov's stage direction reads:

> Larisa enters the circle, begins to dance with passion and abandon.]Then Victor asks her to make way and:[begins with a slow step then, tossing his head, breaks into a wild and furious dance in which one senses a hint of despair. The shouting and clapping of the onlookers almost drown out the music, and Victor and Larisa finish the dance amid stormy applause.[188]

Alexander Lazarev, who played Victor in Okhlopkov's production, was made famous overnight by a dance which he performed at this point. Okhlopkov would appear to have taken his cue from the exchange between Serdyuk and Larisa a little further on, when congratulating her on her dancing, he says: 'You were like a flame', to which she answers: 'Not much fire left, I'm afraid.'[189] This hint was turned into a 'Walpurgisnacht', according to one critic,[190] and Victor's dance became a personification of fire, a tragic monologue performed in silence with the fire separating him from Valya. It was a kind of terrifying confession of passion and despair which put people in mind of the tragic, triangular relationship between Rogozhin, Myshkin and Nastasya Filippovna in Dostoevsky's *The Idiot*.[191] The

28 Scene from *Irkutsk Story* (1960)

characters became translated into elemental forces – the active, the destructive and
the restorative. The action involved a tragic catastrophe but the 'saving' element,
represented by Sergei, finally conquered.

The marriage scene itself was amplified to the extent that it became like a scene
from a Dostoevskyan novel. It was apparent from the moment the bride and groom
entered – the bride's veil extending almost the entire width of the stage. Then both
stood next to each other like statues, unseeing, not touching. It was as if they had
emerged beyond the framework of the simple and everyday and 'stood on the edge
of eternity where questions of life and death were being decided'. What seemed to
be required of the shopgirl was nothing less than a spiritual rebirth, a prospect
which she was both facing and wishing to flee from, so demanding and burdensome
was it. Everything sentimental and banal appeared to have been banished from the
pale face of the little shop cashier, who stood like an image of pale marble. Then
someone in the crowd let fall an insulting remark and she fell to the floor like a white
bird which had been shot. Her white dress covered her and spread wide on the stage
like plumage, or fallen rose petals.[192]

The relationship between Sergei and Valya was presented as a conflict between
a fanatical idealist and someone in whom the initial coquetry just seemed vulgar and
out of place. Even a simple action, such as Sergei's hitting a lad who had insulted
Valya, was performed in a stylised fashion as if the blow were struck in defence of
some ideal, of something sacred, defending it against the assaults of *poshlost*
(vulgarity).[193]

It was precisely this attempt by Okhlopkov to render elements of the play more
abstract in order to heighten their impact, which became the subject of criticism,

especially his use of the chorus in a way other than that prescribed by the author: 'The chorus . . . was unexpectedly stripped of its poetic inspiration, of its lyric lightness, of its philosophical innocence . . . It became heavy, awkward . . . inexpressive.'[194] Writing in *Teatr* Tatyana Bachelis and Konstantin Rudnitsky[195] accused Okhlopkov of over-extending the author's ideas, and of adding an over-abundance of exaltation and temperament: 'Okhlopkov evidently wanted to convince his audience that the heroes of the production, ordinary people of our time, could measure greatness with Faust, Hamlet, Prometheus or Oedipus.'[196]

Some twenty-five years after the date of his first visit, Norris Houghton returned to the Soviet Union and recorded his impressions of the theatre and the man whom he first met at the Realistic Theatre. In the 1960s Houghton compared Okhlopkov unfavourably with his 'master', Meyerhold, although he described their personalities as being alike. Both men were great 'personal showmen' and 'dictatorial' directors. He felt that there was no great subtlety apparent at the Mayakovsky Theatre and that Okhlopkov's boldness and boisterousness, as well as the absence of wit in his productions, made him seem vulgar alongside the remembered image of Meyerhold:

> He is not likely to be accused of 'aestheticism' as was his master for he has kept himself basically unsophisticated. He has kept in touch with the people – including the political powers who in many lands beside Russia are not noted for the sensitivity of their artistic appreciation.[197]

Houghton also referred to the polemic which Okhlopkov was conducting with his opponents, led by the chief director at the Bolshoi Drama Theatre, Leningrad, Georgi Tovstonogov who, like Houghton, made unflattering comparisons between Okhlopkov and Meyerhold, albeit in a rather different spirit.

Okhlopkov initiated the debate with two articles in *Teatr* in November and December 1959, entitled 'On the Conventional', in which he described 'realism' as just one of many conventions, and that 'conventionalism', which is apparent in all art forms, was not in itself subversive of realism. It was the limited definition of realism which shackled the imagination of the dramatist. There was nothing that the theatre could not show by virtue of the means peculiar to it. How could small-scale 'realism' cope with dramatisations of the Bible, Hemingway's *The Old Man and the Sea*, Goethe's *Faust* or Dante's *Divine Comedy*? Tovstonogov, in an 'open letter' to Okhlopkov, replied the following year, accusing him of broadening the understanding of realism to encompass anything and everything and, with a clear side-swipe at Okhlopkov's teacher, Meyerhold, referred to 'a production' of *The Government Inspector* which transferred the location of the play from the Russian provinces to St Petersburg and contained a performance of Khlestakov by Sergei Martinson which was 'the purest formalism'. Attempts to revive theatre forms of the past had all been tried and to little effect, according to Tovstonogov. 'What use was the popular form of the *balagan* in a world in which Palaces of Culture and city theatres reigned? How could the *balagan* bring pleasure to a tractor driver with ten years education behind him, or a worker who had recently been listening to Shostakovich's eleventh symphony?' asked Tovstonogov rhetorically. In answer,

29 Project for a new Mayakovsky Theatre (unrealised)

one might point to Tovstonogov's own evident recantation on this score in borrowing devices from the despised *balagan* for his own production of Shakespeare's *Henry IV* (1969) as well as his use of 'formalist' elements in his production of *The Government Inspector* (1972). In another clear reference, this time to *Irkutsk Story*, Tovstonogov added balefully: 'Unfortunately, we often see how directors "enrich" a play with their own vision of life, without considering the author's "angle of vision".'[198]

The project for a new 'universal' theatre had been maturing in Okhlopkov's mind since around 1950, a 'theatre of the future' based on the Greek amphitheatre but with the project for Meyerhold's new theatre designed by Vakhtangov and Barkhin in the 1930s very much in mind. Okhlopkov had been very impressed by a *son et lumière* presentation he had seen at the Palace of Versailles and imagined staging something similar devoted to the life of Lenin.[199] Plans and models were drawn up by Okhlopkov working with the architect V. Bykov and the engineer I. Maltsyn but, like so many of Okhlopkov's plans, it failed to come to fruition in his lifetime. However, it is highly significant that he selected a Greek tragedy for what was to be his last major production and chose to stage it in the Tchaikovsky Concert Hall, which is what Meyerhold's new theatre project became when plans to build it were abandoned after his arrest in June 1939. This fact alone has prompted some commentators to suggest that the sub-text of this production of Euripides' *Medea* related to Stalinism and its victims as it concerned a 'character of indomitable will and total ruthlessness [which] would not let her spare her own children – and she too came from Colchis, i.e. Georgia.'[200] For others, the production was a polemic against those who sought to deprive the theatre of pathos and emotion, stating the case of a barbarian woman who had been cruelly wronged by a 'civilised' Greek.

Many critics took issue with Okhlopkov's interpretation of Medea as 'a social victim' (which is a long way from comparing her with Stalin!). Others felt that the 'social victim' angle was especially meaningful in a Soviet context, as a consequence of the country's attempt to 'russify' both 'civilised' and 'uncivilised' national groupings. Bearing in mind that Russians make up only about 50 per cent of the total population of the Soviet Union, there had been and still was a good deal of resentment among those national minorities who felt that their culture was being effectively extinguished. In spite of the cultural autonomy granted to minority nationalities, russification had been presented as the only path to social progress and even republics like the Ukraine felt that their national heritage was threatened in the context of a socialist federation. According to these commentators, it seemed likely that 'Okhlopkov's unique treatment of Medea was criticised precisely because it appeared to set such social grievances in relief.'[201] According to Okhlopkov, he chose to stage the play because he was attracted to Euripides' humanism and his protest against moral monstrousness, lies, arbitrariness and social injustice. The action of *Medea* concerned the suffering individual, insulted by society, the people and the Gods. It was a play about Man rebelling so unconstrainedly against the injury done to him that, in despair, he destroyed everything, including his own happiness.[202]

Other critics stated that Okhlopkov saw the clash between Medea and Jason as one between human and non-human elements (rather than between the 'barbaric' and the 'civilised'). In this sense, Euripides had been the first in the ancient world to pose the question about the search for evil in man and to discover that its origin lay outside in society – in the way in which society was constructed, its property values, money and gold. In *Medea*, the concept of property was given moral expression. Medea herself was the aboriginal expression of the property instinct and became its sacrificial victim. Medea ordered everything for the sake of this passion. In her person, society, devoid of a moral idea, crumbled from within. Medea was like Jason in being a general idea of a type, rather than a specific character.

In these terms, Okhlopkov saw the production as a manifesto in defence of grand feelings and ideas and the play as a protest against those social relationships which give rise to crime, evil and even 'demonism' – a mythological hyperbole for the destruction of all human connection. Medea was a combination of reality and myth – the terrifying hypothesis of someone created by a world of evil and self-interest, violence and lawlessness. Medea expressed, through her actions how arbitrariness and violence became 'naturalised', as well as the indissoluble contradictions which she experienced: 'Don't protest and you will perish. Protest and you will perish also.' According to Okhlopkov, the meaning of *Medea* was by way of a warning, which is why it should have been staged prior to the rise of fascist dictatorships. Euripides' tragedy declared that lawlessness was terrible, not through its direct threat physically to destroy people, but through its dissolution of the moral bases of life. Lawlessness gave birth to the destruction of the inner laws of personality, of those laws which assert that life is good only if it is based on goodness and reason.[203]

Okhlopkov tried to convert the Tchaikovsky Concert Hall into an indoor

30 Scene from *Medea* (1961)

amphitheatre by removing the stalls and placing a full symphony orchestra in the 'orchestra'. The setting, on a raised platform surrounded on three sides by the audience, consisted of a simple portico of columns flanked by images of the deities and with steps on either side. Towards the rear, stood a huge statue of Euripides himself, holding a scroll in one hand and a mask in the other. The chorus of Corinthian women was schooled by N.V. Grishina and, at times, filled the entire acting area. An interesting feature was the fact that the chorus was masked throughout whereas the principal performers were only masked at moments of high drama, when a stage servant appeared and held the mask in front of the performer's face. In addition to the chorus, a choir was placed along the sides of the acting area. The music used was taken from Taneyev's operatic trilogy *The Oresteia*.

The production began on a high tragic note. No sooner had the sounds of the orchestra died away than the nurse appeared, dressed in black, to deliver the news of Jason's deceit. As she moved rapidly about the stage, waving her arms despairingly whilst lamenting the terrible fate of Medea, the audience could glimpse Medea herself moving between the thick columns of the portico at the rear, pressing against them with her whole body. When she appeared, she descended the steps directly, as if unseeing, her head crowned with flaming red hair raised in pride, her mouth formed in a convulsive cry. As she pronounced her curse on Jason the timid chorus of Corinthian women retreated in terror. Then, as the nurse ran up the steps to escape the wrath of Medea, the former's black cape fell and fluttered to the ground like a mourning veil.[204]

This was followed by Jason's entry from above, accompanied by a military escort. With a few light steps Jason ran on to the upper platform from where he overheard Medea's final words. Okhlopkov wanted there to be something fantastic and animal-like about Jason's movement, reminiscent of a prancing fawn – a personification of instincts other than human. Everything about the set of his face and his carriage bore the stamp of indomitable self-assurance and a sense of a masculine right to determine his own fortunes at the expense of female suffering. There was a triumphant absence of doubt in his own rightness. Having stood there for a while, facing one another, Jason behaved as if he had not seen Medea, turned away from her and drew the string of an imaginary bow, before performing the action of recoil (this was taken from one of Meyerhold's bio-mechanical exercises). There followed a demonstration of a throw with an imaginary discus. Everything about Jason spoke of the mighty, magnificent Hellene. He was a terrifying 'superman', who considered human feeling, especially feminine feeling, merely an obstacle in his path.[205] At the same time, in the performance of E. Kozyreva's Medea, there was a sense, in her suffering, of something similarly destructive of nature, such as can be felt in Gogol's *The Viy* or *A Terrible Revenge*.[206]

The murder of the children was symbolised by a dagger with a blood-red ribbon streaming from it. This was quite deliberate, as Okhlopkov did not want to portray the murders as a fact but as a metaphor of the extreme depths to which the spirit could stoop. The murder scene became a demonstration, a tragic metaphor of horror, utilising the mask in the manner of Japanese theatre. With the accomplishing of the murder, the chorus fled like birds along the steps of the portico, transmitting the dynamic of a perturbed city which understood that its end had come, like the final hours of Pompeii. In the distance, children's gentle voices cried and black capes flapped like sails. Yuri Yuzovsky, reviewing this, the last Okhlopkov production he saw before his death, described this scene as being 'done with genius'. Reminiscing on his thoughts after the first night, the dramatist Alexander Shtein recalled Lenin's remarks made to M.I. Kalinin to the effect that 'apart from the theatre, there is no single institution or organ which could be a substitute for religion', adding, 'In *Medea*, Okhlopkov created just such an atmosphere.'[207] It is some tribute to the production that the Greek tragic actress Aspasia Papatanassiou agreed to appear as Medea for a few guest performances in 1967. By 1981, the production had been seen more than one thousand times in fifty different cities of the USSR.[208]

It seemed only natural that Okhlopkov should turn his attention at some point to the operatic stage and it is somewhat surprising that he did not do so prior to the late 1950s and early 1960s, and then only on three occasions. His production of Khrennikov's opera *The Mother* at the Bolshoi Theatre had, according to Norris Houghton, 'a magnificent epic sweep to it'.[209] In addition to this, he also staged an operatic version of *The Young Guard* by Meytus at the Maly Opera Theatre in Leningrad as well as a version of Yuri Shaporin's *The Decembrists*, again at the Bolshoi. In the six years which remained of Okhlopkov's life he accomplished little more and was to suffer increasingly from the debilitating illness which finally killed him, although he did not take permanently to his bed until a week before his death. In May 1963, he staged an unsuccessful production of another play by Arbuzov,

For Us Somewhere They Wait . . .' and, on 16 May 1964, a production of another play by Alexander Shtein, *Between the Floods*.

Between the Floods dealt with the Kronstadt rising of 1921 and featured Lenin (the first time he had appeared in any Okhlopkov production), a part played by Maxim Shtraukh with great success. In each of the scenes in which Lenin appeared, he was alone. Despite the fact that what Shtein had written amounted in many respects to a 'chamber' play, Okhlopkov inevitably tried to find a scenic equivalent for the epoch-making events with which it dealt and introduced a number of mass scenes. The sets by Kovalenko and Krivoshein conjured up the vast icy expanses of the Gulf of Finland or depicted the fashionable drawing room in the house of Baroness Rilken. An article appeared in *Pravda* on 12 July 1964, criticising Shtein and, through him, the production for 'the absence of genuine historicism in the approach to the image of V.I. Lenin'.[210]

Between 1940 and 1951 Okhlopkov was a recipient of State Prizes on seven different occasions and, in 1958, had been honoured as a 'People's Artist'. When he died on 7 January 1967, as is the custom when a famous actor or director dies, his body lay in an open coffin on the stage of his own theatre. As he was being borne there, observers were struck by a likeness between the present *mise-en-scène* and Okhlopkov's own for the final scene of *Hamlet*. It was a cold winter's day when the catafalque bearing his coffin drove through the snowy streets of the capital to its final resting place in the Novodevichy cemetery. That spring, Okhlopkov would have been sixty-seven, the same age as the century.

Notes

General introduction

1 Before 1918, Russia used the Julian ('Old Style') calendar, which was thirteen days behind the Gregorian ('New Style') calendar. Hence, what is referred to as the 'October' revolution is now celebrated, officially, in November.

2 The Alexandrinsky Theatre, founded in 1756, was one of the two Imperial Theatres in St Petersburg (the other being the Marinsky, built in 1860). Since the revolution they have been renamed the 'Pushkin' and the 'Kirov' respectively. The Maly Theatre in Moscow acquired 'Imperial' status in 1806. It is called the 'Maly' (Small) as distinct from its opposite number the 'Bolshoi' (Big) Theatre.

3 A full account of E.P. Karpov's production at the Alexandrinsky is given by S.D. Balukhaty in *'The Seagull' produced by Stanislavsky. Production Score for the Moscow Art Theatre by K.S. Stanislavsky*, ed. with an introduction by Professor S.D. Balukhaty; translated from the Russian by David Magarshack (London: Dennis Dobson, 1952), pp. 20–33.

4 In addition to being dramatists and prose writers, both Gogol (1809–52) and Turgenev (1818–83) had a great deal of importance to say about theatre as an art form and what needed to be done to ensure its fruitful development in Russia. An account of their theatrical theories can be found in N. Worrall, *Nikolai Gogol and Ivan Turgenev* (London: Macmillan, 1982 pp. 31–47. The best account of the life and work of Mikhail Shchepkin (1788–1863) and the important influence which he exercised on acting styles and production methods in the nineteenth-century Russian theatre is Laurence Senelick's *Serf Actor – The Life and Art of Mikhail Shchepkin* (Connecticut: Greenwood Press, 1984). One of the fullest accounts in English of the life and work of the nineteenth-century dramatist A.N. Ostrovsky (1833–86) can be found in Marjorie L. Hoover, *Alexander Ostrovsky* (Boston: Twayne Publishers, 1981).

5 The Russian 'vaudeville' is something quite distinct from its English counterpart (associated with the early theatrical work of Chaplin and Keaton, for example). Vaude-villes were, in fact, more like our eighteenth-century dramatic 'after-pieces' – light comedies offered in addition to the main bill involving spoken dialogue and song. They were extremely popular throughout the nineteenth century, but especially between about 1830 and 1880. Shchepkin, like Garrick, with whom he has often been compared, was equally at home in the lighter form as in more serious plays. A useful account of the Russian vaudeville is given by B.V. Varneke in his *History of the Russian Theatre, 17th–19th Century*, trans. Boris Brasol (New York: Hafner Publishing Co., 1971), pp. 188–99.

6 A second-rate actress of the provincial theatre who is a central character in Chekhov's *Seagull*.

7 See, for example, Chekhov's account of the first night of his play *Ivanov*, given to his brother Alexander on 20 Nov. 1887, in *Letters of Anton Chekhov*, selected, introduced and with a commentary by Simon Karlinsky (London: The Bodley Head, 1973), pp. 72–3.

8 *The Seagull* was chosen for her own benefit performance by the actress E. Levkeyeva but then, instead of appearing in that play, she appeared on the same bill in a 'vaudeville' – N. Solovyov's *A Happy Day*, which was more her style. The first night audience for *The Seagull* consisted mostly of Levkeyeva's admirers who anticipated seeing her in a light comedy, which *The Seagull* was not. Chekhov was, of course, to insist, following the Moscow Art Theatre's successful 1898 production of the play staged in a serious, dramatic vein, that this was a misinterpretation and that he had, in fact, written 'a comedy'.

9 Alexander Blok (1880–1921) was a leading figure in the Russian symbolist movement and one of Russia's finest modern poets, as well as an interesting dramatist and essayist.

Translations of Blok's influential play can be found in *An Anthology of Russian Plays*, 2 vols., vol. 2, *1890–1960*, ed., trans. and introduced by F.D. Reeve (New York: Vintage Books, 1963). It is also included as an appendix to an article by Virginia Bennett, 'Russian *Pagliacci*: Symbols of Profaned Love in *The Puppet Show*', *Themes in Drama*, vol. 4, ed. James Redmond (Cambridge University Press, 1982), pp. 141–79. The play is also included in *The Russian Symbolist Theatre – An Anthology of Plays and Critical Texts*, ed. and trans. Michael Green (Ardis, Michigan, 1986). The latter collection also includes another of Blok's plays, *The Rose and the Cross*, as well as some of his theatre essays. His play *The Female Stranger*, sometimes referred to as *The Unknown Woman*, has been translated as *The Stranger* in *Doubles, Demons, and Dreamers: An International Collection of Symbolist Drama*, ed. Daniel Gerould (New York: PAJ Publications, 1985).

10 The 'Silver Age' of Russian culture refers to that second period of efflorescence which took place around the turn of the twentieth century and continued until the revolution. Its forerunner, the so-called 'Golden Age', is the remarkable period during the first half of the nineteenth century which saw an unprecedented flowering of the Russian arts – in literature, music and painting especially.

11 George II, Duke of Saxe-Meiningen (1862–1914), ran a theatre company, together with the actor Ludwig Chronegk, at the Duke's own Court Theatre, achieving European renown in the late nineteenth century as a result of tours which introduced their revelatory 'historical–naturalist' style to audiences unfamiliar with theatrical ensemble work of this quality. The company paid two visits to Russia, in 1885 and 1890, the second of which, especially, left an abiding impression on Stanislavsky.

André Antoine (1858–1943), a former gas company employee, founded the Théâtre Libre (Free Theatre) in Paris in 1887 for the production of the new naturalist drama. His example was followed by Otto Brahm (1856–1912), a German literary critic who founded the Freie Bühne (Free Stage) Theatre in 1889, named after his journal of the same title.

12 An account of the establishment of the People's Art Theatre, as it was originally called, can be found in Constantin Stanislavski, *My Life in Art*, trans. J.J. Robbins (Harmondsworth: Penguin, 1967) and in Vladimir Nemirovich-Danchenko, *My Life in the Russian Theatre*, trans. John Cournos (London: Geoffrey Bles, 1968). A useful synoptic account, 'Stanislavsky's and Nemirovich-Danchenko's Quest for a New Theatre: Foundation of the People's Art Theatre', can be found in Balukhaty, 'The Seagull' produced by Stanislavsky, pp. 34–48.

13 Vera Komissarzhevskaya (1864–1910) was the daughter of the opera singer F.P. Komissarzhevsky and one of the great actresses of the late nineteenth – early twentieth century. She first appeared on the stage of the Alexandrinsky Theatre in 1896 before leaving the company in 1902 to tour for two years. She established her own theatre in St Petersburg in 1904, together with her brother Fyodor, where Meyerhold and Evreinov worked as directors and Tairov worked, briefly, as an actor.

Fyodor Komissarzhevsky (1882–1954), brother of Vera, was a director, teacher and theoretician of theatre. He ran his own theatre studio in St Petersburg from 1914 to 1918 and later organised his own theatre studio at the KhPSRO (The Artistically-Enlightened Union of Workers' Organisations) in Moscow in 1918. He emigrated in 1919 but continued to stage plays as well as teach in London, Stratford, New York, Paris and Vienna. Komissarzhevsky wrote an autobiography, *Myself and Theatre* (1929) as well as several other works, including an important book on theatrical costume. He was married for a short time to the British actress Peggy Ashcroft.

K.N. Nezlobin (1857–1930) was a provincial actor and director who established a theatre named after him in Moscow in 1909, where a number of important directors acquired initial experience, including Fyodor Komissarzhevsky and Konstantin Mardzhanov. The theatre was also an excellent training ground for actors before the revolution.

F.A. Korsh (1852–1923) founded his own theatre in 1882 in Moscow as a direct consequence of the abolition of the Imperial Theatres' monopoly and built his reputation on the skills of fine actors in his company.

14 The standard work on the art movements of the period is Camilla Gray, *The Great Experiment: Russian Art 1863–1922* (London: Thames and Hudson, 1962).

15 The 'World of Art' was a group of artists who came together around the end of the nineteenth century and who co-existed until about 1924. During the course of the group's existence, it included some of the greatest artists and theatre designers of the period, including Benois, Bakst, Bilibin, Dobuzhinsky, Golovin, Korovin, Kustodiev and Serov. They were responsible for the sumptuous decor which accompanied productions at private opera houses and many of them became associated with the Moscow Art Theatre, Meyerhold, Diaghilev's ballet company and Tairov's Kamerny Theatre. The ballet impresario, Sergei Diaghilev, together with Alexandre Benois, edited a magazine called *World of Art* (Mir Iskusstva) between 1899 and 1904, which tended to encourage the symbolist trend in the art of the period.

16 Georg Fuchs (1868–1949), founder of the Munich Art Theatre, directed a season of plays there in 1907–8; he wrote two highly influential books, *The Theater of the Future* (1906) and *The Revolution of the Theatre* (1909), the latter of which was translated into Russian in 1911. He believed that traditional, middle-class theatre would give way to a new theatre of festival (*Festspiel*). He was enthusiastic about Wagner's productions at Bayreuth and thought the stage should be broken down into separate planes, with the actors using their bodies as well as their voices. He also proposed far-reaching reforms in stage lighting and wanted to reveal the process of theatre production through the exposure of its 'machinery'. These ideas exercised considerable influence on Meyerhold, Tairov and Vakhtangov.

17 Fyodor Sologub (1863–1927), poet, writer and dramatist, was a leading light of the Russian symbolists. His essay *The Theatre of a Single Will* (1908) and his play *The Triumph of Death*, staged by Meyerhold in 1907, are to be found in *The Russian Symbolist Theatre*, ed. Green. For further information see Daniel Gerould's article 'Sologub and the Theatre', *The Drama Review*, 21: 4 (T-76) (December 1977).

18 Alexander Tairov, *Notes of a Director*, trans. with an introduction by William Kuhlke (Florida: University of Miami Press, 1969), p. 41.

19 Vyacheslav Ivanov (1866–1949) was a poet, dramatist, theatre historian and theoretician. Ivanov became influenced by Nietzsche's ideas on the origins of tragedy whilst studying in Berlin. He wrote works on Hellenic religion and the cult of Dionysus and contributed to the symbolist magazines *Apollo* and *The Balance* (Vesy), as well as writing plays– *Tantalus* (1905) and *Prometheus* (1919). He sought a communal theatre of ecstasy where the barriers between audience and actors would be broken down. Although his ideas were on a grand scale, most of the experiments in which he was involved took place at the intimate 'Tower' Theatre situated in his own private apartments in St Petersburg. It was here that Meyerhold staged some of his own small-scale 'fringe' productions whilst he was head of the Imperial Theatres between 1908 and 1917. Ivanov emigrated to Italy in 1924. Two extracts from his theatre essays have been translated in *The Russian Symbolist Theatre*, ed. Green, while an extended exegesis of his philosophy of art is contained in James West, *Russian Symbolism; A Study of Vyacheslav Ivanov and the Russian Symbolist Aesthetic* (London: Methuen, 1970). Ivanov's essay, 'The Essence of Tragedy', has been translated in *Russian Dramatic Theory from Pushkin to the Symbolists: An Anthology*, trans. and ed. Laurence Senelick (Austin: University of Texas, 1981).

20 Valeri Briusov (1873–1924) was a poet, essayist and another important figure in the Russian symbolist movement. His essay 'Unnecessary Truth' was first published in the *World of Art* magazine in 1902 and his essay 'Realism and Convention on the Stage' was published in 1908 (it appears in *Russian Dramatic Theory*, ed. Senelick). His drama *Earth* is an interesting work with an apocalyptic theme summarised by Harold B. Segel in *Twentieth Century Drama from Gorky to the Present* (New York: Columbia University Press,

1979), pp. 66–7. The play was staged in the Soviet Union in 1922 and in 1923. Briusov's historical novel, *The Fiery Angel*, on which Prokofiev based his opera of the same title, was reissued in English translation in 1975. An extract from Briusov's essay 'Unnecessary Truth' appears in *The Russian Symbolist Theatre*, ed. Green, pp. 25–30.

21 Maurice Maeterlinck (1862–1949), Belgian poet, dramatist and philosopher, was a major figure in the European symbolist movement who exerted a powerful influence on theatre practice in Russia and was much respected by Chekhov, Stanislavsky and Meyerhold, among others. His essay 'The Tragic in Everyday Life', from his book of essays *The Treasure of the Humble* (1896), was widely read.

22 Sometimes translated as *The Scales*.

23 Andrei Bely (pseudonym of Boris Bugaev, 1880–1934) was a novelist, poet and essayist and one of the most distinguished symbolist theorists. His novel *St Petersburg* is considered by Vladimir Nabokov to be one of the greatest works of 'modernism'. It was composed between 1913 and 1916, then revised again during the 1920s. A dramatised version of the novel was staged by Michael Chekhov at the Second Moscow Art Theatre in 1925. An expert on the work of Gogol, Bely devoted a monograph to Meyerhold's production of *The Government Inspector* (1926) entitled *Gogol and Meyerhold* (1927). His essay 'Theatre and Modern Drama' appears in *Russian Dramatic Theory*, ed. Senelick, together with his essay 'The Cherry Orchard', which also appears in the anthology *The Russian Symbolist Theatre*, ed. Green, alongside another essay of his, 'Against Reviving the Greek Theatre'.

24 In a volume entitled *Theatre: A Book About the New Theatre* (1908).

25 Alexandre Benois (1870–1960), painter, theatre designer, art historian, theatre critic, theatre director, was a member of the 'World of Art' group. He designed sets for the Hermitage and Marinsky Theatres in St Petersburg as well as working for Diaghilev's company in Paris. One of his most famous settings was for Igor Stravinsky's ballet *Petrushka* in 1911. He also designed for Stanislavsky at the Moscow Art Theatre immediately prior to the First World War. He lived and worked abroad from the mid 1920s onwards, mainly in Paris and in Italy. He is the author of *Reminiscences of the Russian Ballet* (1941) and great-uncle of the British author, raconteur, actor and playwright, Peter Ustinov.

26 Anatoli Lunacharsky (1875–1933), dramatist, theatre and literary critic, was the Soviet Union's first Commissar for Education and the Arts. His plays include *Oliver Cromwell* (1921) and *Faust and the City* (1920) while his theatre essays run to two sizeable volumes (1958). A truly cultured and enlightened man, he was much respected by the major figures of the Russian theatre of the 1920s whose work he supported and encouraged even when he disagreed with aspects of it. The State Institute of Theatre Art, in Moscow (GITIS), is named after him as are a number of theatres in the Soviet Union.

27 V.E. Meyerhold (1874–1940) was the major figure in the history of modern Russian/ Soviet theatre alongside Stanislavsky. The standard work on Meyerhold is Konstantin Rudnitsky's *Meyerhold the Director*, trans. G. Petrov, ed. S. Schultze with an introduction by E. Proffer (Michigan: Ardis, 1981). A distinguished British study is that of Edward Braun, *The Theatre of Meyerhold: Revolution on the Modern Stage* (London: Eyre Methuen, 1979).

28 Extended extracts from Meyerhold's essay, including 'The Naturalist Theatre and the Theatre of Mood', where the Chekhov references can be found, are translated in *Meyerhold on Theatre*, ed. Edward Braun (London: Methuen, 1968).

29 Nikolai Evreinov (1879–1953), playwright, director and theatre historian, is someone whose work has been treated quite extensively by English-speaking theatre researchers – see especially, C. Moody, 'Nikolai Nikolaevich Evreinov', *Russian Literature Tri-Quarterly*, 13 (1975); Spencer Golub, *Evreinov: The Theatre of Paradox and Transformation* (Michigan: UMI Research Press, 1982) and Christopher Collins, 'Nikolai Evreinov as a

Playwright', *Russian Literature Tri-Quarterly*, 2 (1972). Evreinov's 'Introduction to Monodrama' is translated in *Russian Dramatic Theory*, ed. Green, pp. 183–99 and his general theatrical credo can be traced in his *The Theatre in Life*, ed. and trans. A.I. Nazaroff (London: Geo. G. Harrap & Co., n.d.). His play *Theatre of the Soul: A Monodrama*, staged by Edith Craig at the Little Theatre in 1915, was published the same year in a translation by Christopher St John and Marie Potapenko. His 'harlequinade', *A Merry Death*, appeared in a volume of *Five Russian Plays*, trans. C.E. Bechofer, in 1916. A more recent collection of his plays in translation, including what is probably his most notable effort, *The Main Thing*, is *Life As Theatre: Five Modern Plays by Nikolai Evreinov*, trans. and ed. Christopher Collins (Michigan: Ardis, 1973).

30 The history of the Studio on Povarskaya Street can be found in Stanislavski, *My Life in Art*, pp. 393–405.

31 Leonid Andreyev (1871–1919), prose writer and dramatist, was a major figure in the Russian symbolist movement. Probably his best-known play in the symbolist genre is *The Life of Man*, staged by Meyerhold in 1906 and by Stanislavsky in 1907. The play of his most widely known and performed abroad is the extravaganza, set in a circus, *He Who Gets Slapped* (trans. F.D. Reeve in *Russian Plays*, vol. 2). Andreyev failed to come to terms with the revolution and lived in Finland after 1917. The standard work in English on Andreyev is James B. Woodward, *Leonid Andreyev: A Study* (Oxford University Press, 1969). A volume of three plays, *The Black Maskers*, *The Life of Man* and *The Sabine Women*, was published by Duckworth in 1915. Some of his theatre essays are translated in *The Russian Symbolist Theatre*, ed. Green, while his 'Letters on the Theatre' appear in *Russian Dramatic Theory*, ed. Senelick.

Knut Hamsun (1859–1952) was a Norwegian writer and dramatist. His plays betray a Nietzschean influence and tend to portray the 'exceptional individual' towering above the mass, such as the hero of his trilogy *At the Gates of the Kingdom* (1895) staged by Moscow Art Theatre in 1909, *The Game of Life* (1896) staged by Moscow Art Theatre in 1907, and *Red of Evening* (1898). The Art Theatre also staged his *In the Grip of Life* in 1911, the year after it was written.

32 For an account of the production of *A Month in the Country* see *My Life in Art*, pp. 499–503. See also N. Worrall, *Nikolai Gogol and Ivan Turgenev*, pp. 180–5.

33 For an account of the production see Laurence Senelick, 'The Craig–Stanislavsky "Hamlet" at the Moscow Art Theatre', *Theatre Quarterly*, 6:22 (Summer 1976). See also the more extended account in the same author's *Gordon Craig's Moscow 'Hamlet': A Reconstruction* (Connecticut: Greenwood Press, 1982).

34 These include S. Yushkevich, S. Przybyszewsky, H. von Hofmannsthal, and F. Sologub.

35 The designers he worked with included Golovin, Bakst, Dobuzhinsky, Bilibin, Sudeikin, Sapunov. Fellow artists included the dancer Fokine, the singer Chaliapin, the actors Yurev, Varlamov and Savina; the composers Glazunov, Stravinsky and Kuzmin; the conductors Nikolai Malko, Edward Napravnik and Albert Coates. His operatic productions included Gluck's *Orpheo*, Wagner's *Tristan and Isolde*, Mussorgsky's *Boris Godunov* and Strauss's *Elektra*. He also staged major productions of Molière's *Don Juan*, Ostrovsky's *The Thunderstorm* and Lermontov's *Masquerade*.

36 Many of the bio-mechanical exercises which Meyerhold incorporated into his training had their origins in the stylised acting forms of his symbolist period. Bio-mechanics drew its inspiration from gymnastics, the circus, the observation of the movements of animals, from time and motion studies, from Pavlovian theories of reflexology, from the American psychologist, William James's, theory of the emotions and from the stylised example of Oriental theatre. For a fuller account of bio-mechanics see Mel Gordon, 'Biomechanics', *The Drama Review*, 18: 3 (T-63) (September 1974), 77–88; see also Marjorie Hoover, *Meyerhold: The Art of Conscious Theatre* (Amherst: University of Massachusetts Press, 1974), pp. 311–15.

37 Eisenstein was conducting acting classes in Moscow when Meyerhold revived his production of *Masquerade* in 1938 and encouraged his pupils to make the trip to Leningrad to see it.

38 The RSFSR (Federation of Soviet Socialist Republics) became the USSR (Union of Soviet Socialist Republics) in 1922 as part of an attempt by Lenin to prevent the weakening of the Federation which the introduction of NEP threatened to bring about.

39 St Petersburg had been russified as 'Petrograd' during the First World War. It was renamed Leningrad following the death of the Soviet leader.

40 *Mystery-Bouffe* was first staged by Meyerhold and Mayakovsky, with a largely amateur cast, at the Luna-Park theatre in Petrograd, and with settings by the suprematist artist, Kasimir Malevich, on the occasion of the first anniversary of the October revolution. Mayakovsky also acted in the production.

41 As Meyerhold is depicted in B. Grigoriev's famous satirical portrait of him.

42 The movement had its own journal *The Theatre Messenger* (Vestnik Teatra) which Meyerhold also edited.

43 The first casualties were the Nezlobin and Korsh Theatres, which became RSFSR Theatres No. 2 and 3.

44 Meyerhold's plans to stage *The Dawns* went back as far as 1907. One of Vakhtangov's projects, after the revolution, was to have multiple productions of *The Dawns* running consecutively at his People's Theatre, staged in varying ways by each of Moscow's major theatre companies.

45 One of the most scathing criticisms was made by Lenin's wife, Nadezhda Krupskaya, reviewing the production in the pages of the Communist Party newspaper, *Pravda*.

46 Constructivism was very popular with Soviet stage directors during the first years of the revolution. The stage forms which V.V. Dmitriev provided for Meyerhold's *The Dawns*, Lyubov Popova for ·his *The Magnanimous Cuckold* (1922), Varvara Stepanova for his production of *Tarelkin's Death* (1922), were revelatory as well as revolutionary. Meyerhold's example was taken up by others, including Tairov, whose set for G.K. Chesterton's *The Man Who Was Thursday* (1924), designed by Alexander Vesnin, vied for constructivist supremacy with V.A. Shestakov's setting for Meyerhold's production of Faiko's *Lake Lyul* at the Theatre of the Revolution (1923). See John E. Bowlt, 'Constructivism on the Russian Stage', *Performing Arts Journal*, 1:3 (Winter 1977), 62–84.

47 Sergei Eisenstein (1898–1948) was a film and theatre director/designer. He worked with travelling theatre groups at the civil war front before joining the Proletkult Theatre in 1920, where he put his theories of 'montage' into practice, most notably in a re-worked version of Ostrovsky's nineteenth-century classic *Enough Stupidity in Every Wise Man*. He was a great admirer of Meyerhold and acted as his assistant on the production of *Tarelkin's Death* (1922) before leaving the theatre to establish a world reputation as a cinema director. For an account of Eisenstein's work at Proletkult, see Daniel Gerould, 'Eisenstein's *Wiseman*', together with a translation of Eisenstein's essay 'Montage of Attractions', *The Drama Review*, 18:1 (T-61) (March 1974). See also Mel Gordon, 'Eisenstein's Later Work at Proletkult', *The Drama Review*, 22:3 (T-79) (September 1978).

48 For a detailed account of the production of *The Magnanimous Cuckold*, see Alma H. Law, 'Meyerhold's *The Magnanimous Cuckold* (1922)', *The Drama Review*, 26:1 (T-93) (Spring 1982), 61–86, and N. Worrall, 'Meyerhold's *The Magnificent Cuckold*', *The Drama Review*, 17:1 (T-57) (March 1973), 14–34. For a detailed, illustrated account of the production of *Tarelkin's Death*, see Alma H. Law, 'The Death of Tarelkin: A Constructivist Vision of Tsarist Russia', *Russian History*, 8, parts 1–2 (1981), 145–98; also N. Worrall, 'Meyerhold and Eisenstein' in *Performance and Politics in Popular Drama*, ed. D. Bradby, L. James and B. Sharratt (Cambridge University Press, 1980), pp. 173–88.

49 Vladimir Mayakovsky (1894–1930) was a poet, playwright, painter, actor, propagandist, director, film scenarist and founder, with Velemir Khlebnikov, Osip Brik and David Burlyuk of the Russian futurist movement, whose manifesto *A Slap In the Face of Public*

Taste (1912) advocated throwing Pushkin and Tolstoy overboard from 'the steamship of history'. He wrote short works for circus performance but his main contribution to dramatic literature are his three plays – *Mystery-Bouffe* (an 'Heroic, Epic, and Satiric Representation of Our Era') and his satires on a renaissant bourgeoisie, *The Bedbug*, and on Soviet bureaucracy, *The Bathhouse*. The latter two were staged by Meyerhold in 1929 and 1930 respectively. See *The Complete Plays of Vladimir Mayakovsky*, trans. Guy Daniels (New York: Simon & Schuster, 1968). See also Frantisek Deak, 'Agitprop and Circus Plays of Mayakovsky', *The Drama Review*, 17:1 (T-57) (March 1973). Mayakovsky committed suicide shortly after the opening of *The Bathhouse*.

50 In December 1917 Lunacharsky issued an invitation to some 120 artists, writers and others to attend a conference on the future organisation of the arts under the new regime. Only five people answered the invitation, three of whom were Mayakovsky, Blok and Meyerhold.

51 At his own Musical Studio, Nemirovich-Danchenko staged, amongst other things, a version of Bizet's *Carmen* and Offenbach's *La Périchole*. Accounts of these productions are given by Oliver M. Sayler in *Inside the Moscow Art Theatre* (New York: Brentano's, 1925).

52 Michael Chekhov (1891–1955) was an actor, director, teacher, and nephew of Anton Chekhov. He joined the Moscow Art Theatre in 1913 and gave memorable performances at the First Studio as Malvolio in *Twelfth Night* (1920) and Khlestakov in *The Government Inspector* (1921), both directed by Stanislavsky; as Erik XIV in Strindberg's play, directed by Vakhtangov (1921) and, later, as Hamlet, at the Second Studio in 1924. He emigrated in 1928.

53 LEF (Levy Front Iskusstva) was a group of avant-garde artists centred round the journal *Lef*, whose leading members included Vladimir Mayakovsky, Sergei Tretyakov, Osip Brik and Boris Arvatov. The journal was replaced by *Novy Lef* (New Left) in 1927.

54 Adapted in 'montage' form by Sergei Tretyakov from Marcel Martinet's novel with a First World War setting, *La Nuit*. See also Frantisek Deak, 'Russian Mass Spectacles', *The Drama Review*, 19:2 (T-66) (June 1975); and Rene Fülop-Müller, *The Mind and Face of Bolshevism: An Examination of Cultural Life in Soviet Russia*, trans. F.S. Flint and D.F. Tait (London: G.P. Putnam's Sons Ltd, 1927), pp. 133–51.

55 Konstantin Mardzhanov (1872–1933) was founder of the Free Theatre in Moscow in 1913, where Tairov was employed as a director. Mardzhanov went on to establish the Soviet theatre in Georgia where the principal theatre in the capital, Tbilisi, is named after him.

56 In his production of *Bubus the Teacher*, Meyerhold experimented with what he called a system of 'pre-acting' (see *Meyerhold on Theatre*, p. 205). His production of Gogol's *The Government Inspector*, in 1926, marked a break with the dominant style of his post-revolutionary productions and an apparent return to the stylised grotesquerie of aspects of his pre-revolutionary work. For a detailed account of the Gogol production, see N. Worrall, 'Meyerhold Directs Gogol's *Government Inspector*', *Theatre Quarterly*, 2:7 (1972), 75–95.

57 P.M. Kerzhentsev (1881–1940), one of the most important theorists of the Proletkult organisation, he set out its theatrical beliefs in two books published in 1918, *The Creative Theatre* and *The Revolution and the Theatre*. From 1936 to 1938 he held the post of president of the Central Committee for the Arts. An article which he wrote in *Pravda* in December 1937, describing Meyerhold's theatre as 'alien', precipitated its closure in January 1938.

58 Sergei Esenin (1895–1925) was a peasant poet described as an 'unlettered genius'. His connection with the theatre is through a verse play about the peasant rebel Emilian Pugachov, which he wrote in 1921, and through two marriages – one to the American dancer, Isadora Duncan, and the other to the actress Zinaida Raikh, who later became the wife of Meyerhold. Esenin took his own life.

59 V.F. Pletnyov (1886–1942), dramatist, essayist and leader of Proletkult, served as its president from 1921 to 1932.

60 See especially Trotsky's remarks on futurism in Leon Trotsky, *Literature and Revolution* (Ann Arbor: University of Michigan, 1968), pp. 126–61.

61 The proceedings of the conference are contained in the volume *Soviet Writers' Congress 1934 – The Debate on Socialist Realism and Modernism* (Lawrence & Wishart, London: 1977).

62 The classic spokesmen for the 'realist' and 'modernist' positions in the 1930s are the Hungarian literary critic, Georg Lukacs, and the German dramatist and theorist, Bertolt Brecht. The essence of their dispute is contained in the volume *Aesthetics and Politics – Debates Between Ernst Bloch, Georg Lukacs, Bertolt Brecht, Walter Benjamin, Theodor Adorno* (London: New Left Books, 1977).

63 Meyerhold's 'eccentric' production of *The Forest* was staged in the manner of an Eisensteinian 'montage of attractions' in a setting more reminiscent of a playground than a landowner's estate (where the play's action is set). The fullest account of the production in English is in Rudnitsky, *Meyerhold the Director*. For Tairov's production of *The Thunderstorm*.

64 *Storm* was directed by E.O. Lyubimov-Lanskoi (1883–1943) and *Virineya* by Alexei Popov (1892–1961).

65 FEKS (The Factory of the Eccentric Actor) was founded in Petrograd in 1921 by G.M. Kozintsev, L.S. Trauberg and G.K. Kryzhitsky, who declared that 'eccentrism' was the highest form of theatrical art, based on dynamic forms involving the 'electrification' and 'Americanisation' of the theatre. Their most famous productions were an 'electrified' version of Gogol's *Marriage* and a production, in 1923, of Cocteau's *The Wedding on the Eiffel Tower*. The members of the group turned their attention increasingly to film after 1924. For further information see the article on FEKS in *The Drama Review*, 19:4 (T-68) (December 1975).

66 Sergei Radlov (1892–1958) was a student at Meyerhold's St Petersburg Studio on Borodinskaya Street before becoming a member of the Petrograd Theatre Section and organising theatre brigades at the civil war front, as well as mass spectacles in the cities. From 1920 to 1922 he headed the theatre of Popular Comedy in Petrograd where he also staged a number of expressionist-influenced productions at the Leningrad State Dramatic Theatre between 1923 and 1927. For further information, see Mel Gordon, 'Radlov's Theatre of Popular Comedy' and Radlov's article 'On the Pure Elements of the Actor's Art', *The Drama Review*, 19:4 (T-68) (December 1975).

67 Nikolai Foregger (1892–1939) was a director and ballet master. Influenced by futurism, constructivism and bio-mechanics, Foregger established Mastfor (Masterskaya Foregger – The Foregger Workshop) in Moscow during the early 1920s. Here he formulated a programme of 'machine dances' on revolutionary and satirical themes, employing techniques derived from the circus and gymnastics and often employing jazz accompaniment.

68 Yuri Zavadsky (1894–1977) was an actor, director, teacher and protégé of Vakhtangov. He ran his own studio in Moscow between 1924 and 1936 and, in the experimental mood of the times, staged a controversial, expressionistic production of Gogol's *Marriage* at the Art Theatre's Third Studio in 1924.

   Igor Terentyev (no dates available) staged a notoriously anarchic production of Gogol's *The Government Inspector* at the Press House, Leningrad, in 1927.

69 The Moscow Art Theatre was away between 1922 and 1924, during which time they toured Western Europe and paid two successful visits to the United States.

70 Other significant productions at the Art Theatre in this vein were of K. Trenyov's *The Pugachov Rebellion* (1925), A.R. Kugel's *Nicholas I and the Decembrists* (1926), M. Bulgakov's *Days of the Turbins* (1926), Leonid Leonov's *Untilovsk* (1928) and Vsevolod Ivanov's *Blockade* (1929).

71 Soon after the revolution, the government created the title 'Academic' to replace the

'Imperial' title of those theatres which had formerly gone under royal patronage. The title was evidence of the respect which the government sought to accord these theatres, and was an indication of the educative function which they hoped they would serve in passing on the cultural heritage of a previous era as the foundation of the new workers' state. The title was also conferred on institutions, such as the Moscow Art Theatre and the Kamerny Theatre, as a mark of recognition of their achievement, and was accompanied by a government grant.

72 This excellent civil war play was later staged at the Moscow Art Theatre in 1936 (directed by Nemirovich-Danchenko and I. Sudakov). It is available in translation in Konstantin Trenyov, *In a Cossack Village and Other Stories* (London: Hutchinson International Authors, 1946).

73 The play, although derived from Bulgakov's own novel *The White Guard*, is not a dramatised version of the novel but a completely original work in its own right. English productions of the play have tended to retain the title of the novel.

74 The 'restoration' referred to here includes aspects of a pre-revolutionary past including, presumably, the monarchy.

75 One of the strongest critics of 'Meyerholditis' (Meierkholdovshchina) was Meyerhold himself, who delivered a lecture 'Meyerhold Against Meyerholditis', in March 1936.

76 For an account of Akimov's production of *Hamlet*, see Alma H. Law, '*Hamlet* at the Vakhtangov', *The Drama Review*, 21:4 (T-76) (December 1977).

77 *Much Ado About Nothing* was directed by I. Rapoport; *The Taming of the Shrew* by Alexei Popov.

78 What we have come to know as two separate works, *An Actor Prepares* and *Building a Character* were, in fact, published as a single volume in two sections under the title *An Actor's Work on Him/Herself* (Rabota Aktyora Nad Soboy). The word *soboy* contains both male and female possibilities in Russian.

79 The attack had the ironic, and happy, consequence of producing an apologetic reply from Shostakovich in the form of his magnificent Fifth Symphony (1937) the score of which is headed with the words – 'A Soviet artist's response to just criticism'. Shostakovich had previously been resident pianist at the Meyerhold Theatre where he had composed a piece for *The Bedbug* scored for 'Firemen's Band'. He also provided an orchestral score for Akimov's *Hamlet*.

80 For details of Meyerhold's 'universal' theatre, see Mikhail Barkhin and Sergei Vakhtangov, 'A theatre for Meyerhold', trans. Edward Braun, *Theatre Quarterly*, 2:7 (July–Sept 1972), 69–73.

81 The reason, it has been assumed in the West, for Meyerhold's arrest arose from a speech he is purported to have given at the conference attacking socialist realism and Soviet theatrical conformity. This version was first promulgated by an emigré source – Yuri Elagin, *Tyomny Genii* (The Dark Genius) (New York: Chekhov Publishing House, 1955). This account has subsequently been repeated by other emigré sources and can be found in Nikolai A. Gorchakov's *The Theatre in Soviet Russia* (Oxford University Press, London, 1957), pp. 363–4. However, more recently, Western researchers such as Edward Braun have thrown doubts on the authenticity of this account, doubts which have been substantiated by the appearance of the official transcript of the speech (admittedly with some gaps) in *Teatr*, 2 (1974), 39–44. It is highly unlikely that the three and a half 'verbatim' pages quoted by Elagin could have constituted one or more of the gaps in the official, edited transcript, so out of keeping is it with the general tenor of the latter version. Elagin's dubious account remains unaltered in a reissue of his book in 1982.

82 Les Kurbas (1887–1942) was a Ukrainian actor and director who organised the 'Berezil' Theatre in Kharkov, which he headed from 1922 until 1933 and where he staged interesting experimental productions of *Oedipus Rex*, *Macbeth*, Kaiser's *Gas* and *Jimmy Higgins* (based on the work of Upton Sinclair). His productions frequently involved a reworking of the text in the interests of Kurbas's imaginative vision of the work.

Sergei Tretyakov (1892–1939), poet, dramatist and translator, came to Moscow after the revolution and became joint founder, with Mayakovsky and others, of LEF. He wrote two plays for Eisenstein at the Proletkult Theatre – *Are You Listening, Moscow?!* and *Gasmasks*. He also adapted Marcel Martinet's novel *La Nuit* for Meyerhold's theatre as *Zemlya Dybom* (Earth Rampant). Tretyakov also wrote a play based on his own experiences in the Far East, *Roar, China!*, also for Meyerhold's theatre, in 1926. He composed screen titles for Eisenstein's silent film *Battleship Potemkin*. He became editor of *Novy Lef* (the journal of the New Left Front of the Arts) in 1928 and befriended Brecht during the latter's visits to the Soviet Union in the 1930s, translating some of his plays. Tretyakov was arrested in 1937 and subsequently disappeared.

83 The invasion flouted a non-aggression treaty between Germany and the Soviet Union which had been signed in August 1939.

84 All three of Mayakovsky's plays were jointly directed by Sergei Yutkevich, a well-known film-maker and former associate of Kozintsev and Eisenstein, together with a former actor at Meyerhold's theatre, Valentin Pluchek, who became Artistic Director of the Moscow Theatre of Satire.

85 Georgi Tovstonogov (b. 1915) began his career at the Children's Theatre in Tbilisi, Georgia, before becoming head of the Griboyedov Theatre in that city from 1938 to 1946. He was principal director of the Lenin Komsomol Theatre in Leningrad from 1950 to 1956, during which time he staged a memorable 'guest' production at the Pushkin Theatre of Vishnevsky's civil war classic *Optimistic Tragedy*, in 1955. Since 1956 he has been artistic head of the Gorky Theatre in Leningrad. He conducted a public argument with Okhlopkov in the pages of the theatre journal *Teatr* in 1959 and 1960 over the perennial and vexed question of what constitutes 'realism' in the theatre. The article which sparked the debate, Okhlopkov's *Ob Uslovnosti* (On the Conventional), can be found in translation as 'On Convention' in *Socialist Realism in Literature and Art* (Moscow: Progress Publishers, 1971), pp. 103–26.

86 A collection of these plays was published as *Contemporary Russian Drama*, selected and translated by Franklin D. Reeve, with a preface by Victor Rozov (New York: Pegasus, 1968).

87 Andrei Zhdanov (1896–1948) was head of the Leningrad party organisation from 1934 to 1944 and secretary to the central committee of the Communist Party in charge of ideological affairs. His name is synonymous with militant philistinism in all matters connected with the arts during the Stalin period.

88 Oleg Efremov (b. 1927), actor and director, began his career at the Central Children's Theatre in Moscow before founding the Studio of Young Actors in 1957, which became the basis for the Sovremennik (Contemporary) Theatre Studio in 1958. Their productions established a new climate in post-war Russian theatre based on youthful optimism and belief in human values. In addition to producing work by a new generation of Soviet dramatists – Rozov, Volodin, Zorin, they also staged significant productions of important Western plays, including Osborne's *Look Back in Anger* (1965) and Wesker's *Roots* (1971). In 1971 Efremov was appointed Artistic Director of the Moscow Art Theatre.

89 Yuri Lyubimov (b. 1917) was Artistic Director of the Theatre of Drama and Comedy in Moscow from 1964 to 1983. The Taganka Theatre (as it is better known) staged a number of important innovatory productions under Lyubimov's aegis inspired by the cultural climate of the mid 1960s and the rediscovery of the experimental vibrancy of the Soviet theatre in the early 1920s. In this respect, the Taganka led the way in the Soviet Union to establish itself as one of the outstanding world theatres, as well as one of the most popular with young people. The company's leading male actor, Vladimir Vysotsky, also commanded a popular following as a singer who combined the talents of Bob Dylan and John Lennon with the acting ability of an Albert Finney. Following the sad and untimely death of Vysotsky and state interference in a production which was designed to pay homage to him, Lyubimov decided, in 1983, to live and work abroad.

1. Alexander Tairov, 1885–1950

1 No. 7 in the 'Books of the Theatre' series, ed. H.D. Albright, trans, and with an introduction by William Kuhlke (Florida: University of Miami Press, 1969).

2 Reference to Tairov can usually be found in general histories of twentieth-century theatre practice – see, for example, James Roose-Evans, *Experimental Theatre From Stanislavsky to Today* (New York: Avon Books, 1970), pp. 46–9, but there has been little else available in English to date.

3 A. Ya. Tairov, 'V poiskakh stilya', *Teatr i Dramaturgiya*, 4 (1936), 202, quoted in *Istoriya sovetskogo dramaticheskogo teatra* (6 vols.), vol. 1, 1917–1920, ed. K. Rudnitsky (Moscow: Nauka, 1966), p. 164.

4 The brothers Robert and Rafail Adelgaim commenced their joint work in the Russian theatre during the mid 1890s before forming a touring company which, during the course of the next forty years, brought the world's classics before a very wide audience, including the work of Shakespeare, Schiller and Goethe. Robert died in 1934; Rafail in 1938.

5 'Shekspir i narod', *Segodnya*, 17 December 1907, quoted in A. Ya. Tairov, *Zapiski rezhissyora, stat'i, besedy, rechi, pis'ma* (Moscow: VTO, 1970), p. 506, hereafter referred to as *TOT* (Tairov on Theatre).

6 Yuri Golovashenko, *Rezhissyorskoe iskusstvo Tairova* (Moscow: Iskusstvo, 1970), p. 214.

7 Ibid., p. 104.

8 Tairov planned a production of another Wilde play, *Lady Windermere's Fan*, in 1948, but this only got as far as the public dress rehearsal.

9 Operetta was an extremely popular form in Russia during the late nineteenth century. For example, Offenbach's *Belle Hélène* was staged on 124 separate occasions between 1855 and 1881. For further details see especially Andrew Donskov, *Mixail Lentovskij and the Russian Theatre* (Michigan: Russian Language Journal, 1985), pp. 19–24.

10 Rene Fülop-Müller and Joseph Gregor, *The Russian Theatre* (reprinted New York: Benjamin Blom, 1965), p. 55.

11 N.F. Monakhov (1875–1936) gained his acting experience on the amateur and popular stages of the 1890s as a song and dance performer and was especially fine in operetta. After the revolution he helped form the Bolshoi Drama Theatre in Leningrad in company with Maxim Gorky and Marya Andreyeva, where he proved to be an equally excellent actor of serious roles.

12 Arthur Symons, 'Pantomime and the Poetic Drama', *Studies in Seven Arts* (London: Martin Secker, 1924), p. 241.

13 M.M. Bonch-Tomashevsky, 'Pantomima A. Shnitslera v svobodnom teatre', cited in *TOT*, p. 508.

14 Alisa Koonen, *Stranitsy zhizni* (2nd ed, Moscow: Iskusstvo, 1985), p. 177.

15 Ibid., p. 179

16 *Notes of a Director*, p. 52.

17 Bonch-Tomashevsky, 'Pantomima A. Schnitslera'.

18 There is an interesting parallel here with Okhlopkov's use of the same conventional device, more than twenty years later, in his production of *Aristocrats*.

19 E. Gugushvili, *Kote Mardzhanishvili* (Moscow: Iskusstvo, 1979), pp. 171–4.

20 A Japanese company had first visited Russia as early as 1902 and its influence, as part of an overall anti-naturalistic tendency, can be noted among the more important theatre leaders and practitioners.

21 *Notes of a Director*, p. 58.

22 N. Ya. Berkovsky, *Literatura i teatr* (Moscow: Iskusstvo, 1969), p. 312. Konstantin Balmont (1867–1942) was a leading Russian symbolist poet who also published collections of Egyptian, South American and Indian folklore. He emigrated in 1921 and died in France.

23 Golovashenko, *Rezhissyorskoe iskusstvo Tairova*, p. 72.

24 Natalya Goncharova (1881–1962) and Mikhail Larionov (1881–1964) together elaborated the artistic theory of 'rayonnism' during the early years of this century and were both associated with the Russian cubo-futurist movement before the revolution. They both lived abroad after the revolution and ended their days in France.

25 Koonen, *Stranitsy zhizni*, pp. 209–10.

26 Nikolai Mikhailovich Tseretelli (1890–1942) worked for a while with Max Reinhardt at his Deutsches Theater before returning to Russia and working at the Kamerny Theatre from 1916 to 1928 where he played most of the leading male roles opposite Alisa Koonen. After leaving the Kamerny he worked for a while as a director at the Operetta Theatre in Moscow. From 1934 onwards he worked mainly in the provinces.

27 Henri Forterre was a French conductor and composer who played an important part in establishing music as a key ingredient of Tairov's early productions at the Kamerny where he worked from 1915 to 1920.

28 *Notes of a Director*, p. 63.

29 The play is available in translation, with an introduction to the work of Annensky, in *The Russian Symbolist Theatre – An Anthology of Plays and Critical Texts*, ed. and trans. Michael Green (Michigan: Ardis, Ann Arbor, 1986).

30 Alexandra Exter (1882–1949) was a leading member of the Russian avant-garde art movement who founded her own studio in Kiev, in 1918, and who worked in both Odessa and Moscow as a theatre and film-set designer (*Aelita*, 1924). Emigrated to France in 1924.

31 *Zaum* – short for *zaumny yazyk* or 'transrational language' – was exploited by the formalist school of poets who considered the sound of language to be as interesting as (if not more interesting than) its sense. Tairov cites an example on p. 88 of *Notes of a Director*.

32 A.A. Salzmann worked with Adolphe Appia and Jaques Dalcroze at Hellerau before the First World War.

33 An extended description of the lighting effects in this production can be found in Oliver M. Sayler, *The Russian Theatre Under the Revolution* (Boston, 1920), pp. 164–9.

34 Golovashenko, *Rezhissyorskoe iskusstvo Tairova*, p. 28.

35 *Notes of a Director*, p. 120.

36 Marc Slonim, *Russian Theater from the Empire to the Soviets* (London: Methuen, 1963), p. 260. For a more extended account of this production in English, see Sayler, *Russian Theatre*, pp. 152–62. There are also references to be found in N.A. Gorchakov, *The Theatre in Soviet Russia* (London: Oxford University Press, 1957), pp. 138–40, and in Hallie Flanagan, *Shifting Scenes of the Modern European Theatre* (London: Harrap, 1929), pp. 148–51.

37 *TOT*, p. 203.

38 B.A. Ferdinandov (1889–1959) was an actor, director and stage designer who worked for a season at the Moscow Art Theatre (1911–12) before working as both actor and designer at the Kamerny between 1917 and 1925. He also founded and headed his own 'experimental–heroic' theatre in Moscow between 1921 and 1923 where he produced work based on his theory of 'metro-rhythm'.

39 M. Lyubomudrov, 'Evolyutsiya tvorchestvo A. Ya. Tairova', *Problemy teorii i praktiki russkoi sovetskoi rezhissury, 1917–1925* (Leningrad: LGITMiK 1978), p. 127. The best account of this production in English is contained in Sayler, *Russian Theatre*, pp. 173–6.

40 Also of interest to Vakhtangov.

41 *Sovetskii teatr – dokumenty i materialy. Russkii sovetskii teatr 1917–1921*, ed. A.Z. Yufit (Leningrad: Iskusstvo, 1968), note 14, p. 179.

42 G.B. Yakulov (1882–1928), an artist profoundly interested in theories of light, became active as a stage designer after 1918, principally at the Kamerny Theatre but also in Paris where he produced the decor for Diaghilev's production of Prokofiev's *Le Pas d'Acier*. Died of pneumonia in Moscow.

43 Not to be confused with A.V. Alexandrov, founder of the famous Red Army Ensemble, who was chorus master at the Kamerny Theatre from 1926 to 1930.

44 *Dokumenty i materialy 1917–1921*, p. 167. See also Koonen, *Stranitsy zhizni*, p. 252.

45 *Istoriya sovetskogo dramaticheskogo teatra*, vol. 1, p. 168. One of the best accounts of the production is Koonen's own in *Teatr*, 3 (1968) and in *Stranitsy zhizni*, pp. 248–52.

46 *Notes of a Director*, p. 54.

47 Koonen, *Stranitsy zhizni* pp. 253–4. For an account of the production's debt to styles and techniques of *commedia dell'arte*, see *Dokumenty i materialy 1917–1921*, pp. 168–78.

48 Alexander Vesnin (1883–1959) was the youngest of three brothers who worked on several architectural and design projects between 1910 and the early 1930s. As a member of Inkhuk (Institute of Artistic Culture) he contributed to the famous constructivist exhibition in Moscow in 1925 '5 × 5 = 25'.

49 Berkovsky, *Literatura i teatr*, p. 347.

50 *Sovetskii teatr – dokumenty i materialy. Russkii sovetskii teatr 1926–1932* (part 1), ed. A. Ya. Trabsky (Leningrad: Iskusstvo, 1982), p. 347.

51 Lyubomudrov, 'Evolyutsiya tvorchestvo Tairova', p. 128.

52 N.A. Andreyev (1873–1932), was a sculptor, graphic artist and stage designer. As well as sculpting many famous public monuments, Andreyev also designed for the stage, probably his best-known settings being those for Stanislavsky's production of Byron's *Cain* (1920).

53 Narkompros – acronym for 'Narodny Komitet Prosveshcheniya (People's Commissariat of Enlightenment).

54 *Dokumenty i materialy 1917–1921*, p. 161.

55 *Notes of a Director*, p. 41.

56 *Notes of a Director*, p. 52.

57 Ibid., p. 77.

58 *TOT*, p. 192.

59 Ibid., pp. 284–91.

60 John Bowlt, *Russian Stage Design: Scenic Innovation 1900–1930* (Mississippi Museum of Art, 1982), p. 137.

61 Ibid., p. 31.

62 *Istoriya sovetskogo dramaticheskogo teatra* (6 vols.), vol. 2, *1921–1925*, ed. K. Rudnitsky, Moscow: Nauka, 1966), p. 142.

63 *TOT*, p. 206.

64 Koonen, *Stranitsy zhizni*, p. 268.

65 Ibid., p. 269.

66 P. Markov, 'O Tairove' in *TOT*, pp. 21–2.

67 A.V. Lunacharsky, *O teatre i dramaturgii* (2 vols.), vol. 1, *Russkii dorevolyutsionnyi i sovetskii teatr* (Moscow: Iskusstvo, 1958), p. 411.

68 Golovashenko, *Rezhissyorskoe iskusstvo Tairova*, p. 289.

69 Gorchakov, *The Theatre in Soviet Russia*, p. 228.

70 For an account of the production of *The Daughter of Madame Angot*, see Oliver M. Sayler, *Inside the Moscow Art Theatre* (New York: Brentano's, 1925), pp. 62–76.

71 L. Sabaneev, quoted in *Istoriya sovetskogo dramaticheskogo teatra*, vol. 2, p. 146.

72 Lyubomudrov, 'Evolyutsiya tvorchestvo Tairova', p. 147.

73 Ibid.

74 Koonen, *Stranitsy zhizni*, p. 291.

75 Ibid., p. 292.

76 Huntly Carter, *The New Spirit in the Russian Theatre* (reprinted New York: Benjamin Blom, 1970), pp. 228–9.

77 G.A. Stenberg (1900–33) and V.A. Stenberg (b. 1899) were members of Inkhuk and champions of constructivism in the early 1920s and closely associated with Lef.

78 *TOT*, pp. 295–8.

79 *Sovetskii teatr – dokumenty i materialy. Russkii sovetskii teatr 1921–1926*, ed. A. Ya. Trabsky (Leningrad: Iskusstvo, 1975), note 2, p. 257.

80 *TOT*, pp. 299–301.

81 Repertkom (or Glavrepertkom) Glavny Repertyarny Komitet, later known as Glavny Komitet Po Kontrolyu Za Zrelishchami i Repertyarom (Chief Committee for the Control of Spectacles and Repertoire), was established in 1923 as a kind of watchdog for all dramatic, musical and cinematographic productions intended for public distribution and consumption.

82 Lunacharsky, *O teatre i dramaturgii*, vol. 1, pp. 265–70.

83 Koonen, *Stranitsy zhizni*, pp. 301–2.

84 Herbert Marshall, *The Pictorial History of the Russian Theatre* (New York: Crown Publishers, 1977), p. 107.

85 *TOT*, p. 211.

86 *Dokumenty i materialy 1921–1926*, p. 256.

87 Ibid., note 4, p. 258.

88 Markov, *TOT*, p. 28.

89 The recent production by Peter Stein of *The Hairy Ape*, seen at the National Theatre in London in 1987, would appear to have been influenced by Tairov. It is interesting to note that, prior to this, in 1972 Stein had staged a version of Vishnevsky's *Optimistic Tragedy*, one of Tairov's most famous productions. Writing in *The Observer* on 16 February, 1986, Peter Stein said of *The Hairy Ape* 'I see it as the complementary half of a diptych with Vishnevsky's *Optimistic Tragedy*' (p. 23).

90 Lunacharsky, *O teatre i dramaturgii*, vol. 1, p. 423.

91 Ibid., p. 424.

92 Ibid., p. 425.

93 Ibid., p. 426.

94 *Istoriya sovetskogo dramaticheskogo teatra* (6 vols), vol. 3, *1926–1932*, ed. M.N. Stroeva (Moscow: Nauka, 1967), p. 106. An *agitka* is shorthand for a schematic, propagandist 'agitational' work.

95 Markov, *TOT*, p. 29.

96 *TOT*, pp. 302–6.

97 Koonen, *Stranitsy zhizni*, pp. 309–12.

98 However, Walter Benjamin noted in his diary on 30 December 1926: 'The production was very poor, and Koonen was especially disappointing, completely uninteresting. What was interesting . . . was the fragmentation of the play into single scenes (cinematization) by means of curtain falls and lighting changes. The tempo was far more rapid than is usually the case here and was further accelerated by the dynamism of the decor. The set consisted of a cross-section view of three rooms: on the ground floor, a large room with a view to the exterior and an exit. At certain points, one saw its walls slide up at an 180-degree angle and the outdoors seemed to stream in from every side. there were two more rooms on the second floor, reached by a stairway that was partitioned off from the audience's view by laths. It was fascinating to follow the characters making their way up and down the stairs behind this lattice.' Walter Benjamin, 'Moscow diary', *October*, 35 (Winter, 1985), pp. 55–6.

99 Golovashenko, *Rezhissyorskoe iskusstvo Tairova*, p. 220.

100 *Istoriya sovetskogo dramaticheskogo teatra*, vol. 3, pp. 106–7.

101 *Dokumenty i materialy 1926–1932*, p. 348.

102 *TOT*, pp. 218–19, 307–10.

103 *Dokumenty i materialy 1926–1932*, p. 339.

104 Gorchakov, p. 233.

105 *Dokumenty i materialy 1926–1932*, p. 335.

106 V.A. Ryndin's first work in the theatre dates from 1922. He joined the Kamerny

Theatre in 1925, becoming its chief designer in 1931. He later worked with Okhlopkov on the latter's productions of *The Young Guard* (1947) and *Hamlet* (1954).

107 *Teatr*, 2 (1969), 89.
108 P.A. Markov, *O teatre* (4 vols.), vol. 3 (Moscow: Iskusstvo, 1976), p. 485.
109 O. Litovsky, *Glazami sovremennika* (Moscow: Sovetskii Pisatel', 1963), p. 94.
110 Koonen, *Stranitsy zhizni*, p. 312.
111 Ibid., p. 315.
112 Ibid., p. 315.
113 Quoted by and translated from Golovashenko, pp. 294–5. The text of a letter from Tairov to O'Neill dated 7 May 1942, was published in *Teatr*, 5 (1985), 74–5 in which he describes work on his current production of Paustovsky's *Until the Heart Stops Beating* and also refers to commencing work on Leonid Leonov's play, *Invasion*. However, the latter appears never to have reached the stage.
114 Edward J. Brown, *Russian Literature since the Revolution* (London: Macmillan, 1969), p. 191.
115 As revealed in letters written by Tairov to Semyonov in January and April 1929 – see *TOT*, pp. 568–71.
116 *TOT*, pp. 484–6.
117 Ibid., p. 263.
118 Koonen, *Stranitsy zhizni*, p. 340.
119 P. Markov, *Teatral'nye portrety* (Moscow–Leningrad: Iskusstvo, 1939), pp. 177–8.
120 *Teatr*, 2 (1969), 91.
121 P. Markov, *TOT*, p. 28.
122 From a review by V. Mlechin quoted in *TOT*, p. 520.
123 *TOT*, pp. 208–20.
124 *Teatr*, 6 (1969), 108.
125 *Soviet Theatre*, 3 (1983), 40.
126 V. Beryozkin, 'Ryndin – khudozhnik Kamernogo Teatra' in *Voprosy teatra*, ed. V. Frolov (Moscow: VTO, 1965), p. 260.
127 *Istoriya sovetskogo dramaticheskogo teatra*, vol. 3, p. 109.
128 Which dealt with revolutionary events in Russia in 1905.
129 Mikhail Zharov, *Zhizn', teatr, kino* (Moscow: Iskusstvo, 1967), p. 227.
130 *TOT*, p. 319.
131 Ibid., p. 320.
132 Ibid., p. 321.
133 1928, directed by Arthur Hopkins and starring Clark Gable. See *The Drama Review*, 26: 1 (T-93) (Spring 1982), 87–100.
134 *TOT*, p. 552.
135 Koonen, *Stranitsy zhizni* p. 345.
136 Golovashenko, *Rezhissyorskoe iskusstvo Tairova*, p. 196.
137 I. Kruti, cited in *TOT*, p. 523.
138 *TOT*, pp. 487–8.
139 Ibid., p. 331.
140 Ibid., p. 332.
141 Yu. Golovashenko, *Mnogoobrazie realizma* (Leningrad: Iskusstvo, 1973), p. 207.
142 *TOT*, p. 341.
143 Ibid., p. 524.
144 *Dokumenty i materialy 1926–1932*, p. 337.
145 *TOT*, p. 370.
146 Ibid., p. 554.
147 Norris Houghton, *Moscow Rehearsals* (London: Allen and Unwin, 1938), pp. 140–1.
148 'Uriel', cited in *TOT*, p. 526.

149 Denis Bablet, *Edward Gordon Craig* (London: Heinemann, 1966), p. 192.
150 Golovashenko, *Rezhissyorskoe iskusstvo Tairova*, p. 14.
151 Joseph Macleod, *The New Soviet Theatre* (London: Allen and Unwin, 1943), p. 94.
152 Koonen, *Stranitsy zhizni*, p. 367.
153 Ibid., pp. 386–7.
154 *Istoriya sovetskogo dramaticheskogo teatra* (6 vols.), vol. 4, ed. E.I. Polyakova (Moscow: Nauka, 1968), p. 162.
155 Golovashenko, *Rezhissyorskoe iskusstvo Tairova*, p. 177.
156 Ibid., p. 182.
157 G. Boyadzhiev, quoted in *TOT*, p. 530.
158 A.G. Obraztsova, unpublished paper given at Anglo-Soviet Colloquium 'Chekhov on the British Stage', Robinson College, Cambridge, August 1987.
159 Quoted in *TOT*, pp. 531–2.
160 P.I. Novitsky, quoted in *TOT*, p. 564.
161 Golovashenko, *Rezhissyorskoe iskusstvo Tairova*, p. 136.
162 Ibid., p. 137.
163 G. Boyadzhiev, *Ot Sofokla do Brekhta za sorok teatral'nykh vecherov* (Moscow: Prosveshchenie, 1969), pp. 291–2.
164 *TOT*, p. 455.
165 Ibid., p. 463.
166 *Izvestiya*, 5 July 1946.
167 Berkovsky, *Literatura i teatr*, p. 390.
168 Boris Filippov, *Actors Without Make-up* (Moscow: Progress, 1977), pp. 151–3.
169 Ilya Ehrenburg, *Men, Years, Life* (6 Vols.), vol. 2, *First Years of Revolution 1918–1921*, trans. Anna Bostock (London: MacGibbon and Kee, 1962), pp. 167–71.
170 An obituary appreciation, by Pavel Markov, appeared in *Teatr*, 11 (1974), 81.

2. Evgeni Vakhtangov, 1883–1922

1 From Vakhtangov's diary, Vsekhsvyatskii Sanatorium, 26 March 1921. Published for the first time, in full, in *Evgenii Vakhtangov* (Sbornik), compiled, edited and with a commentary by L.D. Vendrovskaya and G.P. Kaptereva (Moscow: VTO, 1984), p. 333. The two previous Soviet editions of Vakhtangov's notes and articles do not publish this particular entry in full. The earliest of these is *Vakhtangov: zapiski:pis'ma:stat'i*, compiled and with a commentary by N.M. Vakhtangova, L.D. Vendrovskaya and B.E. Zakhava (Moscow/Leningrad: Iskusstvo, 1939); and *Evg. Vakhtangov: materialy i stat'i*, compiled and edited by L.D. Vendrovskaya (Moscow: VTO, 1959). A translation of the complete diary entry is given in English in *Evgeny Vakhtangov*, compiled by Lyubov Vendrovskaya and Galina Kaptereva, trans. Doris Bradbury (Moscow: Progress, 1982), p. 141.
2 Letter to Stanislavsky from Zakhar'ino Sanatorium, 29 March 1919, published for the first time in *Materialy i stat'i*, p. 158 and in trans., p. 116.
3 Notebook entry for 12 April 1911.
4 From Vakhtangov's notebook (1921).
5 From Vakhtangov's notebook, 26 March 1921.
6 Letter to Serafima Birman, 8 August 1921, published for the first time in *Materialy i stat'i*, pp. 192–3 and included in *Evgenii Vakhtangov*, pp. 362–3 and in trans., pp. 143–4.
7 From Vakhtangov's notebook, 26 March 1921, published for the first time in *Evgenii Vakhtangov*, pp. 333–5 and in trans., pp. 140–3.
8 'Two Conversations between Vakhtangov and his Pupils', 10 April 1922. First pub-

lished in *Zapiski: pis'ma: stat'i*, pp. 254–62, with all references to Meyerhold omitted, but included in full in *Materialy i stat'i*, pp. 206–14 and *Evgenii Vakhtangov*, pp. 429–37 and in trans., pp. 151–8. The term which Vakhtangov uses towards the end of the transcript, 'fantasticheskii realizm', has hitherto been literally translated as 'fantastic realism' but has been amended to 'imaginative realism' in the most recent, Soviet translation, a preferable rendering.

9 Michael Chekhov, *To the Director and Playwright*, compiled and written by Charles Leonard (New York: Harper and Row, 1963), pp. 47–8.

10 This 'meeting' between Meyerhold's anti-inspirational approach and Stanislavsky's 'method of physical actions' is now a commonplace of contemporary Soviet criticism.

11 *Brecht on Theatre*, trans. and with notes by John Willett (London: Methuen, 1964), p. 238.

12 MAT is the normal abbreviation for the Moscow Art Theatre in English; MXAT in Russian (MKhAT) Moskovskii Khudozhestvennyi Akademicheskii Teatr (Moscow Art Academic Theatre).

13 *Brecht on Theatre*, p. 238.

14 Boris Zakhava (1896–1977) was an actor, director and author of books on Vakhtangov and Meyerhold and on theories of acting. He worked as an actor with Vakhtangov before the revolution and with Meyerhold after it before becoming a director at the Vakhtangov Theatre and staging several noteworthy productions there during the 1920s and 1930s. He continued to be a highly influential figure in Soviet theatre for the remainder of his life.

15 Richard Boleslavsky (real name Strezhesnitsky (1887–1937) was an actor and director who worked at the Moscow Art Theatre between 1908 and 1918 and was one of the organisers of the First Studio. Among his more significant roles were those of the tutor Belyaev in Stanislavsky's production of *A Month in the Country* (1909) and Sir Toby Belch in *Twelfth Night* (1917). He emigrated in 1920, finally settling in the United States where his book *Acting. The First Six Lessons*, based on the Stanislavsky system, was published in 1935.

16 *Poem of an Axe* (1931), *My Friend* (1932), and *After the Ball* (1934).

17 Boris Sushkevich (1887–1946), actor and director, was one of the founders of the First Studio and a member of its directorate from 1912 to 1933. He played Stratton in Vakhtangov's production of *The Deluge*, Mortensgaard in *Rosmersholm*, and Persson in *Erik XIV*. From 1933 he worked in Leningrad, mainly as a director.

18 The Bat (Letuchaya Mysh') was one of the first and best pre-revolutionary 'miniature' theatres. It was opened in 1908 by N.F. Baliev and became a base for cabaret performances by members of the Moscow Art Theatre – the 'cabbage parties' described by Stanislavsky in *My Life in Art*. After 1912 it became a more broadly-based cabaret theatre, concentrating on satire and parodies of the Russian classics. Baliev emigrated with a section of his troupe in 1920 and continued to perform abroad, mainly in Paris and New York.

19 This notion of a reversion to nature and the metamorphosis of life into art also inspired the early work of Copeau, Michel Saint-Denis, and others.

20 Notebook entry, 7 April 1921, included in all Soviet editions but not in 1982 translation.

21 There are interesting analogies to be drawn here with a work such as Synge's *Riders to the Sea*, first performed in 1904.

22 N. Zograf, *Vakhtangov* (Moscow–Leningrad: Iskusstvo, 1939), p. 17.

23 N.I. Smirnova, *Evgenii Bagrationovich Vakhtangov* (Moscow: Znanie, 1982), p. 9.

24 A. Diky, *Povest' o teatral'noi yunosti* (Moscow: Iskusstvo, 1957), pp. 283–4.

25 Zograf, *Vakhtangov*, p. 17.

26 Ibid., p. 18.

27 B. Zakhava, *Sovremenniki* (Moscow: Iskusstvo, 1969), p. 22.

28 Lyubov Gurevich, quoted in Zograf, *Vakhtangov*, p. 17.

29 Zograf, *Vakhtangov*, pp. 153–4.
30 Serafima Birman (1890–1976), actress and director, was a member of the Moscow Art Theatre company and of its First Studio. From 1924 to 1936 she was a member of MAT 2. She played the principal role in her own production of Gorky's *Vassa Zheleznova* in 1936. She acted and directed at the Lenin Komsomol Theatre in Moscow from 1938 to 1958.
31 Serafima Birman, 'Sud'ba Talanta' in *Materialy i stat'i*, p. 314, trans. as 'A Talented Life' in *Evgeny Vakhtangov*, p. 190.
32 *Zapiski: pis'ma: stat'i*, pp. 269–70.
33 Zakhava, *Sovremenniki*, p. 87.
34 B. Zakhava, 'Tvorcheskii put' E.B. Vakhtangova' in *Zapiski: pis'ma: stat'i*, p. 335.
35 *Sovremenniki*, p. 87.
36 'Tvorcheskii put' E.B. Vakhtangova', p. 335.
37 B. Vershilov, 'Stranitsy vospominaniya' in *Materialy i stat'i*, p. 380.
38 *Sovremenniki*, p. 99.
39 Ibid., p. 98.
40 Ibid., p. 98.
41 There does not appear to have been an anti-smoking policy as such.
42 'To Studio Members and Associates', 14/15 November 1918.
43 N. Volkov, quoted in Zakhava, 'Tvorcheskii put' E.B. Vakhtangova', pp. 339–40.
44 Zograf, *Vakhtangov*, p. 29.
45 Ibid., p. 34.
46 Ibid., pp. 35–6.
47 Plot adapted from Huntly Carter, *The New Theatre and Cinema of Soviet Russia* (London: Chapman and Dodd, 1924), pp. 220–1.
48 P.A. Markov, 'Vakhtangov v studii khudozhestvennogo teatra' in *Evgenii Vakhtangov*, p. 468, also in *Evgeny Vakhtangov* trans. as 'Vakhtangov at the First Moscow Art Theatre Studio', p. 176.
49 *Sovremenniki*, pp. 106–7.
50 Zograf, *Vakhtangov*, p. 22.
51 Diky, *Povest' o teatral'noi yunosti*, p. 279.
52 'Canadians' in some accounts.
53 Markov 'Vakhtangov v studii khudozhestvennogo teatra', p. 469 (trans. pp. 176–7).
54 *Sovremenniki*, pp. 107–8.
55 Marc Slonim, *The Russian Theater From the Empire to the Soviets* (London: Methuen, 1963), pp. 187–8.
56 R. Simonov, 'Mikhail Aleksandrovich Chekov' in *Ruben Simonov: tvorcheskoe nasledie*, ed. N.G. Litbinenko (Moscow: VTO, 1981), p. 289.
57 V. Gromov, *Mikhail Chekhov*, (Moscow: Iskusstvo, 1970), pp. 38–42.
58 'Suler' – affectionate abbreviation of Sulerzhitsky.
59 Christian name and patronymic of Stanislavsky.
60 B. Sushkevich, 'Vstrechi s Vakhtangovym' in *Materialy i stat'i*, p. 367. This paragraph is omitted from *Evgeny Vakhtangov*, p. 198.
61 Zakhava, 'Tvorcheskii put' E.B. Vakhtangova', p. 352.
62 Ibid., pp. 346–7.
63 'S khudozhnika sprositsya . . .' (April 1919). The article was published for the first time on 29 May 1924. It appears as 'The Artist Will Be Asked . . .' in *Evgeny Vakhtangov*, p. 131. A better translation might be 'It Will Be Asked (Demanded) of the Artist . . .'
64 Zakhava, 'Tvorcheskii put' E.B. Vakhtangova', pp. 355–6.
65 P. Novitsky, *Sovremennye teatral'nye sistemy* (Moscow: Izd. Khudozhestvennoi Literatury, 1933), note 6, p. 202.
66 A. Matskin, 'Delo i mysl' Vakhtangova', *Teatr*, 2 (1983), 61.
67 Letter to A.I. Cheban, 3 August 1917.

68 Lyubov Freidkina, 'Nemirovich-Danchenko and Vakhtangov' in *Evgeny Vakhtangov*, pp. 212–13.
69 'Chego mne khotelos' by dostdignut' v Rosmerskholme' (1918), translated as 'What I Would Like to Achieve in *Rosmersholm*' in *Evgeny Vakhtangov*, p. 49.
70 Sophia Giatsintova quoted by Freidkina in *Evgeny Vakhtangov*, p. 214.
71 Boris Zakhava, *Vakhtangov i ego studiya* (Moscow: Teakinopechat, 1930), p. 53.
72 *Evgeny Vakhtangov*, p. 46.
73 Ibid., p. 47.
74 Markov, 'Vakhtangov v studii khudozhestvennogo teatra'. There are slight discrepancies between the Russian original and the English translation in *Evgeny Vakhtangov*, p. 179. For example, the sentence in English: 'When he speaks to Rebecca about the severed finger, his [Brendel's] voice is mysterious and cold', is missing from the Russian.
75 *Evgeny Vakhtangov*, pp. 46–55.
76 Zograf, *Vakhtangov*, p. 60.
77 *Evgeny Vakhtangov*, p. 133.
78 A device Vakhtangov would appear to have borrowed from Gordon Craig's designs for the court scene in act 1 of *Hamlet*, where he imagined a sea of courtiers' heads poking through a gold cloth which cascaded from a centrally elevated throne and covered the entire stage.
79 Zograf, *Vakhtangov*, pp. 63–4.
80 Ibid., note 96, p. 159.
81 Zakhava, *Vakhtangov i ego studiya*, pp. 94–108.
82 Letter to Oleg Leonidov, 23 October 1918.
83 Smirnova, *Vakhtangov*, p. 40.
84 From Vakhtangov's notebook, 26 March 1921.
85 Zakhava, 'Tvorcheskii put' E.B. Vakhtangova', p. 376.
86 Smirnova, *Vakhtangov*, p. 4.
87 Ruben Simonov, *S Vakhtangovym* (Moscow: Iskusstvo, 1959), p. 21; trans. and adapted by Miriam Goldina as *Stanislavsky's Protégé: Eugene Vakhtangov* (New York: DBS Publications, 1969), p. 21.
88 Ibid., pp. 45 and 54.
89 Ibid., pp. 45–55; 54–69.
90 Ibid., pp. 45–55; 54–69.
91 Vershilov, 'Stranitsy vospominaniya', p. 392.
92 Simonov, *S Vakhtangovym*, pp. 55 and 69.
93 Zakhava, 'Tvorcheskii put' E.B. Vakhtangova', p. 375.
94 Zograf, *Vakhtangov*, p. 48.
95 Zakhava, *Vakhtangov i ego studiya*, p. 51.
96 Ibid., p. 51.
97 Ibid., p. 52.
98 Rehearsal notes for 17 September 1916 in *Zapiski: pis'ma: stat'i*, p. 305.
99 Rehearsal Notes for 29 September, ibid., p. 306.
100 Smirnova, *Vakhtangov*, p. 34.
101 Ibid., p. 38.
102 Zograf, *Vakhtangov*, p. 109.
103 *Stanislavsky's Protégé*, p. 110.
104 Zograf, *Vakhtangov*, p. 108.
105 Zakhava, *Vakhtangov i ego studiya*, p. 125.
106 *Stanislavsky's Protégé*, p. 87.
107 Ibid., pp. 95–6.
108 Ibid., p. 99.
109 Simonov, *S Vakhtangovym*, p. 97.

110 L. Shikhmatov, *Ot studii k teatru* (Moscow: VTO, 1970), p. 101.
111 Yu. Smirnov-Nesvitsky, 'Revolyutsionnaya teatral'nost' Vakhtangova' in *Problemy teorii i praktiki russkoi sovetskoi rezhissury 1917–1925* (Leningrad: Lgitmik, 1978), pp. 105–6.
112 Zograf, *Vakhtangov*, p. 93.
113 *Sovremenniki*, p. 280. (He is quoting remarks made by B. Sushkevich.)
114 From Vakhtangov's notebook, 26 March 1921. The sentence reads: 'Of course, Stanislavsky is a less talented director than Meyerhold. Stanislavsky has no individuality. All his stage productions are banal.' This sentence is omitted from all Soviet Russian editions of Vakhtangov's writings but is included in the Soviet English-language edition, *Evgeny Vakhtangov*, p. 140.
115 Quoted by E. Polyakova in *Stanislavsky* (Moscow: Progress, 1982), p. 265.
116 J.W. Roberts, *Richard Boleslavsky – His Life and Work in the Theatre* (Michigan: UMI Research Press, 1981), p. 76.
117 *Evgeny Vakhtangov*, pp. 340–2. The article on *Erik XIV* was first published, in shorter form, in *Kul'tura Teatra*, 4 (1921).
118 Quoted in Smirnova, *Vakhtangov*, p. 19.
119 Hallie Flanagan, *Shifting Scenes of the Modern European Theatre* (London: Harrap, 1929), pp. 138–9.
120 Smirnova, *Vakhtangov*, pp. 18–28.
121 Ibid., pp. 18–28.
122 *Evgeny Vakhtangov*, p. 139.
123 Zograf, *Vakhtangov*, p. 96.
124 Ibid., p. 97.
125 Ibid., p. 101.
126 Gromov, *Mikhail Chekhov*, pp. 75–86.
127 *Zhizn' Iskusstva*, 758–60 (1921), quoted in G. Boyadzhiev, *Ot Sofokla do Brekhta za sorok teatral'nykh vecherov* (Moscow: Prosveshchenie, 1969), p. 247.
128 Boris Alpers, quoted in N. Gorchakov, *The Theatre in Soviet Russia* (London: Oxford University Press, 1957), p. 438.
129 Smirnov-Nesvitsky, *Problemy teorii i praktiki*, p. 110.
130 Zakhava, 'Tvorcheskii put' E.B. Vakhtangova', p. 360.
131 See Huntly Carter, *The New Spirit in the Russian Theatre* (reprinted New York: Benjamin Blom, 1970), p. 182, where he refers to 'a very talented young Jew named Vakhtangov'.
132 Mendel Kohansky, *The Hebrew Theatre – Its First Fifty Years* (Israel Universities Press, Jerusalem: 1969), pp. 20–2.
133 Letter to the Student Studio, 5 May 1915.
134 Pearl Fishman, 'Vakhtangov's *The Dybbuk*', *The Drama Review*, 24:3 (T-87), (September 1980), 43–58.
135 *The New Theatre and Cinema of Soviet Russia*, p. 176.
136 Yuri Zavadsky, 'Oderzhimost' tvorchestvom' in *Materialy i stat'i*, pp. 295–6.
137 Cited in Kohansky, *Hebrew Theatre*, p. 45.
138 Akim Valinsky, quoted in Kohansky, *Hebrew Theatre*, p. 44.
139 Kohansky, *Hebrew Theatre*, p. 45.
140 Smirnov-Nesvitsky, p. 115.
141 *Lubok* – woodcut broadsides, dating from the seventeenth century and deriving their name either from the limewood block from which they were printed or from the bast baskets from which they were hawked. Grotesque and satirical in nature they combine Russian iconographic mannerisms with a crude copying of Western European engravings.
142 N. Volkov, quoted in *Sovremenniki*, p. 288.
143 A. Kugel, cited by Kohansky, *Hebrew Theatre*, p. 46.

144 Stark Young, *Immortal Shadows* (New York: Hill and Wang, 1948), p. 62.

145 Smirnov-Nesvitsky, p. 111.

146 Quoted by Kohansky, *Hebrew Theatre*, p. 43.

147 Letter to Nikolai Yanovsky, *Evgeny Vakhtangov*, p. 145.

148 The account of the production which follows is based mainly on the following: N. Gorchakov, *Rezhissyorskie uroki Vakhtangova* (Moscow: Iskusstvo, 1957), translated as *The Vakhtangov School of Stage Art*, ed. Phil Griffith (Moscow: Foreign Languages Publishing House, n.d.); Simonov, *S Vakhtangovym/Stanislavsky*'s *Protégé*.

149 Theodore Komisarjevsky, *Myself and the Theatre* (Heinemann, London, 1929), p. 93.

150 V.N. Solovyov (1887–1941) was a close collaborator of Meyerhold's in studio work during his pre-revolutionary St Petersburg period, with a particular interest in *commedia dell'arte*. Yu. M. Bondi (1889–1926) designed sets for Meyerhold between 1912 and 1915 as well as being a close collaborator in Studio work.

151 *Vakhtangov School of Stage Art*, p. 104.

152 Boris Zakhava, 'Turandot' in *Evgeny Vakhtangov*, p. 251.

153 Zograf, *Vakhtangov*, p. 142.

154 'Stenogramme of Two Discussions between Vakhtangov and his Students', *Evgeny Vakhtangov*, p. 158.

3. Nikolai Okhlopkov, 1900–67

1 *Vstrechi s Meierkhol'dom: sbornik vospominanii*, ed. L.D. Vendrovskaya (Moscow: VTO, 1967).

2 Igor Ilinsky and Boris Ravenskikh became important figures at the Moscow Maly Theatre; Mikhail Tsaryov went on to become a director of the Maly Theatre, president of the All-Union Theatre Society and president of the Soviet section of the International Theatre Institute; Erast Garin and Sergei Martinson had long and distinguished careers in both theatre and cinema, while Valentin Pluchek became artistic director of the Moscow Theatre of Satire.

3 In the film *Alexander Nevsky* (1938), A *bogatyr* is a Russian epic hero.

4 Jay Leyda, *Kino – A History of the Russian and Soviet Film* (London: Allen and Unwin, 1960), p. 350.

5 Nina Velekhova, *Okhlopkov i teatr ulits* (Moscow: Iskusstvo, 1970), p. 276.

6 In his home town of Irkutsk in 1921. The city's main theatre is now called the Okhlopkov Theatre.

7 Staged in Minsk.

8 Z. Vladimirova, 'Nasledstvo i nasledniki', *Teatr*, 4 (1971), 46.

9 Ibid., p. 47.

10 Nina Velekhova, 'Razgovory s Okhlopkovym', *Teatr*, 6 (1975), 79.

11 Isidor Shtok, *Rasskazy o dramaturgakh* (Moscow: Iskusstvo, 1967), p. 205.

12 Velekhova, *Okhlopkov i teatr ulits*, p. 179.

13 Nikolai Okhlopkov, *Vsem molodym* (Moscow: Molodaya Gvardiya, 1981), pp. 88–9.

14 Ibid., p. 89.

15 GITIS – Gosudarstvennyi Institut Teatral'nogo Iskusstva (State Institute of Theatre Art).

16 Vs. Malashenko, 'Okhlopkov i molodye aktyory', *Teatr*, 5 (1982), 98.

17 *Vsem molodym*, pp. 69–70.

18 N. Okhlopkov, 'O tsenicheskikh ploshchadkakh', *Teatr*, 1 (1959). Trans. as 'Creative Interplay' in *Directors on Directing*, ed. Toby Cole and Helen Krich Chinoy (New York: Vision Press, 1964), pp. 257–63.

19 See O. Schlemmer, L. Moholy-Nagy, F. Molner, *The Theatre of the Bauhaus*, ed. with an introduction by W. Gropius (London: Eyre Methuen, 1979).

20 Velekhova, *Okhlopkov i teatr ulits*, p. 107.

21 See especially, Norris Houghton, *Moscow Rehearsals* (New York: Harcourt, Brace and Co., 1936; London: Allen and Unwin, 1938); and André van Gyseghem, *Theatre in Soviet Russia* (London: Faber and Faber, 1943).

22 Rehearsals of a dramatised version of Nikolai Ostrovsky's famous novel and called *One Life* (Odna Zhizn´) began in mid November, 1936, and the production was given a single, closed performance in November 1937. Platon Kerzhenstev's *Pravda* article 'An Alien Theatre' appeared in December, and Meyerhold's theatre was closed the following January.

23 Lee Strasberg, 'Russian Notebook (1934)', *The Drama Review*, 17:1 (T-57) (March 1973), 121.

24 Nikolai Abalkin, in his introduction to *Vsem molodym*, quotes Okhlopkov as saying that, 'When I have a volume of Mayakovsky's poems with me, I am armed to the teeth' (p. 3).

25 N.P. Okhlopkov, 'Ya ishchu teatr potryaseniya', *Teatr*, 8 (1969), 102.

26 Ibid. p. 102.

27 *Vsem molodym*, p. 6.

28 A.V. Fevralsky (1901–1987) spent many years as literary manager at Meyerhold's theatre and did a great deal, during the 1960s and 1970s to revive interest in the work of Meyerhold and Mayakovsky.

   P.V. Tsetnerovich (1894–1963) was a student of Meyerhold's in Moscow in 1922, together with Okhlopkov, then worked alongside Meyerhold as a director's assistant until 1932, when he joined Okhlopkov at the Realistic Theatre. Worked at the Central Red Army Theatre from 1934 to 1937.

29 Velekhova, *Okhlopkov i teatr ulits*, p. 52.

30 A. Fevralsky, 'Okhlopkovskii teatr', *Teatr*, 6 (1980), 108.

31 Velekhova, *Okhlopkov i teatr ulits*, p. 52.

32 Ibid., pp. 52–3.

33 Sergei Eisenstein, *Film Form*, ed. and trans. Jay Leyda (New York: Harcourt, Brace and World, 1949), p. 16.

34 Letter to Okhlopkov, 10 August 1929, in *V.E. Meierkhol'd – perepiska* (Moscow: Iskusstvo, 1976), pp. 300–1.

35 Abram Room was invited by Meyerhold to work at the Theatre of the Revolution in 1923; he soon turned his attention to film making and was responsible for the extremely entertaining and popular film *Bed and Sofa* (Tretya Meshchanskaya) (1927).

36 In which Okhlopkov had acted the role of a commissar.

37 Victor Shklovsky (1893–1984) was a formalist critic who worked in the literary department of Sovkino where he produced film scripts for, among others, Abram Room and Lev Kuleshov, including the latter's *By the Law* (1926).

38 Nikolai Erdman (1902–70) was the brother of Boris Erdman, an actor at Tairov's Kamerny Theatre during the 1917–18 season. Erdman's first play, *The Mandate*, was staged by Meyerhold with great success in 1925. Attempts to stage a second satire, *The Suicide*, during the early 1930s, were less successful and the play was not produced in the Soviet Union until the 1980s. Erdman earned his living as a film scenario writer and adapter. He adapted Lermontov's novel *A Hero of Our Time* for the Taganka Theatre in 1965. He also composed a number of music-hall sketches.

39 *Kino*, pp. 218–19.

40 Ibid., p. 273.

41 Alexander Medvedkin was director of the remarkable 'socialist' film comedy *Happiness* in 1934 with its debts to Chaplin, Dovzhenko and Russian folklore and filmed in a bizarre style mixing surrealist and expressionist elements.

42 Velekhova, *Okhlopkov i teatr ulits*, p. 81.

43 Ibid., p. 82.

44 *Sovetskii teatr – dokumenty i materialy. Russkii sovetskii teatr 1926–1932*, ed. A. Ya. Trabsky (Leningrad: Iskusstvo, 1982), p. 255.

45 F.I. Panfyorov (1886–1960) was a novelist and dramatist who wrote plays on village themes but whose novel *And Then the Harvest* (1939) is probably his greater claim to fame. M.A. Sholokhov (1905–1984) was a novelist and short-story writer whose greatest work is *Tikhii Don* (And Quiet Flows the Don) the four separate books of which appeared between 1928 and 1940. His other main work, consisting of two books published in 1932 and 1959, is *Virgin Soil Upturned* which concerns the development of socialist consciousness among the Don Cossacks. Sholokhov was awarded the Nobel Prize in 1965.

46 *Vsem molodym*, p. 7.

47 *Directors on Directing*, ed. Cole and Chinoy, p. 258.

48 Strasberg, 'Russian Notebook', p. 121.

49 *Directors on Directing*, ed. Cole and Chinoy, p. 262.

50 Ibid, p. 258.

51 Strasberg ('Russian Notebook', pp. 109–10) points to a connection between Okhlopkov's working methods and those of Grotowski. There is also a link between Okhlopkov's work at the Realistic Theatre and that of Ariane Mnouchkine's Théâtre du Soleil, for example the methods employed in her production of *1789* (1970).

52 Fevralsky, 'Okhlopkovskii teatr' p. 110.

53 Velekhova, *Okhlopkov i teatr ulits*, p. 7. The model for the set of *I Want a Child*, which was never staged, is preserved in the Bakhrushin Theatre Museum, in Moscow. An illustration can be found, facing p. 257, of *Meyerhold on Theatre*, trans. and ed. with a critical commentary by Edward Braun (London: Methuen, 1969).

54 Quoted in Velekhova, *Okhlopkov i teatr ulits*, p. 92.

55 Velekhova, *Okhlopkov i teatr ulits*, p. 86.

56 Boris Kornilov (b. 1903) and Nikolai Zabolotsky (b. 1903) were two comparatively minor Soviet poets whose themes tend to be the relationship between man and nature. They both share a tendency to depict natural phenomena disguised in human form as in Zabolotsky's poem *Sever* (The North) 1938.

57 Velekhova, *Okhlopkov i teatr ulits*, p. 86.

58 Fevralsky, 'Okhlopkovskii teatr', p. 110.

59 Velekhova, *Okhlopkov i teatr ulits*, p. 97.

60 *Ideinost*, together with *narodnost, partinost, tipichnost* and *klassovost* are the basic constituent elements demanded of a work of 'socialist realism'. See C. Vaughan James, *Soviet Socialist Realism: Origins and Theory* (London: Macmillan, 1973), esp. pp. 1–14.

61 Bakhno was the hero of *Running Start*, whose character and personality appear to be based on that of the anarchist Makhno, who broke with Lenin shortly after the revolution, hence the critic's hostility to anything in the production which might have rendered him attractive.

62 Velekhova, *Okhlopkov i teatr ulits*, p. 95.

63 *Dokumenty i materialy 1926–1932*, p. 255.

64 Natan Zarkhi (1900–35) was a film writer and dramatist. His play *Joy Street* paints a grim picture of the poverty of urban life in the United States as well as a lyrical prospect of proletarian solidarity. The play was extremely popular in the Soviet Union during the early 1930s. Zarkhi also provided the screen adaptation of Gorky's novel for Pudovkin's film *Mother* (1925) and the scenario for *The End of St Petersburg* (1926).

65 Velekhova, *Okhlopkov i teatr ulits*, pp. 98–100.

66 Houghton, *Moscow Rehearsals* (1938), p. 172.

67 van Gyseghem, *Theatre in Soviet Russia*, p. 193.

68 Houghton, *Moscow Rehearsals*, p. 175.

69 Ibid., p. 176.
70 Strasberg, 'Russian Notebook', pp. 117–18.
71 Fevralsky, 'Okhlopkovskii teatr', p. 110.
72 van Gyseghem, *Theatre in Soviet Russia*, p. 196.
73 Yu. Yuzovsky, *Zachem lyudi khodyat v teatr* (Moscow: Iskusstvo, 1964), pp. 65–6.
74 van Gyseghem, *Theatre in Soviet Russia*, p. 196.
75 Fevralsky, 'Okhlopkovskii teatr', p. 111.
76 Vera Alexandrova, *A History of Soviet Literature 1917–1964*, trans. Mirra Ginsburg (New York: Doubleday, 1964), p. 33.
77 Yu. Yuzovsky, *Spektakly i p'esy* (Moscow: Khudozhestvennaya Literatura, 1935), p. 112.
78 van Gyseghem, *Theatre in Soviet Russia*, p. 190.
79 Houghton, *Moscow Rehearsals*, p. 37.
80 Yuzovsky, *Spektakly i p'esy*, p. 112.
81 Ibid., p. 115.
82 van Gyseghem, *Theatre in Soviet Russia*, p. 192.
83 N. Okhlopkov, 'O tsenicheskikh ploshchadakh', *Teatr*, 1 (1959), 41.
84 Yuzovsky, *Spektakly i p'esy*, p. 116.
85 Ibid., pp. 115–16. This sentence is missing from the reprinted version of the article in *Zachem lyudi*, pp. 53–66, as is the earlier reference to 'pornography' on p. 114.
86 Ibid., pp. 116–17.
87 Ibid., pp. 117–18.
88 Ibid., p. 119.
89 Fevralsky, *Okhlopkovskii teatr*, p. 111.
90 N. Okhlopkov, 'On Convention' in *Socialist Realism in Literature and Art*, trans. C. Vaughan James (Moscow: Progress, 1971), p. 124.
91 Yuzovsky, *Spektakly i p'esy*, p. 126.
92 Velekhova, *Okhlopkov i teatr ulits*, p. 117.
93 van Gyseghem, *Theatre in Soviet Russia*, p. 199.
94 Houghton, *Moscow Rehearsals*, p. 171.
95 van Gyseghem, *Theatre in Soviet Russia*, p. 205.
96 Ibid., pp. 201–2.
97 Yuzovsky, *Spektakly i p'esy*, p. 126.
98 Ibid., p. 125.
99 Velekhova. *Okhlopkov i teatr ulits*, p. 121.
100 Ibid. p. 120.
101 *Veniki* are small bundles of birch wands, tied together, with which partakers of a steam bath beat the skin to bring the blood to the surface.
102 Velekhova, *Okhlopkov i teatr ulits*, p. 120.
103 Ibid., pp. 122–3. This description would seem to be derived from the revised version of the production in 1956. It is not clear whether the scene existed, or took this form, in the original.
104 *Istoriya russkogo sovetskogo dramaticheskogo teatra*, vol. 1, *1917–1945* eds. Yu. A. Dmitreva and K.L. Rudnitsky (Moscow: Prosveshchenie, 1984), p. 209 (hereafter referred to as *IRSDT*).
105 A. Ya. Vyshinsky (1883–1955) was Soviet foreign minister during part of the cold war 1953–5 but, more significantly, deputy public prosecutor and then public prosecutor between 1935 and 1939 when the notorious so-called 'show trials' were held.
106 Boris Filippov, *Actors without Make-up* (Moscow: Progress, 1977), pp. 164–5.
107 Ibid., pp. 164–5.
108 Velekhova, *Okhlopkov i teatr ulits*, p. 120.
109 Yuzovsky, *Spektakly i p'esy*, p. 126.

110 This admonitory suggestion of Yuzovsky's, made in 1935, was excised from the reprint of the article which appeared in 1964 in *Zachem lyudi*, p. 63.

111 Filippov, *Actors Without Make-up*, pp. 165–7.

112 Velekhova, *Okhlopkov i teatr ulits*, p. 129.

113 A. Mikhailova, 'Prostranstvo dlya igry. Iz opyta B. Knobloka', *Teatr*, 4 (1983), 94–101.

114 B. Glan, 'Poslednee vystuplenie N.P. Okhlopkova', *Teatr*, 8 (1969), 100–1.

115 N.P. Okhlopkov, 'Ya ishchu teatr potryaceniya', *Teatr*, 8 (1969), 104.

116 Boris Shchukin (1894–1939) was acknowledged as one of the great actors of the Soviet theatre. After working with Vakhtangov he continued to act at the Vakhtangov Theatre where he included among his many roles, historic performances as Egor Bulychov in Gorky's play of that title (1932) and as Lenin in Pogodin's *The Man With the Rifle* (1937). The acting school attached to the Vakhtangov Theatre is named after him.

117 Velekhova, *Okhlopkov i teatr ulits*, p. 127.

118 *Vsem molodym*, p. 13.

119 Ibid., pp. 13–15.

120 Mikhailova, 'Prostranstvo dlya igry', p. 97.

121 *Teatr*, 8 (1969), 104.

122 P.A. Markov, *O teatre* (4 Vols.), vol. 4 (Moscow: Iskusstvo, 1977), p. 166.

123 *Vsem molodym*, p. 57.

124 M.N. Kedrov (1893–1972) joined the Moscow Art Theatre in 1924 and became one of their leading actors and directors. He played the name part in Stanislavsky's production of *Tartuffe* (1939). V.O. Toporkov (1889–1970) joined the Moscow Art Theatre in 1927 and acted Orgon in *Tartuffe*. His book *Stanislavskii na repetitsii* appeared in 1950 (trans. *Stanislavski in Rehearsal: the Final Years*, New York: Theater Arts Books, 1979).

125 VTO – Vsesoyuznoe Teatral'noe Obshchestvo (All-Union Theatre Society).

126 Velekhova, *Okhlopkov i teatr ulits*, p. 137.

127 A.D. Diky (1889–1955), actor and director, joined the Moscow Art Theatre in 1910 and founded his own studio in 1931. R.N. Simonov (1899–1968) was a leading actor and senior artistic director at the Vakhtangov Theatre, succeeded by his son, Evgeni. I.M. Rapoport (b. 1901), actor and director, joined the Art Theatre Third Studio in 1924.

128 *Vsem molodym*, p. 58.

129 Harold B. Segel, *Twentieth-Century Russian Drama* (New York: Columbia University Press, 1979), p. 302.

130 V.V. Dmitriev (1900–48) was an outstanding theatre designer of the Soviet period who worked with Meyerhold as well as at the Moscow Art Theatre. B.R. Erdman (1899–1960), actor and theatre designer, was the brother of the playwright Nikolai Erdman. He designed the setting for the Vakhtangov Theatre production of Olesha's play, based on his story, *Three Fat Men* (1930).

131 Velekhova, *Okhlopkov i teatr ulits*, p. 141.

132 G. Boyadzhiev, *Poeziya teatra* (Moscow: Iskusstvo, 1960), pp. 53–4.

133 *Teatr im. Evg. Vakhtangova – 55 sezonov 1921–1971* (Moscow: Iskusstvo, 1971), no pagination.

134 *IRSDT*, pp. 328–9.

135 Tatyana Tess, 'Voskreshchenie Sirano', *Izvestiya*, 24 December 1943, quoted in *Ruben Simonov: tvorcheskoe nasledie* (Moscow: VTO, 1981), p. 543.

136 Boyadzhiev, *Poeziya teatra*, p. 50.

137 Velekhova, *Okhlopkov i teatr ulits*, p. 145.

138 Ibid., p. 145.

139 Marya Babanova (1900–82) worked with Komissarzhevsky in Moscow after the revolution then at Meyerhold's Theatre. Maxim Shtraukh (1900–72) worked with Eisenstein at the Proletkult Theatre in the early 1920s before going to work with Meyerhold. His interpretation of the role of Lenin was reputed to be the best. Babanova

and Shtraukh both worked at the Mayakovsky Theatre during the eras of Okhlopkov and Goncharov.

140 V. Ya. Dubrovsky, *Moskovskii Akademicheskii Teatr imeni Vl. Mayakovskogo 1922–1982*, ed. N.A. Velekhova (Moscow: Iskusstvo, 1983), pp. 67–8.

141 *Theatre in Soviet Russia*, p. 398.

142 *IRSDT*, p. 310.

143 Boyadzhiev, *Poeziya teatra*, p. 50.

144 *IRSDT*, p. 311.

145 M. Turovskaya, *Babanova – legenda i biografiya* (Moscow: Iskusstvo, 1981), p. 276.

146 Dubrovsky, *Moskovskii Akademicheskii Teatr*, p. 68.

147 van Gyseghem, *Theatre in Soviet Russia*, p. 398.

148 Pyotr Vilyams (1902–47) began work as a theatre designer in 1929 at the Moscow Art Theatre and was head of design at the Bolshoi Theatre from 1941 to 1947.

149 Filippov, *Actors without Make-up*, p. 168.

150 Turovskaya, *Babanova*, p. 284.

151 Dubrovsky, *Moskovskii Akademicheskii Teatr*, p. 68.

152 Decree of 26 August in *Bolshevik*, 16 (1946), 45–9.

153 The account of the production is derived mainly from Boyadzhiev, *Poeziya teatra*, pp. 165–81.

154 Joseph Macleod, *A Soviet Theatre Sketch Book* (London: Allen and Unwin, 1951), p. 125.

155 V. Komissarzhevsky, *Teatry Moskvy*, trans. as *Moscow Theatres* (Moscow: Foreign Languages Publishing House, 1959), p. 159.

156 Velekhova, *Okhlopkov i teatr ulits*, p. 166.

157 Gail Lenhoff, 'The Theatre of Okhlopkov', *The Drama Review*, 17:1 (T-57) (March 1973), p. 99.

158 Ibid., p. 99.

159 Velekhova, *Okhlopkov i teatr ulits*, p. 201.

160 Dubrovsky, *Moskovskii Akademicheskii Teatr*, p. 84.

161 Ibid., p. 84.

162 Starring Innokenti Smoktunovsky, Lenfilm, 1964.

163 Dubrovsky, *Moskovskii Akademicheskii Teatr*, p. 88.

164 Reprinted in English translation as 'From the Producer's Exposition of *Hamlet*, in *Shakespeare in the Soviet Union: A Collection of Articles*, trans. Avril Pyman (Moscow: Progress, 1966), pp. 182–203.

165 R.M. Samarin, 'International Notes – U.S.S.R.' in *Shakespeare Survey 9*, ed. Allardyce Nicoll (Cambridge University Press, 1956), pp. 117–18.

166 *Shakespeare in the Soviet Union*, p. 193.

167 Lenhoff, 'Theatre of Okhlopkov', pp. 99–101.

168 Faubion Bowers, *Entertainment in Russia* (New York: Thomas Nelson, 1959), p. 101.

169 Velekhova, *Okhlopkov i teatr ulits*, pp. 226–7.

170 Ibid., p. 314.

171 Turovskaya, *Babanova*, p. 306.

172 Houghton, *Moscow Rehearsals*, pp. 167–8.

173 *Teatr*, 8 (1960), 98.

174 Bowers, *Entertainment in Russia*, pp. 123–8.

175 Velekhova, *Okhlopkov i teatr ulits*, p. 206.

176 Anatoli Efros (1925–87) began work as a director in 1954 but made his first significant mark when he assumed directorship of the Moscow Drama Theatre on Malaya Bronnaya in 1967. His work was seen widely abroad, and included a visit to the Edinburgh Festival in 1978. He staged guest productions at the Taganka Theatre prior to taking over its artistic directorship from Yuri Lyubimov when the latter failed to return to the Soviet Union from abroad in 1983.

177 G. Tovstonogov, *Krug myslei* (Leningrad: Iskusstvo, 1972), pp. 93–4.

178 A.G. Obraztsova, 'Rezhissyor' in *Novatorstvo sovetskogo teatra*, ed. A. Anastasev (Moscow: Iskusstvo, 1963), p. 393.

179 Segel, *Twentieth-century Russian drama*, pp. 296–7.

180 Dubrovsky, *Moskovskii Akademicheskii Teatr*, pp. 92–3.

181 Alexei Arbuzov (1908–86) wrote his first play in 1930 but made his mark with *Tanya* (1939) which starred Marya Babanova at the Theatre of the Revolution. After the war he was the first Soviet dramatist to acquire a world reputation with his plays *Moi bednyi Marat* (trans. *The Promise*) and *Irkutsk Story*. Several of his plays have been translated into English and performed in Britain.

182 Norris Houghton, *Return Engagement* (London: Putnam, 1962), p. 32.

183 Ibid., p. 33.

184 Velekhova, *Okhlopkov i teatr ulits*, p. 181.

185 Ibid., p. 181.

186 Alexei Arbuzov, 'Irkutskaya istoriya' in *Dramy* (Moscow: Iskusstvo, 1969), p. 311.

187 Velekhova, *Okhlopkov i teatr ulits*, p. 215.

188 Arbuzov, *Dramy*, p. 314.

189 Ibid., p. 315.

190 Velekhova, *Okhlopkov i teatr ulits*, p. 187.

191 Ibid., p. 189.

192 Ibid., p. 203.

193 Ibid., p. 237.

194 Lenhoff, 'Theatre of Okhlopkov', p. 102.

195 Tatyana Bachelis (b. 1918) and Konstantin Rudnitsky (1920–88) are both formidable theatre critics and historians, and are also husband and wife. Rudnitsky's major study of Meyerhold, *Rezhissyor Meierkhol'd* (Meyerhold the Director), was published in 1969.

196 Velekhova, *Okhlopkov i teatr ulits*, p. 332.

197 Houghton, *Return Engagement*, p. 103.

198 Tovstonogov, *Krug myslei*, p. 107.

199 *Teatr*, 8 (1969), 104.

200 Herbert Marshall, *The Pictorial History of the Russian Theatre* (New York: Crown Publishers, 1977), p. 147.

201 Lenhoff, *Theatre of Okhlopkov*, p. 103.

202 Dubrovsky, *Moskovskii Akademicheskii Teatr*, p. 99.

203 Velekhova, *Okhlopkov i teatr ulits*, pp. 239–41.

204 I. Solovyova, 'Medeya' in *Spektakl' idyot segodnya* (Moscow: Iskusstvo, 1966), pp. 134–5.

205 Velekhova, *Okhlopkov i teatr ulits*, p. 203.

206 Ibid., p. 341.

207 Ibid., pp. 341–2.

208 Dubrovsky, *Moskovskii Akademicheskii Teatr*, p. 101.

209 Houghton, *Return Engagement*, p. 106.

210 *Ocherki istorii russkoi sovetskoi dramaturgii* (3 vols.) vol. 3, *1945–1954*, ed. S.V. Vladimirov (Leningrad: Iskusstvo, 1968), p. 116.

Select bibliography

Beilin A., *Nikolai Pavlovich Okhlopkov*, Moscow, Goskinizdat, 1953
Berkovsky N. Ya., *Literatura i teatr*, Moscow, Iskusstvo, 1969
Boyadzhiev G., *Poeziya teatra*, Moscow, Iskusstvo, 1960
    Ot Sofokla do Brekhta za sorok teatral'nykh Vecherov, Moscow, Prosveshchenie, 1969
Carter, Huntly, *The New Spirit in the Russian Theatre*, repr. New York, Benjamin Blom, 1970
    The New Theatre and Cinema of Soviet Russia, London, Chapman and Dodd, 1924
Cole, Toby and Chinoy, Helen Krich (eds.), *Directors on Directing*, New York, Vision Press, 1964
Derzhavin, D.K., *Kniga o Kamernom Teatre*, Leningrad, Khudozhestvennaya Literatura, 1934
Diky, A., *Povest' o teatral'noi yunosti*, Moscow, Iskusstvo, 1957
Dubrovsky, V.Ya., *Moskovskii Akademicheskii Teatr imeni Mayakovskogo 1922–1982*, ed. N.A. Velekhova, Moscow, Iskusstvo, 1983
Efros, E.A., *Kamerny Teatr i ego khudozhniki 1914–1934*, Moscow, VTO, 1934
Flanagan, Hallie, *Shifting Scenes of the Modern European Theatre*, London, Harrap. 1929
Golovashenko, Yu.A., *Rezhissyorskoe iskusstvo Tairova*, Moscow, Iskusstvo, 1970
Gorchakov, N.A., *The Theatre in Soviet Russia*, London, Oxford University Press, 1957
Gorchakov N., *Rezhissyorskie uroki Vakhtangova*, Moscow, Iskusstvo, 1957
Gorchakov, Nikolai, *The Vakhtangov School of Stage Art*, ed. Phil Griffith, Moscow, Foreign Languages Publishing House, n.d.
Grossman, L., *Alisa Koonen*, 'Academia', Moscow/Leningrad, 1930
Houghton, Norris, *Moscow Rehearsals*, New York, Harcourt, Brace and Co., 1936; Allen and Unwin, London, 1938
    Return Engagement, London, Putnam, 1962
Istoriya sovetskogo dramaticheskogo teatra (6 vols.), Moscow, Nauka, 1966–71
Ivanov, O. and Krivitsky, K., *Vakhtangov i Vakhtangovtsy*, Moscow, Moskovskii Rabochii, 1984
Khersonsky, Kh., *Vakhtangov*, Moscow, Molodaya Gvardiya, 1963
Knebel, M., *Vsya zhizn'*, Moscow, VTO, 1967
Kohansky, Mendel, *The Hebrew Theatre – Its First Fifty Years*, Jerusalem, Israel Universities Press, 1969
Koonen, Alisa, *Stranitsy zhizni*, Moscow, Iskusstvo, 1975; 2nd edn 1985
Lunacharsky, A.V., *O teatre i dramaturgii* (2 vols.) Moscow, Iskusstvo, 1958
Macleod, Joseph, *The New Soviet Theatre*, London, Allen and Unwin, 1943
    A Soviet Theatre Sketch Book, London, Allen and Unwin, 1951
    Actors Cross the Volga, London, Allen and Unwin, 1946
Markov, P., *O teatre* (4 vols.), Moscow, Iskusstvo, 1974–7
    Pravda teatra, Moscow, Iskusstvo, 1965
Marshall, Herbert, *The Pictorial History of the Russian Theatre*, New York, Crown Publishers, 1977
Novitsky, P., *Sovremennye teatral'nye sistemy*, Moscow, Izd. Khudozhestvennoi Literatury, 1933
Okhlopkov, Nikolai, *Vsem molodym*, Moscow, Molodaya Gvardiya, 1981
N.P. Okhlopkov: stat'i, vospominaniya, ed. E.I. Zotova and T.A. Lukina, Moscow, VTO, 1986
Problemy teorii i praktiki Russkoi sovetskoi rezhissury 1917–1925, Leningrad, 1978
Rudnitsky, K.L. (ed.), *Rezhissyorskoe iskusstvo A. Ya. Tairova*, Moscow, VTO, 1987
Rudnitsky, Konstantin, *Russian and Soviet Theatre – Tradition and the Avant-Garde*, London, Thames and Hudson, 1988
Sayler, Oliver M., *The Russian Theatre Under the Revolution*, Boston, 1920
Shikhmatov, L., *Ot studii k teatru*, Moscow, VTO, 1970

Simonov, Reuben, *S Vakhtangovym*, Moscow, Iskusstvo, 1959
  Stanislavsky's Protégé: Eugene Vakhtangov, trans. Miriam Goldina, New York, DBS Publications, 1969
Slonim, Marc, *Russian Theater from the Empire to the Soviets*, London, Methuen, 1963
Smirnova, N.I., *Evgenii Bagrationovich Vakhtangov*, Moscow, Znanie, 1982
Smirnov-Nesvitsky, Yu., *Vakhtangov*, Leningrad, Iskusstvo, 1987
Sovetskii teatr – dokumenty i materialy. Russkii sovetskii teatr 1917–1921, ed A.Z. Yufit, Leningrad, Iskusstvo, 1968
Sovetskii teatr – dokumenty i materialy. Russkii sovetskii teatr 1921–1926, ed. A.Ya. Trabsky, Leningrad, Iskusstvo, 1975
Sovetskii teatr – dokumenty i materialy. Russkii sovetskii teatr 1926–1932, ed. A.Ya. Trabsky, Leningrad, Iskusstvo, 1982
Tairov, A.Ya., *Zapiski rezhissyora, stat'i, besedy, rechi, pis'ma*, Moscow, VTO, 1970
Tairov, Alexander, *Notes of a Director*, Florida, University of Miami Press, 1969
Tovstonogov, G., *Krug myslei*, Leningrad, Iskusstvo, 1972
Vakhtangov: zapiski: pis'ma: stat'i, eds. N.M. Vakhtangova, L.D. Vendrovskaya, B.E. Zakhava, Moscow/Leningrad, Iskusstvo, 1939
Evg. Vakhtangov: materialy i stat'i, ed. L.D. Vendrovskaya, Moscow, VTO, 1959
Evgenii Vakhtangov (Sbornik), eds. L.D. Vendrovskaya and G.P. Kaptereva, Moscow, VTO, 1984
Evgeny Vakhtangov, eds. Lyubov Vendrovskaya and Galina Kaptereva, trans, Doris Bradbury, Moscow, Progress, 1982
van Gyseghem, André, *Theatre in Soviet Russia*, London, Faber and Faber, 1943
Velekhova, Nina, *Okhlopkov i teatr ulits*, Moscow, Iskusstvo, 1970
Yuzovsky, Yu., *Spektakly i p'esy*, Moscow, Khudozhestvennaya Literatura, 1935.
  Zachem lyudi khodyat v teatr, Moscow, Iskusstvo, 1964
Zakhava, B. *Sovremenniki*, Moscow, Iskusstvo, 1969
  Vakhtangov i ego studiya, Moscow, Teakinopechat, 1930
Zograf, N., *Vakhtangov*, Moscow–Leningrad, Iskusstvo, 1939

INDEX